LEARNING TO
DIVIDE THE WORLD

Engraving in G. E. Rumphius, D'Amboinische Rariteitkamer
(Amsterdam, 1741). Courtesy University of British Columbia Library.

LEARNING TO
DIVIDE THE WORLD
Education at Empire's End

- OUR NEED TO ORDER & CATEGORIZE THE IS A DIRECT RESULT OF OUR ENCOUNTERS w/ THE OTHER (VIA BRITISH IMPERIALISM)

- IMPERIALISM INCLUDES AN EDUCATIONAL PROJECT WHICH SEEKS TO MAKE "SENSE" OF THE OTHER

John Willinsky

 University of Minnesota Press
Minneapolis
London

Paul, David, and Aaron, once more

The publication of this book was assisted by a bequest from Josiah H. Chase to honor his parents, Ellen Rankin Chase and Josiah Hook Chase, Minnesota territorial pioneers.

CONTENTS

ACKNOWLEDGMENTS

For the exceptional research assistance I received over the years of this project, I extend my thanks to Denise Buchner, Chris Denholm, Mark Frein, Jumin Hu, Pam Johnston, Tan Phan, Margot Rosenberg, Avner Segall, and Lynn Thomas. The staffs of the New York Public Library, the British Museum, Yoka's, and the University of British Columbia Library are to be commended for their helpfulness and dedication. For the voices of teachers and students in this book, I am indebted to Lorri Neilsen and the students involved in the Learning Connections Project; the biology teachers who agreed to participate in this book; Jim Greenlaw and his class of high school students; Leslie Roman, Tim Stanley, and the students who participated in Leslie's antiracism course project reported here; Susan Inman and her drama class; and Lynn Thomas and the students of the Pacific Cultural Literacy Project. Various chapters received decidedly helpful readings (to which I fear I have not fully done justice) from Clayton Burns, Kieran Egan, Roy Graham, Helen Harper, Jumin Hu, Peter McLaren, Sonia Macpherson, Wilma Maki, Ranjini Mendis, Edward Robeck, Leslie Roman, Avner Segall, Peter Seixas, Suzanne Sherkin, Roger Simon, and Handel Wright.

At the outset of this project, I took much from discussions with Peter Chin and Sharilyn Calliou, and I'm sure this book would not have turned out the way it has, if it were not for what I and those who know her well have learned from Airini. I also convey my appreciation for the contributions of Vivian Forssman, who attended to the whole and the parts on behalf of a broader community of readers; Anne Hawson, who once again did much to teach me the fault lines and lines of resistance to this work; and Roger

Simon, with whom this book might be said to have begun more than once—certainly with a walk through San Francisco during the Columbus countercommemoration.

Micah Kleit at the University of Minnesota Press, along with Jennifer Moore and Tammy Zambo, have served this book very well indeed, and I thank Pam Willinsky for her support of this work. This project was generously underwritten by the Social Sciences and Humanities Research Council of Canada and supported by the William Allen Endowed Chair of Education at Seattle University, with special thanks for the assistance of Jennifer Hoffman.

Earlier versions of chapters 6 and 9 were published in the *Journal of Curriculum Studies* and *Canadian Children's Literature,* respectively, and appear by permission of the publisher. Among the illustrations from the New York Public Library, the Galle print is courtesy of the Print Collection in the Miriam and Ira D. Wallach Division of Art, Prints, and Photographs; and the others are courtesy of the Rare Books Division of the Astor, Lenox, and Tilden Foundations.

digital imaging & graphics art direction:
Ed Lee. Angelhood/Dimestore Philosophy; Kim Graff. Riot Girl Studios

ONE

WHERE IS HERE?

I t is hard to know what to do about a world beset by struggles of ethnic nationalism, hardening of racial lines, and staggering divides between wealth
and poverty. For my part as a teacher, I have to wonder at what we are to
teach the young about such a world. How do we help them understand why
differences of color and culture, gender and nationality continue to have such
profound consequences? It won't do to fall back on the old lessons, to tell students that such differences are simply a fact of life, to tell them that the sus-
picion and distrust with which these differences are often regarded are the
product of sheer ignorance. They are unlikely to be reassured that only for
want of an education much like the one they are receiving, the world suffers
such discord and division. They might, however, appreciate how this faith in
education would help teachers through their own day.

Perhaps it is time to turn the tables on education in trying to make sense
of this divided world. After all, our schooling has not been so much the great
redeemer of prejudices as the tireless chronicler of what divides us. Education
is no small player in giving meaning to these differences. We are schooled in
differences great and small, in borderlines and boundaries, in historical struggles and exotic practices, all of which extend the meaning of difference. We
are taught to discriminate in both the most innocent and fateful ways so that
we can appreciate the differences between civilized and primitive, West and
East, first and third worlds. We become adept at identifying the distinguishing features of this country, that culture, those people. We are educated in
what we take to be the true nature of difference. Yet if education can turn a
studied distance between people into a fact of nature, education can also help

I

us appreciate how that distance has been constructed to the disadvantage of so many people. What has been learned can be learned again, and the time is right for such a project.

On June 30, 1997, the already wasted British Empire could be said to have gasped its last. Making a good show of closing one of history's great acts, Great Britain ceremoniously returned Hong Kong, the last of its major colonial outposts, to China. The territories were restored to China after 158 years of occupation, having been ceded to Britain following the infamous Opium War that revealed, among the many guises of British imperialism, the empire's role as drug pusher. Of course, the events of that final day in June were largely symbolic, as the sun had set on the British Empire long before the British government offices turned out the lights for the final time. Most of the attention was spent on what China would do with this cosmopolitan, international city. The whole thing might have been mistaken as a celebration of imperialism's accomplishment. Britain's foreign secretary during those final years, Douglas Hurd, boasted, "What we gave back at midnight on June 30 was one of the miracles of achievement in the modern world. Achievements, I hasten to add, not primarily by the British but by the people of Hong Kong" (1997).

Although minor British colonies remain to this day, from Bermuda to the Falkland Islands, the empire was not to survive the century it began at the height of its powers, when it spanned roughly a quarter of the globe in population and land mass. Britain was the largest of a series of European empires that in the last five centuries managed to annex the Western Hemisphere, foster a global slave trade, divide the African continent, and create a revolution in the arts and sciences. What so recently came to an end on Hong Kong Island in the South China Sea, in the colony that hung on the lip of the great divide between East and West, is something we will have to live with well into the next millennium. The empire is no more, in fact. Long live the Empire.

In more than one sense, the educational project of postcolonialism in the West is only beginning. Although the process of decolonization began in earnest after the Second World War with the repeated successes of the independence movements, the West has barely begun to see beyond the divisions generated by the same sensibilities that drove imperial expansion over the face of the globe. This book on education at empire's end examines one powerful source of those divisions. It is about imperialism's influence on the educated view of the world that the West cultivated during the era of empire. We need to learn again how five centuries of studying, classifying, and ordering humanity within an imperial context gave rise to peculiar and powerful ideas of race, culture, and nation that were, in effect, conceptual instruments that the West used both to divide up and to educate the world. This can help us understand why the rather inept explorer and missionary David Livingstone insisted on having a magic lantern among the scientific instruments, clothing, and other supplies hauled by his twenty-seven porters: it wasn't enough for him to attempt to fill in the European map of Africa; he had also, as one biographer puts it, "to blind his African audiences with science and Christianity" (T. Holmes, 1993, p. 75).

Given the enormity of imperialism's educational project and its relatively recent demise, it seems only reasonable to expect that this project would live on, for many of us, as an unconscious aspect of our education. After all, the great colonial empires came to a reluctant end only during the years when I and the rest of the postwar generation were being schooled. It may take generations to realize all that lies buried in this body of knowledge as a way of knowing the world. In attempting to make a small contribution to that process, this book has postcolonial, or, perhaps more precisely, postimperial pretensions, even as it maintains a decidedly Eurocentric focus on the West's educational project for the world.[1] But then, such a contribution seems to me to be the responsibility of one who has been so thoroughly shaped by this legacy and whose work as a teacher has been to be part of its shaping of others.

I have to say that this concern with imperialism's educational project has also fostered in me an appreciation for imperialism's learned achievement. There can be little question of the scientific value of James Cook's expeditions to the Pacific and Darwin's voyage on the *Beagle* for fields as diverse as entomology and astronomy. This is not, however, all that their endeavors have to teach us. And I now realize that for every Cook and Darwin, there were thousands of other earnest and adventurous souls gathering pieces of what was seen as the great jigsaw puzzle of nature. What comes, we now have to ask, of having one's comprehension of the world so directly tied to one's conquest of it? Much of the knowledge achieved through conquest and colonization was understood to legitimate the political and cultural domination of imperialism. The resulting perspective on the world formed an educational legacy that we have now to reconsider. We cannot readily sort through and discard the

---

[1] See Samir Dayal for a review of "postcolonialism's possibilities," which he poses warily against the postmodern assumption that postcolonialism is the work of the "Third World": "Thus, a fundamental task for the postcolonial must be to finger these double disjunctions, to disturb the reification of a Third World as a symptom of the First World and trouble the appropriation gesture that domesticates the non-West as other" (1996, p. 124). Gayatri Spivak (1991) insists on using "neocolonial," which does not betray the continuation of colonialism in the way that "postcolonialism" does.

colonially tainted understandings we carry, without devoting attention to how our view of the world has been shaped by imperialism's educational projects, which included fostering a science and geography of race; renaming a good part of the world in homage to its adventurers' homesick sense of place; and imposing languages and literatures on the colonized in an effort to teach them why they were subservient to a born-to-rule civilization.

Given the wonderful spectacles of learning, from arboretums to zoos, that were established under imperialism's patronage, it is not hard to argue that the whole venture had about it something of a great public education project intent on bringing the world together under the roof of European learning. I think it is fair to say that what Edward Said wrote of the field of study known as orientalism is no less true of imperialism as a whole: "It is . . . a distribution of geopolitical awareness into aesthetic, scholarly, economic, sociological, historical, and philological texts" (1978, p. 12). The educational itinerary of the extended and profoundly successful field trip of imperialism is rendered in Said's own exuberant cataloging of orientalism's scholarly project:

> to dignify all knowledge collected during the colonial occupation with the title "contribution to modern learning" when the natives had neither been consulted nor treated as anything except as pretexts for a text whose usefulness was not to the natives; to feel oneself as a European in command, almost at will, of Oriental history, time, and geography; to institute new areas of specialization; to establish new disciplines; to divide, deploy, schematize, tabulate, index, and record everything in sight (and out of sight); to make out of every observable detail a generalization and out of every generalization an immutable law about the Oriental nature, temperament, mentality, custom, or type; and above all to transmute living reality into the stuff of texts, to possess (or think one possesses) actuality mainly because nothing in the Orient seems to resist one's powers. (p. 86)

This book seeks, then, to extend Said's inspiring critique of orientalism to what I am framing as the educational legacy of imperialism, a legacy that has shaped many of our ideas about education, a legacy that continues to play a small but significant part in what the young learn of the world.

The problem today is not that schools are insensitive or unresponsive to the legacy of imperialism as it takes the form, for example, of a scientifically underwritten racism. I will examine how the textbooks used in biology, history, and English classes, which once could be expected to depict stereotypical racial types and national identities, now display a new multicultural sensitivity that teaches students about race as a form of culture in social studies, whereas the topic of race has been largely dropped from their biology classes.

In English classes, students read works that movingly depict personal struggles against discrimination, without gaining any sense of how English literature was used to teach people their distance from the center of civilization. The textbooks of my own school days made it apparent that the academic disciplines were in the front lines when it came to fixing the distinctions between the natives and the Europeans; they made it clear that the educational project was about extending the gift of civilization. By ignoring how the arts and sciences have contributed to the significance of race, culture, and gender, the school leaves students to wonder how in the world these differences took on the considerable significance they still hold. This book speaks to the educated about their education in the ways of the world, and it does so on behalf of the yet-to-be-educated.

I do not imagine that such critical scrutiny will dry up the wells of racism or end the neocolonial forms of exploitation that remain imperialism's aftermath. But whatever its impact, I think that the young are owed an explanation of how such divisions have come to mean so much and of how the schooling of only a generation ago, during the final days of the colonial empires, was still teaching us to divide the world in very troubling ways. One may argue that dragging up this past can only spoil the chances that the young will start with a clean slate. Yet educators would seem obliged to consider their sources, to consider how the forces of good and evil have worked their way through education. I think we have to consider how this, too, forms part of the past that we have inherited, part of what has prevailed in our finest educational institutions. Schools have offered students little help in fathoming why this sense of difference in race, culture, and nation is so closely woven into the fabric of society. As a result, students have been relatively unaware of such government measures as the racial restriction of access to voting, immigration, and public services until not so long ago.[2] They need to see that such divisions have long been part of the fabric and structure of the state, including the schools, and they need to appreciate that challenging the structuring of those differences requires equally public acts of refusing their original and intended meanings.

How these sometimes subtle imperial themes of difference and identity

---

[2] In Canada, for example, a Civil Liberties Association survey on historical awareness of discrimination found that among two hundred high school students in the Toronto area, only 9 percent were aware that blacks had been refused entry to the country on the basis of race; 11 percent knew that Chinese and 32 percent that First Nations peoples had once been denied the vote; 20 percent knew of racial discrimination against Jews in immigration, business, and higher education; and 25 percent knew that there had been slavery in Canada (Grange, 1995).

continue to play themselves out in the lives of the young can be heard in the words of a group of students with whom I worked in a Vancouver high school on a study of electronic communications.[3] Kathy Chin, for example, was preparing an introductory E-mail message for a student in Australia when I stopped to talk to her about the process, only to find her opening lines catching me off guard as they raised for me the issues of identity and location: "First let me tell you about myself. My parents came here from Hong Kong (I'm Chinese) about twenty years ago and I was born here in Vancouver. I have never lived anywhere else but I have traveled a lot."

The point Kathy made about who she was struck me as both banal and extraordinary. This was who *she* was, yet what she said spoke to a history that was still present for all of us. To identify oneself as having been born in Canada while remaining parenthetically Chinese echoes a colonial history that determined whose home Canada was to be, even as imperialism engaged the Chinese of the diaspora in the business of empire; it speaks to the barriers that imperialism constructed between East and West out of a compound of race, ethnicity, and nationality, as well as gender in the West's feminized conception of the Oriental as other. This may be too much to make Kathy's comments bear, but she was not alone in this self-identification; others among her classmates recognized themselves as indelibly Chinese in Canada:

> As to my appearance I'm chinese and very short 5'2", or 5'3" actually. Obviously I have long black hair parted down the middle and brown eyes. (Anne Lee)

> I have black eyes and hair. As you can tell from my last name you should know that I am Chinese. . . . I was born in Taiwan and moved to Costa Rica when I was in grade two. Later when I was in grade four I moved to Canada. (Sarah Huang)

> You probably wouldn't know that [I] am Chinese. I have one of the strangest names in the world, but at least if someone asked, "Where's Sterling?" nobody would say, "Sterling who?" (Sterling Tan)

What lessons should the school be teaching, I wondered, about the historical depth and intricacy of the great divide that these students continue to live out? How might it help them understand the histories carried in these innocent acts of self-identification? It was not that the question of identity

---

[3] For a description of the project, conducted in collaboration with Lorri Neilsen, see Neilsen and Willinsky (1993); for the qualities of that communication among Japanese and Canadian students, see Greenlaw (1993). Pseudonyms are used for the students studied in this and other research projects reported in this book; the students are quoted with their permission.

was missing from the school curriculum. Students have long had lessons on who is and who is not a member of this imagined community known as Canada.[4] These lessons do their share to make each student, in effect, "a précis of all the past," as Antonio Gramsci framed it: "For each individual is the synthesis not only of existing relations, but the history of these relations" (1971, p. 353). A strong source of light that the schools can throw on "the history of these relations," I argue, is found in reviewing imperialism's educational project.

One student in Kathy's class framed her identity in terms of ethnicity— "My ethnic background is Chinese but I was born in Vancouver and have lived here all my life" (Karen Yu)—yet there is still the strength of the contrast, established by her use of "but," of her Chinese background and her life in Vancouver.[5] The Kiplingesque division between East and West remains firmly a part of this city's vision of itself as the gateway to the Asian Pacific, a city in which half of the students speak English as their second language. Although the city is often given to celebrating its multiculturalism, the newspaper boxes a few blocks from Kathy Chin's school are occasionally defaced with "Chinks go home," and stickers placed on telephone poles in a local suburb at one point read, "Save a Young Mind, Stop Multiculturalism." The city's leading newspaper has run headlines on the order of "Immigrants Form Pool for Disease, Doctors Say" and "Cost of Providing ESL [English as a Second Language] Classes Is Eating Up the Education Dollar." Clearly, the graffiti would be a lot easier to deal with—as messages of misguided hate and ignorance—if they did not appear to be underwritten at times by the city's newspapers and doctors.[6]

Of course, there were also students in Kathy's class who did not appear to have to face such issues:

> I am 15 (turning 16 on April 7) with blonde hair and blue eyes. I'm pretty short. I was captain of the cheerleading squad for a football team. (Susan Harris)

---

[4] In his insightful treatment of nations as "imagined communities," Benedict Anderson speaks of how "in everything 'natural' there is always something unchosen," as "nation-ness is assimilated to skin-color, gender, parentage, and birth-era—all those things one cannot help" (1983, p. 143).
[5] On whether "Chinese" is a reference to race or ethnicity, it may be worth noting that the People's Republic of China is said to be the home of fifty-six ethnic groups (C.-C. Cheng, 1992, p. 163).
[6] The headlines are from Wigod (1993) and Boyd (1994). This new-wave xenophobia was candidly conveyed by one Vancouverite in a nationally distributed newspaper when she wrote about the loss of her "little exclusive Anglo-Saxon world . . . [having been] replaced by a thriving Chinese community from Hong Kong, sporting BMWs and Mercedes

> Hello, my name is James Statley. I live in Vancouver, British Columbia. I like sports a lot. I hate school. (Jim Statley)

> My name is Robert Campbell, and I am a Libra. (Robert Campbell)

It would seem that the play of race and ethnicity in identity is not necessarily everyone's affair, and this, too, signifies a gap in the students' education. All students need to understand the historical legacy of these self-identifications. They need to see how it is that white is a color that need not name itself. No one makes this more apparent than the antiracist educator Peggy MacIntosh when she speaks of the "invisible weightless knapsack" of white privilege, out of which she pulls some twenty-six instances, including, "I can be sure that my children will be given curricular materials that testify to the existence of their race," and, "I am never asked to speak for all the people of my racial group" (1990, p. 35). MacIntosh's last point strikes home all the more as this speaking-for-my-race is what I've done on behalf of Kathy Chin and her classmates, just as they have used this racial/ethnic identification out of a sense of history for which I am holding education accountable in this book.

The real issue is obviously not how Kathy and her classmates chose to identify themselves. My concern is with whether the schools can do more to help the young understand the educational formation of worldly divisions that carry with them a profound sense of who belongs where. The postimperial migration of people around the world today poses profound challenges to what we once knew and assumed of the world. Just as the changes involve Kathy Chin, I would argue, so also they include, and must become a part of the education of, her classmate Robert Campbell. He also needs to understand how the community he lives in is changing as part of a history that has long involved the sort of dislocations that first brought the Scots to Canada even as they displaced the people who had lived here for thousands of years before that. Imperialism does not tell the whole of students' stories, but it does figure in what they will learn of the world.

The Canadian literary critic Northrop Frye, whose work I focus on in chapter 9, wisely commented that that great identity question "Where is

---

Benzes," with the distressing irony of the colonized having profited by British colonialism. "Old houses were torn down at an unprecedented rate," Karen Krucik (1995) goes on to write, "to be replaced by 'monster houses,' huge three-level brick mansions with brick fences that now tower over hollows of older, smaller, one- or two-story Tudor style houses and cottages." Who lives in monster houses, one wants to ask, if not monsters? Chung Wong (1995) wrote back to the newspaper that house deeds in some Vancouver neighborhoods banned the sale of houses to "Orientals" until as late as 1972, an agreement that held, I have been told, for Jews as well.

here?" was less perplexing than "Who am I?" (1971a, p. 220). The geoidentity question "Where is here?"—which in Matthew Arnold's "Stanzas from the Grande Chartreuse" takes the form "And what am I, that I am here?" (1895, l. 66)—does have a way of linking our various histories as indigenes, colonials, immigrants, expatriates, tourists, citizens, refugees, and displaced persons. It is easy to see that many of the disputes that threaten the future of Canada, as well as those that concern broader questions of national identity, are about the nature of "here."

What Imperialism?

The Columbus quincentenary, celebrated a few year ago, was staged as a great marketing opportunity for blockbuster art shows and epic movies, yet for many the event amounted to what performance artist Guillermo Gómez-Peña called "a dance on the wound of history."[7] It was also a grim reminder of how students in the West have long been asked to honor the inflicting of that wound. We might take the familiar classroom mnemonic "In fourteen hundred and ninety-two / Columbus sailed the ocean blue" as proof of how Columbus has long been at the heart of what it means to be schooled. A new account, if not a new rhyme, of imperialism's misadventures, which has been long overdue in the schools, has begun to be written for the classroom, as I will point out presently. What also needs to be reviewed is imperialism's record of learned achievements, which was to shape our modern sensibility.

Such accounts need to begin with the often-taught pursuits of the Portuguese along the coast of Africa, Columbus in the Caribbean, the Spanish in America, Cabot and Raleigh across the Atlantic and their countrymen in India, the Dutch in Southeast Asia, and later the Germans in Africa and the Americans in the Pacific. They need to include imperialism's influence through Europe's age of exploration and the Renaissance, the founding of colonies and the Enlightenment, the opening of the Pacific and the rise of Romanticism, the Victorian age and the scramble for Africa. They need to confront a trade in human beings that forced 12 million people from sub-Saharan Africa on a deadly journey into slavery in the Western Hemisphere. They need to address the devastation of indigenous populations through military campaigns, economic exploitation, and the spread of epidemics. They also need to consider the encyclopedic project of mapping and naming all

---

[7] On performance artist Gómez-Peña, see Sawchuk (1992, p. 24) and chapter 3 of this book. On the "insurgent commemorations" of Columbus's voyage, see Roger Simon (1992), who deals with the challenges posed for educators by this way of celebrating history.

that the world contained, bringing it within a single system of thought. They need to realize the spread of education from the missionary schools of the New World to the universities of Japan.

Of course, the label "European imperialism" does not in any sense represent a systematic movement, a sustained campaign, or a coherent body of thought. Nowhere is this more clear than with the British Empire. Although by the turn of this century the empire encompassed more than one-quarter of the world's people, the British liked to think that it had been acquired over a five-century period in a "fit of absence of mind," as the British historian John Seeley put it in the last century (1884, p. 10). The empire was made up of a makeshift assortment of Crown colonies, white dominions, mandates, naval bases, trading ports, and the unique Indian raj. To name what was common to all of these arrangements is difficult, and so the term *imperialism* will have to operate as a loosely conceived historical phenomenon that covers a myriad of ventures directed at extending the dominion of Europe around the globe.[8]

At the risk, then, of lending too much coherence to the forces of European imperialism and of seeming to belittle the violence and injustice that accompanied the exploits of these "gentlemanly capitalists," as they have been characterized, this book focuses on the activities that were conducted in the name of imperialism's intellectual interests, which I take to be its educational project.[9] Beginning in earnest during the eighteenth century, the research and development arm of imperialism was gradually staffed by increasingly professional cadres of geologists, naturalists, astronomers, ethnographers, philosophers, historians, geographers, painters, and poets (many of them holding day jobs as sailors, soldiers, missionaries, and bureaucrats). The whole thing resulted in a Victorian "obsession with gathering and ordering information," as Thomas Richards describes it, that was closely connected to the "administrative core" of the British Empire through such educational institutions as the British Museum, the Royal Society, the Royal Geographic Society, the Royal Botanical Gardens, and the India Survey, as well as the universities (1993, p. 9). It produced an imaginary "imperial archive," in Richards's

---

[8] Trying to pin down the meaning of *imperialism* gives proof to Nietzsche's observation that "only that which has no history is definable": "All concepts in which an entire process is semiotically concentrated elude definition; only that which has no history is definable" (1969, p. 80). Add to this the imperialist injunction "Start the forgetting machine!" which Aimé Césaire claimed accompanied too many of Europe's colonial campaigns, and you have a sense of why imperialism offers a diffuse array of motives and intentions (1972, p. 32). On the relative lack of historical work on British imperialism, see Cannadine (1993, p. 184).

[9] Cain and Hopkins identify imperialism's new class of merchants and bankers that began to take shape in the early eighteenth century as "gentlemanly capitalists" (1993, p. 116).

terms, which amounted to "a fantasy of knowledge collected in the service of state and empire" that was thought capable of turning the world into a comprehensive order (p. 6). It was the duty and pleasure of these learned men and women, as this book will detail, to make the whole of the world coherent for the West by bringing all we knew of it within the imperial order of things. So it was that this order dictated all that future generations were going to learn of the world.

Today, that order may seem to be a thing of the past. The great colonial empires collapsed after the Second World War, undone by the politics of self-determination, the cold war, and transnational capitalism. A hundred nations were born, legalized segregation was declared unconstitutional in America, apartheid was finally ended in South Africa, and the Soviet Union was broken up. Transnational capital remains a global force, an imperialism of a different order, that extends beyond the scope of this book, which is taken up with the particular manifestations of the colonial legacy.[10] Yet the West is still dealing directly with the colonial legacy on a number of fronts. Consider Australia, where Aborigines' land claims met with considerable resistance until, only recently, the courts corrected one of colonialism's great myths by conceding that the British had not found a *terra nullius,* that is, an unoccupied land, when they first arrived (Milliken, 1993). In Canada, the Quebecois and First Nations peoples are each still working on forming postcolonial associations within or apart from the dominion (and are often at odds with each other in this struggle). The First Nations peoples in Canada do not hesitate to speak of a "colonialism on trial" in addressing unsettled land claims now before the courts (Monet and Skanu'U, 1992).

In America, the legacy persists in a deepening of the "color line," with increasing segregation in schools and discrimination in health care ("Race," 1993; "Segregation's Threat," 1993). Bob Herbert (1995) writes in the *New York Times* of "a besieged black population" facing restricted voting rights, dimin-

---

[10] Aijaz Ahmad addresses the process of decolonization as a struggle within and against the cold war and out of which has emerged what he identifies as "Super Imperialism" based on how "advanced capital has now reached a level of global self-organization" that has "given the imperialist countries a kind of unity that was inconceivable even fifty years ago" (1992, p. 313). He provides this helpful "rough periodization" for the end of colonization: "A very large number of sovereign states emerged in Asia and Africa during the twenty years after the Second World War, mainly under the hegemony of the national bourgeoisie and subordinated to regimes of advanced capital. The next decade, 1965–75, was dominated by the wars of national liberation which had a distinctly socialistic trajectory, even though the level of prior economic development and the scale of imperialist devastations preempted the possibility that socialist construction would have a reasonable chance. The two phases of the anti-colonial movements were over by the mid 1970s" (p. 30).

ished affirmative action, education, and job training opportunities, and curtailed support for the poor (largely the black poor) in housing, health, and food. For Herbert, the "increasingly harrowing times" that face the African American people bear "the foul legacy of 200 years of slavery and nearly a century and half of violent and grotesque racism." Meanwhile, a rising nativism uses the specter of an "immigration crisis" to advocate restrictive legislation for newcomers and a pitting of one minority group against another (Rayner, 1996; F. R. Lee, 1993). "The Asian invasion" (and its variations) whether in the *New Yorker* or in *Sports Illustrated,* is just one of the racial clichés that have returned to prominence (W. Wong, 1994). Immigration also preoccupies Europe, with its internal colonization of guest workers facing a rising xenophobia that sustains, for example, the demand for blood citizenship in Germany and talk of a fortress Europe, which, having made so much of the world, now closes its door to it.[11]

Beyond the economic and political legacy of the colonial era, the West has also been busy producing a colonial nostalgic that speaks to the lost style and seeming grace of those heady days. *The African Queen, A Passage to India, Raiders of the Lost Ark,* and *Indochine* are but a few films serving up a fascination with the exotic, with Walt Disney making it a speciality. Disney's *Aladdin* perpetuates the charmingly despotic Eastern other in a cartoonish orientalism, and *The Jungle Book* and *Pocahontas* extend the characterizations of this colorful period (Karim, 1993). Red Rose tea announces that its company's agents "comb the backwaters of Ceylon (sic), India, and Africa in search of the most treasured tea leaves" for "tea that means the world to you." Colonial imagery wafts through the perfume ads for Ralph Lauren's "Safari," and the *New York Times* spread on "Indo-Chic," with fashions by Chanel and Armani, was shot in Vietnam, one "of the rare places where one can still experience true glamour. . . . There's something otherworldly about the place" (O'Neill, 1993). For the home, colonial nostal-chic can be had from Domain Home Fashions: "No one went farther to make themselves comfortable than the British," its ad explains. "From the West Indies to East India, their traditional furnishings were enriched by the tropical cultures of the colonies, and now you can reclaim this adventurous and romantic era for yourself. . . . After all, it's your empire."

---

[11] On immigration and citizenship restrictions, see Whitney (1996) and A. Phillips (1993). On neocolonialism, see Warren Bello (1992) on the Pacific and the new world order; Noam Chomsky (1993), who pursues American policies of imperialism without colonies per se; and Frank Furedi (1994), who discusses the moral rehabilitation of imperialism.

But if our empire has left us with the rewards of (former) membership, it has also left us with liabilities of an educational nature. Imperialism afforded lessons in how to divide the world. It taught people to read the exotic, primitive, and timeless identity of the other, whether in skin color, hair texture, or the inflections of taste and tongue. Its themes of conquering, civilizing, converting, collecting, and classifying inspired educational metaphors equally concerned with taking possession of the world—metaphors that we now have to give an account of, beginning with our own education.

Educational Accountability

In thinking about how schools are ill prepared to address the history of identities that imperialism has bestowed upon us, I think we need to begin with the intersection between imperialism's legacy and education within our own lives. When my great-grandmother's family arrived in America in the 1880s, they were in search of a Europe they had not been able to find in Russian Poland.[12] After centuries of internal colonization in Eastern European shtetls, the Jewish people were being depicted at the time of their emigration as a race apart from Europeans. They were said to be a "secret race" and a "nation within a nation," as new scientists of race were obsessively given to measuring Jewish feet, noses, and gait.[13] It hardly needs to be added that this shift culminated in the Nazi campaign to eliminate a defiled, mongrel race, a rootless Jewish nation.

Fortunately, long before the *shoah,* my family were making their way across the New World on what might be taken to be a journey away from anti-Semitism and toward whiteness.[14] It often meant joining in on the displacement of others, such as American Natives and African Americans. While holding to their religion (although conversion was embraced by some), Jews sought to deracialize their family's lives through the language they spoke and

---

[12] The town my great-grandmother's family left, Grabova, now exists, as far as I can tell, only as a name engraved at the Holocaust Museum in Washington, D.C., as one of the Jewish communities that were eliminated by the Nazis.

[13] Ella Shohat, for one, has linked this persecution to the colonial project that began to unfold in 1492: "The campaign against the Muslims and Jews, as well as against heretics and witches, made available a mammoth apparatus of racism and sexism for recycling in the newly 'discovered' continents" (1992–93, p. 96). On the development of a medieval colonialism through the Crusades, see Robert Ignatius Burns (1975). On racialized physiology, see Gilman (1991); and on the Jew in Victorian literature, see Ragussis (1994).

[14] The racial assignation of Jewishness continues to drive anti-Semitism in, for example, the Church of Jesus Christ Aryan Nation, whose pastor, Richard Butler, publicly denounces those who fail to support the superiority of the white race as "traitors who are white outside, black inside and have Jewish minds" (Janofsky, 1995).

the education they sought.[15] My mother recalls formally debating in her Saturday Hebrew school class whether Judaism was a religion or a race. She held with religion, but the racial barriers would take another generation to fall. My grandfather was barred from the post that he coveted and qualified himself for on the faculty of the University of Toronto, for as late as the 1940s there were no Jewish professors in Canada (A. I. Willinsky, 1961; Abella, 1996). In the decade leading up to the Second World War, Canada had the worst record of any nation in restricting Jewish immigration; and during the war, riots in Montreal led to the smashing of Jewish shop windows.[16] While I was growing up, after the war, my parents were still not able to join the local golf and country club, but for my family these were the last such outposts of racial privilege associated with defining and maintaining the whiteness of here. Although it would not have occurred to my family to hold the forces of imperialism responsible for racial discrimination, imperialism had fostered and been well served by the science of race that through the nineteenth and into the twentieth century gave a thoroughly modern legitimacy to anti-Semitism and other forms of racism (more to follow on this).

My own education felt race-free, outside the occasional school-yard slander. Still, I kept my Jewishness protected and quiet well into my days as a schoolteacher. What could this aspect of my "background" have to do with the wonders of Western culture that I studied and ended up teaching to others? It didn't occur to me that "the best that had been thought and said," in Matthew Arnold's famous phrase (1896), was based, as he also put it, on discriminating between Hebraic and Hellenic influences in favor of the glory

---

[15] Sander Gilman portrays this urge to escape a racial identity as a form of self-hatred that could amount to a self-defeating preoccupation with the essential otherness of the Jew (1986, pp. 11–13). In his psychopathology of colonial racism, Frantz Fanon contrasts "the Jew [who] can be unknown in his Jewishness" and the African who is "overdetermined from without"; as he also puts it, "I am the slave not of the 'idea' that others have of me but of my own appearance" (1967, pp. 115–16). He bitterly concludes that between Jew and African, "we have one point in common. Both of us stand for evil" (p. 180). In America's landmark school desegregation decision, *Brown v. Board of Education,* the psychologist Kenneth Clark's research on racial self-hatred (1955) was used to persuade the U.S. Supreme Court that separate was not equal in education.

[16] At the time, Canada's best-loved humorist, Stephen Leacock, whose *Sunshine Sketches of a Little Town* remains a staple of school readers, insisted in his capacity as professor of economics at McGill University that the nation close off immigration for certain races of people: "But for continental Europe we should go slow and for some areas shut out their people as we would a bubonic plague. For all the Orient the only policy is and must be exclusion. Where we cannot marry, where we cannot worship, where we cannot eat, there we cannot live. The Eastern and Western races cannot unite. Biologists tell us that where they intermarry their progeny is an ill-joined product, two brains rattling in one skull" (1941, pp. 241–42).

that was Greece. On the rare occasions in this race-unspoken education when the Jew made an appearance, it was in the form of Shylock in my introduction to Shakespeare, or Fagin featured in my first Dickens, and there was scarcely a comment from anyone, least of all me, on what had been made of these characters. In science class, it's true, there was the inevitable poster of the wild-haired Albert Einstein as eccentric scientist-hero. Meanwhile, I took my history and geography lessons on a world split between civilized and primitive, West and East, male and female. So, keeping my Jewishness for the Woody Allen moments in my life, I went on to make an Arnoldian education my business and my life. It must have been a common experience for teachers in current and former British colonies around the globe, except that through one generation and a terrible war, I had been freed of the racial designation.

Only now have I finally come to ask how I so eagerly acquired an education that was indifferent, where it was not negative, toward aspects of my life and generations of my family. Who was I to be, what was I to make of this culture that was not meant to be mine, a culture that had been built, after all, on realizing such discriminations of character and identity? I had been taught to think the world of Ezra Pound, T. S. Eliot, and D. H. Lawrence, and did— only to learn sometime later that they would have found in me a distasteful and racialized Jewishness. I realized then that I had distanced myself from the Jewish culture that T. S. Eliot and Co. did not care much for.

This critical return to what our education makes of us is one that feminist scholars have been pursuing for some time, following Virginia Woolf's disquieting footsteps through the British Museum and Oxford University in *A Room of One's Own* (1929), all the while asking how it is that we make ourselves worthy of the West's best arts and sciences. Such reconsideration is, of course, what one should be about as an educator, always being drawn back to one's own never-adequate education, as if to affirm Eliot's all too well-known lines:

> We shall not cease from exploration
> And the end of all our exploring
> Will be to arrive where we started
> And know the place for the first time.

Yet when I now recall these lines from *Four Quartets* (1971b), they speak both to the age of exploration and to "where *we* started" in a new way ("for the first time").[17] They speak to an education in who I was to be, for all appearances,

---

[17] Cornel West, facing a similar point, allows for both a respect and a calling into question of one's education: "Yet all evaluation—including a delight in Eliot's poetry despite his

and who I was not to be: "What might have been and what has been / Point to one end, which is always present."

Against this historical and global backdrop of a world imagined as empire and race, I seek to achieve with this book a degree of educational accountability. Although this phrase typically refers to holding teachers responsible for student achievement scores on standardized tests, what I have in mind is that educators *owe* those they teach some *account*—if always partial—of what we have taught them about the world. The ethics of accountability, as I would cast it here, is about examining what this form of schooling has underwritten and who it has denied. It is about giving an account of education's and scholarship's role in a recent historical phenomenon that has had incalculable global ramifications. The account called for here concerns the significance of such divides as East and West, primitive and civilized; it concerns how the world has been constructed around centers and margins, and how these divisions were bolstered through forms of scholarship supported by imperialism. As I am a teacher, I owe students an account of my work within the educational project that sought to put the world together in this way. I owe them an account of why education has not done more good in the world, why it has not done more to realize fully the democratic promises that continue to underwrite public education. I owe them an account of why I remain committed to expanding the concerns of education to include this reflective and self-critical function.

What might such an account sound like? Leon Litwick, in his presidential address to the Organization of American Historians in 1987, captured the spirit of educational responsibility that I am invoking here, when he called upon historians to acknowledge that "no group of scholars was more deeply implicated in the miseducation of American youth and did more to shape the thinking of Americans about race and blacks than historians" (cited by Hughes, 1993, p. 123). This particular burden of scholarship does not fall, of course, on historians alone. It is distributed *across* the educational experiences that, in all likelihood, we and our children have gone through. However one wants to label this work—and Litwick would not use *postcolonial* to describe his position—there is a need to examine education's continuing contributions to what were and continue to be colonizing divisions of the world. Everywhere in this work there is a worrying about the consequences of knowing

---

reactionary politics, or a love of Zora Neale Hurston's novels despite her Republican party affiliations—is inseparable from, though not identical or reducible to, social structural analyses, moral and political judgments and the workings of a curious critical consciousness" (1990, p. 31).

that might have been inspired by the ethical compass set out in the eighteenth century by Montesquieu:

> If I knew something useful to myself and detrimental to my family, I would reject it from my mind. If I knew something useful to my family but not to my homeland, I would try to forget it. If I knew something useful to my homeland and detrimental to Europe, or else useful to Europe and detrimental to Mankind, I would consider it a crime. (Cited by Kristeva, 1991, p. 130)

This book is about the accumulation of learning that proved eminently useful to Europe and often detrimental to the larger body of humanity. It is concerned with what remains of that crime, as Montesquieu would have it, in the lessons we continue to teach the young and in the way many of us still see the world.

To let students in on how their education may still be marked by European imperialism resembles the project proposed by the literary scholar Gerald Graff (1992) when he calls on scholars to "teach the conflicts." Rather than following the typical pedagogical tack of "conflict evasion," Graff recommends that university classes explore the contest of ideas that dominate public forums and scholarly enclaves.[18] Perhaps the recent controversy surrounding Stanford University's Western civilization courses would be a good place to start in trying to understand the politics of imperialism's educational aftermath.[19] However, when it comes to excluding dissenting voices, few institutions can best the public high school, which is the educational home to a far wider range of the public than is the university. To hold off "teaching the conflicts" of imperialism's educational legacy until college, or to treat it simply as an intellectual contest, diverts our attention from how the ideas of the primitive and the civilized become part of a commonsense division of the world by race, culture, and nation. The common sense of these divisions, I will argue, can be attributed to the success of this legacy, from primary grades to graduate school, from television's *Wild Kingdom* to *National Geographic*. This book turns to the less glamorous site of the public school because this is where most people form their ideas about history, science, literature, and other disciplines.

---

[18] Graff's point, that the majority consensus and sense of shared culture upheld by those he identifies as "educational fundamentalists" emerged by virtue of little more than the "clubiness" of educators and educated, is well taken. As he points out, "It is not too hard to get a consensus if you start by excluding most Jews, blacks, immigrants, women, and others who figure to make trouble" (1992, p. 58).

[19] Among the accounts of the struggle at Stanford is D'Souza (1991), to which I have responded (1996).

The aim of this account giving is to afford students (and readers of this book) a critical distance from their own education, which may well, in turn, be in need of revision itself one day; the aim is to hasten and focus changes that are already under way in creating a multicultural curriculum by offering readers a review of the history and the sort of education that have brought us to this point. I do not intend the intellectual legacy of imperialism to be the whole of anyone's education, but neither should it go completely missing in a dozen years of schooling. Such teaching as I propose is not about realizing, or teaching to, the true identity of the student. It is intended, rather, to help students understand their own education and the education of others as a worthy object of inquiry. Whatever criticisms of education this inquiry raises, it still reflects a faith in learning.

In writing this book, I have sifted through the rich history of imperialism, drawing on primary documents and firsthand accounts as well as contemporary polemics and advances in critical theory; I have worked with students, teachers, and textbooks in today's schools. The pattern I follow in this book is to move from the larger historical record of imperialism to specific components of today's classrooms. Along the way, I pause at the 1960s as the critical juncture when the current generation of baby boomers that swell the ranks of today's teaching force was schooled and when twenty-eight nations, from Algeria to Zaire, successfully struggled through war and diplomacy to wrest their independence from the imperial powers. It was a time when Frantz Fanon published his scathing indictment of colonialism, *The Wretched of the Earth* (1963); and Great Britain attacked the UN for pursuing "a new and dangerous path" of decolonization as it pressured Portugal to grant independence to Angola, Mozambique, and Portuguese Guinea. Meanwhile, the United States was amassing some fourteen thousand military "advisers" in Vietnam while at home it faced, as *Time* put it, "the pressures of Negro revolution bursting out all over." Federal troops had to accompany African American students to school in Little Rock, Oxford, and Tuscaloosa, while two hundred thousand people gathered during the triumphant March on Washington to hear Rev. Dr. Martin Luther King Jr. tell the world, "I have a dream that my four little children will one day live in a nation where they will not be judged by the color of their skin but by the content of their character."[20]

---

[20] Citations are from *Time,* respectively, as follows: "United Nations: Words of Dissent," January 5, 1962, p. 25; "United Nations: Against the Last White Strongholds," August 9, 1963, p. 30; "South Viet Nam: Search for Answers," August 9, 1963, p. 30; "Civil Rights: More Anticlimax than Crisis," September 20, 1963, p. 20; "Civil Rights: The March's Meaning," September 6, 1963, pp. 15–17. This was also the year that *Time* switched from the topical heading "Races" to "Civil Rights."

To give a sense of the intellectual climate of those formative years in the education of many of us, I draw on three powerful scholarly statements in the chapters ahead: William McNeill's *The Rise of the West* (1963), Carlton Coon's *The Origin of Races* (1962), and Northrop Frye's *The Educated Imagination* (1963). Even as the European empires were dissolving, these major scholars and educators bolstered the case for a unequaled culture and race, whatever civil rights and political independence might finally be achieved in the world. Taken with Fanon's *The Wretched of the Earth,* these works make for a fascinating intellectual moment in the legacy of a collapsing imperialism that was as important as the Beatles, dare one say, in the education of the postwar baby boom generation now assuming the reigns of power in the West. At the very least, we need to reconsider how a person coming of age in the West in those years, whether in grade school or graduate school, was raised in the aftermath of colonialism among imperial habits of mind that now need to be identified, as they might still contribute to the educated imagination.

To establish the degree to which our current ideas of education may have been influenced by the global forces of imperialism, I lay out, in the following three historical chapters, the different ways in which imperialism was bent on taking a knowing possession of the world, on setting that world on public display for the edification of the West, and on developing the principal forms of schooling that might serve both colonial state and colonized native. Having secured education's historical place in imperialism, I then begin a detailed treatment of five of the academic disciplines that have become staples of the school curriculum: history, geography, science, language, and literature. Each of these subject areas is accorded its own chapter (chaps. 5–9), which is devoted to identifying traces of the colonial imagination that form part of how we have learned to divide the world. Each chapter begins with the subject's historical formation within the age of empire, pauses over the form this legacy took during the early 1960s, and then takes a close look at the lingering elements of this legacy in today's classrooms, whether in America, Britain, Canada, or elsewhere.

Education remains a voyage of discovery, a journey in search of a larger world. So it is that the philosopher Ernst Cassirer insists, in his discussion of Rousseau, that the student "understands the world only inasmuch as he acquires and conquers it step by step" (1989, p. 119). That the age of exploration furnished the commonplace metaphors of educational rhetoric is obviously, for me, more than an imaginative borrowing. Imperialism was an educational venture that captured and captivated the imagination of the West. From its interests in tourism to interior design, the West still lives within the spell of the imperium, and what follows in this book is a disquisition on what it might take to distance ourselves from that spell. When Toni Morrison opened her Massey lectures on American civilization at Harvard in the year of the Columbus quincentenary, she described her hope to "draw a map, so to speak, of a critical geography and use that map to open as much space for discovery as the original charting of the New World—without the mandate for conquest" (1992, p. 3). In this way, we need to grow curious about what we have made of the world, beginning with a critical geography of our own map-coloring and -labeling days in school that did so much to define our place in the world. We owe students today an account of the historical divisions out of which we have fashioned ourselves as educated people, even as we work together to move beyond our current understanding of an inexorably divided world.

PART I
EDUCATIONAL IMPERATIVE

The Landing at ERRAMANGA one of the NEW HEBRIDES.

Representation of the Heiva at Otaheite

Two engravings capturing the explorations of Captain Cook in the Pacific. Above: The Landing at Erramanga, by Sherwin, in Captain Cook's Voyage towards the South Pole (London, 1777). Below: Representation of the Heiva at Otaheite, by Royce, in Rickman's Journal of Captain Cook's Last Voyage to the Pacific Ocean (London, 1781). Courtesy Rare Books Division, New York Public Library, Astor, Lenox, and Tilden Foundations.

TWO

AN ADVENTURE IN LEARNING

For the learned and scholarly members of the European community, the big news during the age of exploration did not arrive with the ships returning from the New World loaded with wonders and riches. They were as fascinated by these unprecedented sights as the next person, but the real discovery was that what these scholars had made of the world for a thousand years was sinking beneath the expanded horizon, sinking beneath the weight of the cargo and concepts gathered through this exploration. They came to realize that the world was not simply one or two continents larger than the best of them and their books had imagined, it was no longer the same world. What they knew so well of that world did not contain—nor could it readily account for—the newfound places, plants, and peoples. They now had the challenge of accommodating all that these new worlds offered within their familiar world of learning. Much of their learning had been shaken, if not undone, and they needed to rebuild that world anew.

It had not taken long for the first signs of trouble to appear. Within hours of Columbus's arrival in the Caribbean, he was noting the absence of "monsters," thereby not only discounting popular legend but also undermining Pliny's encyclopedic *Historia Naturalis* that had stood as fact for close to fourteen centuries (Columbus, 1969, p. 121). The other great pillar of European learning, the Bible, was also to prove geographically shortsighted in its ability to serve as a guide to the discoveries made abroad. That was hardly the end of things, however, and there was more than a short period of transition in which mythical creatures from Pliny were used to illustrate new maps of the world and biblical prophecies were seen as fulfilled in new lands; the classics and Christianity had shown a vulnerability in the face of what had been found in the New World. More than a few of the cognitively adventuresome scholars recognized that here, amid such an amassing of new evidence, was an opportunity for rethinking what this earth was and could now be. "O, what arrogant poverty of intellectual humility, not to be moved to wonder," the Italian physician Girolamo Cardono chastised those who failed to realize what was before them (cited by Lach, 1977, p. 556).

Many of the learned were too preoccupied with the religious schisms and the classical revival of the Renaissance to give much thought to news from abroad. They comfortably clung to the learning of ages past and taught the young the same, so that toward the end of the sixteenth century, Richard Hakluyt reports having been instructed on "the division of the earth into three parts [Europe, Asia, and Africa] after the old account" (1972, p. 31). But Hakluyt and others had already figured out that something was amiss and that it was up to them to "prosecute that knowledge and kind of literature" (p. 31). His *Principal Navigations, Voyages, Traffiques, and Discoveries of the English Nation,* published in 1589–90 with corporate sponsorship from the English Virginia Company, dared the intellectually intrepid to sail toward and embrace that new knowledge under their nation's flag. The adventurer-scholar would bring order to what was strange, dividing up nature and world by name and map as if to make them over anew. Like architects after an earthquake, many lettered Europeans saw a chance to rebuild a world that had been lost, and to build it with greater strength and integrity than were possessed by the world they had inherited. And in five centuries of this reconfiguration, they managed to take hold of the whole world in ways that those schooled in Western ways continue to inherit. As Anthony Grafton quips, "The encounter with naked inhabitants of a new world, in short, enabled intellectuals to make naked experience take the place of written authority" (1992, p. 5).

In a sense, then, the conquest was intellectually staged alongside imperialism's other exploits. For example, consider how Michel de Certeau names, among the technologies turned to imperial conquest, a "*writing that conquers,*" which was to "use the New World as if it were a blank 'savage' page on which Western desire was to be written" (1988, p. xxv; de Certeau's emphasis). This writing was, above all, to inscribe a New World of learning. "Rhetorically, the New World replaced the ancient texts," Anthony Grafton adds to this discussion. "It had become the prime metaphor for the right way to discover new facts about the world and the prime source for new theories about human society" (1992, p. 252). Making sense of the New World became an enormous educational project in which an age had to reconstruct itself, not only by using the new materials at hand but also by transforming its past into a new resource, a process that Grafton captures with some grace:

> Even though [the ancient texts] retain their position in education and their claim to supreme age and beauty, their period of real cultural authority has passed. What began as weapons in an arsenal wind up as exhibits in a museum; what had been articles to be used with deadly seriousness become things of beauty to be visited on holidays. (p. 254)

The question we face today is how the lessons that were drawn from the centuries of European expansion continue to influence the way we see the world. Even as imperialism's "period of real cultural authority" has been eclipsed by forms of neocolonialism and the new transnationalism of science and technology, many of the ideas of the world generated by imperial designs on it "retain their position in education." The colonial era is the stuff of museums visited on holidays, yet Grafton fails to note that weapons in museums, like lessons in classrooms, still work upon the mind, instilling a nostalgic sense of how the world was once meant to be.

To appreciate what might persist of that imperial age in our educated imaginations, we need to return to its original lessons, to what was first made of the *discovery* and the *new.* The legacy begins with the distance between primitive and civilized peoples that gave rise to a science of our humanity. The dichotomy not only made Europe's place in the world sensible and secure after it was temporarily unsettled by the discovery of new worlds, but also left it with a mandate for distributing its civilization to the rest of the world in return for governing that world. In 1620, Francis Bacon set out the divine distance between European and native, using the West Indies as his measure:

> Let anyone but consider the immense difference between men's lives in the most polished countries of Europe, and in any wild and barbarous region of the new Indies, he will think it so great, that man may be said to be a god unto man, not only on account of the mutual aids and benefits, but for their comparative states—the result of the arts, and not of the soil and climate. (1855, p. 109)

Just how those "arts" could be thought to reflect a "[Western] man [who] may be said to be a god unto [non-Western] man" is part of an education in education that I try to achieve with this book. In our efforts today to make new sense of what are still understood as "immense differences," it seems naive and ill fated to proceed without recognizing the history of their making. It will not do to try to forget a past that is not past.

By the time the age of empire was all over, no branch of learning was left untouched. New academic disciplines of anthropology and orientalism were born, and the old ones of geography, philology, and anatomy were recast in the ordering of the new world. Colonial rule gave rise to a new class of knowledge workers in universities, government offices, industry, and professions devoted to colonial conquest by classification and categorization. They traveled, formed learned societies, created experimental gardens, and established laboratories. They joined in building the military, political, religious, and economic structures of global empires. If imperialism proved to be the political emancipation of the bourgeoisie, as Hannah Arendt has suggested (1951), with businessmen assuming the role of international statesmen, it was no less liberating for the attending scholars and educators. The learned helped fashion an imperial design on the world, and they arranged to have the splendid spoils of this adventure in learning exhibited in lectures, circuses, museums, zoological and botanical gardens, and written and illustrated accounts, each providing its own lesson on the wonders of empire. Imperialism proved a keen sponsor of an extensive public education on the benefits of global domination. How could such a sustained and sweeping effort help but end up defining the whole of the world for the West?

The educational history of imperialism is told in this and the following two chapters as it moves through a focus on learning, exhibition, and schooling. The chapters deal with those who sought a rational and self-affirming mastery of the world and those who found in that mastery a further proof of God's Christian will on earth. These eager students of the world were delighted with the meeting of economic and intellectual advantages that came of conquest and colony. They achieved innumerable scientific advances, as well as a wide array of cultural and historical understandings. It was a five-century-long adventure in learning that did not fail to help humankind in practical and philosophical ways, even as its dividing up of that humanity continues to haunt us to this day—which leaves for those who have formed their lives around this educational legacy to acknowledge the accomplishment while coming to terms with the troubling and persistent aspects of imperialism's regard for the world.

Willful Knowledge

The intellectual interests of imperialism could be characterized as reflecting a particular "will to know." At its root was a desire to take hold of the world, and it was the equal, in its acquisitiveness, to any financial interest in empire. If this desire had amounted to nothing more than an unrelenting enthusiasm for learning, a healthy curiosity about the world and its wonders, then I would not be writing this book. But this will to know became an integral part of the economic and administrative apparatus of imperialism, and in the process it was far too often dedicated to defining and extending the privileges of the West. In *The Order of Things* (1970), Michel Foucault identifies a major shift in European thought that took place at the close of the sixteenth century. In its crudest form, this shift meant that knowledge was no longer sought in looking for the semblance among things; rather, the aim of scholarship was to determine differences: "Resemblance, which had for long been the fundamental category of knowledge—both the form and content of what we know—became disassociated in an analysis based on terms of identity and difference" (p. 54). Knowledge had originally been found in what was mirrored, reflected, and echoed within the heavens and the earth. Then, with the seventeenth-century leadership of Bacon and Descartes, "thought cease[d] to move in the element of resemblance" (p. 51). In support of this shift, Foucault cites Bacon's critique of resemblance: "The human intellect, from its peculiar nature, easily supports a greater order and equality in things that it actually finds" (p. 52). Semblance was a false idol that could lead one to gloss over the distinguishing differences and defining essences of things. Descartes, for his part, declared that all knowledge "is obtained by the comparison of two or more things with each other" (p. 52). The will to know during the seventeenth century and thereafter pursued, in Foucault's words, a "calculable form of identity and difference" (p. 53). This phrase could easily take us back to Kathy Chin's grade 10 classroom, introduced at the opening of chapter 1 of this book. The "calculable form of identity and difference" is what those students were inscribing in their E-mail messages about who they were; it is what their social studies class continued to teach about Canada and China.

In poststructuralist fashion, Foucault does not contemplate the causes of this sixteenth-century shift in thinking. Yet it is hard to miss how the turn to identity and difference served the interests of imperialism. When Europe was the whole of the world, anyone wanting in resemblance could be expelled, as the Jews were from Spain in 1492 for failure to convert; or they could be beaten back, as were the Moors from Spain that same year. A century later, Europe was beginning to develop new sciences of difference for making sense of a new world. "The sciences always carry within themselves the project, however remote it may be," Foucault offers, "of an exhaustive ordering of the world" (1970, p. 74). He pronounces, with a typically majestic sweep, that "the center of knowledge, in the seventeenth and eighteenth centuries, is the *table*" (p. 75; Foucault's emphasis). The scientific table encouraged increasingly fine calculations of differences, row by row, column by column; and those who engaged in imperialism's adventure in learning used tables, graphs, and diagrams aplenty to enumerate, order, and identify a world of differences. The identification of difference was always read against the extreme polarities of primitive and civilized, East and West, just as certainly as it had already been set out between woman and man. That these differences stood was never in question; there was no danger of blurring the boundaries, weakening the hierarchies. This knowledge of difference served, as Edward Said states, to "help the mind intensify its own sense of itself by dramatizing the distance and difference between what is close to it and what is far way" (1978, p. 55).[1]

In 1800, three centuries after Columbus landed in the Americas, a young Frenchman named Joseph-Marie Degérando presented a treatise entitled *Considerations on the Various Methods to Follow in the Observation of Savage Peoples* (1969) to the newly formed Société des observateurs de l'homme in Paris. What had come naturally to Columbus was, by the beginning of the nineteenth century, transformed into a scientific method that combined travel with observation and record keeping: "The Science of man is a natural science, a science of observation, the most noble of all" (p. 61). The scientific aim is reflection, for "none is more fascinating, more fruitful in useful trains of thought" when it comes to knowing "the work of nature" than "peoples at very different degrees of civilization" (p. 62). The scientific morality at work here falls between using others to know oneself better and coming, through this knowledge, to "a better awareness of all the bonds that unite us to our fellows" (p. 61). The aim was to witness the evolutionary history of the species that culminated in the West, and the method was the form of time travel afforded more civilized peoples: "The philosophical traveler, sailing to the ends of the earth, is in fact traveling in time; he is exploring the past; every step he makes is the passage of an age. Those unknown islands that he reaches are for him the cradle of human society" (p. 63).[2]

When it came to the imperial pursuit of identity and difference, to return to Nietzche's warning, examples abound of justice placing a distant second to the earnest pursuit of knowledge. The will to know became part of the seafaring Europeans' code of conduct. For a 1553 journey to China, Sebastian Cabot, "governor of mystery and company of the Merchant Adventurers," as Hakluyt named him, compiled just such a set of ethically dubious ordinances to govern the meeting of an unknown nation of people:

> It is to be considered how they may be used, learning much of their natures and dispositions, by some such person, as you may first either allure, or take to be brought aboard your ships, and there to learn as you

---

[1] Said points to how the Orient was depicted as unchanging and "absolutely different" from the West (1978, p. 96).

[2] The advantage of depicting these cultures as outside time, as Johann Fabian has pointed out, is that it avoids the irrevocable changes visited on these peoples' lives by imperial expansion (1983, p. 32).

may, without violence or force, and no woman to be tempted, or en-
treated to incontinence, or dishonesty. . . .

If the person may be made drunk with your beer, or wine, you shall
know the secret of his heart. . . .

The names of the people of every island, are to be taken in writing, which the commodities of the same, their natures, qualities, and
dispositions, what commodities they will most willingly depart with,
and what metals they have in hills, mountains, streams or rivers, in, or
under the earth. (Cited by Hakluyt, 1972, pp. 57–58)

How well this questionable respect of other peoples was upheld amid the desire to learn "without violence or force" may be judged by comparing it to
the probable success of Cabot's forbidding "detestable swearing" among the
crew. His call to record the dispositions of the people visited is akin to the
data quest of later anthropological inquiries, with a hint, in this case, of labor-
market and natural-resource research. His singling out of native women
speaks to the mix of license and learnedness that traveled these "places unknown." In 1589, Cabot's ordinances were published as part of the proud
record of British exploration that Hakluyt presented in his *Principal Navigations* (1972).

British scientific efforts received a significant boost during the seventeenth century when a group of scientifically minded Londoners and Oxford
dons formed the Royal Society, devoted to promoting the new experimental
philosophy developed by Bacon. Although the early achievements reported
to the Royal Society from the physics laboratories, anatomical theaters, and
astronomical observatories of the age owed little enough to imperialism,
inklings of imperialism's subsequent impact on the success of the scientific
worldview were apparent in the drawing up of the society. The opening line
of the charter issued by Charles II in 1662 certainly posited the close association between the sciences and the empire: "We have long and fully resolved to
extend not only the boundaries of Empire but also the very arts and sciences"
(cited by Ornstein, 1963, p. 105). The society itself cast its pursuit of knowledge in the service of all humankind and, as Thomas Sprat records, was leery
of the temptations of empire: "For to increase the Powers of all Mankind and
to free them from the bondage of Errors, is greater Glory than to enlarge *Empire,* or to put Chains on necks of Conquer'd *Nations*" (1959, n.p.; Sprat's emphasis). In ranking beneficial knowledge over empire, the society sought to
take advantage of the opportunities of this worldly travel by publishing "Directions for Seamen Bound for Far Voyages" in the first edition of its *Philosophical Transactions.* English sailors were pressed into the service of science,
and these newfound students of nature proved ready contributors to the in-

tellectual riches of the nation. Sprat noted how "in short time, there will scarce a Ship come up the *Thames,* that does not make some return of *Experiments,* as well as *Merchandise*" (p. 86). As these seamen collected samples of what they beheld while traveling abroad, they contributed to the society's pursuit of a "Universal History of Nature." Sprat describes one of the "Principal Intentions of the Society" to be assembling "a General Collection of all the Effects of *Arts,* and the Common or Monstrous *Works* of *Nature*" (p. 251). The society's cabinet of curiosities, or "Musaeum," was to include specimens of that monstrous work of race, judging by a comment from the time cited by Ornstein: "Amongst the curiosities, the most remarkable are . . . an ostrich . . . an herb which grew in the stomach of a thrush; and the skin of a moor, tanned, with the beard and hair white" (1963, p. 115). The skin of the Moor was a small enough curiosity, third after the ostrich and the intestinal herb, but both scientific and popular culture would increasingly make of the skin of the other a spectacle of significance through to this century.

The society did not hesitate to remind its more sedentary members that it was "the design of the *Royal Society . . .* to study *Nature* rather than *Books,*" calling on them to consider "how much they may increase their *Philosophical* stock by the advantage which England enjoyes of making Voyages into all parts of the World" (Sprat, cited by B. Smith, 1960, p. 8). The metaphorical reference to commerce is suggestive. The arts and sciences profited by the nation's earnest investment in imperialism, and they repaid the investment by advancing the technologies of conquest, gathering relevant information, and articulating the ideologies of superiority, all of which were necessary for seeing through this drive to possess of the world.[3]

One source of insight into the scholar-adventurers' esprit de corps is Denis Diderot's whimsical "supplement to Bougainville's *Voyage*" (1991). First published in 1773, the "supplement" takes the form of a dialogue between two gentlemen discussing the recent travel book *Voyage around the World,* by the mathematician-turned-explorer Louise-Antoine de Bougainville. Bougainville made the career switch, one of Diderot's characters explains, because "he is a true Frenchman, ballasted on the one side by a treatise on calculus and on

---

[3] David Philip Miller writes that "if the voyages of exploration could dispatch or bring back to Europe measurements of latitude and longitude; charts of coastlines, harbors, and seaways; collections of flora and fauna; depictions of people; and accounts of their language, then future emissaries could deal from a position of strength with the places and peoples encountered on subsequent occasions" (1996, p. 23). In *Machines as the Measure of Men* (1989), Michael Adas argues that by the mid-eighteenth century, the West understood its global display of scientific and technological accomplishment as proof positive of its preeminence among civilizations and therefore of its right of global dominance.

the other by a voyage around the world" (p. 61). Bougainville is imperialism's ideal student. We are told that he has "the right intellectual outlook and the qualities needed for success," which include "philosophy, courage, truthfulness; an eye skilled in and swift in the art of observation; caution, patience; the desire to see, to understand, to learn; a grasp of calculation, mechanics, geometry, and astronomy, and a sufficient smattering of natural history" (p. 61). Thus it is made to seem that only on imperialism's immense playing fields and watery expanses can a well-rounded and well-educated Frenchman be truly exercised. In return, Bougainville is said to offer his nation three assets: "a better knowledge of our ancient domicile and its inhabitants; improved security on the seas, which he traversed plummet in hand; and more accuracy in our maps" (p. 61). The improved security was surely as much psychic as military, coming from possession of a superior knowledge.[4]

For all that he credited the adventuresome Bougainville, Diderot was not above directing this acquired knowledge of the colonies against the imperial state. He makes reference at one point to "the most primitive of people, the Tahitians, [who] seem to have come nearer good legislation than any civilized nation," insofar as they have avoided, among other nasty civilized aspects, "the tyranny of Man, who has turned possession of a woman into a property right" (1991, pp. 104, 107). The educational imperative of this scurrying about the oceans, for Diderot, is still to make something at home of the differences.[5] The learned of the day took the lives and artifacts of others as their principal texts for reconfiguring the New (and expanded) World in their own image. When Europeans wrote about the importance of freedom, it was in the light of colonial slavery, just as they came to write about love inspired by the "primitive," "uninhibited" coupling they imagined taking place on South Seas islands.

---

[4] Charles de la Condamine, eighteenth-century geographer and leader of scientific expeditions sponsored by both France and Spain, put it this way: "Whilst his Majesty's [Louis XV's] armies flew from one end of Europe to the other, his mathematicians dispersed over the surface of the earth, were at work under the Torrid and Frigid Zones, for the improvement of the sciences, and the common benefit of all nations" (cited by Pratt, 1992, p. 18). By the next century, it was imperial France's military forces that possessed scholarly presence abroad, serving, in Pyenson's estimation, as "the largest reservoir of astronomical talent in France" (1993, p. 18).
[5] The anticolonial side of Diderot is seen in his preparing a surreptitious edition of the notoriously popular L'histoire des deux Indes en Europe et en Amérique au XVIII siècle, by the abbé Raynal, in 1780. This encyclopedic work, cobbled together out of colonial detail and scathing polemic, inveighed against the overlords of imperialism: "Tremble! you who feed men with lies, or make them groan beneath oppression. You are going to be judged" (Diderot, 1992, p. 185). The Parlement of Paris hastily consigned the book to shredding and burning, "as impious, blasphemous, seditious, and as inciting the masses to rebel" (cited by Aravamudan, 1993, p. 49).

Whether for increasing or threatening the security of the state, the will to know fostered by imperialism proved to be the force of ideas and learning in the world. The increasing traffic in ideas, crucial to the success of imperialism, was acutely observed in the closing years of the eighteenth century by George Forster, who had sailed with Cook on his second scientific expedition to the Pacific. On looking out onto the busy Amsterdam harbor, Forster noted how the sciences on which the West prided itself had fashioned their own imperial economy:

> The eagerness of greed was the origin of mathematics, mechanics, physics, astronomy and geography. Reason paid back with interest the effort invested in its formation. It linked faraway continents, brought nations together, accumulated the products of all different regions— and all the while its wealth of concepts increased. They circulated faster and faster and became more and more refined. New ideas which could not be processed locally went as raw materials to neighboring countries. There they were woven into a mass of already existent and applied knowledge and sooner or later the new product of reason returns to the shores of the Amstel. (Cited by Fabian, 1983, p. 96)

This imperial traffic was a form of *intellectual mercantilism* that drove the learned version of empire.[6] News of the untapped riches of fact and artifact abroad encouraged intellectual mavericks and inquisitive adventurers to seek their fortune among the little-mapped regions of the world. They were followed in their journeys by less daring sorts who undertook more systematic forms of cultural and scientific strip-mining of the colonial terrain. There was so much to be named and known, so much that stood to be brought within the compass of European learning. The practice of science and scholarship in the colonies meant sweeping up barrelfuls of specimens to feed the serious work of synthesis and theory, as well as public education, reserved for the "invisible colleges" of the metropolis (Macleod, 1987). What this mercantilism produced was universal theories of knowledge, which were later sold back to the colonies at a premium that would largely teach them their place at the periphery of learning. To be educated within this circulation of ideas, as Frantz Fanon noted in the closing days of Algerian colonialism, was only to

---

[6] In describing European scientific institutions overseas, typically set up in the later phases of imperialism, Pyenson develops a three-dimensional model for the strategies of cultural imperialism, including mercantilist, research, and functionary aspects. The mercantilist strategy "would have scientists serving business interests" and is described more literally and narrowly than I intend here (1989, p. 276). Along similar lines, Bruno Latour speaks of the European "centers of calculation" that made sense of all that was acquired in the great "cycle of accumulation" provoked by imperial ventures abroad (1987, pp. 222, 232).

be further dispossessed: "The educated native is referred to as 'having acquired the habits of a master'" (1965, p. 132).

The World in a Name

The scientifically minded and peripatetic Peter Martyr offers a sense of what
it was like in the New World facing the overwhelming excess and profusion
of these newly discovered regions. His early-sixteenth-century account of
Peru reflects a certain exasperation over the proliferation: "And now enough
of quadrupeds, birds, insects, trees, grasses, essences and other things of this
sort. Let us turn our attention to the doings of men and their way of life"
(cited by Gerbi, 1985, p. 68). One early hope for restoring the natural order of
things was to treat the New World as an extension of the known world. Thus
we come to the onset of the Foucauldian divide between semblance and difference as a way of knowing. The burning botanical question of the century,
for Peter Martyr and others, was whether the seemingly exotic plants and animals were truly different. Did they warrant original names, or variations of
existing ones? Where were the lines to be drawn that divided one plant from
another, an old-world monkey from a new-world one? Such questions invited
a new system, a rationalizing of nature's realm.

It is little wonder, then, that Linnaeus's *Systema Naturae* was greeted with
enthusiasm when it was published in 1735. Here was a scientific structure for
naming the natural realm, bringing order to the relationship among things,
genus by species. The true names of things, which Adam had first bestowed
on beast and plant, was about to be restored, in the priestly and learned language of Latin. One of Linnaeus's students, Anders Sparrman, writing of his
visit to South Africa during the 1770s, refers to himself as "a-botanizing . . . in
the same dress as Adam wore in his state of Nature" (cited by Pratt, 1992, p.
52). It was as if these adventuresome students might arrive at a time before
the fall, before Adam hid his nakedness, although they seemed as destined as
he had been to taste the apple that held the knowledge of good and evil, especially as they would bring to the world an ordering that included the racial
identification of humankind.

"The method, the soul of science, designates at first sight any body in
nature in such a way that the body in question expresses the name that is
proper to it," Linnaeus wrote in the *Systema Naturae*, "and this name recalls
all the knowledge that may, in the course of time, have been acquired about
the body thus named: so that in the midst of extreme confusion there is revealed the sovereign order of nature" (cited by Foucault, 1970, p. 159). To designate at first sight becomes "the soul of science," in an ABC of epistemology

that linked Adam, Bacon, and Columbus in a biblical and scientific order.[7] Foucault calls it "this essential nomination" (p. 159). This scientific mission presumes that it falls to the West to name the world properly. In setting out to name the world anew, science acts as a principal on behalf of the sovereign order of nature. It would thus structure identity and difference into a grid that could span the whole of the earth and keep a good number of Europeans, with their colonial assistants, employed.

Linnaeus insisted, with some pride, that his system could be acquired and applied by anyone (with a Latin education). It was a ready way of deputizing those with a passing interest in natural history, whether they were at home or traveling abroad, to join in this global project. Linnaeus's system offered an amateur naturalist an identification kit for reading difference, beginning with parts related to "fructification" (cited by Foucault, 1970, p. 140). Linnaeus set in motion his own curriculum experiment in public education, which was eagerly pursued by amateur students of natural history with a penchant for adventures in learning and travel. This effort to name—and often to rename, in the face of local nomenclature—the whole of the living realm ranks among the more ambitious and presumptuous projects in science (and it is not over yet).[8]

The Swedish East India Company offered Linnaeus's students free passage aboard its ships. Those students of natural history who were inclined to stay at home were amply served by such enthusiastic and widely traveled naturalists as Nathaniel Wallich, a Dutch surgeon who had given up his practice in 1809 to earn his keep as a botanist for the British government. After years of scouring the Indian countryside in the mid-1830s, he arrived back in England with some thirty barrels of dried plants, which he generously distributed among scientists and institutions throughout the nation (Kumar, 1990, p. 53). When one of the great biologists of the Victorian age, Richard Owen, took charge of the natural history collection at the British Museum in 1856, he ensured that the country's colonial naturalists at work in nearly every corner of the globe sent their specimens to him, creating what Janet Browne refers to as "the cataloging hub of the English dominions" and further asserting "Britain's

---

[7] Sprat states in his history of the Royal Society, "So true is that saying of my Lord Bacon, That by a little knowledge of Nature men become Atheists; but a great deal returns them back again to a sound and Religious mind" (1959, p. 351).

[8] The naming project goes on to this day with the recent formation of the Systematics Agenda 2000 project, which intends to devote twenty-five years and $75 billion to collecting and cataloging the still unnamed species. Unnamed insects alone are estimated at 8 to 100 million in number, with some 950,000 already described by this point (McDonald, 1994, p. A8). The aim this time is to track the extent of extinction among species.

right of sovereignty" over what must have seemed to some Nature herself (1994, p. 3).

This relabeling of the world added greatly to the educational value and responsibility of travel for Europeans. In her late-nineteenth-century travels through West Africa, Mary Kingsley captures the consternation of not being in possession of the proper names for the local flora and fauna, as well as the danger of such knowledge: "It is like being shut in a library whose books you cannot read, all the while tormented, terrified and bored. And if you do fall under its spell, it takes all the color out of other kinds of life" (1965, p. 165). Naturalists and other scientists were not above chastising travelers for not keeping better records of the world they visited (Lach, 1977, p. 444). Kingsley was not above mocking this earnestness, giving just that school-like sense of having received a field trip assignment:

> The last words a most distinguished and valued scientific friend had said to me before I left home were, "Always take measurements, Miss Kingsley, and always take them from the adult male." I know I have neglected opportunities of carrying out this commission on both banks, but I do not feel like going back. Besides the men would not like it, and I have mislaid my yard measure. (1965, pp. 244–45)

Kingsley had traveled abroad with the special "Collectors Outfit" issued by the British Museum, and she made good use of it, returning home with sixty-five species of fish and eighteen species of reptiles, many of them in pickling jars, all of which were gratefully received by the British Museum (Robinson, 1990, p. 138). As a result of her successes as a naturalist, three species of fish were named after her.

This interest in naming the world, however, was hardly restricted to flora and fauna. On the one hand, Donald Lach reports how, during the early years of imperialism, the Portuguese proudly paraded in their writing the names of the places their sailors had visited—Goa (India), Cilan (Ceylon), and Japão (Japan)—as a tribute to Portugal's navigational achievement (1977, p. 526). Columbus, on the other hand, after noting what the natives called their islands, went on to rename them (1969).

Naming a place is about staking and extending a verbal claim to it, which returns us to the theme "Where is here?" Here is what is named. The unnamed is nowhere. To name is the sovereign act. Even when a name, such as Canada, had originated with indigenous peoples, it was not adopted out of recognition of their claim to the land. Local names were often misheard, misunderstood, or deliberately transformed by the interlopers from abroad: *China* for *Ch'in; mongoose* for *mangus.* These escapades of naming not only brought thousands of new words into the European languages but also must have seemed to deliver the places themselves, as they were named and mapped, within the reach of imperialism's educated imagination. Naming was to think about the world, one might say, on one's own terms.

If a place was unmarked on the map, it awaited only a word pronounced and written down in an unceremonious christening. This point has fascinated Paul Carter, and in his *The Road to Botany Bay* (1987), he pauses over Captain James Cook's manner of assigning names to places. During a voyage to the Pacific, Cook recorded in his journal how he was so impressed by "the great quantity of new plants etc. Mr. Banks and Dr. Solander collected in this place" (along the coast of Australia) that it "occasioned me giving it the name of Botany Bay" (1993, p. 411). With "place-naming," as Carter refers to Cook's practice, "space is transformed symbolically into a place, that is, a space with a history" (1987, p. xxiv). That history is not about the land itself nor of those who have long lived there. It is about the power to place-name against those who previously named it and have lived on it for centuries. Carter notes how Cook's sighting of an eagle was enough to create Eagle Island, whereas Green Island might refer to the ship's astronomer or perhaps the island's look (p. 7). What is certain, in looking back over the process, is that Cook's assignment of names was an assertion of sovereignty over the land. The names along the east coast of Australia, from York Cape to Botany Bay, "preserved the trace of [Cook's] passage," in Carter's final analysis (p. 32). That these traces preserve the imperial passage, even as they form the much-studied order of the world for schoolchildren, could stand as my theme.

Finally, this odyssey of renaming the world was also about honoring the heroes of empire, so that a loyal soldier of empire such as the Victorian scientist Sir Roderick Murchison, after initiating the Geological Survey and heading up the Royal Geographical Society, could expect to look over maps in his final years marked with Mount Murchison and Murchison Bay. It was more than merely a fitting tribute for one who filled in many of the blank places on the map. The world was assumed to be a tabula rasa that awaited inscription by the West and its soldiers, administrators, scientists, and educators, a new class of professionals who found their boyhood fantasies fulfilled by this vocation in just the way that Joseph Conrad relates Marlow's childhood in *Heart of Darkness:* "At the time there were many blank spaces on the earth, and when I saw one that looked particularly inviting on a map (but they all look like that) I would put my finger on it and say, When I grow up I will go there" (1973, p. 11). Wittgenstein's aphoristic observation that the limits of one's language are the limits of one's world becomes transformed here into the political maxim that the limits of one's world are one's limits in naming it (1961, 5.6). That the world was then labeled in the name of scientific order, colonial occupation, childhood curiosity, and imperial honors was no less a part of the adventure in learning that students everywhere must return to, although without, perhaps, the same original sense of delight at the mastery of an otherwise unlimited world.[9]

The Floating Fortress-Lab

I want to return to James Cook at this point, because his famous and ultimately fateful expeditions to the South Pacific, commissioned by the Royal Society between 1768 and 1780, launched a British age of scientific travel. Bernard Smith, in his history of the South Seas, points to how Cook's ships "combined the values of a fortress and a traveling laboratory" (1960, p. 2). For all of their scientific interests, such interdisciplinary expeditions were also conducted under secret orders from the British Crown and were directed at claiming the lands of the South Pacific for the British Empire (D. Livingstone, 1992, p. 129). Just what sort of laboratory these ships presented is captured in a contemporary letter sent to Linnaeus, which provides a brief inventory of the ships' scientific inventory, beginning with the ships' library:

> No people ever went to sea better fitted out for the purpose of Natural History. They have got a fine library of Natural History; they have all sorts of machines for catching and preserving insects; all kinds of nets, trawls, drags and hooks for coral fishing; they have a curious contrivance of a telescope, by which, put into the water, you can see the bottom at great depth. (Cited by Gregory, 1994, p. 18)

From the first voyage onward, the scientific accomplishments of the expedition were diverse and substantial: "The transit of Venus was accurately observed," David Livingstone begins his catalog of Cook's achievements, "kangaroos were discovered, ethnographic studies of indigenous peoples carried out, the New Zealand coastline was charted and a vast amount of material collected and shipped back to the Royal Society—thousands of plants, five hundred fish preserved in alcohol, five hundred bird skins, and hundreds of mineral specimens" (1992, p. 127). The ships' naturalists, with Joseph Banks foremost among them on the initial voyage, proudly returned home with

---

[9] Some communities in Canada are refusing this naming and returning to their original, native names. This process began in 1950 with the renaming of Port Brabant in the western Arctic to its original and long-standing Tuktoyaktuk. Places being returned to their native names, largely in the far north, include Fort Chimo and Port Simpson, both of which date back to the 1830s (Rayburn, 1994, pp. 136–39). For a deconstruction of the proper name—"the original myth of transparent legibility present under the obliteration"—see Derrida (1974, p. 109).

specimen-filled barrels and crates, as well as stacks of notebooks, which amply served the Royal Society's interests in natural history. For his part during the voyage, Banks practiced his own form of scientific ecology on the many trips ashore he took "in order to shoot anything I could meet," as he records in his journal (1993, p. 409).[10] The expedition naturalists turned Cook's ships into a Noah's ark of the preserved and dead, bringing home to England the Pacific's contribution to nature's order. In addition, anthropological records were made of the indigenous peoples encountered, including Captain Cook's appreciation for the navigational finesse of the Pacific islanders, which he accurately speculated was based on a skilled reading of the stars.

An original and remarkable aspect of these voyages was the Royal Society's use of trained artists and draftsmen to supplement the acquisition of scientific specimens and data (B. Smith, 1960, pp. 130–31).[11] This had the effect of turning the scientific arm of imperialism into a prominent patron of the arts, with artists put to work capturing, as Smith refers to them, "the sciences of visible nature, geology, botany, zoology, anthropology, meteorology" (p. 255). The artists so commissioned added a detached scientific demeanor to their work, successfully investing it with a new level of documentary authority that appealed to both "the scientist and the man of taste" (p. 255). More than just nature's bookkeepers, expeditionary artists lent their vision to celebrating the extent and wonders of the empire-building project. They brought home to Europe a new landscape that, in its artistic accessibility and appeal, evoked another dimension of this imperial will to know. This meant that John Ruskin's formula—"If you can paint a leaf, you can paint the world"— could be reasserted as, in Smith's estimation, "The painters of leaves had painted the world" (p. 257). The artists' watercolors of the tropical Pacific established the luxuriant and voluptuous beauty of the islands, so uninhibited and uninhibiting, on this otherworldly other side of the earth. These new-found sites of masculine desire spoke to a longing for Eden. In a theme that dates back to Columbus's voyages, Banks noted in a 1770 journal entry off the Australian coast: "Of all these people we had seen so distinctly through our glasses we had not been able to observe the least signs of clothing; myself the best of my judgment plainly discerned that the women did not copy our mother Eve even in the fig leaf" (1993, p. 408).

---

[10] On coming across a flock of quail on the day of that journal entry, Banks did pause to reflect that really his "business was to kill variety and not too many individuals of any one species" (1993, p. 409).

[11] Smith notes that "a great deal of artistic talent was absorbed between 1750 and 1850 in thus serving the biological sciences as they sought to perfect the descriptive and systematic phases of their respective disciplines" (1960, p. 3).

The sexual allegory had long formed its own conceit in the depiction of the imperial adventure. Two centuries earlier, Théodore de Bry's famous copperplate engravings of rapacious conquest had been used in a Protestant attack on the licentiousness of the Spanish conquistadors (who were also attacked by the English for failing to educate the natives).[12] When Sir Walter Raleigh returned from his rather dismal explorations of South America at the end of the sixteenth century in his search for El Dorado, he held out the promise of Guyana as an invitation to rape (which may have seemed ill advised, given his devoted service to the virginal Queen Elizabeth): "Guiana is a countrey that hath yet her maydenhead, never sackt, turned, nor wrought, the face of the earth hath not bene torne" (cited by Montrose, 1993, p. 188).

It was clear that the far and wild reaches of the earth, where such scientific and artistic enterprises were taking place, were surely no place for a well-bred woman. These expeditions formed another reason for directing Western women away from one of the leading intellectual activities of the day. Fortunately, however, this did not prevent Lady Mary Wortley Montagu from taking a great interest in the use of inoculations to prevent smallpox while she accompanied her husband on a diplomatic mission to Turkey in the early eighteenth century. On returning to civilized England, she had to campaign anonymously, because of her gender, in trying to convince the medical profession to introduce this preventive procedure (1909). Moreover, this proscription against women joining the great quest did not prevent British naval ship commanders from having live-aboard women count among a ship's amenities in the nineteenth century (de Kay, 1995). Yet women were not permitted to become full members of the Royal Geographical Society, despite their record of contributions to the geographical sciences and the advocacy of longtime society president Sir Roderick Murchison, until 1913 (Stafford 1989, p. 215).[13] The gender hypocrisy and sexual double-dealing was common to the age, of course, and imperialism merely threw this play of European power and privilege onto a global stage.

In Bernard Smith's final analysis, Cook's voyages formed a leading edge for European intellectual history: "The opening of the Pacific is numbered among those factors contributing to the triumph of romanticism and science in the 19th-century world of values" (1960, p. 1). The artist and scientist

---

[12] On Théodore de Bry, see Bucher (1981). Thomas Sprat notes that "the Spaniards . . . permit not the *Natives* to know more than becomes their slaves" (1959, p. 383; Sprat's emphasis).

[13] See G. Rose on how "only the 'objective' gaze of white men could explore and describe other places in appropriate scientific detail" (1993, p. 9); and S. Mills on the "excising of women's involvement in colonialism" (1991, p. 58).

closed the circle of the globe, bringing the immense Pacific Ocean within the European ken, and they prospered by it. Smith would have it that Cook's voyages in opening of the Pacific to the British imagination benefited the planet as a whole, a claim that demonstrates for me how we are still coming to terms with the political economies of our ways of knowing the world. The planetary consciousness fostered by imperialism contained what I think can be fairly characterized as a distinctly educational fascination with the world. I do not mean that Europeans had an exclusive claim to educational or scientific interests, a view that would fall into imperialism's own presumption. Nor, as I have already stated, do I see it as helpful to think of all educational interests as inherently imperialist. From Banks's shooting sprees to the island watercolors, there is both innocence and complicity to this learning. These images of exploration and discovery represented the paradigmatic educational act both on the grand scale of the floating, fortified laboratory, like the space shuttles of today, and on the more modest scale of the devoted amateur collector.

The Learned Colonial Administration

Having given natural history its imperial due through the example of Cook's expeditions, it's important to recognize that the humanities were to play no less a role in imperialism's adventure in learning. In the shaping of the British raj in India, for example, the Persia scholar Warren Hastings stood for a most notable collaboration of governance, commerce, and learning. After becoming the first governor-general of British India in 1772, he sponsored the formation of the Royal Asiatic Society and commissioned the translation of *A Code of Gentoo [Hindu] Law,* in his largely successful effort to secure the place of Hindu law in the legal system of the colony (Rocher, 1993, p. 226). Moreover, Hastings initiated the Calcutta Madrassa, an Islamic education center, at the request of the Moslem community for, as it was put at the time, "the sons of Mohamadan gentlemen" who sought an education that would prepare them for "responsible and lucrative" government jobs (cited by Ghosh, 1993, p. 176). Thomas Macaulay was to pay the rare compliment to Hastings that although he may have failed to introduce "the learning of the West" to India (a task that was to fall to Macaulay), Hastings "was the first foreign ruler who succeeded in gaining the confidence of the hereditary priests of India and who induced them to lay open to English scholars the secrets of the old Brahminical theology and jurisprudence" (1907, p. 616).

Hastings's scholarly respect for Indian culture convinced him that the English translation of the *Code* would show those living in Britain that "the inhabitants of this land are not in a savage state . . . [and] do not require our

AN ADVENTURE IN LEARNING   41

aid to furnish them with a rule of conduct, or a standard for their property"
(cited by Rocher, 1993, p. 221). Of course, by producing a compilation of laws
based on ancient manuscripts, Hastings was providing just the sort of "aid"
and "rule of conduct" that he thought was necessary for these people to re-
store their decaying civilization. Hastings's *Code* also had the effect of dis-
placing more recent developments in Indian law and banishing local adaptations of it, thereby devaluing native pundits and legal scholars who attended
the court. It ended up enshrining the power of the Brahman caste, to which
the translators of the *Code,* working from the British model, accorded the
legal status of the Church of England. From his scholarly seat of authority,
Hastings saw himself as protecting the country from its own decline, as well
as from the less learned among the British. This proved in practice to be more
than a noble scholarly application of a healthy educational interest.

   Well into Hastings's second decade as governor-general, his command
was called to account before the British Parliament for engaging in acts of "arbitrary power" in what had become "the great theater [of] abuse," as Edmund
Burke described in setting out the charges against Hastings (cited by Suleri,
1992, p. 45). In 1787, Burke convinced the Commons to instigate impeach-
ment proceedings against Warren Hastings. Among the charges were instances of outright torture and sexual abuse of Indian women by Hastings's
minions in the Courts of Justice. Burke rendered the violation to great effect,
prefacing his statement to Parliament with "The treatment of females could
not be described," before offering the graphic details of the horrors: "In the
face of the Ministers of Justice, in the face of the spectators, in the face of the
sun, those tender and modest virgins were brutally violated" (p. 60).[14] The
scholarly construction of difference turned out to have a role in Hastings's
successful defense of his regime. What measures one might expect and live
by in England were bound to be different from those that were—some would
say had to be—instituted in this far-off land. Burke characterized this as a
"geographical morality" (p. 46). During the eight long years of the trial, Hastings claimed that the despotic tenor of his regime was no more than indigenous to the political landscape of the Orient, and he had done the homework

---

[14] Sara Suleri finds that Burke's dwelling on the harrowing violation of the female body
turns the audience's eye away from imperialism itself as a penetrating incursion: "When
the colonial dynamic is metaphorically represented as a violated female body that can be
mourned over with sentimentality's greatest excess, its rape is less an event than a deflection
from a contemplation of male embattlement, the figure of which more authentically dictates the boundaries of colonial power" (1992, p. 61). Suleri also sees the colonial "as the
landscape upon which the intimacy of homoerotic invitation and rejection can be enacted"
(p. 17).

to prove it. Burke tried to expose this reading of India as a poor excuse for acting badly. He argued from a basic equality among peoples: "I must do justice to the East; I must assert that their morality is equal to ours" (p. 46). But such claims, which might ultimately have undermined the entire ethical economy of colonialism, were not to hold. The key point here is how Hastings's scholarly construction of the difference between Indian traditions of authority and English liberty managed to license the abusive and autocratic treatment of the East India Company's Indian employees and families by the otherwise just English.

A further chapter of greater scholarly accomplishment and consequence to this learned occupation of India came with the arrival of William (Oriental) Jones. Jones was a distinguished linguistic scholar and minor poet, as well as a reputable lawyer. In 1783, he received his Indian commission as a judge of the supreme court in Fort William. Once he settled in, it did not take Jones long to combine his interests in jurisprudence and learning. He was the founding president of the Asiatic Society and editor of *Asiatic Researches,* both devoted to promoting a broad European understanding of that part of the world.[15] Through his legal study of Sanskrit, Jones arrived at a model of the Indo-European family of languages that proved a founding moment for modern linguistics. His further translations of the law, along with editions of other Sanskrit manuscripts, continued to emphasize the earlier "purity" of this ancient language after the model of classical Greek. Here was the European scholar playing the true benefactor and executor of the historical legacy of the colonized, drawing validating connections to other ancient civilizations.

Jones's philological investigation of Indo-European languages gave rise to the study of Aryanism, which was formally introduced into Great Britain by Friedrick Max Müller, who served as Oxford's first professor of comparative philology and translated the Vedas into English. Müller eventually renounced the tendency to treat "Aryan" as a racial designation rather than a philological term. But by that point, it was closely associated with Hellenic values, especially as they were set in counterdistinction to Semitic traditions by such prominent figures as Matthew Arnold.[16] Müller was the product of

---

[15] Deepak Kumar reports that Indians weren't accepted into such societies until 1829, and there were cases of their scientific papers first being received and accepted as a basis for membership in the London branch, well before their being allowed to join the colonial Indian society (1990, p. 60).

[16] Matthew Arnold's *Culture and Anarchy* follows the German leads of Hegel and Heine by setting Hellenism, with its "aèrial ease, clearness, and radiance . . . of what we call sweetness and light," apart from Hebraism, marked by its "prodigious space for sin" (1896, pp. 116–17).

Germany's leading role in the development of Indology as a field of study through the nineteenth and twentieth centuries, demonstrating that colonial control was not absolutely necessary for the excellence of national scholarly undertakings. This seemingly distant and removed field of inquiry proved in the 1930s to be extremely valuable to the political fiber of fascist Europe.[17]

In addition to studying the country's ancient texts and languages, the colonial administration of India also worked hard to create a statistical rendering of the country during the nineteenth century. The establishment of this elaborate process of enumeration was to serve, in Ajun Appadurai's estimation, "a pedagogical and disciplinary function," which replaced the imperial sense of "land is to rule" with "land is to teach" (1993, p. 325). More specifically, there was once again a field-testing of a scholarly pursuit, now combining demographics and human geography, that was to inform the political apparatus of colonial rule:

> The measurement and classification of land was the training ground for the culture of number in which statistics became the authorizing discourse of the appendix (giving direct weight to the verbal portion of the text) at the same time that it gave higher level officials a pedagogical and disciplinary sense of controlling not just the territory over which they sought to rule but also the native functionaries through which such rule needed to be effected. (p. 325)

The British were working out the basis of an empire of information that, like any system of governance, shaped the ruler and the ruled. As a result of the census, distinctions of caste received greater attention than they might have otherwise (with some 2,378 castes and tribes identified by the British), while also emphasizing the distribution of religious differences between Hin-

---

In discussing Arnold's debt to Heine, Lionel Gossman brings to light a fascinating meeting point between the Hellenic and the Hebraic suggested by Heine, that Arnold decided not to bring forward to the British public: "Shakespeare is at once Jew and Greek" (cited by Gossman 1994, p. 17). Nonetheless, Gossman describes Arnold as a solid supporter of modern Jews, pointing to his instrumental role in obtaining state aid for the Jews' Free School, and his vehement attack of what was termed "the sacred theory of the Aryans," which denied the Semitic roots of Christianity (pp. 34–35).

[17] National Socialism's interests in Indology, in Sheldon Pollock's estimation, led to "some of the most politically deformed scholarship in history" (1993, p. 81). In public forums, a number of scholars used the study of Aryanism to separate "Indo-German" and "Semite" citizenry in Germany, which required an explanation of the "degeneracy of South Asia Aryans" in the plea for greater racial purity among the redeeming Germanic peoples (p. 81). Pollock offers the image of a Sanskrit professor addressing an SS officer corps on the topic of the "hereditary, long term tradition" linking the Führer and the Buddha.

dus and Muslims. This earnest counting of people and their place in Indian society created statistical divisions among people that became a function of colonial governance (Rocher, 1993).[18]

The British established a tradition of scholarly enterprise in administering the Indian jewel in its colonial crown. Even with its military and technological advantage, the colonial administration found itself drawn to developing new areas of philology and demographics that ultimately assisted it in governing the Indian subcontinent. Knowledge operated as a force, with *mastery of the subject* the operative educational metaphor and faith. The colonial administrators' interests in Indian culture provided their work with a mantle of respectability and an ennobling recreational interest, as well as a warrant, in Hastings's case, for the otherwise unseemly activities of governing an empire. It was all part of the British Empire's development of what we would call a global information system, with extended data feeds, lines of credit, and international postings. Its ongoing association of power and knowledge was dedicated to the viability of such categories as colony and empire. Out of this governing knowledge of Indian culture, with its Sanskrit texts, Aryan linguistics, and caste demographics, India was indelibly cast as a decayed and despotic society, and the empire as the remedy to these failings. Colonial administrators stationed in India, no less than naturalists aboard Cook's scientific expeditions to the Pacific, were part of an imperial adventure in learning that was also conducted by military campaigns and learned missionaries.

The Egyptomania Military Campaign

Napoleon's ultimately unsuccessful Egyptian campaign easily stands as the leading instance of an imperial army's contribution to a single field of popular and serious study, namely, Egyptomania and Egyptology. In 1789, Napoleon launched his campaign against Egypt with a massive fleet of four hundred French ships that arrived on the coast of Alexandria, carrying with them a team of 151 scientists, engineers, medical men, and scholars from the Commission of Science and Arts (Gillispie, 1994). This invading and inquiring

---

[18] See Inden (1988, pp. 49–84) for the British analysis of caste in "imagining India." Appadurai (1986) has found it necessary to expose the continued exaggeration of caste distinctions in Indian society in such distinguished scholarly works as Louis Dumont's *Homo Hierarchicus* (1966). Although Appadurai does not record the Indian response to the importance added to these categories, they did not go unchallenged in Britain. From 1887 to 1895, Catherine Impey edited the magazine *Anti-Caste*, with a masthead declaring its contributors to be "advocates of the brotherhood of mankind irrespective of color or descent" (cited by Ware, 1992, p. 186). The magazine exemplified the daring work of feminists and other social activists, dating back to the abolitionist movement earlier in the century, who were committed to educating the British public about the terrible cost of imperialism.

army, after successfully occupying Egypt, soon found itself cut off from return to France by Admiral Nelson's fleet, which had destroyed and chased away the attending French ships. The French were trapped in Egypt for a dozen years until the British finally expelled them in 1801, but those years were not wasted on the French artists and scholars among the trapped expedition. During that time, they worked with the army, gathering material on every aspect of Egyptian history and countryside. Naturalists made anatomical drawings of fish while scholars unearthed and packed up the Rosetta stone. Engineers who were sent to study the Nile's influence on fertility surveyed ancient monuments, reconstructed on paper their former glory, and, when their pencils were used up, the story goes, turned the lead of their bullets into drawing instruments (Ziegler, 1994, p. 257). The expedition demonstrated the vast educational benefits that could be produced by what Said has characterized as "an entire corps of savants backed by a modern army of conquest" (1995, p. 3).[19] Egypt was now theirs to collect, to appreciate, and ultimately to render for European consumption.

The first step of incorporation was to pack up Egypt—specimen by artifact—for intellectual export to Paris. When the expedition finally returned to France with its sweeping collection intact, it inspired new domains of knowledge, new realms of science, and new fashions for the architecture of monuments and the furniture of bourgeois drawing rooms (Humbert, 1994). For the naturalist standing before the uncrated drawings of dissected lungfish and ibis, the close renderings of butterfly and hexapod jaw, it no longer seemed enough to perform the typical taxonomic classifications. For those examining such careful renderings, the organisms appeared to be "the subject matter of a science in the absence of the science," in the words of Charles Gillispie, a modern editor of the campaign's major publishing project, *Description de l'Ègypte* (1994, p. 81). The naturalist responded by undertaking new forms of morphological study that related form and structure within and across species. Working with beautifully detailed drawings, as well as thousands of well-preserved specimens, naturalists were able to mount a convinc-

---

[19] The expedition's secretary, Jean-Baptiste Fourier, claimed that the team had been sent to Egypt for purposes of "extending irrigation and agriculture . . . [and] improving the standard of living of the inhabitants and procuring them all the advantages of an improved civilization . . . [through] the continual application of science and the technical arts" (cited by Gillispie, 1994, p. 85). This would take place, however, only after the arrival of the British in 1803. The model was thought to be enough of a success that when Napoleon III invaded Mexico in 1861, he also included an army of savants, who carried out large-scale excavations of ancient Aztec sites. Yet this invasion was another military fiasco. The exported artifacts did not lead to an Aztecomania, but the expedition did further enrich the Louvre as well as many private collections (E. A. Williams, 1985, p. 150).

ing case for what Gillispie calls "a fundamental unity of plan" among the organization of all classes of vertebrates (pp. 82–83). This form of morphological investigation was to dominate nineteenth-century biology.

Description de l'Ègypte began to appear in 1809 as a result of a formation of a joint stock company devoted to that purpose. It laid out Egypt's antiquities, presented the full range of its natural history, and described ten centuries of Arab life. It took up twelve volumes and included three thousand illustrations, some folding out to one meter in length. It was one of the great publishing projects of the nineteenth century, if not, as Christine Ziegler has recently commented, "the most monumental work ever published" (1994, p. 257). It was not long before engravings of pyramids and temples set amid palm trees were featured in both the cheap press and finely honed folios. The pharaohs became the subject of museum exhibitions, marketing efforts, and schoolbooks. There was no less fascination with Egypt's mysterious preservation of the dead and cryptic forms of worship. It must have seemed plain to everyone that expanding the empire paid excellent educational dividends. This occupation of the land afforded a scholarly industry devoted to interpreting every natural and historical feature of this mysterious land. Ancient Egypt became the special possession of the French, and although the fruits of Napoleon's expedition did little for the French Empire, it demonstrated the national and cultural benefits of the imperial campaign as an educational event. Meanwhile, the Egyptians of the day were judge incapable of appreciating their country's importance.[20]

In setting the achievement of France's scientific campaign in Egypt within the context of the British in India, the Dutch in Indonesia, and the Spanish and Portuguese in America, Gillispie concludes that "the spread of European science and its appurtenances to African and Asian societies under the aegis of military conquest and political power began with the French conquest of Egypt" (1994, p. 85). Napoleon's military campaign certainly turned Egypt into a fantastic field of play for France's Commission of Sciences and Arts, and such exercises meant the conceptual and territorial expansion of European sciences. Yet one wants to ask Gillispie just what sort of human engagement with African and Asian societies this expansion entailed. These so-

---

[20] This sense of Egypt as a civilization in decay was also exploited by tourists such as Gustave Flaubert who traveled there with the photographer Maxime Du Camp in 1849, after acquiring official commissions "to enjoy every possible advantage while traveling"; Flaubert's commission was from the Ministry of Agriculture, and Du Camp's was from the Ministry of Public Instruction, to photograph "views of the monuments and copies of the inscriptions" (Flaubert, 1972, pp. 22, 23). Flaubert's letters home leave little to the imagination about his sexual fascination with difference.

cieties could expect to benefit from what was, at best, a trickle-down theory. Here again is that delicate ambiguity that we now take for granted: "The spread of European science . . . to African and Asian societies" was about the forces of science taking advantage of and contributing to a global project of domination. We can now assume that this is safely an aspect of the imperial past, or, in the name of a greater vigilance and accountability, we can consider it part of a necessary education in the sciences and in related forms of learning.

The Traffic in Ideas

Having acknowledged the intellectual enterprise of imperialism's expeditionary naturalists and colonial administrators, it would be unfair not to credit the learned contributions of the missionaries and the church. Foremost among those who included the world of learning within their imperial mission was the Society of Jesus. The Jesuits' integration of Christian and classicist training with a rigorous grounding in the mathematical sciences served their missionaries well in their efforts to establish a concurrent spiritual dominion over the globe while assisting the colonial regimes. Not long after Columbus sailed, the Jesuit historian Gian Pietro Maffei asserted that the spread of Christianity through imperialism fulfilled God's wishes for the world, and he concluded that all that was left to the Lord was to bring this now completed world to an end (cited by Spence, 1983, p. 123). The Jesuits intended to remain busy up to that final moment.

In China, Madagascar, and Lebanon, Jesuits "disseminated the research ethos," as Lewis Pyenson describes their scholarly contribution, among "institutions in every kind of imperial administrative regime" (1993, p. 14). To take one important instance, the careful anthropological observations captured in the long-running annual *Jesuit Relations* from New France initiated the construction of "culture" as a scholarly and accepting way of dealing with heathen differences: "Christianity serves as the plane of emergence," Bernard McGrane offers in his critique of anthropology, "upon which the Other can appear and be described and deployed in a system of knowledge" (1989, p. 52). The assembling of knowledge about the "savages," no less than their conversion, attested to the simultaneously subordinating and civilizing mission of the Western accumulation of knowledge.

The Jesuit accord between proselytizing and scholarship found its clearest expression in Matteo Ricci, a Jesuit priest whose story Jonathan Spence engagingly tells in *The Memory Palace of Matteo Ricci* (1983). Ricci first carried his training in the mathematical sciences, including astronomy, geography, and engineering, to China in 1573, becoming a widely respected Western scholar at the commercial center of Nanchang. This priest's exemplary life of devotion and scholarship, it was hoped, would win converts among the court scholars of the Ming Dynasty, who would in turn convince the rest of the court and then the country. The key was the admirable degree of Jesuit learning, and the approach had worked in the earliest days of the church. The Roman emperor Constantine had been converted through such counsel. It was to be a conquest, for Ricci, by (intellectual) virtue. On his arrival in Canton, among the gifts he gave out were sundials, striking clocks, maps, and a celestial sphere. In Li Yan and Du Shiran's analysis, given China's strength at the time under the Ming Dynasty, "science and technology therefore were used as a means of penetration" rather than a source of force (1987, p. 190). The learning was generously and respectfully shared with the Chinese as a demonstration of what the West had to offer. Learning, however genuinely given, was a loss leader, an instrument of trade and conversion.

The Chinese scholars were clearly impressed by Ricci and his learning, so much so that one might wonder at the faith of the scholars who chose to convert to Catholicism. One who did was Xu Guangpi, a high official in the Ming court and grand secretary of the Wen Institute, who had studied Western methods of calendar calculation and weaponry. "He was a scientist who loved his country," write Li Yan and Du Shiran in their history of Chinese mathematics (1987, p. 193). Xu befriended Ricci and worked with him to elaborate a new series of Chinese mathematical terms necessary to translate Euclid's *Elements of Geometry,* which was completed in 1607.[21] Although Xu was eager to have the whole of the work in Chinese, Ricci limited the project to the first six of the thirteen books, suggesting that they wait to see if "it proves useful," as Ricci put it in his preface (cited by Li and Du, 1987, p. 194). They did not finish the project, nor did Xu use his new faith to convert the emperor. He did, however, have his Jesuit colleagues assist the Imperial Board of Astronomy in reforming the Chinese calendar, which at the time was failing to predict solar and lunar eclipses (Jami, 1992, p. 80).

At one point, the celebrated Confucian scholar Guo Zhengyu wrote to Ricci after examining the Jesuit materials sent to him by the priest. Reporting that he had read Ricci's work with some joy, Guo asked him, in comparison with "the works of our sages and of the Confucian scholars who came after them, which have all been recorded completely and in the greatest detail; can you agree with me that there is no difference [between Catholicism and Con-

---

[21] It is worth noting that this classic Greek treatise had found its way into Latin only in the tenth century A.D., when it was translated from the Arabic, where it is commonly said to have been "preserved" (Li and Du, 1987, p. 193).

fucianism]?" (cited by Li and Du, p. 151). Guo was taking a position on difference, and his challenge to Ricci is blunt and forthright: "Can you agree with me that there is no difference?" Well, no, Ricci would have to say. He could not agree. His religious mission was based on the significance of the difference, but then, difference was the intellectual engine of empire. The mastery of difference enabled students of imperialism, whether they traveled abroad or followed published accounts at home, to possess the world-as-knowledge.

The Chinese scholars were not oblivious to differences between Ricci's spiritual and intellectual missions. Those who converted must have understood that the translations of Euclid's *Elements of Geometry* and Christoph Clavius's *Epitome of Practical Arithmetic,* the world map, and the improvements of the calendar were going to have a far more lasting influence on Chinese society than Catholicism. This may be why Guo's question catches one off guard. One can imagine a level at which differences disappear between Jesuit and Confucian philosophies, where the world is seen as one. But this sense of no-difference seems to call into question the point of Ricci's arduous journey to China. Imperialism's great adventure in learning was also about the trading of forms of civilization, adding to the riches of the West. Ricci's use of learning as an instrument of conversion adds another dimension to the will to know, to the desire for domination. Yet there is still another side to this traffic in ideas.

While Ricci was toiling over translations of Euclid and Aquinas with the best-trained minds in China, Francis Bacon was defining the scientific spirit of the European Renaissance and its imperial exploits. When Bacon argued in 1620 for creating a new science based on observation and experiment, he pointed to the discovery of printing, gunpowder, and magnetism as perfect demonstrations of "the force, virtue and consequences of discoveries." He claimed that the "origin, [of these three discoveries], though recent, is obscure and inglorious" (1855, p. 110). Each of these obscurities was, of course, a glorious Chinese discovery.[22] Through well-traveled trade routes, a wide range of important Chinese breakthroughs, from gunpowder to the horse stirrup, found their way into eager European hands. By the sixteenth century, many of these discoveries had been absorbed and their sources obscured. The Europeans who set out during the age of exploration thought of the East as little more than a source of porcelains, lacquers, and textiles (Lach, 1977, p. 405).[23]

---

[22] The Chinese origins were not totally unknown in Europe, as Lach is able to trace recognition of the Chinese origin of fireworks back to 1589 (1977, p. 404 n. 28).

[23] Lach allows that "whether movable type printing came at this time from China or Korea to Europe is a question still being debated" (1977, p. 400).

Meanwhile, the West had marshaled these once-Chinese inventions and other developments for the organizational skills and naval forces necessary to begin asserting its interests around the globe. Donald Lach credits the competition present among the European nations and missing with China as a motivating force for this growth. Yet his more telling point for my project is that "the aim of European invention began to be directed more and more toward comprehension of the ordered cohesion of the universe" (pp. 404, 400). Such order and cohesion are no more than is attempted by any system of thought, with this particular *ordo universalis* being distinguished by its integration of scientific objectivity and Western dominance.

The West has come to understand the achievements and contributions of Chinese science largely through the still-incomplete work of the biologist Joseph Needham, who found himself drawn in the 1950s into the history of Chinese science by accusations that Asia had appropriated Western science in ways that could, according to one historian, "destroy in the end all that is profound and essential in [European civilization's] spirit and morality" (cited by Needham, 1964, p. 235 n. 1). It was assumed that science was foreign and dangerous for a people with a tradition of despotism. Needham devoted himself to writing, in collaboration with Wang-ling and other Chinese colleagues, a multivolume history of that country's scientific achievements (1954), which includes its often obscured but significant scientific contributions to the West.[24] To give a crucial instance from the navigational arts, Needham credits "the faithful and magnificent experimenters of medieval China" with laying the groundwork for the scientific study of magnetism: "All the preparation for Peter de Maricourt, and hence of the later ideas of Gilbert about the earth as a magnet and of Kepler on a role of magnetism in astronomy, had been Chinese" (1986, p. 59).

With Bacon, there was an ignorance of China's contributions, which have now been largely put to rest. But now, after Needham, we might say, another sort of obscuring sets in, one that equally sustains the great divide between West and East. It is not just that science is uncomfortable with history. Science textbooks include boxed biographies of Bacon and Newton; some

---

[24] In a later summary, Needham catalogs China's scientific triumphs: "In technological influences before and during the Renaissance, China occupies a quite dominating position[:] . . . the efficient equine harness, the technology of iron and steel, the inventions of gunpowder and paper, the mechanical clock, and basic engineering devices such as the driving-belt, the chain-drive, and the standard method of converting rotary to rectilinear motion, together with segmental arch bridges and nautical techniques such as the stern-post rudder" (1964, p. 238). In addition, Needham discusses Chinese thinking on action at a distance, the principle of vaccination, and the setting of astronomical coordinates.

offer sidebars on Chinese discoveries in astronomy and technology. Yet those stories stand apart from the knowledge at hand, which, once discovered, is ahistorical. To encourage students to reflect on science's place within the order of human interests has recently been construed by a number of scientific organizations as an attack on the truth that it has made of the world (see Harding, 1993; and Haraway, 1989). Still, we need to see how these articles of faith took shape as part of a global project that we have vastly benefited from and thus have some responsibility for rethinking. This chapter has gone about that rethinking by describing the imperial quest as an expression of the will to know that was directed at the construction of identity and difference. Historian George Levine explains this imperial obsession as the product of a Cartesian mind-body dualism. This split separated the decidedly European mind from nature's body: "To know nature, one must make it alien, perceive it as fundamentally other" (1993, p. 370).[25] The amateur naturalists, weathering the most trying of expeditions, suffered an alienation from the body, according to this scheme, that facilitated taking in these new worlds. Science was imperialism's fellow traveler, even as its agents tried to remain aloof from its aggressive political and economic agendas. The scientific separation of meaning from value was to reach maturity in Victorian science.[26] One can imagine how the degree of detachment afforded by distance might lighten concerns about imperialism's subjugation of peoples and territories. They were objects of study, the knowledge of which benefited humankind.

This will to know was thoroughly implicated in the desire for power. It is, in Said's words, "power using knowledge to advance itself" (1995, p. 4). As an education in the world, the study of lettered relics and pickled specimens was fully part of the exercise of power. The planetary consciousness that arose through these global exploits always had designs on the world. As we saw with Ricci, the West was prepared to trade in knowledge as a point of conversion to Christianity, a trade which, if it was initiated by, was not to be restricted to the Jesuits. This was to become a basic educational principle, especially concerning literacy learning. The West created an intellectual mercantilism that

---

[25] Focusing on the instance of Darwin, Levine argues that the displacement of God by the theory of natural selection was "still deeply inflected with the language of natural theology" (1993, p. 386).

[26] Levine finds his epistemological model of alienation and possession in Darwin's making detailed observations of his own children. The debilitated and aging scientist simply worked with the resources at hand; it was as much an integration of his work and family as anything else. The more telling model of the detached but still highly acquisitive frame of mind comes with the exploratory voyages of the HMS *Beagle,* one of 107 survey ships that proved to be floating science schools for junior naturalists such as Thomas Huxley and Joseph Dalton Hooker.

mined the worldly reservoir of facts and artifacts to fuel its theories and its powers to survey, name, and bring the world to reason. If the West has tended to forget the origin of ideas outside itself, there has nonetheless been an inspiring flow of ideas through history and around the globe that call into question the boundaries by which science effectively divides humankind.

Now clearly, the learning that came of those long shipboard days was not wholly or endemically evil. The individual acts of courage and commitment that drove those who undertook such expeditions always entailed a complex set of motivations. To appreciate how easy it is to overlook the human nuance of these adventures, one has only to stumble across the fact that the first American scientific expedition to Africa in 1859 was led by Martin Delany, the son of a slave and eventually a teacher at the "colored school" in Chatham, Ontario (Gilroy, 1993, pp. 19–29). Behind the twists of individual stories, however, it still seems fair to examine the patterns that repeatedly link colonization and knowledge in ways that continue to influence how we learn about the world. The response to this earlier association that I am trying to formulate is obviously not a righteous will to ignorance, as if there could be some sort of flat refusal to have any traffic with the vast storehouse of gathered knowledge that can be attributed to imperialism. Nevertheless, there is something to be said for the ethical issues that have been raised in recent times, issues that focus on the values entailed in securing various forms of knowledge. The lightning-rod case has been the medical information on hypothermia and other topics published by Nazi doctors who conducted their grisly experiments on concentration camp victims. At the very least, it seems educationally worthwhile to ask after imperialism's enormous and earnest production of knowledge, to inquire into the means by which celebrated forms of learning have been gathered and used, and to wonder what has been erased and written over in the making of the modern world.

The European arts and sciences that blossomed from the Renaissance onward were inspired by decidedly more than the exploits of imperialism. Yet amid all of that flowering, the colonial imaginary formed a constant backdrop to the intellectual life of Europe. Imperialism's humanist ideal might be summarized in something of a moral equation—this degree of learning warrants this level of oppression. The responsibility of an "advanced civilization" was assumed to be to make the world fathomable and sensible for the benefit of all humankind. A parallel can be drawn with a good deal of the imperial action in the Near East, which was intended to protect precious trade routes and colonial advantages in the rest of Asia. Thus, it must have seemed that the accomplishments in natural history and other forms of inquiry required a similar level of support and protection. Such an assumption, however, only begs the question whether learning on this scale requires a colonial empire to sustain it. After all, one hardly need invade and occupy a country to study its language or identify its flora and fauna. Europeans did carry out scientific work in China and Siam with the cooperation, rather than the colonization, of local populations.

To ask after learning's dependency on imperialism from another angle, consider the pre-imperial successes of Marco Polo's journey to Cathay. Although questions are still being raised about the reliability of the records, they suggest that one might accomplish much by way of trade and learning in what might have become the model for a cost-recovery global venture. Or, consider how, during the heyday of imperialism, countless students from Asia and Africa found much to study and learn in Europe, studies which they happily pursued amid local prejudices without feeling compelled to exploit the local economy, convert the native children, or take charge of the government. It seems obvious enough that global forms of inquiry, scientific exchange, and scholarly investigation neither require nor redeem five centuries of imperial exploitation and subordination of the world outside Europe. What had first threatened the European world of learning with the discovery of unaccounted-for peoples and places, grew into its primary intellectual adventure, and for half a millennium the learned worked in a meeting of power and knowledge to reconfigure, define, and center the known world on European learning.

If imperialism has been transformed in recent years into a new form of globalized economy no longer dominated by a handful of European powers, what then of the systematic educational apparatuses established by those powers over the centuries? Have they been equally transformed? A sensible starting point for answering that question is to review how Europeans, in taking hold of the whole of the world, first chose to portray and display it for their own affirming edification.

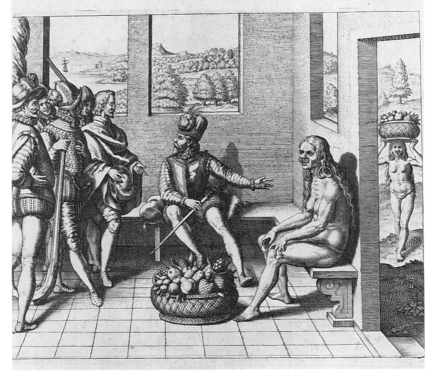

Ad Præfectum Erreram feruntur munera III.
ab vxore Reguli Prouinciæ Cumanæ.

"It was the ugliest and most hideous sight I have ever seen; she appeared more like a monster than a human being" (Benzoni, cited by Bucher, 1981, p. 66). Indian Woman from Cumana Province, *Engraving in Théodor de Bry's America (Frankfurt, 1590, ill. 8a, 4:3). Courtesy Rare Books Division, New York Public Library, Astor, Lenox, and Tilden Foundations.*

THREE

IMPERIAL SHOW-AND-TELL

Although most everyone knows that Christopher Columbus took possession of the New World by a simple act of proclamation in 1492, few realize that before the end of that first day, he went on to outline what is arguably the educational dynamics of empire in his logbook. His entry for that historic October 12 includes a thumbnail ethnography of the Arawak natives whom he encountered in the newly named San Salvador, noting that they are "well built with fine bodies and handsome faces," as well as friendly, naked, and, in color, "neither black nor white" (1969, p. 55). Here, then, is the first educational vector: the educational dynamic begins with a witnessing and positioning of the other. The expansion of experience and conquest educates the conqueror, as we saw in chapter 2. Columbus goes on to record his intention to "bring half a dozen of them back to their Majesties, so that they can learn to speak" (pp. 55–56). The initial act of self-education is repaid through a second vector: educating the unknowing natives, raising them through education to the level of the human "so that they can learn to speak." This is done to make them worthy of servitude: "They should be good servants and very intelligent, for I have observed that they soon repeat anything that is said to them" (p. 56). Finally, Columbus advances a third dynamic in his optimistic approach to converting the Arawak: "And I believe," he notes, "that they would easily be made Christians, for they appeared to me to have no religion" (p. 56).[1] The weight of Columbus's initial observations

---

[1] Columbus may be making a veiled reference to how converting the Arawak would be far less trouble than converting Jews in Spain who had been forced into exile earlier that year for failing to become Catholic.

consigned the seemingly unspoken and godless Arawak to be studied, educated, governed, and converted. The educational dynamic laid out by Columbus that fateful day inscribes the better part of a standard that, if rarely achieved, given how notoriously apt educational designs are at falling short of realization, was still to capture imperialism's educational project.

As it turned out, however, Columbus did not yet have the whole of it. Only on his return to Spain did he come upon the final vector of imperialism's educational dynamic, the one that occupies this chapter (with the second and third vectors reserved for chapter 4). He found the Spanish drawn en masse to the spectacle of this newfound and alien side of their humanity. His son reports that as his heroic father made his way through Spain from Seville to Barcelona, "everyone came from everywhere in the vicinity to gaze at him, and at the Indians and other strange objects that he had brought back with him" (Columbus, 1969, p. 114). The people were gathering together for the *exhibition* of empire, which was to be a constant educational element of the experience of imperialism. The native-on-display was to be both spectacle and object lesson for the European imagination. The Arawak must have been filled with wonder and apprehension at the sight of the Spanish lining the streets to see them pass, and the native who was kept at the Spanish court is said to have expired of sadness after two years had passed.[2]

What began along those Spanish streets was harnessed into various forms of public instruction over the next five centuries. This chapter focuses on the educational institutions in Europe that took shape around putting on display the world possessed through imperialism. Museums and international expositions filled their glass cases with the spoils of empire. Public gardens and zoos were stocked with specimens from abroad and occasionally exhibited natives as living displays. The encyclopedias of Europe organized the lasting wonders of empire in alphabetical order, and the illustrated newspapers carried articles and etchings on the latest adventures of exploration. These forms organize the structure of this chapter as I examine the contribution that each made to generating an informed public at the center of a global empire. Although much attention has been paid to how imaginative works—namely, novels, plays, poetry, and, later, films—educated the public about its empire,

---

[2] In Foucault's terms, the display of the native at court represents the meeting of two eras of power: "Traditionally, power was what was seen, what was shown and what was manifested [such as at court]. . . . Disciplinary power, on the other hand, is exercised through its invisibility; at the same time it imposes on those whom it subjects a principle of compulsory visibility. In discipline, it is the subjects that have to be seen"(1979, p. 187). Although Foucault is writing about the birth of the prison here and refers specifically to the power of the examination and the school, the extraordinary subjection of the aboriginal to public examination would appear to offer a parallel process.

I focus primarily in this chapter on the processes of exhibition and documentation, both popular and learned, profane and sublime, that were used to organize the display of empire. What has been described in the previous chapter as an animated adventure in learning for intrepid Europeans was fed into the multifaceted teaching machine at the centers of empire. The idle spectators of Columbus's parade of Arawak were gradually transformed into the educated public of the bourgeois state. The transformation was supported by educational institutions that were constructed largely around that imperial purpose, and which we are now having to rethink, given what they once made of the world.

These instruments of public instruction, including museum, garden, encyclopedia, exposition, and travel, took shape under the auspices of private enterprise, corporate concerns, nation-state, and church. Their imperial display educated the eye to divide the world according to the patterns of empire. As the eye was disciplined, so was the body. A public was lining up for these institutions, and it was leaving them amused, amazed, informed, and committed to, among other things, the future of national empires and the institutions of public education. The best that the arts and sciences could offer in dividing the world, whether between primitive and civilized or East and West, was used in the formation of a public that was learning to see the world in these imperial terms. In the previous chapter, I discussed the scientific importance placed on vision; educating the eye became an equally important topic in the seventeenth century when René Descartes claimed that perception is was above all habits of understanding that shape people's vision: "I now know that our perception of bodies is due neither to the senses nor to the imagination, but solely to the understanding, and they are known to us not because we see them or touch them, but because we conceive them in thought" (1960, p. 116). To gaze into the captioned display case of bushman weaponry was to learn as much about Western hegemony over the world as could be learned by reading about the nation's military presence abroad. The West's way of putting the world on display, whether for museum-goer, spectator, or sightseer, was an education in how to hold the world in mind, with little thought given to the power required to mount such exhibits.

This education by museums and travel turned the world into an exhibit. Or so it has occurred to Thomas Mitchell, who writes of Egypt, "In the end, the European tried to grasp the Orient as though it were an exhibition of itself" (1988, p. 29). The philosophical sense of the world-as-exhibition was articulated some years ago, as Mitchell points out, by Martin Heidegger in his lecture "The Age of the World Picture," given in Breisgau in 1938. For Heidegger, it is just this perspective on "the world conceived and grasped as pic-

ture" that permits science to assume its objectivity: "Truth has been transformed into the certainty of representation . . . the objectiveness of representing" (1977, pp. 127–28). Within the context of my study, the world-as-
picture becomes the educational privilege of the West, closely tied to its
colonizing efforts and civilizing mission. For Heidegger it defines the modern
age: "The world picture does not change from an earlier medieval one into a
modern one, but rather the fact that the world becomes a picture at all is what
distinguishes the essence of the modern age" (p. 130). This metaphysical
transformation needs its own picture-framing, one that captures how Heidegger himself lectured a purged student body and faculty in the Nazi Germany of 1938 amid the triumph of those racial visions and divisions that had
arisen out of the imperial project and that thus were no less part of the modern world picture. Here Nietschze's will to knowledge makes its fearsome appearance in the perverse Nazi pursuit of racial purity. The picture is framed
through the close association of power and knowledge that affords a seeming
disengagement from the world in the name of science and education, with
the result, as my colleague Derek Gregory notes, that we now see "the world
at a distance—from a platform, seen through a window, displayed on a
screen" (1994, p. 66).

The Educational Spectacle

Within a century of Columbus's triumphant return to Spain, the spectacles of
empire had become a source of common mockery on the Elizabethan stage.
In Shakespeare's *Tempest,* one of the first ideas to cross the mind of the jester,
Trinculo, on stumbling upon Caliban is to put the aboriginal on display back
home, for "not a holiday fool there but would give a piece of silver" to witness
this "strange fish." Trinculo appreciates the economies of fascination to be
had of empire: "When they give not a doit to relieve a lame beggar, they will
lay out ten to see a dead Indian" (2.2.30–32).

By the turn of the eighteenth century, William Wordsworth was looking
back in anger at how his visits to London's St. Bartholomew's Fair had been
marred by such spectacles. In his long, autobiographical *Prelude,* this contemplative poet describes such an exhibit as "hell for eyes and ears," the "anarchy and din / Barbarian and infernal" (7.686–87). Among the imperial figures of this "spectacle," he names the "chattering monkeys dangling from
their poles" and "the silver-collared Negro with his timbrel" (7.694, 703).
They stand among the "movable wonders," presenting a lesson in the outer
limits of life, the possibilities of perversity, which are as surely drawn to London, the city at the center of the empire, as were the dried specimens and
crated artifacts of Cook's journey:

All movable wonders, from all parts,
Are here—Albinos, painted Indians, Dwarfs,
The Horse of knowledge, and the learned Pig,
The Stone-eater, the man that swallows fire,
Giants, Ventriloquists, the Invisible Girl,
The Bust that speaks and moves its goggling eyes,
The Wax-work, Clock-work, all the marvellous craft
Of modern Merlins, Wild Beasts, Puppet-shows,
All out-o'-the-way, far-fetched, perverted things,
All freaks of nature, all Promethean thoughts
Of man, his dulness, madness, and their feats
All jumbled up together to make up
This Parliament of Monsters. (7.706–18)

Wordsworth's parliament of monsters represented the popular expression of natural history, lacking the discipline and order that distinguished the more formally educational displays of nature. If the fair was driven by a desire for sensationalism, the same monkey, Negro, and Indian were later featured in the instructive displays of international exhibitions and national museums. One might say that after Wordsworth, given the wild, irrepressible anarchy of the carnival, the leading lights of the bourgeois state and industry were bound to back a different "horse of knowledge." Yet the state-sponsored expositions that arose in the nineteenth century and continued into our own also drew on the spectacular, as we shall see, knowing how readily the eye lights on novelty, drawn like a moth to a flame.[3]

What might be readily taken as the most monstrous instance of the nineteenth-century spectacle is the exhibition and dissection of Saartjie Baartman, a Xhosa from South Africa. In 1810, at the age of sixteen, she was brought to London, where she was shown as the "Hottentot Venus." Her steatopygia, or protruding buttocks, were the principal focus of attention. They were thought to identify a primitive level of sexuality, and they became the subject of cartoons and vaudeville plays (Gilman, 1985, p. 215). This crude display of Baartman's person drew the attention of abolitionists, and letters of protest appeared in local papers. The African Association, "a Society of

[3] The carnival's challenge to authority, its reversals of the order and celebration of the perverse, have been championed most notably in Mikhail Bakhtin's work on Rabelais (1968); and in Peter Stallybrass and Allan White (1986), who make much of it a category of transgression. This romantic treatment of the carnival as a licensed affair and "a permissible rupture of hegemony, a contained blow-off" has been countered by Terry Eagleton (1981, p. 148).

Benevolent and highly respectable Gentlemen," launched an unsuccessful legal suit "to release her from confinement." However, the court was persuaded by her promoter that Baartman was sharing in the profits and performing of her own accord (Altick, 1978, p. 270).

After the show moved to Paris, Baartman contributed to France's ethnological record of Africa by being painted in the nude at the Jardin du Roi. Then, at the age of twenty-five, after nine years of this exhibitionary life, Baartman succumbed to smallpox. The fascination with her sexuality became the object of further scientific attention, and detailed autopsy reports were published by Henri de Blainville and the famous zoologist Georges Cuvier, founder of comparative anatomy. They took this opportunity to compare the "lowest" human species to the highest primate (orangutan), dwelling on what was regarded as her anomalous "organ of regeneration" (cited by Gilman, 1985, p. 213). This focus on her genitalia led to their preservation and presentation to the Académie Royale de Médecine, "prepared in such a way," in Cuvier's words, "as to allow one to see the nature of the labia" (pp. 215–16). The "Hottentot apron," portrayed in the anatomical diagrams as extended labia minora, served as an icon of African perversity, deformation, and pathology; it was a projection of primitive sexual appetite and lack of moral turpitude that bore anatomical comparison with the assumed deformities suffered by prostitutes and lesbians.

This scientific fascination with the African female led to numerous other autopsies performed on women identified as Hottentots. Their seemingly abnormal physiological and moral disposition was added to the scientific literature on the distance between the races, or their "non-unity," as one American scientist put it in 1868 (Gilman, 1985, p. 216). The cruel journey that Baartman suffered, from the vaudeville stage to the dissecting table, from "Venus" to "apron," demonstrates the spectacle's iconic quality, which brutally reduces aspects of the world to disengaged objects of anxious desire and knowledge for the powerful. Gilman concludes that "the 'white man's burden' thus becomes *his* sexuality and its control, and it is this which is transferred into the need to control the sexuality of the Other, the Other as sexualized female" (p. 237).[4] It is both discouraging and instructive that Baartman's genitalia remain to this day on display at the Musée de l'homme in Paris.

The heartless spectacle that science proved capable of creating had its

---

[4] For a critique of Sander Gilman's reading of Saartjie Baartman's life as largely a masculine "lack of distance between the object of his critique and his own view," see Mieke Bal (1991, p. 32).

match in the exotic exhibitions sponsored by scholars in the humanities. At the late-nineteenth-century International Congress of Orientalists, the educational display of the other attracted, at least on one occasion, somewhat less than sympathetic disdain, as this reviewer reveals in an 1897 issue of *Hellas:*

> The grotesque idea was started of producing natives of Oriental countries as illustrations of papers; thus the Boden Professor of Sanskrit at Oxford produced a real live Indian Pandit, and made him go through the ritual of Brahmanical prayer and worship before a hilarious assembly. . . . Professor Max Müller of Oxford produced two rival Japanese priests, who exhibited their gifts; it had the appearance of two showmen exhibiting their monkeys. (Cited by T. Mitchell, 1988, p. 2)

What had begun as tragedy with the Arawak culminated in the pathos of these presentations at the International Congress of Orientalists. To illustrate one's point with the very human beings under discussion takes the educational device of the visual aid to what now readily seems an inhuman degree. The Japanese priests and Indian pandit are reduced to pure spectacle, unable to be other than objects of the fascinated and knowing gaze of the West, as they are explained and made sensible, like puppets, by their learned presenters.

In more recent times, a number of writers, artists, educators, and curators have made it their business to challenge the spectacle that is made of racial and cultural difference, whether in biology textbooks or Disney cartoons, although they are faced with charges of "political correctness" from those who, not wanting to have their own educations disturbed, seek to trivialize their concern for these acts of misrepresentation. Yet, clearly, some form of political correction is called for when such punishing imbalances of power can account for the treatment of the Arawak, Baartman, the Indian pandit, and the Japanese priests. The correction begins by making the relations of power and knowledge explicit in matters of display and characterization.

For example, when Coco Fusco teamed up with Guillermo Gómez-Peña in the performance piece "Two Undiscovered Amerindians," their display of themselves in a cage challenged the educational spectacle that had long been made of indigenous peoples. To make explicit the voyeuristic relationship endemic to what they termed the "imperialist classification and the fetishizing of the exotic body," the two of them "exhibited" themselves as the mock natives El Aztec High-Tech and Miss Discovery 1992, in a cage placed on display in plazas, museums, and universities (Sawchuk, 1992, p. 24). Their performance, in Fusco's words, "was based on the once popular European and North American practice of exhibiting indigenous people from Africa, Asia, and the Americas in zoos, parks, taverns, museums, freak shows and circuses" (1995, p. 40).[5] Their play on imperialism's *educational* theme is also hard to turn away from. One of the more difficult moments during their tour of Europe and America, Fusco notes, was coming upon a diminutive African American at the Minnesota State Fair who was billed as "Tiny Teesha, the Island Princess." "Not even my own performance," Fusco records, "prepared me for the sadness I saw in her eyes, or my own ensuing sense of shame" (p. 58). The year was 1992.

The Museum

To realize how the museum relates to the spectacle, it helps to return to the sixteenth century, when the Italian grand duke Francesco I, assembled his secret, windowless *studiolo* with landscapes painted on the walls and treasures from afar on display. Francesco had a desk placed in the middle of the room to situate himself at the contemplative center of the known and possessed world. Florentine scholars and physicians were also known to have far more modest cabinets of wonders, which further suggests that the origin of the museum lay in private display (Hooper-Greenhill, 1992, p. 126). The collection of wonders and curiosities, often from abroad, took on greater scientific importance with the encouragement of Francis Bacon and others who saw the importance of having the display of nature at hand for their experimental philosophy. Bacon recommended that even the "most perfect and general library" of the modern scholar be supplemented by "spacious, wonderful gardens" and a stable for "all rare beasts" and "all rare birds; with two lakes adjoining, the one of fresh water the other of salt. . . . And so you may have in small compass a model of the universal world of nature made private." Bacon also recommended "a goodly huge cabinet" and a "still-house" for instruments and furnaces "as may be a palace fit for a philosopher's stone" (cited by Impey and MacGregor, 1983, p. 1). This all-encompassing, private model of the universe, so necessary for driving the empirical engine of modern science, proved equally effective in attracting and instructing a paying public.

What started as the duke's secret pleasure chamber and the scholars' studied objects gradually evolved into the public display of the museum. By the nineteenth century, museums were regularly open to the public, with free ad-

---

[5] Gómez-Peña and Fusco also performed at the Field Museum in Chicago, where, a century before, at the Columbia Exposition, "living dioramas" of "dying savages" in the Congress of Evolution were set up outside the "White City" celebrating Western science and industry. Maureen Sherlock reports that at some sites of this conceptual artwork, "tourists asked to have their pictures taken with the two 'natives,' and many believed them to be real aborigines on display for their entertainment and edification" (1994, p. 33).

mission days beginning in 1810 at the British Museum to ensure that those who needed to benefit the most would not be prohibited from attending. Private museums also thrived in England, along the lines of Reimers's Anatomical and Ethnological Museum, which advertised of its Aztec Lilliputians in 1854 that "the great sensation which these extraordinary little human creatures have excited during their stay in London, has induced Mr. Reimers to model them, that the Public may have further opportunity of inspecting their singular form" (cited by Altick, 1978, p. 342). The movement from exciting sensations to inspecting singular forms describes the educational arc of the museum. I would ask the reader to think about how the museum placed its visitors at the center of a world to be known and possessed, how a museum might use its collection of African masks, Ming vases, and Egyptian mummies to teach visitors about past and present civilization and empire, and about their place within that order. This process can be contrasted with the habits of medieval Europe, when the church incorporated Arabic pieces of inlaid ivory and enameled glass, brought back from the Crusades, into its religious iconography (Raby, 1983, p. 251). However acquired, these early artifacts did not come to stand for a domination of the world in the same way that museum artifacts did. Like Marco Polo's legendary Chinese porcelain, they represented a different order of acquisition, far less intent on teaching about difference and identity.

The museum's particular disciplining of the spectacle not only took place in the West but was also staged in the colonies. The Indian Museum in Calcutta was the largest among colonial collections, opening its doors to the public in 1878. Rudyard Kipling's Anglo-Indian novel *Kim* begins with another of these museums, as the book's young hero sits astride a great bronze cannon, (having "kicked off" an Indian lad), which stood opposite "the Wonder House as the natives called the Lahore Museum" (1939, p. 1). The educational dynamic of empire was doubly applied at the Madras Central Museum, where a certain superintendent's interests in anthropometry led him to stand at the door with his calipers and other tools with which he would take the measurements of native visitors, occasionally paying them for this notable contribution to science (Prakash, 1992, pp. 155–56).

By the nineteenth century, museums in London, Berlin, and Paris were issuing helpful guides to seamen on the gathering and preserving of specimens (Ritvo, 1990, p. 5). Sailor, naturalist ("herborizer"), and missionary alike were caught up in a scientific fervor that sought new specimens, classifications, and causes, as if this great cataloging of nature might form a rock on which to found a new faith. These amateur collectors sent dried, pressed, pickled, caged, or housed artifacts to museums and universities, as well as the zoos and circuses, of an eagerly awaiting Europe. Although the museums began as largely private, sometime-philanthropic, sometime-commercial enterprises, the government was not long in getting involved, introducing a new force into the global search for artifacts, as E. M. Forster sardonically notes in his essay "For the Museum's Sake":

> In the nineteenth century, the soil was scratched all over the globe, rivers were damned, rocks chipped, natives tortured, hooks were let down into the sea. What had happened? Partly an increase in science and taste, but also the arrival of a purchaser, wealthier than cardinals and quite as unscrupulous—the modern European state. (1967, p. 309)

Meanwhile, the museum curator, confronted with the task of arranging greater and greater arrays of artifacts, found a wonderful story line in Darwin's theory of evolution. Here was a way of placing the public not only at the center of the known world, but at its culminating evolutionary moment as well. One result of pursuing this evolutionary narrative, Tony Bennett reports in his study of the museum, is that British, American, and Australian museums were soon looting Aboriginal sacred sites for materials to fill gaps in the chronology of the story they told (1995, p. 79). For a contemporary social critic such as Bennett, the museums during the nineteenth century were designed for easy absorption and were intent on demonstrating the "improving force of culture to the working class" (p. 8).[6] In this, they joined with the church in competing against the alehouse. Bennett cites Sir Henry Cole, who wrote in 1884 that for the working man, "the Museum will certainly lead him to wisdom and gentleness, and to Heaven," compared to the "brutality and perdition" of the "Gin Palace" (p. 21). The glass cases and labeled displays of the museum served, in Bennett's words, "as a space of emulation in which civilized forms of behavior might be learnt and thus more widely diffused through the social body" (p. 24). These lessons were not restricted to London. The number of museums open to the public in Britain increased from fifty in 1860 to two hundred in 1900. This array of museums obviously carried more than artifacts of imperialism, but such exotica were always a strong draw.

In his mock travelogue of yesteryear's Pax Britannica ("Let us ourselves, guide in hand, wander around"), James Morris puts this fixation on imperial objects into sobering perspective with his visit to the Victoria and Albert Museum collection of Indian art, first assembled by the East India Company.

---

[6] Edward Gray, the British Museum's keeper of zoology, pointed out in 1858 that the museums were organized from the beginning "to afford the greatest amount of information in a moderate space, and to be obtained, as it were, at a glance" (cited by Bennett, 1995, p. 41).

The most fascinating and popular exhibit of the late nineteenth century, in Morris's estimation, was "Tipu Sultan's famous Tiger-man-organ, an ingenious toy which represents an Indian tiger eating an Englishman, the tiger growling and the sahib feebly gurgling from an interior mechanism" (1968, p. 437). What Morris fails to mention, as I realized on coming across a picture of this toy, is that not only is it life-size, but it also has a strange sexual ambivalence, beginning with the soldier's skintight uniform. The tiger is poised on the soldier's thighs and shoulders, his mouth at the soldier's neck (Kiernan, 1969, p. 65). Their deadly embrace carries its own lesson in the fears and desires of the colonial encounter.

Yet if I had to point to one device that linked the museum to the unfettered spectacle of empire, it would be the general use of the painted and dressed-up mannequin, which proved to be the museum's way of giving in to a certain visual fascination with the exotic body. Mannequins first turned up in commercial exhibitions, such as the Chinese Collection, which opened in 1842 in London. In the 1890s, when the anthropologist Franz Boas was called upon to design "life groups" of northwestern Native Americans for the American Museum of Natural History in New York, he worked with a "life group preparator" who made casts of native body parts using the Native Americans who performed in circuses visiting New York, and students of the Carlisle Indian School. On occasion, anthropologists would gather body casts while collecting artifacts among Native Americans in the field. A photograph from the preparation of one exhibition shows Boas "demonstrating a pose of the Kwakiutl hamatsa dancer for the model maker at the U.S. National Museum in 1895" as he crouches on a tabletop, dressed in a suit and cravat, with his arms spread out and his mouth in the shape of an O while he looks heavenward (Jacknis, 1985, p. 99). Ira Jacknis notes the great additional expense, as well as the "problems they presented in scientific and artistic veracity," that came with using plaster-cast simulacra, although plaster took the paint needed for skin tones better than wax or papier-mâché (p. 98).

The natives, it appeared, could be effectively represented by a hollow, painted casting, but their tools and clothing had to be authentic possessions of the museum. The educational interests of the museum called for a boxing and preserving of natives' lives within a spectacular three-dimensional family album that preserved their place in the past. The displays certainly proved effective with visitors, Boas noting that "when the Public leave the Lecture Hall, they invariably look at the group" (cited by Jacknis, 1985, p. 100). The real measure, for Boas, however, was that people would "stop to read the labels" at the exhibits (p. 100). With his concern for the pedagogy of exhibition, Boas was distressed at how the architectural presence of the museum—

he refers to its columns and stairways—could defeat the desired effect of entering another world, of fully realizing the scope of difference these lives represented (p. 101). This desire to teach from a nature that existed outside the institution had been Rousseau's great dream in *Émile* (1979). Boas did his share to bring a scientific quality to the museum's realization of that dream. Not long afterward, the study of anthropology and other sciences moved out of the museum and into the university, leaving the museums o focus on public instruction and edification.[7]

The museum's educational influence came to be felt in the department store as it began to encourage extended browsing, so that, in Michael Kimmelman's analysis, "shopping at a department store became a form of connoisseurship for the average man and woman" (1995, p. H43). In the United States, this exhibitionary mix of the educational and the commercial reached a fine art by the turn of the century. Stewart Cullin, ethnology curator of the Brooklyn Museum, was at that time setting up displays of the museum's artifacts in the Bonwit Teller and Abraham & Straus department stores, while the owners of such enterprises were funding expeditions to collect Amerindian artifacts. The public was raised to appreciate the finest fruits of empire, as Bonwit Teller advertised that its 1923 "sports attire of Congo fabrics" was "on exhibit . . . in collaboration with the Brooklyn Museum" (p. H43). Both the museum and the department store were participating in a form of consumer democracy that came of recognizing that women formed an audience and a market.[8]

Another legacy of the ethnological exhibition and, in many senses, a dilemma yet to be resolved comes of what Elizabeth Williams (1985) describes as "the opposition between art and artifact." Williams notes that the Louvre began in the nineteenth century to serve as a repository of pre-Columbian artifacts. The case was soon made to remove these artifacts from the realm of high culture to a site devoted to anthropological study. In the 1820s, E. F. Jomard, curator of the Bibliothèque Royale, complained that "there was no

---

[7] By 1907, Boas had concluded that "the psychological as well as the historical relations of culture, which are the only objects of anthropological inquiry, cannot be expressed by any arrangement based on so small a portion of the manifestation of ethnic life as presented by specimens" (cited by Jacknis, 1985, p. 108). Perhaps, one might then suggest, it was the relation *between* cultures that was being expressed or manifested by these presentations of specimens.

[8] Turning the analogy around, Marianna Torgovnick proposes that the museums' display of primitive objects at the turn of the century "resembled department stores during clearance sales: items were displayed en masse in no special order; they were on view but not exhibited lavishly or enticingly" (1990, p. 75). Nancy Armstrong discusses this democratic consumerism through a postcolonial reading of *Alice in Wonderland* (1990, p. 17).

question of beauty in these arts . . . but only of objects considered in relation to practical and social utility" (cited by Williams, 1985, p. 147). These practical objects came into their own with the Universal Exposition of 1878 in Paris, which featured a massive exhibition of Americana, decorated mannequins, and staged vignettes. After the exposition closed, the site of the Americana exhibit was transformed into the Museé d'Ethnographie du Trocadéro. Some thirty years later, the story goes, Picasso wandered into the Trocadéro, where he had a profound encounter with the "primitive" in the form of Kota reliquary figures from the Congo. Picasso's reflections on his visit to the Trocadéro emphasize these artifacts' break with the traditional aesthetics of Western art, invoking in him a profound engagement with what he saw as the magic and hostility of the world:

> At that moment I realized that this was what painting is all about. Painting isn't an aesthetic operation; it's a form of magic designed as mediation between the strange, hostile world and us, a way of seizing power by giving form to our terrors as well as our desire. When I came to this realization, I knew that I had found my way. (Cited by Rhodes, 1994, p. 116)

A 1908 photograph of Picasso shows the artist in his Parisian Bateau-Lavoir studio, sitting by a coal stove and surrounded by what appear to be West African artifacts (Rhodes, 1994, p. 112). His *Nude with Raised Arms* from 1907 brings an infusion of this designated primitiveness to the cubist denial of Western perspective, with the figure's mask-like, football-shaped eyes sitting askew in the extended face. This was the artist's unmasking of what was, for him, both primal and duplicitous in the female. It is art after ethnography. A remote culture is reassembled in Paris, feeding the viewer's desire for a primitive break from the tired spirit of the metropolis. The ethnographic artifact, torn from the culture of the African village, enters the Western imagination through the museum display, with little thought for the colonialism that has made it all possible. The Trocadéro affords the West a cultural exchange mediated, as Picasso writes of painting's purpose, "between this strange, hostile world and us." The ethnographic display in the museum domesticates "our terrors as well as our desires" for an empire over the primal (cited by Rhodes, p. 116). What has been wrenched from one community is placed within the museum's quietude of order, grace, and instruction. The object's careful mounting neatly belies the imperial violence, symbolic and otherwise, that has afforded this ethnographic display. The museum's lessons are always partial.

The studied primitiveness achieved by artists from Gauguin through Matisse, Klee, and Modigliani to Hepworth and Moore transformed artifacts into art. This elevated the public's appreciation of ethnographic mask and totem, but, as Sally Price observes, "much of the recent valorization of Primitive Art has simply been a matter of removing selected Masterpieces from one realm and depositing them in the other, without in any way narrowing the great divide that separates them" (1989, p. 99). Even the museum that houses both art and artifact manages to keep them apart through its educational efforts. Think of how the museum labels a work of art with the year of its completion, the name of the artist, the place of birth; the ethnographic artifact is typically identified by tribe, region, or nation, and is dated by century. The framed and hung artwork celebrates the artist's transcending moment of sublime achievement, whereas the array of artifacts in the glass case signifies an aspect, whether spiritual or culinary, of a remote culture. Does the allure of these artifacts come from this educated sense of approaching a great divide across time and space?

The dialectical push and pull of Western art being what it is, the dadaists turned back against the spiritualizing of a primitive sexuality earlier in this century, with Hannah Höch producing the collage series *From the Ethnographic Museum* in 1926. It included African sculptures intercut with women's lipsticked lips and fashion-model legs in high heels, mocking the treatment of both the primal and the well-made-up woman as other (Rhodes, 1994, p. 147). Such work becomes part of the museum's ability to encompass modernity's central tension between the ubiquitous institution and the critique of its dominance. Art, in that sense, is still about itself.

Another countermove against the museum tradition includes the National Museum of the American Indian, which, since its opening in 1994 at the Smithsonian Institution in New York, has featured labels for some of its exhibits in three colors, with art historians, anthropologists, and Native Americans each providing commentary. It also leaves some objects undated to show their continuing life within an ongoing culture ("On Native Ground," 1994). To have Native Americans curating, advising, and repatriating artifacts may disturb without completely unsettling the museum's placement of the Western visitor at the center of a universe. Rather than seeing their own perspective and knowledge unrelentingly celebrated or seeing the museum as a ledger of ownership, here Western visitors are just that, visitors to a familiar institution that is now in the hands of those whom it once simply put on display.

Although museums are becoming more self-conscious about their rendering of the world, the public's expectations have only very slowly been following suit. The Africa 95 celebration in Great Britain featured a number of exhibitions, including as its principal showpiece and the largest of its kind *Africa: The Art of a Continent,* sponsored by the Anglo American Company,

De Beers, and Minorco. One reviewer of the show at the Royal Academy of Arts in London, John Ryle, after critiquing the use of the term *art* as a Western imposition, expressed his disappointment that in "visiting the Royal Academy, you do not feel you have been to Africa. To tell the truth, the light is so low and the rooms are so gloomy, it is more like a visit to the land of the dead" (1995, p. 19). The idea of the museum somehow *delivering* Africa affords a clear vision of how the museum's imperial legacy lives on in those it effectively educated over a lifetime. All is not lost for Ryle in this exhibition, however, as he finally claims to feel closer to "a contemporary Akan carver, trading in an international market" than to his own forebears, who as colonists engaged in a "triumphant, ill-informed appropriation of Akan ritual furniture" (p. 19). The curator of the exhibition was the painter Tom Phillips (1995), who expressed the hope that the show would put an end to talk of the primitive: "Certainly after this exhibition I hope never to hear the word again."[9] Hoping not to hear of what has been made of the past is not helpful.

There remains much to be said about the "primitive" if we are to understand what we have been taught by the museum. Although the museum preserves, honors, and informs in ways I do not want to disparage or lose, we need to be able to imagine what the museum presumes, how that presumption informs our education, and how that presumption has been fed by the very specific material and historical relations that fall under the name "imperialism."

The Botanical and Zoological Gardens

The spectacle and the museum were both caught up in a fascination with the human, but it was actually the study of plants that formed the earliest of the imperial sciences, a study that would lend itself to magnificent collections, gardens, and illustrations. The naturalists who traveled the seas were especially keen about the pharmacological and agricultural uses of newfound plants. They preserved, dried, and kept living instances of the world's botanical variety. As early as 1540, gardens stocked with plants from around the globe were being added to European estates for their beauty, oddity, and scientific value (Lach, 1977, p. 441). The Portuguese physician Garcia da Orta

---

[9] Among the responses to the exhibition that Alan Riding reports are comments by William Packer in the *Financial Times*—"We shall never look at African art in our old innocent, patronizing naiveté again"—and Simon Jenkins in the *Times*: "They look exotic, exciting, colorful but primitive. . . . But we are not supposed to say that" (cited by Riding, 1995, pp. 43, 46). Torgovnick notes that "we conceive of ourselves as at a crossroads between the civilized and the savage; we are formed by our conceptions of both these terms" (1990, p. 17).

was among the earliest to plant systematic gardens for studying the life of tropical plants, including cannabis, choosing Goa and Bombay Island for the establishment of his gardens. This led to his treatise on the uses of some fifty-seven plants and "simples" in the preparation of spices, foods, and medicines (p. 433). Lach notes how, in those pre-Linnaean times, Orta labeled the plants with their common names in as many languages as possible, as if to capture what was then a multicultural claim to a naming of the world.[10]

By the end of the eighteenth century, the Calcutta Botanic Garden offered a profusion of some 22,000 plant species and 800 tree types, all carefully labeled for the visitor's edification (Kumar, 1990, p. 52). Meanwhile, as I mentioned in the previous chapter, the famous Jardin du Roi was established in Paris in 1635, and the pleasure gardens at Kew in London were rechristened as the Royal Botanic Gardens in 1841, when they were officially recognized for their contribution to the study of natural history. As Lucile Brockway summarizes it, "Through its research, its dissemination of scientific information, and its practical activities, which included plant smuggling, Kew Gardens played a major part in the development of several highly profitable and strategically important plant-based industries in the tropical colonies" (1979, p. 6). Joseph Banks and those who followed him in administering Kew Gardens set up satellite gardens from St. Vincent to Calcutta to support the gardens. Brockway compares the Royal Botanic Gardens, with its "semiamateur" horticulturalists, to the modern research laboratory: "These new plantation crops complemented Britain's home industries to form a comprehensive system of energy extraction and commodity exchange which for a time, in the nineteenth and early twentieth centuries, made Britain the world's superpower" (p. 6). And this from a garden that continued to fill the Sunday afternoons of Londoners with earthly delights.

Although the state-sponsored gardens of Europe typically sought a balance between scientific inquiry and public pleasure, those who made it their business to profit by empire's spectacle were less equivocal about the intent of their exhibitions. The private zoos, which by midway into the nineteenth century were postering the streets of major European and American cities with notices of their great menageries, were strong on colonial lessons in identity and difference. The Royal Menagerie of London billed itself as "the grandest National Depot of Animated Nature in the World" (Altick, 1978, p. 308). For a shilling, visitors to the Royal Menagerie were able to see "the African Lion—Nero" and the "Noble Lioness—Charlotte," along with "the

---

[10] After introducing a standard nomenclature, Linneaus honored Orta's early work by naming a number of plants after him (Lach, 1977, p. 434).

Striped or Untamable Hyena," "a Variety of the Monkey Tribe," "an Oriental Porcupine," and on the list goes, with each animal suggesting the corresponding human savagery of untamable oriental tribes. Londoners with a little pocket change could see the caging of the strange and the savage in an animal version of the colonial drama. The Royal Menagerie's Ne(g)ro, accompanied by his noble Charlotte, suggested the fearsome emperor of the jungle lording over the natives before succumbing to the true colonial masters of the land.[11]

But it was not just the showman who was in it for the money. The French government sought to exploit the economic potential of the research garden when it established the Jardin zoologique d'acclimatation in 1854, a venture that continues to this day in Paris. The Société zoologique d'acclimatation sought to revitalize France's agricultural situation by domesticating exotic plants and animals, with the whole process put on display for the information of the public. The *société*, largely made up of amateur naturalists, imported yaks, ostriches, and alpacas in the hope that such animals, in adapting to French soil and climate, could be used to revitalize the country's languishing agriculture enterprise.[12] The *société's jardin* also had an active educational component, with occasional and highly "successful" ethnological exhibits. These spectacles included, at different times, small numbers of Africans, Inuit, Argentine gauchos, and Laplanders set among displays of relevant animals (Osborne, 1994, pp. 126–27).

By the twentieth century, the Jardin zoologique d'acclimatation had declined as a public attraction, and the efforts to acclimatize kangaroos and llamas proved, in almost all instances, disastrous. This desire to see animals adapt to different climates was another take on reordering the world. It was a selective go at shuffling what-belonged-where to the advantage of the French. Augustine Hardy, director of the corresponding Jardin d'essai at Algiers, declared in 1898, "The whole of colonization is a vast deed in acclimatization" (cited by Osborne, 1994, p. 145). Acclimatization was about establishing a new order over the nature of the world. Certainly, the colonial powers devoted considerable scientific energies not only to preparing llamas for alpine pastures, but also to increasing the ability of white men to govern and profit in the tropics. The initial colonial forays into the region of the equator in the

---

[11] Edgar Rice Burroughs's Tarzan novels, perhaps most notably *Lord of the Jungle,* were to sustain this theme. Donna Haraway argues in her *Primate Visions* (1989) that symbolically elevating the animals of Africa over the Africans who live with them is part of what ethnologists have done in their study of primates.

[12] Ten percent of the Société zoologique d'acclimatation's membership was made up of engineers, physicians, scientists, and teachers (Osborne, 1994, p. 20).

early nineteenth-century had been disastrous, claiming the lives of seventy-eight out of one hundred British physicians stationed in tropical Africa before they had completed their two years of duty (p. 93).

The acclimatization theme was about thriving within the expanded horizons of this exotic and vital nature. It meant learning to be at home in the world, in the sense of being its lord and master. The imperial garden and the zoo set nature on display for the cosmopolitan, creating miniature Edens within the urbanity of civilization. They encouraged the public to step off the street and into the scientific and colonial mastery of nature that attested to the wonder and beauty of the West's dominion.

The Encyclopedic Urge

In eighteenth-century France, the encyclopedists were among those calling for the movement of the royal collection of art and artifacts from its refuge at Versailles to a Louvre open to the public (Bennett, 1995, p. 37). Such was the commitment of true citizens of the Enlightenment to the spread of reason and knowledge among the people. The great expression of that ideal, of course, was Diderot's magnificent publishing project, the *Encyclopédie,* undertaken by a "Society of Men of Letters." It was originally contracted to be a translation of Ephraim Chambers's recently issued *Cyclopedia,* but Diderot was not long in convincing his backers that they could all do much better by going with an original and thoroughly French ordering of knowledge. The resulting *Encyclopédie ou dictionnaire raisonné des sciences, des arts, et des métiers,* the first volumes of which appeared in 1751, was the bound and portable showcase of Western civilization. Although the French Empire plays only a minor part in the content of the *Encyclopédie,* Diderot did not hesitate to appeal to imperialism's planetary consciousness in describing the intent of this work: "The purpose of the Encyclopedia is to assemble the knowledge scattered over the face of the earth; to explain its general plan to the men with whom we live and to transmit it to the men who come after us" (Gillispie, 1959, p. ix). Gathering what was otherwise dispersed and scattered, to educate those among whom "we" live, with the ambiguous question just who is being named here, carries its own sense of the imperial educational mission.

Here was a work that advertised itself as a "detailed system of human knowledge" that could be set out on a large page, with the whole of "Understanding" divided among "Memory," which ran to "the working and uses of silk," through "Reason," and on to "Imagination," including "theoretical, practical, instrumental, and vocal music" (d'Alembert, 1995, pp. 144–45). Jean le Rond d'Alembert, Diderot's collaborator, contributed a "Preliminary Discourse," which set out the *Encyclopédie*'s commitment to empiricism: "All our direct knowledge can be reduced to what we received through the senses; whence it follows that we owe all our ideas to our sensations" (p. 6). French efforts to gather up the world's scattered knowledge, to expand the range of its sensations, named the intellectual debt owed to imperialism in the *Encyclopédie*. D'Alembert goes on to offer an ethics governing the will to knowledge: "The mere fact that we have occasionally found concrete advantages in certain fragments of knowledge, when they were hitherto unsuspected, authorizes us to regard all investigations begun out of pure curiosity as being potentially useful to us" (p. 16). The *Encyclopédie* stood for the authorized use of the world by the guardians of human understanding, out of that world's potential usefulness to the European mind and body. It spoke eloquently to what was learned, inventive, innovative, and industrious in the French. In a colonial vein, it provided an illustrated guide to the indigo, manioc (the source of arrowroot), tobacco, cotton, and sugar plantations of the French colonies, which were "disposed according to the dictates of reason and a slave economy," as Charles Gillispie puts it in his edition of the *Encyclopédie*'s illustrations for the trades and industry (1959, pl. 37). The plantation landscapes depicted are thoroughly idyllic. Slaves walk in from the fields in pairs, while another is catching a fish in the pond for dinner. The main house sits off on a hill.

For Roland Barthes, the *Encyclopédie*'s illustrations are forebears of the international expositions that began in the next century. Barthes speaks of how the "Encyclopedic man mines all nature with human signs. . . . The object is the world's human signature" (1980, p. 24). The human signature is in a French hand, a signature that, in the encyclopedic appetite for order and knowledge, extends to the entire world. The *Encyclopédie* becomes, for Barthes, "a huge ledger of ownership" that distinguishes the Enlightenment, in his mind, from the Renaissance's "animated spirit of an adventurous knowledge." Although Barthes makes no direct reference to imperialism in his analysis, he does identify "a learning of appropriation" in which "to appropriate is to fragment the world, to divide it into finite objects subject to man." For Barthes, "we cannot separate without finally naming and classifying, and at that moment property is born" (p. 27). This seems at once to identify (to name and classify) the coinciding spirits of imperialism and scholarship that seek to possess the world, bringing it within the (French) signature. The questions that I keep returning to in this book are, how dependent was learning on taking possession of the world in this way, and what is the legacy of this possessive education, this right of ownership and property? At some level, I suppose, any work that aspires to encompass the known world could be said to suffer from imperialist aspirations. With this encyclopedic urge of the Enlightenment, however, the rhetoric and ambition are underwritten by a literal, rather than a literary, aspiration to take hold of the world.

This is perhaps no less the case with the great encyclopedias of imperial China, which were equally far-reaching and equally given to fragmentation, classification, and, ultimately, a sense of the emperor's ubiquitous ownership. Pliny's *Naturalis historia,* from the time of the Roman Empire, had for centuries possessed the same confident claim on learning. Diderot's *Encyclopédie* was not, then, the invention of European imperialism. It was part of a larger tradition of compiling and collating all that is known of the world. Yet it and its English companions *Cyclopedia* and *Britannica,* did define a world that readers could assume they possessed as their sets stood in their special bookcases. We have inherited an encyclopedic tradition, with its sense of having gathered up "the knowledge scattered over the face of the earth [in order] to explain its general plan to the men with whom we live." As the great exposition of the Enlightenment, the encyclopedia constituted the whole of a civilization in the Western mastery of nature, reason, and the world at large, organized into an alphabetical arrangement of knowledge's discrete divisions. How much of that has changed? The reassuring and ultimate message of the *Encyclopédie,* for Barthes, is that "a glance suffices—ours—for the world to be eternally complete" (1980, p. 39). The legacy of imperialism is about forms of knowledge that preserve and complete the hegemony of the knower.

The Great Exhibitions

By the middle of the nineteenth century, the amassed wealth and treasures of imperialism must have seemed to cry out for demonstration and display, at least for those who felt the pride of this accomplishment. The fairs, museums, and libraries proved insufficient to the welling up of pride and the desire to focus people's attention on the nation's accomplishments abroad. In Great Britain, the industrial classes had just come through the social unrest of the Chartist movement and were settling in for the long haul toward full democratic participation, while living in the "two nations" that identified the gap between the industrial and the propertied classes at the time. Where the industrial classes had yet to secure their democratic due, the first of the Reform Bills advanced the powers of the emerging middle class. Thus, the enfranchised classes might think well of staging a glorious national lesson in empire and commerce.

Such was the Great Exhibition of the Industry of All Nations held in 1851, drawing 6 million visitors to its Hyde Park site in London. The exhibition's architectural centerpiece, the Crystal Palace, set the world within a magnificent ironwork and glass display case presenting Great Britain's imperial hold on the world with reassuring abundance (Breckenridge, 1989, p. 202). If the English people's knowledge of India up to that point had been restricted to the sweeping panoramas of battle scenes on display in London, the Great Exhibition presented the subcontinent through the regalia of past splendors and current crafts, including the ivory throne of the raja of Travancore brought as a present to Queen Victoria and surrounded by fine carpets, saddles, and parasols. "Like everything else at the Great Exhibition," Paul Greenhalgh notes, "Empire was a commodity, a thing more important than but not dissimilar to shawls, ironwork, flax, or indeed sculpture. . . . Countries within the empire were exhibited, as quantifiable batches of produce rather than as cultures" (1988, p. 54). The exhibition cultivated an appetite for the world.[13] It offered proof of the nation's historical and geographical place as a center of advanced civilization. The exhibition was intended to serve as a rallying point for a nation still deeply divided along class lines, and among those attending the display of industrial progress were delegations of French workers, who traveled to London for the exhibitions of both 1851 and 1862. These educational ventures were arguably precursors to the formation of Marx's International Workingmen's Association and perhaps the beginning of labor's troubled history around the support for and challenges to empire (Benjamin, 1978, p. 152).

There were exhibitions aplenty during this era on science and technology, arts and crafts, and waxworks and clockworks—and, when it came to making a spectacle of the world, especially the world outside Europe, the triumph of imperialism for colonizer and colonized was the constant theme (Altick, 1978). Following the Great Exhibition, one after another of the great European metropolises created the most engaging educational experiences out of distant lands and peoples. Timothy Mitchell has pointed out how the exhibition positioned its public as an observer "separated from the physical world and from his own physical body," with the effect that "the true nature of the human being . . . was to learn to be industrious, self-disciplined and closely attentive" (1988, p. 19).[14] Yet the exhibition was something more as well.

---

[13] Among the educational marketing spin-offs was the Crystal Palace Game, which offered "a voyage around the world, an entertaining excursion in search of knowledge whereby geography is made easy" (Whitfield, 1994, p. 123). Carol Breckenridge refers to such objects as "sumptuary technologies of honor, prestige, and blood" (1989, p. 204).

[14] Tony Bennett is another who is less than sanguine about the exhibitions: "After 1851, world fairs were to function less as vehicles for the technical education of the working classes than as instruments for their stupefaction before the reified products of their own labor" (1995, p. 81). The fairs may have been poor sources of technical education, but they remain fascinating displays of industrial accomplishment that were meant to stand in stark contrast to the exhibitions of the less civilized world.

The United States found a late-nineteenth-century enthusiasm for international exhibitions and world fairs that allowed it to celebrate its emerging involvement in global affairs and imperialist ventures, especially for those Americans who envisioned themselves as the rightful heirs of the new world order that Europe had created. Although that order was shot through with themes of science and progress, it also proved to be deeply mired in replicating the racial divisions so central to what imperialism made of the world. The Centennial Exhibition held in Philadelphia in 1876 featured pavilions divided into what were, in effect, racial zones, and the 1893 World's Columbian Exposition in Chicago split the world between the White City, as the pristine pinnacle of civilization, and the Midway Plaisance, as the baser home of such ethnological exhibits as "Darkest Africa," set amid the belly dancers and strip shows. Prominent anthropologists were consulted in constructing the native village, which became a common feature of American fairs after the Columbian Exposition. Some professors took advantage of the site to teach university summer school classes at the exposition (Rydell, 1993, p. 21). The educational features of the exposition were trumpeted by the *Chicago Tribune,* which claimed it offered an adventure in social Darwinism: "An opportunity was here afforded to the scientific mind to descend the spiral of evolution," the paper advised (cited by Bederman, 1995, p. 35).

The exposition's cloaking of racial prejudices in the robes of science, progress, and liberty, which all Americans were not permitted to enjoy, did not pass without public comment. Outraged by this elaborate display of hypocrisy, the social activists Ida B. Wells and Frederick Douglass responded with the pamphlet *The Reason Why the Colored American Is Not in the World's Columbian Exposition.* Some ten thousand copies of the pamphlet were distributed during the fair through the Haitian Building, where the former slave Douglass was later able to find a place as a representative. The pamphlet attacked the "barbarism and race hate" of an America that dared to boast of "liberty and civilization" while excluding the "colored American" from the exposition (cited by Bederman, 1995, p. 39). Wells and Douglass were especially dismayed by the "Darkest Africa" midway show: "As if to shame the Negro, the Dahomians are also here to exhibit the Negro as a repulsive savage" (p. 39). What was being commemorated of the four hundred years that had passed since the arrival of Columbus was not only the triumph of the West in conquering the better part of the world, but also the growing gap between this achievement and the place of other peoples.

The exhibitions of this century, no less than in the last one, rallied their respective nations around their place within this triumphant civilization. The fair's spectacular architecture of knock-down buildings and mock-up displays was clearly designed to simulate the experience of being at the center of a world in which one could as readily gaze into its farthest reaches as well as into its past and future. The international exposition made a spectacle of the world, turning it into a lesson on the ability of advanced scientific civilizations to reap great educational and consumer benefits from colonial empires. These massively attended public events represented the educational formation of what Guy Debord describes as "the society of the spectacle," in which "the spectacle is the existing order's uninterrupted discourse about itself, its laudatory monologue" (1977, p. 24). From the Arawak whom Columbus paraded down the streets of Seville to the living exhibitions of the international exposition, a public lined up to witness the spectacle of empire and to expand its own world. The world's fairs and expositions have continued past the demise of the West's vast empires, and if they now represent something more of a united-nations assembly of showplaces, we need to wonder at how much of their original exhibition of a crudely divided world still works on the educated imagination.

Curious and Competitive Travel

For all of the exhibitions, fairs, and museums that brought the bounty of the empire home, there were still those Europeans who longed for the real thing, longed to play their own version of Christopher Columbus and be part of the empire's recording and image-making apparatus. As a result, there were always, especially from the last century onward, peripatetic Europeans climbing with guidebook and journal in hand to the heights of the Great Pyramid of Giza and working their way across the sweeping terraces of the Shalamar Gardens in Lahore. "He whose eyes passively look out and possess" is how Mary Louise Pratt, in her book *Imperial Eyes,* renders the gaze of those who traveled the empire (1992, p. 7). If the travel writer served as recording secretary of empire tourism, many of those who took notes managed to demonstrate what Pratt identifies as an "anti-conquest" sensibility; they sought "to secure their innocence at the same moment as they assert[ed] European hegemony" (p. 7). Many of the sightseers were deeply moved by the suffering they witnessed at the hands of colonial regimes and plantation economies. Even the more disengaged narratives stood in contrast to the political and economic machinations that made the empire possible. Travel writing gave a certain face-to-face quality to this imperial possession of the world, yet, however much it appeared to tell of native life, it was ultimately directed, in an educational sense, inward. The self-improvement of travel was its theme. We have much to learn about ourselves and others, if we only take the time to explore what lies beyond our all too familiar horizons.

Travel's educational value, however, was not above being called into question. It had an unforgiving critic in Jean-Jacques Rousseau, who midway into the eighteenth century was challenging European thinking, more generally, on the nature of learning:

> It is said that we have learned men who travel to inform themselves. This is an error. The learned travel for profit like the others . . . by order of the court. They are dispatched, subsidized, and paid to observe such and such an object which is very surely not a moral object. . . . If in some country there happen to be men who are curious and travel at their own expense, it is never to study men but rather to instruct them. It is not science they need but ostentation. How would they shake off the yoke of opinion in their travels? They only undertake them for the sake of opinion. (1979, p. 454)

Rousseau's questioning of travel's broadening effect—"The learned travel for profit"—comes toward the conclusion of his sustained critique of European educational practices: "But if one wants to study men, is it necessary to roam the entire earth? Is it necessary to go to Japan to observe Europeans?" (p. 451). His answer is a sharp no to both questions. He adds, if not quite accurately, then to great effect, that "the ancients traveled little, read little, and wrote little, and yet one sees in those of their extant works which remain to us that they observed one another better than we observe our contemporaries" (p. 452).

Travel, as a way of finding oneself through a greater knowledge of the other, brings us to perhaps the busiest of intersections between education and imperialism. This traveling theory calls for Europeans to visit Japan to witness the true depth of the divide between the East and West. Not only do we seek the thrill of crossing the line and entering the space of the other, but we see this as a way of knowing ourselves and defining our place as the ones who, hovering above this divide, *can* know the other and ourselves, as if to encompass the whole world. This presumption of knowing, supported by the range of educational apparatuses discussed in this chapter, is what gives travel its colonizing aspect. It is yet another aspect in the assertion of dominion. Mungo Park opens his *Travels in the Interior Districts of Africa* at the end of the eighteenth century not only by acknowledging the "passionate desire to examine the production of a country so little known," but also with a promise to "render the geography of Africa more familiar to my countrymen" so that they may realize through "their ambition and industry new sources of wealth" (cited by D. Lee, 1995, p. 13). Imperial travel was conducted as if to a dreamland with job openings and stock options.

Of all of the educational forms considered in this chapter, travel writing takes us closest to the literary realm, and there was a complex circulation of meaning between literature and travel writing. For example, Debbie Lee (1995) has analyzed how John Keats's poem "Lamia" draws on travel writers, such as Park, to gather the poem's mythic proportions and monsters; the poet would later send his poetry along with the surgeon-explorer Joseph Ritchie, who made his way across Africa. We can envision the romantic poet tapping into the travel writer's imperial experience of the world, only to return the favor by affording later travel writers a heady body of imagery, adding a new dynamic to their writing abroad. There were also those intrepid literary sorts who went along for the ride. David Spurr argues that the body of well-traveled literature that resulted from this trekking about, "from colonial American captivity narratives to the novels of Forster and Malraux, has built itself around the trial of penetration into the interior spaces of non-European peoples" (1994, p. 19). In that interior penetration, literature affords what most travel writing overlooks on its way to taking in the sights. The educational function of both, by dwelling on interiors and exteriors, was to deliver up the land and hand of what was at once foreign and about to be rendered familiar.

Although well forgotten today, and for good reason, Charles Wentworth Dilke's *Greater Britain: A Record of Travel in English-Speaking Countries during 1866 and 1867* (1869) was widely recognized for its influence on readers in its day (Winks, 1969, p. 81). Dilke begins the work plainly and boldly: "In 1866 and 1867 I followed England round the world; everywhere I was in English-speaking, or in English-governed lands." He goes on with disarming candor to offer the racial core of this worldly pursuit: "The idea which in all the length of my travels has been at once my fellow and my guide—a key wherewith to unlock the hidden things of strange new lands—is a conception, however imperfect, of the grandeur of our race, already girding the earth, which is destined, perhaps, eventually to overspread" (1869, p. 2). It is tempting to suggest that what remains of that white grandeur is the Marlboro man, cigarette dangling from his mouth, riding his beloved horse across the billboards of the non-Western world. The book's narrative quality ("A bump . . . roused us from our musings") treats the reader as a traveling companion who aspires to the knowing superiority that comes of seeing the world within the sensibilities of an adventurous and wise guide to a Greater Britain. Dilke takes seriously his pedagogical mandate to instruct and delight.

Dilke may be nothing more than an imperial flag-waver, but we are little further ahead when we consider the travel reflections of one of the century's great scientists, Charles Darwin. His *Voyage of the* Beagle was published to great acclaim in 1839, and among its extensive observations are once again the great imperial themes of identity and difference. He finds the Feuguans, for example, "the most curious and interesting spectacle I ever beheld: I could not have believed how wide was the difference between savage and civilized man: it is greater than between a wild and domesticated animal, inasmuch as in man there is a greater power of improvement" (1962, p. 205). That Darwin, having observed the "savage," could not believe the degree of difference compared to "civilized man" suggests how *empiricism* was linked to the moral economy of *empire,* which depended on such differences. The two concepts, like old friends, had grown up together in the European experience when the world seemed so new to them both.[15]

In the final pages of the book, Darwin sets out the advantages of travel for the young naturalist. He gives a manly air to living in the open by comparing it to the "love of the chase"; he feels travel's primeval appeal: "It is the savage returning to his wild and native habits" (1962, p. 502). The imperial traveler is able to live out a savage passion in pursuit of a civilized knowing, and it leads him to a "glowing sense of happiness," which he assumes every traveler has experienced "when he first breathed in a foreign clime, where the civilized man has seldom or never trod." He has the pleasure of filling in what was the blank map of the larger world: "The map of the world ceases to be a blank. . . . Each part assumes its proper proportions" (p. 502). Those proper proportions are set, of course, in relation to the observer and the center of his world. This extension of the known world takes its place for the scientist who was to turn this trip into the principles of evolution within the accomplishment of the British nation: "The march of improvement, consequent on the introduction of Christianity through the South Sea, probably stands by itself in the records of history. . . . Changes have now been effected by the philanthropic spirit of the British nation." He foresees Australia standing as "empress over the southern hemisphere" while observing that "to hoist the British flag, seems to draw with it as a certain consequence, wealth, prosperity, and civilization" (p. 502). Such were the lessons to be had everywhere for the West, it must have seemed in the nineteenth century. It was no less true when one attended international expositions, visited the zoo, browsed through the encyclopedia, shopped in a department store, or embarked on a journey across

---

[15] William Paterson provides an excellent example of a voyager who used scientific inquiry to advance imperial politics in the contested cape region of Africa during the late eighteenth century. After providing his government with valuable military information, he wrote without a trace of irony in the preface to the widely read record of his journeys, "Greatly excited by the perspective of a land whose products are unknown to us, I left England with resolution to satisfy a curiosity, which, if it is not seen as useful to society, is at least innocent" (cited by Pratt, 1992, p. 57).

the seas. "In conclusion, it appears to me" Darwin wrote, "that nothing can be more improving to a young naturalist than a journey in distant countries" (p. 502).

By the 1920s, travel to the colonies had begun to trouble the empire in ways that E. M. Forster skillfully renders in *A Passage to India* (1924). The imminent threat driving the novel is directed not so much at the unfortunate Englishwoman frightened in the darkness of the Marabar cave, as at the imperial order, which finds its expression in another of the novel's Englishwomen, Mrs. Moore, who has not yet acquired the necessary state of mind for the unpleasant business of colonialism. The educational value of travel lies in keeping one's distance; it depends on approaching one's destination as an exhibition. Mrs. Moore leaves India in a great wave of disappointment— "I have not seen the right places"—whereas her one Indian acquaintance, Dr. Aziz, comes to feel by the book's end that he has been seduced by "this pose of 'seeing India' "; he understands that the desire on the part of the British to see India "was only a form of ruling India; no sympathy lay behind it" (1924, p. 204). The educational dynamic of seeing the right places, of taking in the great treasures, still plays its part in modern travel and in amusement parks. It meets its perfect match in a Disneyland boat tour through lushly decorated and mechanized versions of jungle and village life. The busloads of Japanese students at the Louvre and of Indians touring Oxford, however, suggest that the collapse of empire has really been about repackaging and marketing the metropolitan centers as global tourist attractions. Tourism on a grand scale was once the privileged expression of the Western empire; with Disneyland in Tokyo, the idea is not so much gone as far more globally distributed as a reward of modernization.

Forster's novel also reminds one how travel formed part of the more restricted sphere of Western women's privilege. The sense of overseas travel's imminent and unspeakable dangers did not prevent, however, a great deal of the most adventuresome sort of travel bravely conducted and artfully recorded by women (Robinson, 1990).[16] I presented earlier in this book both the well-traveled accomplishments of Mary Wortley Montagu, which resulted in the introduction of the smallpox vaccination into Europe, and Mary Kingsley's collection of rare fish species. Both women also made notable con-

---

[16] Jane Robinson comments in her introduction to *Wayward Women: A Guide to Women Travellers:* "A female who traveled abroad was a strange creature in any age—although by the nineteenth century perhaps not quite as shocking as before. Then, if she were a Lady, she could go where she pleased, given suitable male protection, as long as it lay within the bounds of civilization (i.e., the British empire), and even if she were a mere woman she need not be entirely useless" (1990, p. viii).

tributions to the Western reader's hunger for travel writing. Among the women who wrote from the colonies, Isabelle Eberhardt offers an early and courageous instance of participant-observer travel. To dress as she did in Arab men's clothing while traveling through North Africa at the turn of the century was to offend both Muslims and Europeans at least as much as did her support for local rebels and dissidents and her embrace of Islamic mysticism. Beginning her desert adventures at the age of nineteen, she was soon producing a steady stream of evocative fiction and political journalism (for, among other sources, *La dépêche coloniale*), only to be caught by a flash flood in the desert and drown at the age of twenty-nine. Her work captured (and her journalism actively defended) a way of desert life intent on resisting the ravages of French colonialism. In her journeying, Eberhardt threw herself across the boundaries that divided the colonized from the colonist, while sending dissenting and colorful dispatches back to the French press. When Eberhardt wrote of why "the blind beggar was so dignified and serene" in the valley of Figuig or why the "Arabs slumber . . . stretched out in the shade of the ancient walls that crumble to dust," she found her explanations in "the harsh splendor of the landscape, the resignation of vague dreams, profound indifference to things of this life, and of death" (1994, p. 126). It was still a sort of travel writing that turned the Arab people into object lessons of an exotic otherworldliness. It probed the mystery of their lives in romantic and radical ways, itself a kind of cross-dressing, much like her outfit, moving across established borders if never quite escaping them. Yet she was the travel writer who stood both apart from and within the empire, catching the eye of Western readers in her enthusiasm and adventuring, if not always turning their heads to her cause. Those who reported on their lives and travels abroad brought a different order of display to the empire, full of ambivalences and nuances that would have rarely shown up in the expositions, museums, and encyclopedias.

The press began to champion travel writing late in the development of imperialism, at a time when it saw the prospect of reawakening the public's appetite for heroic exploration with the conquest of the two poles and the interior of Africa. My guide in this period is Beau Riffenburgh, who sets out to expose the myth of the explorer as imperialism's last great hero:

> By the late 19th century, explorers were being promoted through a number of powerful iconographies. They were widely desired and highly paid as public speakers. They, and the images of the new lands they discovered, were the subjects of painters, sculptors, and early photographers, as well as of artists for popular newspapers or journals, such as *The Illustrated London News* or *Frank Leslie's Illustrated Newspaper*. (1994, p. 2)

Riffenburgh describes the close relationship that developed between the press and explorers, which included sponsorship, the purchase of exclusive interviews, and the staging of dramatic rescues. "The volume and sensational style of press coverage," Riffenburgh surmises, "helped make the exploration of the Arctic, Antarctic, and Africa (as well as the explorers of those areas), significant cultural factors in the developing mass markets of journalism" (p. 3). Among the big stories of this era were the tragic Franklin expedition of 1845 (with the explorers' cannibalized bodies not found until 1854); Henry Morton Stanley's successful three-year search for the missing and inept explorer David Livingstone, which was sponsored by the *New York Herald;* and the race between Robert Peary and Frederick Cook to the North and South Poles in the early years of this century, which turned into a major fight between the *Herald* and the *New York Times*. As the American polar explorer Anthony Fiala explained the drive, "The Spirit of the Age will never be satisfied until the command given to Adam in the beginning—the command to subdue the earth—has been obeyed, and the ends of the earth have revealed their secrets" (cited by Riffenburgh, p. 34). At this point, however, the command was to foster a readership keen for the secrets and struggles of subduing the last reaches of the earth.

Although William Goetzmann (1986) has claimed that the "Second Great Age of Discovery" that occupied nineteenth-century America was largely a scientific enterprise, Riffenburgh treats it as sport as much as science. It was an international competition, both commercial and national, led by the American and British press, with each reaching for new levels of sensationalism in covering the lurid detail of failed explorations, some of which it was sponsoring. The press managed to build a new readership on a remarkable series of twisted tales. Not the least of them is the story of Henry Morton Stanley, who, in the pay of the *Manchester Guardian,* the *Daily Telegraph,* and other papers, rescued Ermin Pasha, the governor-general of Equatoria, who in 1887 had been trapped by the Hahdist uprising, only for Stanley himself to disappear into the Ituri Forest of the northern Congo. Two years later, correspondents from the *Herald* and the *World* found the irrepressible Stanley drinking champagne in the jungle, and they vied for an exclusive interview with the man. The *World* reporter finally obtained the interview for four thousand dollars, spending almost as much for cabling the fourteen-hundred-word story back to New York (Riffenburgh, 1994, p. 112).

The press used the travel adventure to join the educational parade that celebrated the spread of imperialism and its scientific achievement. Whether for the thrill of savage encounters or to find the frozen remains of failed polar expeditions, travel writing was about expanding the horizons of experience for its avid students. The self-improving nature of this education only added to the West's assertion of a well-traveled hegemony over the world.

Where does that leave us today? Although travel is no longer about empire, advertising campaigns for popular destinations can still bring home the legacy of that earlier sensibility, just as it can remind us of what the West still expects of the world, as this travel agency advertisement makes spectacularly clear:

> Where In The World Do You Want To Go? What In The World Do You Want To See? How In The World Can We Deliver Such Low Prices?
>
> The Wonders of The World. Travel Spectacular.

Yet even in the always idyllic world of travel ads, signs of a postcolonial awakening have begun to emerge, with the resulting uneasiness for tourists frankly addressed in this copy for the U.S. Virgin Islands ("They're your islands"):

> Come to an island where
> *the people actually*
> look forward to your visit.
>
> Imagine vactioning in a place where "tourist" isn't a bad word. Where English is the spoken language. By the warmest people in the Caribbean. People who want you to love their island the way they do. For their beautiful beaches and crystal clear bays. Superb snorkeling, diving, windsurfing and sailing. Delicious Caribbean fare. World class shopping. And exciting island histories . . .

Those exciting island histories have come down through colonial times to such invitations as this one to reenact the Columbiad with a credit card. What the welcomed gaze of the tourist costs the rest of the world, against what it pays, is captured by human-rights activist and Nobel Peace Prize winner Aung San Suu Kyi. In an interview that she gave after being released from years of house arrest, she turns to how preparations for tourism have affected her native Burma:

> A large part of the tourist infrastructure . . . has been built with forced labor. . . . Everyone knows how a lot of villagers around Pagan were forced to move because they wanted to make the place look clean and proper for the tourists. A whole lot of the settlers have been removed from the banks of the Irrawaddy to make the docks look very neat. You know, at the Shwedagon [Pagoda] they've started tearing down the stairways that are hundreds of years old. They are going to make it all very new. The roof above the staircase, bits of it were donated by people.

From a Buddhist point of view, it is very wrong to tear these things down because they are the good works of others. You don't tear down the good works of people just to impress tourists. (Cited by Dreifus, 1996, p. 34)

Looking back over this and the previous chapters, it should be apparent that the educational qualities of Western imperialism began with the amateur naturalist gathering specimens and artifacts while recording the lay of the land, and it culminated in the professional showmanship of the world's fair. The expressions of this will-to-display also took the form of learned societies and publishing projects in the colonies and metropolises. The themes of discovery, conquest, possession, and dominion are about ways of knowing the world, of bringing it to order, of surveying, mapping, and classifying it in an endless theorizing of identity and difference. Yet the curating of museums or the editing of encyclopedias is not, in itself, at issue here. Assembling or writing about a collection of meaningful objects is hardly dependent on empire. The West's passion for collecting and putting the world on display over the last few centuries has been part and parcel of a global design on the world. The presumption and appropriation with which it has collected the world reflects an attitude with which many have been educated. Over the last five centuries, the spectacles of empire were harnessed through what might be termed an exhibitionary pedagogy. The West came to see the world as a lesson in its own achievement. An educated public was formed around this natural history of the world. It was a nation-building and race-defining exercise through public instruction, the pedagogical thrust of which an article in *Blackwood's* summed up in 1852:

No better test can be applied to determine the degree of refinement, intelligence, and education of a people than the avidity displayed by them for places of instructive amusement, where not only are shows to be seen, but ideas acquired, and whence visitors retire, not only more happy than they entered, but more knowing. (Cited by Altick, 1978, p. 375)

Today, as a symptom of this postmodern age, progressive museums have begun to address their own history of representing the world.[17] The performance artwork, "Two Undiscovered Amerindians," by Coco Fusco and Guillermo Gómez-Peña is an example of this critical return to what has been made of the museum. But the continuing consequences of imperialism's will

---

[17] See Gerald McMaster and Lee-Ann Martin (1992) for the critique of museum practices that emerges out of the aboriginal mounting of an exhibition.

to knowledge, in its desire to make a spectacle of the world for the benefit of the West, is still not a matter of general education. We need to learn to read again the exhibition of the world, to see the display of the civilized and the primitive as the history of an idea attuned to the benefit of a few. We need to think about how people have been trained to view the gulf between West and East. How has a public been educated in the value of Western hegemony as an expression of civilization? In returning to what museums and exhibitions make of the world, there can be no easy sorting out of this accumulated educational effect, no ready measures of what is politically correct or what needs to be returned to those from whom it was taken. What is called for is a slow steady unpacking of, and thinking back through, the countless displays that we grew up with and that continue to educate. To the question of where museum objects really belong, anthropologist James Clifford responds vehemently "that they 'belong' nowhere, having been torn from their social contexts of production and reception, given value in systems of meaning whose primary function is to confirm the knowledge and taste of a possessive Western subjectivity" (1985, p. 244).

The exhibitionary formation of imperialism presented throughout this chapter sought to amaze, intrigue, titillate, and inform a public who were to see themselves, whatever their station in life, as the benefactors of empire by virtue of their race. This huge educational effort was bound to leave more than a few marks upon a variety of scholarly disciplines and school subjects in ways that I will deal with directly in the second half of this book. Following this and the preceding chapters' partial sampling of what was most educational about Western imperialism, I now turn to the actual schooling associated with imperialism's educational dynamic within the British Empire. Taken together, the three chapters of this section are intended to illustrate the close and complex association of learning and colonialism. In coming to understand how that association worked so effectively in the past, we should be able to identify the remaining traces of it in the ideas circulating around schools and universities today, and to find ways of finally moving beyond the lessons of that earlier era. The moving beyond, as I suggested in the first chapter, begins with giving an account of how the earnest intellectual work of imperialism has brought us to this point.

In the final years of the empires, when Frantz Fanon was nailing his scathing denouncements of colonialism to the gates of the Western metropolises, he identified the educational contradictions that needed to be rethought as a curriculum project for both former colony and colonial power: "The colonist bourgeoisie, in its narcissistic dialogue, expounded by the members of its universities, had in fact deeply implanted in the minds of the colonized intellectual that the essential qualities remain eternal in spite of all the blunders men may make: the essential qualities of the West, of course" (1965, p. 36). The universities and schools have come only very slowly to solving, or at least reducing, the polynomial equation that fixed the West to the eternal, making it, in effect, the Eternal Center of the Universe of Learning. We have to work with this knowledge of the world—for this knowledge is all that many of us have of the world—by understanding the cost at which it was achieved and the ends to which it was exhibited. The lion in the zoo is no less real or true for all that the forces of imperialism did to make such a spectacle a part of our lives, but when we stare into the lion's eyes, what is it we see that has not been touched in some way by the colonial adventure that we have, through myriad forms, learned so well? To catch sight of our education working on us in this way is to begin to change it, disabling some of the ready assumptions that form our idea of the world. If we cannot go back, perhaps we can go forward.

Photograph of Annette Ackroyd with her pupils in 1875.
By permission of the British Library, Oriental and India Collection.

FOUR

THE EDUCATIONAL MISSION

B y the close of the eighteenth century, after three centuries of imperial conquest, the German thinker Johann Gottfried von Herder thought it well to advise Europeans that "the barbarian rules by force; the cultivated conqueror teaches."[1] Although the barbarism continued, Herder's maxim might be taken as guiding a cultivated and instructive strain within the forces of imperialism through the nineteenth century and well into our own. The investment in colonial schooling signaled a move from imperial adventure to colonial consolidation, from the reign of European bandit kings, in Ashis Nandy's formulation, to the dominion of philosopher kings (1983, pp. x–xi). The construction of schoolhouses throughout the colonies brought the weight of imperialism's educational project home to generations of the young around the empire, but it also bore on the idea of education at home for the colonial powers. It is all of a piece, this turn to learning, organizing, exhibiting, and schooling that went on under imperialism's patronage, but the final step in this educational dynamic, the building of the colonial school, has symbolized the staying power of this legacy.

For educators, one encouraging theme of this aspect of imperialism's legacy is that although colonial education was dedicated to extending the regulation and usefulness of the colonized, it also—the human spirit being what it is—contributed to the empire's undoing. This danger was not lost on those who were ruthlessly exploiting the colonized peoples. Fanon speaks of "that bludgeon argument [against colonial schooling] of the plantation-owner in

---

[1] Herder (1909, p. 289) is cited and translated in Olender (1992, p. 42).

Africa: Our enemy is the teacher" (1967, p. 35). His own mixture of colonial and European schooling attests, through his passionate and effective anti-colonialist writings, to what could come of these educational efforts. Colonized students tend to learn more than the teacher seeks to teach. The master's tools, it may be fair to suggest, can take down the master's house.

The colonial school, like much else in the formal structure of Western imperialism, has been dismantled. Around the globe, nations are earnestly pursuing postcolonial forms of education aimed at recovering from the colonial era of schooling. The reviews coming in from those who suffered the years of an imperial education remain mixed, except on the weight of its impact. Nelson Mandela recalls his education in one of Natal's British schools with a measure of irony and diplomacy: "Britain was the home of everything that was best in the world. I have not discarded the influence which Britain and British history and culture exercised on us" (cited by James, 1994, p. 565). Edward Said, on the other hand, speaks of his British schooling in Egypt in terms of "the tremendous spiritual wound felt by many of us because of the sustained presence in our midst of domineering foreigners who taught us to respect distant norms and values more than our own. Our culture was felt to be of a lower grade, perhaps even congenitally inferior and something of which to be ashamed" (1991, pp. 8–9). What sort of residue on our thinking about education, I want now to ask, was left by this enormous exercise of building colonial schools across the Western empires? What impact did this colonial exercise have on the emergence of public education during the same period in the West? Mandela's sense of learning what was best and Said's of feeling induced shame are still very much at play in schools around the world today, from considerations of whether to school in the former colonial languages, to debates pitting the Western classics against the claims of multiculturalism.

This chapter cannot begin to do justice to the variety of schooling that occurred in the centuries-long global process of imperialism. Schooling took on almost as many forms as there were colonies, and its impact was felt both by colonial subjects and by colonial powers. Thus, I move from colonialism's first residential schools, established by the church in New France, to the curtailing of career opportunities at a postcolonial Oxford University. As with the adventure in learning and the exhibition of empire, colonial schooling presumed a right exercised over those to be educated, a right that is present in every educational act yet that represented a special level of presumption in the colonial context.

This presumption is more than adequately rendered in E. B. Sargant's "Educational Problems of the Empire," which is found in the sixth and concluding volume of *The Oxford Survey of the British Empire,* published on the eve of the First World War. In identifying the educational problems of the British Empire, Sargant does not dwell on inadequacies in students' ability to read and write, nor on weaknesses in their computational skills. Rather, in surveying "every part of our Empire," Sargant locates a far more profound educational disability. The children of the British Empire do not grow up thinking like Englishmen. The empire's schools are unable to achieve "the adaptation to other circumstances and other peoples of that habit of mind with regard to law that scarcely ever becomes a matter of formal instruction in our English schools, but is insensibly acquired by our youth at every stage of growth, no less at home or upon the playing fields than in the classroom" (1914, p. 233). The challenge was to instill in the native the very character "insensibly" acquired by civilized peoples at home and on the playground. The problem was to teach one group what others hadn't needed to be formally taught. This was intended, at best, to raise up a people in a studied, and thereby inadequate, approximation of their betters.

Sargant compares this challenge to the church's original educational mission on behalf of British maturity and masculinity: "In the main, those school ideals which were sedulously cultivated by the Church of England at a time when the English nation itself was growing to manhood are still working directly or indirectly to bring the British Empire to maturity" (1914, p. 244). Colonial schooling sought to instill a manly maturity in its students that, within the moral economy of empire, would repay the right of occupation: *We provide a civilizing education in exchange for your lands and selves; this education alone may be able to afford you a level of civilization (or maturity) that will warrant you taking charge in your own house.*[2] The exchange or gift value of education forms part of Bhikhu Parekh's critique of nineteenth-century British liberalism:

> In order to justify colonial rule, liberals needed to show that the British had something to give to the colonies which the latter badly *needed,* were unable to acquire *unaided,* and which was so *precious* as to compensate for whatever economic and political price they were required to pay. The logic of colonial justification required a perfect match between

---

[2] In light of the educational problem, Sargant proposed, to his credit, such corrective measures as dismissing the significance typically placed on "the characteristics and capacities of particular races" while providing more instruction in the native students' vernacular languages, especially when it came, oddly enough, to "dealing with English life," which was to remain an important focus of the colonial curriculum throughout the nineteenth century (1914, pp. 234, 240).

British gifts and colonial needs, between British strength and native deficiency. (1994, p. 11; Parekh's emphasis)[3]

Whether cultivated or barbaric, colonial schooling was part of the larger imperial process, even as it was seen as redressing imperialism's more avaricious moments. Yet claiming that education would raise the colonized along a historical scale toward a level of civilized maturity, as Sargant puts it, is simply to imply that the current society was in an infantile state. Western education stood as a universal standard from which people departed at their own and their children's peril, whether by teaching in an indigenous language rather than a European one, or by fostering traditional crafts that took time away from the demands of science and mathematics. At the very least, we all need to go forward knowing something of the history that first set this educational perspective in place, however strong the temptation to see it as part of the past.

Although colonial education is bound to appear harsh in a review such as this, it was also a meeting place of caring adults and eager children, a middle ground between cultures and a refuge from the ravages of colonialism. To approach it once more from the European perspective, the possibilities and limits of these connections are made vivid in Forster's *Passage to India*. Within the heart of colonial India, Forster sets up the schoolteacher Fielding as the one man capable of realizing the British hope of befriending and understanding the Indian, which forms part of an educational exchange in what is already a crumbling empire. Yet, in having achieved a basis for exchange, Fielding is treated by the other English characters in the book as being thoroughly removed from the colonial reality: "But you see, Fielding, as I've said to you once before, you're a schoolmaster, and consequently you come across these people at their best. That's what puts you wrong. They can be charming as boys" (1924, p. 166). The schools, at some level, were removed from the realities of empire, even as they were implicated in its larger intent and scheming. The flimsy schoolhouse was unable to redeem the empire. If educators did prove, on occasion, protectors of their charges, they offered a teacher's patronage that rarely amounted to an exchange among equals. The schoolhouse was far too often the site of abuse. And whatever ideas the schools instilled of the European nation-state, the young often sought to repay this instruc-

---

[3] This liberal sense of responsibility should be compared to the earlier theology of colonization practiced by Christian missionaries, as described by V. Y. Mudimbe and Kwame Anthony Appiah, "which drew largely on a conception of natural law according to which the most advanced have the obligation to promote their inferior brethren; and, in the name of thus promoting them, allowed itself to dispossess non-Christian countries in order to exploit the wealth meant by God for the use of mankind" (1993, p. 134 n. 5).

tion with articulate, defiant, and sometimes violent expressions of a home-grown nationalism. Fanon, Mandela, and Said, without unduly crediting their schooling for their achievements, represent something of the unforeseen redress afforded by colonial education. Education remains an unpredictable force, and although it is more a source of insight and hope in this book than of wariness, it is a source of wariness nonetheless.

The Missionary School

Colonial education began as missionary work. The instructive Franciscan monks were traveling with Spanish soldiers and sailors to the Caribbean before the turn of the sixteenth century, bringing their lessons of God's grace to the Amerindians in the bloodied wake of the Spanish conquistadors. Although it is easy enough to draw comparisons between conquest and conversion, there were those among the traveling priests who proved defenders of the conquered, especially after witnessing the rapacious excesses of the Spanish forces. The outspoken among these missionaries managed to convince Pope Paul III to issue the bull *Sublimis Deus* in 1537, which declared that the Amerindians were rational beings with souls, worthy of conversion as well as protection rather than the indiscriminate slaughter that was being brought down upon them by Christian soldiers. The best known of these critics of empire was the Dominican Bartolomé de Las Casas, who was the first priest to be ordained in the New World. In 1552, after decades devoted to protesting the abuses that the Amerindians were made to suffer at the hands of the Spanish, he published his *Devastation of the Indies,* which cataloged the horrors committed in the name of civilization: "Yet into this sheepfold, into this land of meek outcasts there came some Spaniards who immediately behaved like wild beasts, wolves, tigers, or lions that had been starved for many days" (1992, p. 29). In what was to become a common moral appeal, Las Casas reverses the sense of who the savage is, placing the priest-educator in a position to redeem both European and native. His arguments, in a contest over souls and bodies, would later contribute to the end of Spanish slavery among the Amerindians.[4]

From the time of the Spanish conquest to this day, missionaries have worked with local populations to build thatched, adobe, log, tin-roof, and

---

[4] It should be kept clearly in mind that everywhere there was an earnestness of intent and a contradiction of purpose. The treasurer of the London Missionary Society, during his sixteen-year term, continued to profit by the slavery of his West Indian plantation (C. G. MacKenzie, 1993, p. 60). Yet he advocated a Christian education for the enslaved at a time when most plantation owners were actively plotting against missionary efforts at educating their workers (B. Holmes, 1967, p. 11).

cinder-block schools that served in colonial times as both buffer and supporter for the larger project of imperialism. Christianity took advantage of
imperial conquest to achieve its own form of global expansion, and it sought,
in ways that could be generous and brutal in turn, to use education to make
Christians. Efforts were made by the East India Company and others to keep
missionaries out of specific colonies—sometimes to protect the local culture,
as in India, and sometimes out of a concern for what education could do for
native populations—yet the missionaries succeeded in gaining access to all of
the colonies and were often welcomed by the local people for their educational efforts (C. G. MacKenzie, 1993, p. 50).

Arguably the most "effective" educational instrument used by the church
on colonial populations was the residential school.[5] In 1635, Jesuit missionaries working in Quebec founded a *collège* for native boys that was intended to
grant the best of them the full benefits of European learning, and the idea
was soon extended to the education of native girls. In conscripting children to
attend the colonial residential school, the Jesuits led them to turn their backs
on learning the ways of their parents' lives (Bitterli, 1989, p. 102). The schools
opened before the pupils a one-way gate to another form of life that left them
suspended between worlds. Students could learn to appreciate, but could
never fully achieve, what the West held out to them. The Jesuits in Quebec,
following a model established by the Portuguese in the Congo, also used the
residential schools to train native missionaries who might return to their people and more effectively complete the Jesuit mission. There were, as well, ill-
fated attempts to have native students complete their education in what
proved to be the consumptive climate of France. Where such an attempt did
succeed, it made the student "quite different from what he was." As one priest
writes of a native student raised in France, "He has become quite obedient,
astonishingly enough." The priest took this as proof that "education alone
[was] lacking in Savages" (cited in Dickason, 1984, p. 219). Here again is that
constant theme of the natives lacking in an education that, once obtained,
would complete them as (pliant) human beings.

Residential mission schools were sponsored and run by the full range of
Christian churches. The result was an educational system that my colleague
Jo-anne Archibald, who has studied such schools in Canada, has described as

---

[5] The 1925 report by the Advisory Committee on Native Education in the British Tropical
African Dependencies did not hesitate in declaring, "The most effective means of training
character . . . is the residential school in which the personal example and influence of the
teachers and older pupils . . . can create a social life and tradition in which standards of
judgment are formed and right attitudes acquired almost unconsciously through imbibing
the spirit and atmosphere of the school" (1979, pp. 131–32).

an unremitting and near-lethal attempt at decimating First Nation identity and community: "Children for over seven decades experienced alienation from their families; varying degrees of emotional, physical and sexual abuse; and shame or denial regarding their cultural heritage" (1993, p. 106). So it was in the beginning of the colonial era, and it persisted down to the lifetimes of those among us who still struggle with this legacy. The basic sense of this educational form as a denial of a native child's life is captured in Shirley Sterling's powerful novel of growing up in an Indian residential school during the 1950s, a dislocating process that began with the first day of school: "After that Sister Maura asked me what my name was. I said my name was Seepeetza. Then she got really mad like I did something terrible. She said never to say that word again. She told me if I had a sister to go and ask what my name was" (1992, p. 18).

It was only in 1973, well over a century after Canada had found its own colonial status unacceptable, that the federal government recognized the possibility of Indian control of Indian education, having been pushed by the National Indian Brotherhood (Archibald, 1993, p. 106). As schooling was applied to colonized peoples, it was made to stand against family and community, against a culture that seemed to fly in the face of the ostensible rationality and enlightenment of the colonial power. Schooling, in this sense, was meant to wean the child from the learning and life associated with what was regarded as an expired era, an eclipsed form of life.[6]

However well-intentioned—and often enough it was not so well-intentioned—this schooling turned the concept of learning into the acquisition of what and who one was *not*. Having to learn a new name for oneself (to return to a theme from an earlier chpater) became something of a colonial universal for native populations. Describing education in Uganda, P. G. Okoth reports that the baptism made necessary for admission to missionary schools meant adoption of "Christian names such as Smith, Welensky[!], [and] Verwoerd" (1993, p. 140). The Nigerian writer Wole Soyinka, whose father was himself a teacher in a church school, tells of the baptism of a girl named Nubi, which took place routinely for all of the non-Christians who joined his household: "After that, we had to call her by her Christian name, Mary" (1981, p. 65). The displacement that accompanied being renamed under colonial education came with the recruitment—some would call it the kidnapping—of identity by the residential school. It was all part of a colonial relationship originally forged among family, community, school, and state that forms part of education's history.

---

[6] For a history of the residential schools in Canada, see Haig-Brown (1988).

It's true that more recently, missionary schools in Brazil and elsewhere have become the protectors of indigenous cultures, teaching the young the myths and ceremonies of earlier generations that might otherwise be lost.[7] As the church's role has changed in the state, so has its sense of responsibility. However, the original desire to take hold of and shape the mind of the new-found souls defined both religious and secular education among the dependencies and beyond. This mission to civilize, as a lifting up, gave an unwavering direction to education, turning the residential school into its own model colony, able to affect, not always with wholesome or beneficial results, the whole of the indigene's life. This desire to unconsciously instill standards and values in the young is not so far removed from what many hope for schooling today, which is why it is worthwhile to consider the original situation of colonial schooling and its legacy. At stake is the very idea of education.

Macaulay's Educational Vision

Thomas Babington Macaulay represents the unusual situation of one of the Victorian era's leading intellectuals taking a direct hand in shaping colonial policy on education. In an 1833 speech to the British Parliament, this distinguished historian reminded the august body that "the most sacred duties which as governors we owe the governed, and which, as a people blessed with far more than ordinary measure of political literacy and intellectual light, we owe to a race debased by three thousand years of despotism and priest-craft . . . [are] an equal measure of freedom and civilization" (1909b, p. 125). Macaulay was to take a most liberal view of the colony. He would recommend that Indians hold positions in the colonial government, as long as this was "effected by slow degrees" (p. 124). More than that, he envisioned an end, through the infusion of British values into Indian culture, to India's colonial dependence on Britain, offering instead an association that unintentionally echoed Napoleon's slur that the British were a nation of shopkeepers. "To trade with civilized men is infinitely more profitable than to govern savages," Macaulay argued, disparaging an economy that "would keep a hundred millions of men from being our customers in order that they might continue to be our slaves" (p. 125). He frankly and prophetically appealed to the market potential of India's hundred millions, while holding out the hope that "we

---

[7] Lévi-Strauss describes how, for the Bororo, the missionaries keep the traditional feather diadems under lock and key, for use only when required, as "they would be increasingly difficult to replace since the macaws, parrots and other brightly colored birds are disappearing (1995, p. 21).

may educate our subjects into a capacity for better government" (p. 126).[8] He was inspired by the belief in the longevity of a cultural imperialism destined to outlive any sort of political control: "An empire exempt from all natural causes of decay . . . that empire is the imperishable empire of our arts and our morals, our literature and our laws" (p. 126). Such imperishable goods were held to be best transported to the people through the graces of education.

Shortly after boldly speaking out against current conceptions of colonialism, Macaulay became a member of the Supreme Council of India and president of the General Committee of Public Instruction. It was during this post that he composed his oft-cited minute of 1835 on Indian education, which led to the "oriental-occidental controversy." The issue at hand was whether to suspend the British support for the teaching of Sanskrit and Arabic languages and literatures that had been instituted in the East India Company's Charter Act of 1813. The alternative proposal was to replace Sanskrit and Arabic with instruction in English. The challenged clause in the act was clearly the work of British orientalists, such as William Jones (as discussed in the previous chapter).[9] In the course of his minute, Macaulay was to make what is now perhaps the best-known statement of English prejudice and presumption from the colonial era. Based on the "valuation of the Orientalists themselves," Macaulay unequivocally declared, "a single shelf of a good European library was worth the whole of native literature of India and Arabia" (1971, p. 182). This is but one of a series of dismissals he offers in the minute as he denounces the "false history, false astronomy, [and] false medicine" that otherwise constituted Indian education (p. 188).

Macaulay saw English literature as part of an education that could only extend and secure the empire: "We must at present do our best to form a class who may be interpreters between us and the millions whom we govern—a class of persons Indian in blood and color, but English in tastes, in opinions, in morals and intellect" (1971, p. 190).[10] Here again is the chilling call to re-

---

[8] A century later, in 1928, the Empire Marketing Board issued posters proclaiming that India was "the world's biggest customer for British goods" (Constantine, 1986, pl. 23).

[9] The clause from the forty-third section of the Charter of 1813 of the East India Company states: "A sum of not less than one lakh of rupees in each year shall be set apart and applied to the revival and improvement of literature and the encouragement of the learned natives of India, and for the introduction and promotion of a knowledge of science among the inhabitants of the British territories in India" (cited by Vasantha, 1992, p. 50). Vasantha discusses the scientific controversy between orientalists and occidentalists and its impact on Indian science.

[10] On the home front, little more than a decade later, Macaulay was arguing before Parliament for the need to support public education, on the grounds that "the education of

form character and to create imperial subjects under the guise of education. Here, too, is the empire's promise to make the world over in its own image through education without diminishing the lines of racial difference.

Not often considered in these remarks is how Macaulay also bases his case for English on the Indian students themselves. First, he compares those Indian students who were all too happy to pay tuition to attend English classes, with those taking Sanskrit and Arabic only because, as he presents it, they received a stipend from the state. Second, he presents petitions from graduates of the sponsored programs in Sanskrit and Arabic complaining of the difficulty in getting work after this training. Finally, he sets out the disastrous efforts of the British to publish in Arabic and Sanskrit against the enormous English-language successes of the School Book Society. For Macaulay, educational expenditures were intended to meet both native deficiencies and native desires and, as such, did nothing to undermine the British raj. In either case, the Indians would see that "the superiority of the Europeans becomes absolutely immeasurable" in relation to the native culture (1971, p. 182). One needs to recall here that the real target of Macaulay's ire was the European orientalists who hoped to preserve the ancient strands of Indian civilization. It was a battle between colonial visions of India. Among the Indians who participated in it were Raja Ram Mohan Roy and his followers, who supported the call for instruction in English out of a desire to reform and modernize Indian society for Indians (Vasantha, 1992, p. 53; Panikkar, 1969, p. 150). As it turned out, Lord Bentinck, governor-general of India, acceded to Macaulay's minute, and state instruction in English language and literature was instituted in the education of the Indian elites, whereas what schooling existed for the lower classes was allowed to continue in their native language.[11]

Decades before English literature was thought worthy of being treated as a distinct discipline in the universities and better schools of Great Britain, it was field-tested in the training of natives and elites intended to serve as colonial administrators. A second feature of literature's colonial role appears with its prominent place on the employment examinations for the East India Company in London. In *Masks of Conquest*, Gauri Viswanathan explores how literary study was intended to convince the Indian people "that their destinies

---

the common people is a most effectual means of securing our persons and our property," for "the gross ignorance of the common people is a principal cause of danger to our persons and property" (1909a, pp. 351–52).

[11] Deepak Kumar offers the example of the Grant Medical College, which opened in Bombay in 1845 but refused to admit students from the lower castes on grounds that "we have come to rule and not to cause social upheaval," as the report of the Bombay Board of Education put it (1995, p. 114).

were guided by men of principle" (1989, p. 72). She describes how this educational process transformed English literature "into an instrument for ensuring industriousness, efficiency, trustworthiness, and compliance in native subjects" (p. 93). The introduction of Indian students to this literature creates an intriguing sense of letting them in on the secrets, vulnerabilities, and heartfelt yearnings of their otherwise distanced colonial administrators. In promoting the teaching of literature, there was not, it appears, a sense of giving the Indian students a competitive advantage, nor of revealing the weaknesses of their masters. Such was the pride of the English.[12]

The popularity of colonial schooling in India, Suresh Chandra Ghosh points out, fostered generations of disillusioned but well-educated Indians and far more than could possibly find suitable work in the colonial administration of the British raj (1993, p. 193). By 1918, Bengal, with roughly the same population as England, had the same number of students—twenty-six thousand—preparing for university degrees. Macaulay was right about the educational ambition of the people, if less so about the willingness of the English to step aside when the Indian people had proved themselves educationally worthy of self-governance (Headrick, 1988, pp. 315–16). This aim of colonial education was to transform natives into colonial intermediaries, turning schools into civil-service training institutions intended to support the administration of the empire.[13] The schools formed an integral part of the governing apparatus, creating a class of half-proud, half-ashamed bureaucrats to serve in that shadowy space between the colonizer and the native, schooled in tattered textbooks devoted to scenes and lessons from the unapproachable motherland, lessons that were thought to make obvious Britain's right to rule and

---

[12] The lasting hold of this literature, as it was thought to constitute the educated imagination, survives to this day in the Indian university with a shift of emphasis to literary theory, as Aijaz Ahmad explains: "So fundamental and even genetic is the Indian university's relation with—indeed, dependence upon—its British and American counterparts that knowledges produced there become immediately effective here, in a relation of imperial dominance, shaping even the way we think of ourselves. . . . Nowhere is the parasitic intellectual dependence of the Indian university upon its metropolitan counterparts so obvious as in the teaching of English" (1992, p. 44).

[13] Rahimaj Haji Ahmad pinpoints the structure and motives, as well as the consequences, that informed a similar colonial education system in Malaya: "The British colonial government set up schools mainly to ensure a steady supply of support staff for its administrative service. This later developed to become a system to provide elite education preparing lower administrative officers subservient to the colonial government, although ironically it became the training ground for the earliest statesmen who ultimately took over the rule of the country from the British" (1992, pp. 5–6). The vernacular schools in Malaya had the double function of preserving the culture and delimiting the aspirations of the students, for, as one official put it in 1915, "Teach them the dignity of manual labor . . . and I am sure that you will not have the trouble which has arisen in India over education"

the colonizer's duty to serve. A century later, from his vantage point in colonial Martinique, the poet and politician Aimé Césaire condemned colonialism's "parody of education" that resulted in "the hasty manufacture of . . . subordinate functionaries, 'boys,' artisans, office clerks, and interpreters necessary for the smooth operation of business" (1972, p. 21).

After Macaulay's minute, yet another tack taken with colonial education in the nineteenth century was initiated by J. P. Kay Shuttleworth, a legendary bureaucrat among Victorian educators. On turning his hand to this imperial arena, he gave practical and hard-nosed advice in the form of "Brief Practical Suggestions on the Mode of Organizing and Conducting Day-Schools . . . as Part of a System of Education for the Colored Races of the British Colonies," delivered to the Privy Council of the British Parliament in 1847. His proposal was "to combine intellectual and industrial education and to render the labor of the children available toward meeting some part of the expenses of their education" (1961, p. 192).[14] The declared aim was not only to instill Christianity in the students but also "to accustom the children of these races to habits of self-control and moral discipline," all through the English language, "as the most important agent of civilization for the colored population of the Colonies" (p. 194). This was also to be an education devoted to instructing the young in colonial policy: "The lesson-books of the Colonial schools should also teach the mutual interests of the mother-country and her dependencies; the rational basis of their connection and the domestic and social duties of the colored races" (p. 194). There could hardly be a more direct statement of education's contribution to the stability of imperialism's world order, a contribution that by this point was widely recognized by the colonial powers. The Act of Union of Great Britain and Ireland in 1800 provided for state-aided primary schools largely intended to staunch the local "hedge schools" given to churning up Irish nationalism. These state-aided schools used the *Irish National School Books,* from 1861, to extol the wonders of Britain and its empire, advising students that if they were to immigrate to "any of these

---

(cited by Watson, 1993, p. 160). At the same time, the students who attended the English schools were asked to take to heart the likes of Stamford Raffles, the great British colonizer of the region. As one textbook described Raffles's generous regard for the Malay peoples, "He welcomed them all from all parts to talk to him of their lives and their homes, and amongst them he made a good many friends" as part of his "dream" to become "the overlord of the whole Malay world" (p. 166).

[14] A second well-known advocate for technical education was John Stuart Mill, who in his East India Company *Dispatch on Education* of 1854 called for an education directed at "useful and practical knowledge suited to every station in life [for] the great mass of people who are utterly incapable of obtaining any education worthy of the name by their own unaided efforts" (cited by Headrick, 1988, p. 325).

settlements, you will find schools there quite as good as our own; and, in fact, the very same books are used in them that you are now reading . . . sent for by the colonial authorities" (Coolahan, 1993, p. 60). These books also answered the question "What makes the difference between any of us Europeans and these poor savages? Evidently it is education" (p. 59). A special place was written into the notorious Berlin Act of 1884, which divided Africa among European nations, for those who exercised the educational functions of imperialism: "All the powers exercising sovereign rights or influence in the aforesaid territories . . . shall . . . protect and favor all religious, scientific, or charitable institutions . . . which aim at instructing the natives and bringing home to them the blessings of civilization" (Winks, 1969, p. 109).

For all of the rhetoric surrounding this civilizing blessing, the results proved more than a little tawdry. Toward the end of the Victorian era, when Charles Dilke produced another of his considered surveys of Greater Britain, he was happy to note the many educational accomplishments of the settler colonies, such as Canada's free, compulsory, and often secular education with features that Dilke noted were clearly in advance of the mother country (1890, pp. 563–77). Yet when it came to the Crown colonies in Africa, the Caribbean, and India, Dilke offered a critical comparison with the United States, which "in spite of [its] strong and general opinion against admitting the negro race, [has] made far better provision for negro education in their Southern states than is the case with us in even the most advanced of our West Indies colonies" (p. 580). Colonial education among the dispossessed was at best an empire-serving process, trumpeted in its intentions and occasionally inspired in its delivery by dedicated teachers and missionaries, but as often sloughed off and halfheartedly bestowed on native populations. Education was a way of bundling together the hopes and fears of its sponsors and recipients, with the question An education for whom? never far from the surface.

Yet it needs to be made clear that among the colonized there were those who were prepared to hold the imperial forces to their educational promises. In Egypt under British rule, Ahmad Lufti al-Sayyid took Lord Cromer to task in the newspaper *al-Jarida* in 1907 for overseeing the "the abandonment of decent education" whereas this representative of Great Britain should, if he were taking his colonial responsibilities seriously, be "establishing the foundations of public education" (al-Sayyid, 1979). It turns out that Cromer, who had drastically reduced scholarships and increased tuition in Egypt, was being driven by fears that any surplus education above the immediate demands of the job market for technical skills would risk creating the sort of unemployed, well-educated agitators for nationalism found in India. Cromer had confided to his officials that his educational plans for the Egyptian people were to be "the three r's in the vernacular, nothing more" (cited by Headrick, 1988, p. 310).

The twin educational themes of paternalism and restricted opportunities were sustained well into this century. Macaulay's original concern for providing native populations with the full scope of an English education "in taste, in opinions, in morals and intellect" was to be overshadowed by far more pragmatic demands (1971, p. 190). The Advisory Committee on Native Education in the British Tropical African Dependencies reiterated in 1925 that "the Controlling Power is responsible as trustee for the moral advancement of the native population" (1979, p. 130). Not long after, Julian Huxley advised the paternal trustees of this and other colonial committees to relate their schooling "to the ideal you have for [the 'primitive' people's] future development . . . to blend what is good in their tradition with what is good in the tradition of Western Civilization" (cited by Russell, 1945, p. 199). What this trusteeship came to mean to the people of Africa was largely a minimization of the educational needs of the colonial economy and regime. The Ugandan historian P. G. Okoth has pointed out that colonial schooling in Africa was typically based on the assumption that it was introducing the very idea of education to the native population, and was largely designed "to instill a sense of deference towards all that was European and capitalist" (1993, p. 139).[15] Documents from the colonial period of this century express caution over exposing native populations to "the onrush of new ideas," in the words of one colonial advisory committee in 1935, which could lead to "unregulated individualism which is destructive of the best elements of communal life" (cited by Headrick, 1988, p. 306). The British at the time pressed for a more strictly technical education, in opposition to the popular support expressed among the African colonies for a more academic approach.

The one consistency within the African colonial education system was that inequities abounded. By 1945, for example, there was still no secondary education in Northern Rhodesia and more than half the children did not go to school at all (Russell, 1945, p. 170). Schooling was provided for boys in Africa far more often than for girls, and the local men who taught were better paid than the women. The young women who attended mission schools in South Africa were prepared for little more than domestic employment in colonial homes (Gaitskell, 1994). The official reports at the time took a line that is perhaps best expressed by the superintendent general of education for

---

[15] Okoth cites Walter Rodney's comment in *How Europe Underdeveloped Africa* that this was "education for subordination, exploitation, the creation of mental confusion, and the development of underdevelopment" (Rodney, 1981, p. 240).

the Cape of Good Hope, who stated in his report of 1941 that "the fear that we are over-educating the colored people has no foundation in fact" (cited by Russell, 1945, p. 172).[16] Colonial education developed into a pathetic realization of Macaulay's already demeaning educational principle of creating Englishmen in all but race. It did little for the good name of education, with many of these efforts at colonial schooling lending weight to Césaire's injunction that "first we must study how colonization works to *decivilize* the colonizer" (1972, p. 13).

Women and Colonial Education

Having delved into the moral bankruptcy of colonial education, I am conscious, in the face of such easy judgments, that circumstances are always more complicated than they may seem. The participation in colonial education by a certain class of women in Europe who were able to find a new life abroad by teaching in the colonies is a good example of such a complication. Here was opportunity to be more than a mother of empire, more than an accompaniment to those who administered the colonies. "It is the Mecca of teachers," one woman wrote of Canada, "or should be. . . . Any girl with a mother . . . may, everyone here says, safely bring her out, as schools are in such abundance" (cited by Trollope, 1983, p. 73). Women with educational interests did more than teach after they arrived in the colonies, however; some set up their own schools, whereas others took a more political role, such as Mary Carpenter, who during her journey through India lobbied British officials for the establishment of normal schools to train secular female teachers for Indian girls, even as she envisioned the schools being run by Englishwomen serving as principals (Ramusack, 1992, p. 121). The most famous instance of the enterprising educator comes from Southeast Asia with Anna Leonowens (1991), who was running a school in India before she entered the employ of King Mongkut of Siam, where she took on the instruction of not only the prince but also the court concubines. If not exactly in the fashion portrayed in Rodgers and Hammerstein's *The King and I,* she used this educational process to introduce a European sensibility to a country that had otherwise resisted colonization. Whatever support she lent to imperialism's educational mission, Leonowens took advantage of her position to oppose the slavery of the harem.

---

[16] Although A. G. Russell has little trouble seeing the irony in the superintendent's remark, he himself is comfortable citing an Oxford University Press publication to the effect that "in the African negro, thinking is 'emotional' and, as such, of shorter duration," before concluding that "few indeed are the Africans who, like Newton, have 'voyaged on the strange seas of thought, *alone*'" (1945, p. 162; Russell's emphasis).

Within the moral space of the schoolhouse, women were able to confound the roles of submission and domination.[17]

The Indian organization Brahmo Somaj proved a source of inspiration for British women who were drawn to teaching abroad. During the closing decades of the nineteenth century, it developed a program of social and political reform in India, supported by eloquent representatives who sailed to England in search of British teaching recruits to assist in rebuilding Indian society for Indians. A special appeal was made to women "capable of doing good to their Indian sisters," as Keshub Chunder Sen put it in his well-received traveling lecture "England's Duties to India" (cited by Ware, 1992, p. 121). Annette Ackroyd, one of those moved by the call of Brahmo Somaj, on arriving in India set up a small school for a dozen or so young women in an effort to blend feminist concerns with an equally determined effort to redress colonialism's racial injustices (Ware, 1992, pp. 149–64). Although Ackroyd's school remained open for only a few years during the 1870s, it set a precedent for far more extensive efforts, such as those of Margaret Noble who a few decades later worked with young Indian women while assuming the life of an orthodox Hindu, becoming Sister Nivedita in a reversal of the naming process discussed earlier (Ramusack, 1992, pp. 124–25). In trying to fathom the sort of dedication and transgression exhibited by Sister Nivedita, Aishis Nandy suggests that she and others like her "found in Indian versions of religiosity, knowledge and social intervention not merely a model of dissent against their own society, but also some protection for their search for new models of transcendence, a greater tolerance of androgyny, and a richer meaning as well as legitimacy for women's participation in social and political life" (1983, p. 36). Yet Sister Nivedita was not inclined to abandon, even if that were possible, the world that she had brought with her to India; her philosophy of education was, in her own words, to "root [students] in their own past" and then furnish them with such measures of modernity as "scientific standards, geographical conception, [and] historical prepossession" (cited by Ramusack, 1992, p. 125).

These colonial forms of schooling offered women the chance to intervene with some compassion on behalf of the young in the otherwise manly business of bringing the colonies into line. Although teaching brought home the claim of the empire on these children's land and minds, it also left the teachers the wiser for the schooling they came to India to provide. After

---

[17] See also Paxton (1992) for a description of Annie Besant, who in 1904 established the Central Hindu Girl's School and worked to reform the treatment of women in Indian society. Hansen (1992) describes women's educational missionary work in Northern Rhodesia.

teaching for only a short period, they were in a far better position to under-stand the vile prejudices that infused the governing of the colonies, prejudices that remained largely invisible in Great Britain. These women also discov-ered, as they moved between continents, how even these modest attempts at schooling challenged inequities of gender in both India and Great Britain. On the home front at this time, the feminist efforts at undermining the em-pire of patriarchy were under way in the hands of writers such as Charlotte Yonge. Her 1890 history textbook, *Westminster Readers,* made the psychology of colonialism available to a wide range of readers. It was not celebratory or triumphant in tone, and it did not deploy the collective sense of accomplish-ment by using the collective and plural first person: "The British did not take pains, as a rule, to show friendly courtesy to the grave and dignified Hindoos, often of high rank . . . and though the native might cringe and obey, he laid up hatred in his heart" (cited by Castle, 1993, p. 34).

Among Indian students, especially young women, such educational ef-forts were regarded locally as both boon and burden, according to Jasodhara Bagchi's research on growing up in colonial Bengal. Bagchi points out that In-dian reformers of the nineteenth century, such as Ishwarchandra Vidyasagar, used the educational principles of "western bourgeois liberal ideology" to argue against the marriage of upper-caste Hindu girls at a very early age (1994, p. 24). Although these efforts were often met by Indian nationalist cries de-nouncing the schooling of women as giving in to the West, many women suc-ceeded in pursuing the Western-influenced education open to men. These women went on, Bagchi notes, to contribute to Indian journals, including a few they edited, debating their right to education within the struggle for na-tionhood (p. 27). Fortunately, colonial forms of education were not fully de-termined in their application or outcomes.

To move to another instance and another continent, during the most in-tense period of the British occupation of Egypt, from 1882 to 1920, the first Egyptian women were licensed as schoolteachers (Hatem, 1992). These women went on to assert their right to public participation in a number of re-lated fields. Malak Nasif, for example, qualified as an elementary school-teacher before taking up a career in journalism, writing on women's issues for the newspaper *Al-Jarida,* where she complained of colonial educational poli-cies that led to the British teaching Arabic grammar to Egyptian students, as if they did not know their own mother tongue (p. 38). Other women used their newly acquired public position as teachers to attack imperialism's claim to be a protector of Muslim women's rights (a charge that has a contemporary ring to it, given the Western press's continuing attack on the treatment of women in the Islamic world). They pointed out how Islamic law was, and could increasingly be, responsive to such concerns as women increasingly participated in education and public life. The colonial education provided to Egyptian women, which was largely devoted to Bible reading and needlework, had not been intended to foster such public participation among its students (Sislian, 1967).

Through the limited educational channels afforded by colonial rule, Margaret Noble's work as Sister Nivedita and the journalism of Malak Nasif managed to disturb colonialism's determination of people's education and lives. These women took charge of what was intended to keep them, as it kept the colonized, on the margins of a governing process and on the receiving end of an educational process.[18] They were part of a movement among women that saw education as a primary concern in redressing the flagrant imbalances of power that were based on a cultivated misconception of women. When Mary Wollstonecraft had called for the reform of women and education, she mockingly apologized for addressing her own sex as rational creatures instead of "viewing them as if they were in a perpetual childhood, unable to stand alone" (1975, p. 81). In much the same spirit as these colonial educators, Wollstonecraft had called for an end "to a false system of education" that she felt only weakened its students, who then became "the objects of pity, and . . . will soon become objects of contempt" (pp. 79, 82). Education among the dispossessed affords another lesson in the school's contribution to the learning of difference and identity. Schooling for women and the colonized made it possible for some to challenge the self that they were intended to learn to be. The Western women who took up teaching in the colonies were participating in the making of the empire without necessarily accepting the pre-set lessons in how certain classes of people could never fully belong to the order of the arts and sciences they were asked to study.

---

[18] "In other words," Chantal Talpade Mohanty writes of the connections among gender, colonialism, and humanism, "it is only insofar as 'Woman/Women' and 'the East' are defined as Others, or as peripheral, that (Western) Man/Humanism can represent him/itself as the center. It is not the center that determines the periphery, but the periphery that, in its boundedness, determines the center" (1991, p. 73). Mohanty warns that "third world women" continue to be colonized by feminism, as an "effect of Western scholarship" that takes a monolithic approach to questions of human rights (p. 53). In concluding her much reprinted essay "Under Western Eyes," from 1984, Mohanty sets out the colonial relationship between scholarship and gender: "In the context of hegemony of the Western scholarly establishment in the production and dissemination of texts, and in the context of the legitimating imperative of humanistic and scientific discourse, the definition of 'the third world woman' as a monolith might well tie into the larger economic and ideological praxis of 'disinterested' scientific inquiry and pluralism which are the surface manifestations of a latent economic and cultural colonization of the 'non-Western' world. It is time to move beyond the Marx who found it possible to say: They cannot represent themselves; they must be represented" (p. 74).

The Lingering Colonial Force of Western Schooling

An obvious danger I face in laying out the educational legacy of imperialism is in overrunning the historical specifics of imperialism and treating education itself as inevitably and incurably a form of cultural imperialism. Certainly, education can always be cast as an act of power, however benevolent in its exercise, between teacher and student. Yet something has to be said for the intent and circumstance that shaped the particular forms of education that arose during five centuries of imperialism. Whereas I have been attempting to demonstrate the influence that the historical project of Western imperialism has had on our ideas about education, Martin Carnoy is one who argues, in *Education as Cultural Imperialism* (1972), that Western education, even after the end of the empires, should still be thought of as a broadly imperial project by design. Without paying much mind to historical causes, he identifies education's ongoing colonizing function as "transmitting the social and economic structure from generation to generation through pupil selection, defining culture and rules, and teaching certain cognitive skills," and this function applies wherever students are schooled in the Western tradition (p. 13). This "colonizing aspect of schooling" has not been restricted, Carnoy is careful to point out in this Marxist critique, to the overseas market:

> Western schools were used to develop indigenous elites which served as intermediaries between metropolis merchants and plantation labor; they were used to incorporate indigenous peoples into the production of goods necessary for the metropolis markets; they were used to help social structures to fit in with European concepts of work and interpersonal relations; and, within advanced capitalist economies such as the United States, schools were used to fit white workers and, later, disenfranchised minorities into economic and social roles defined by the dominant capitalist class. (p. 15)

Carnoy goes on to identify how Western schooling now forms part of a postcolonial heritage, with locally inspired changes in the colonial curriculum and language coming only very slowly and amid much debate. As he found it in the early 1970s, so it stands today; the legacy remains, for example, with the Lesotho high school students who send hard-earned money to Great Britain to pay for the privilege of taking the examinations run by the Cambridge Examination Syndicate, examinations that, in turn, largely organize the curriculum. It reemerges with the current American move to make English the nation's official language as part of an assault on bilingual education programs intended to give recently arrived students greater opportunities. The center is made to hold. In Carnoy's terms, whether the power is vested in examinations or an official language, "knowledge itself is 'colonized': colonized knowledge perpetuates the hierarchical structure of society" (1972, p. 3). For one who claims that social justice can be achieved only through the educational challenge of decolonizing knowledge, Carnoy proves decidedly uninterested in the detailed work of identifying the colonizing aspects of various educational domains, thus leaving it to me to work out in the second half of this book.

In a preview of the curriculum analysis that I undertake in part 2, let me briefly introduce how this might be thought to work with the teaching of mathematics, the discipline seemingly at the furthest remove from politics. Allan Bishop argues that mathematics is "one of the most powerful weapons in the imposition of Western culture" and was carried to the colonies through the three-pronged attack of trade, administration, and education, all involving considerable number work (1990, pp. 51–53). Not only was a standard for all manner of calculation established as centered in the West, but it was also used to establish a global measure that stands to this day, by which both the individual student and the nation can reckon the level of their educational development. The Chinese and Korean students who excel in international mathematical assessments will not find the mathematical contributions of Asian cultures referred to in these tests, nor any mention of the historical aspects of the Western standard.[19] The international standards in mathematics education form another chapter in an intellectual mercantilism through which Europe reprocessed ideas from abroad, including in this case algebraic and other computational techniques using Indian numerals, the Indo-Chinese zero, and the Chinese decimal place value (Needham, 1964, p. 237). In analyzing mathematics' often overlooked multicultural roots, George Ghevarghese Joseph concludes that "it is not generally recognized that practically all topics taught in school mathematics today are directly derived from the work of mathematicians originating outside of western Europe before the twelfth century AD" (1991, p. 50).[20] Mathematics now stands as the quintessential mode of Western rationality, but it, too, possesses a history entwined

---

[19] Frederick Leung, from the University of Hong Kong, explained to me how China's success in recent international mathematics assessments among high school students not only redressed the assumed balance in capabilities between East and West, but also demonstrated the continuing influence of Confucian principles, which could become, he thinks, the next phase of a Chinese contribution to the study of mathematics.

[20] Joseph provides a thorough review of "the indigenous scientific and technological base," which may have been "innovative and self-sufficient" during precolonial times, as well as the European distortion of mathematical history (1990, p. 2). Ubiritan D'Ambrosio (1991) also presents a strong case for ethnomathematics as the proper pedagogy for a less Eurocentric mathematics curriculum.

in the expansion of European interests. In considering how, then, to approach the teaching of mathematics, Joseph recommends a multicultural mathematics sensitive to both practical employment and educational enrichment issues, which will provide "opportunities for all pupils to recognize that all cultures engage in mathematical activity and no single culture has a monopoly on mathematical achievement" (1993, p. 19).

In attempting to find a way beyond colonized forms of knowledge, one has to be careful not to imagine that they invariably colonize the learner. Students can and do turn to their own advantage what they are taught. We need to recognize that for all the cultural domination that Western education came to represent, it proved a useful resource for resisting that very domination. The Indian historian Sardar Panikkar offers an excellent example from social studies when he describes how Indian students were taught during the British raj to appreciate the great moments in Western history, as if these events might fill a void in the nonhistorical East (a theme I will address presently). However, students' detailed study of the storming of the Bastille ensured that the rhetoric of colonial reform directed against European tyranny would be vividly illustrated by such instances as the French Revolution (1969, pp. 149–50). Panikkar notes how, in just this way, native scholars schooled in the West often formed a colonial intelligentsia dedicated to independence and self-determination:

> In every one of the countries of Asia, the leadership of the movement which ultimately displaced European supremacy belonged to those who had been trained under the West in the aegis of imperialism. Not only Mahatma Gandhi and Jawaharlal Nehru, but the founders of the Indian National Congress and the successive generations of Congress leaders were trained in the West. In Japan, it was the group of explorers sent to the West by the Shogunate that led the movement for the reorganization of the State. In China, though the disposition of the Manchus was not the work of the Western-educated people, the building up of the revolutionary movement that followed was led by men of Western training. In Indonesia, Indo-China, Burma and Ceylon, it is the men and women educated in the West . . . that provided the leadership. (p. 153)

Coda: Rousseau

I want to conclude this three-chapter review of imperialism's educational influence on the world with Jean-Jacques Rousseau's *Émile,* because, as central an educational text as it is, it speaks to a reverse in the flow of educational ideas I have represented here. Rousseau claims, more than once, that his ideas are drawn from native thinking, even as the book offers a variation on the theme of an intellectual mercantilism that transformed the New World into Europe's New Idea of the World. Rousseau finds in the native not an affirmation of the civilized superiority of France but the greater truth of nature, a truth that, like the discovery of coffee, was held to quicken the blood of a waning civilization. He does not simply invert the ideas of who the savage is and who the civilized being, as do Las Casas and Montaigne. Rousseau insists on using the life of the savage to generate both a critique and a system of education. In this way, he would arrest the great decline that the West was suffering: "Everything is good as it leaves the hands of the Author of things," *Émile* opens. "Everything degenerates in the hands of man" (1979, p. 37). Civilization bears too much of the handiwork of "man." What has it meant for Western thinking about education to learn from the very way of life that imperialism was destroying in earnest or indifference?

Émile reveals the great debt owed to this philosopher for what are now the standard tenets of progressive education. Here is the argument for treating the child as a child (or at least for treating the wealthy boy child as a child). Here is the case for centering education on the childlike child rather than on the interests of the teacher, for attending to the child's development, and for cultivating the child's individuality apart from the conforming spirit of society. Learning is a matter of doing for Rousseau, and having the child actually do things in the world is necessary to prepare him for the proper exercise of reason and liberty in later life. Rousseau credits these radical and influential lessons to what he has learned of the aboriginal peoples (largely from Buffon and Le Beau). He more generally calls on the constantly ironic example of the "savage" to contrast with the barbaric damage inflicted by society on children in the name of civilization.[21] The savage is nature in the shape of a man, an object lesson in the natural order.

Rousseau uses these ideas to lay low the old order of learning: "It is entirely evident that the learned companies of Europe are only public schools of lies . . . and there are very certainly more errors in the Academy of Sciences than in a whole nation of Hurons" (1979, p. 204). In rejecting the aspiring

---

[21] For Rousseau's use of New World accounts of native life in his writing, especially the *Discourse on Inequality*, see Brandon (1986, pp. 108–11). The "intellectual great-grandfather of the concept of the Noble Savage," according to Anthony Grafton, is the Roman historian Tacitus, whose *Germani* contains "a comparison of the virtues of the allegedly savage people with the corruption of Rome" (1992, p. 43). On this theme in Rousseau, Derrida writes of how "non-European peoples were . . . studied as the index to a hidden good Nature, as a native soil recovered, of a 'zero degree' with reference to which one could outline the structure, the growth, and above all the degradation of our society and our culture" (1974, pp. 114–15).

vanity of learning, Rousseau's modest educational objective is to supplement what the Hurons have achieved by nature: "My pupil is that savage, with the difference that Émile, having reflected more, compared ideas more, seen our errors from closer up, is more on guard against himself and judges only what he knows" (pp. 243–44). But is the "savage" only a projection of Rousseau's imagination? In the founding of a new school on a native sensibility, what sort of unwritten social contract is implied between old and new worlds? What manner of debt did progressive forms of education accrue during the age of empire?

Native scholar George Sioui (1992) is convinced that not only Rousseau but also Diderot and others drew from the accounts of Native American life, especially as they dealt with the spirit of cooperation and consensus found therein. Sioui credits Lom d'Arce de Lahontan as "the discoverer of Americity" on the basis of his *Dialogues avec un sauvage* and *Mémoires de l'Amérique*. "We are born free and united brothers," the Wendat chief of the Turtle Clan, Adario, explains in the *Dialogues,* "each as great a master as the other, whereas you are all slaves of one man" (cited by Sioui, p. 71). Although there is no easy tracking of ideas and origins within this complex encounter and exchange, it seems fair to say that at some level Émile stands as a student of Adario.[22] At the very least, Europe was finding a new language of liberty by using the situation of the Amerindians, even as Europeans initiated the slave trade across the Middle Passage. But then, too, I find the philosopher Ernst Cassirer casting Émile, and what he names "the pupil's business," within the metaphorical reach of the imperium: "He understands the world only inasmuch as he acquires and conquers it step by step" (1989, p. 119).

As modern thinking about education often gives itself up to imperial metaphors, so imperialism was literally a quest for global forms of knowledge. This remains part of imperialism's imaginative value; it is at once the metaphorical and the literal extension and renewal of the Western sensibility. Rousseau lived in a Europe awash in literary, artistic, and philosophical images of new worlds where natural forms of liberty seemed to prevail in contrast to the civilized tyrannies and oppression at home. In thinking about the

---

[22] Jack Weatherford writes, "The original play *Arlequin sauvage* [based on Lahontan's work] had a major impact on a young man named Jean Jacques Rousseau, who set about in 1742 to write an operetta on the discovery of the New World featuring Christopher Columbus's arrival with a sword while singing to the Indians the refrain 'Lose your liberty'" (1988, p. 124). In criticizing native life, Rousseau holds up the Caribs as swaddling their children in an even more preposterous manner than the French, noting sarcastically that "the Caribs are twice as lucky as we are" (1979, p. 43), and he refers, at another point, to a savage laziness (p. 202).

educational legacy of imperialism, it is worth considering the many paths that came of this engagement, from the church's residential schools for natives to the Rousseau-inspired free schools, such as Summerhill, for native Britons.

It would indeed be surprising, after five centuries of this educational imperative, if schooling did *not* carry forward traces of imperialism in former colonies and colonial powers alike. As I have noted, it would be amazing if, after a single generation or two since imperialism ended, such a legacy could be left behind. I have tried to establish, up to this point, how we have to appreciate the full extent of imperialism's educational dimensions and dynamics. From the age of reconnaissance to the collapse of the colonial empires, the West engaged in an enormous educational project of learning and teaching the world. It was surely a formative and formidable experience, giving body and order, discipline and rhetoric to the institution of education that we now live within. We have still to wonder, then, whether educators are asking the young to look at the world through Columbus's eyes, to treat it as a "marvelous possession" in that colonizing sense, as Stephen Greenblatt characterizes the European regard for the New World (1991). Are they learning to see the native as on display? Are they coming to an understanding of identity and difference as the natural divide of humankind, or as resulting from particular histories?

Having completed this general history of imperialism's educational project of classifying, displaying, and teaching the world and its divisions, I now turn to how this imperial past has worked through and continues to operate in the teaching of history, geography, science, language, and literature. There are aspects of the current curriculum that seem to carry forward that imperial history, which was largely determined to learn about the *other*—the one who is so markedly not the one engaged in the study—through subordination and surveillance, conversion and training. We are still in the midst of resolving this extended colonial legacy on a global scale, which means, in part, engaging with the related growth (and belated recognition) of diversity in the classrooms of the West. This diversity manages to confound the traditional self/other distinctions that infused imperialism's curriculum project, with its easy equation of race with nation and colony. It calls into question how well students have been served by the subjectivities celebrated by the assigned literary classics, the history and geography of Western civilization's relentless advance, and the scientific pursuit of the knowing division and conquest of nature. There is, in turning to the legacy of these sometimes monstrous lessons, the potential for a critical and deliberately postcolonial supplement that may hasten the attenuation of, if it does not check, what imperialism made of the world.

PART II

MONSTROUS LESSONS

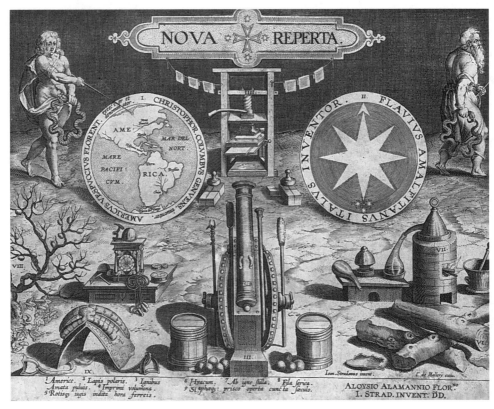

Theodor Galle's Nova Reperta *(Antwerp, ca. 1600).*
Courtesy Print Collection, Miriam and Ira D. Wallach Division
of Art, Prints, and Photographs, New York Public Library,
Astor, Lenox, and Tilden Foundations.

FIVE

HISTORY AND THE RISE
OF THE WEST

I first set up this chapter to read like a response to an imaginary school exercise on great theories of history, only to stumble upon—as life tends to
imitate school—just such an assignment in British Columbia's *History
[Grade] 12 Resources Manual.* The student activity sheet "Theories of History" lists sixteen men, from Thucydides to Nietzsche, for whom students are
to asked to find out, "for each historian they have been assigned . . . the dates
he lived, his major work or works in history, and his theory of history"
(British Columbia Ministry of Education, 1990, p. 79). My choice from the
list is the German philosopher Georg Wilhelm Friedrich Hegel, whose dates
are 1770–1831 and whose major historical work is *The Philosophy of History,*
which has the rise of the West as its theme. In what follows, I track his theory
of history across the centuries and continents, from the daylight lecture theater in the Berlin of the 1820s, to the fluorescent spectrum of contemporary
classrooms in the United States, Canada, and Britain.[1]

Certainly, one could build a fine library of books on the rise of the West,
dating back to the histories of Herodotus. Hegel is but a vivid instance from
the early nineteenth century that, like the radioactive isotopes used in medicine, can be used to trace the descent and digestion of, in this case, an idea
about history. He not only made modernity the project of the West, he also
made the West the sole and final possessor of history. I would point out that

---

[1] The answer guide included in the *Resources Manual* identifies Hegel's theory of history
thus: "History is determined by people's ideas about things" (British Columbia Ministry
of Education, 1990, p. 82).

whether the West rose is not in question here. It certainly did, and it did so within an intellectual tradition, it has been pointed out to me, that affords critiques such as this one.[2] What fascinates me is the degree to which Hegel's suppositions about history and the West's hold on history have become part of what we regard as a commonsense historical understanding. For example, on hearing today of China's efforts to "modernize," we imagine a people finally about to enter the flow of modern history by Westernizing its economy and education system, if not its political system. Equally so, the celebrated "end of history" debate, sparked by Frances Fukuyama in 1989, began with the premise that communism had collapsed with the demise of the Soviet Union, again seeming to place China beyond the web of history.[3] Hegel had no qualms about placing China outside history, as we shall see, and outside history it has largely remained for Western eyes, even at the very end, it would appear, of history.

Hegel's *Philosophy of History,* although lacking the philosophical stature of his *Phenomenology of Spirit* and *Philosophy of Right,* proved to be his most popular work during the nineteenth century and into the twentieth. Hegel's *Philosophy of History* was transcribed from lectures he delivered on the history of the world in Berlin during the 1820s. What makes this a philosophical approach to history, Hegel begins in an introduction he is thought to have added to the book, is its concern with the underlying Reason of the World. "Reason is the Sovereign of the World" is how Hegel puts it, using the emphatic and Germanic capitalization of J. Sibree's popular 1899 translation (1956, p. 9). This Reason, as Sovereign of the World, governs History. We are not, according to Hegel, moving through time without rhyme or reason. We are progressing through History guided by Reason in the form of a Spirit or self-contained essence that defines any given age. Historical progress is there-

---

[2] When historians such as Eric L. Jones (1981) and Paul Kennedy (1987) speak of the rise as the "European Miracle," I have to wonder whether this is meant to emphasize the unlikeliness of the rise without something approaching divine intervention, or to evoke the sense of gratitude and grace that is to be associated with such intervention. In *The Rise and Fall of the Great Powers,* Paul Kennedy places "the long-range and armed sailing ship" at the center of that miracle, giving the West the ability "to control the oceanic trade routes and to overawe all societies vulnerable to the workings of sea power" (p. 26). For a critique of the "miracle" as resulting, "essentially, from historical forces generated within Europe itself," see J. M. Blaut (1993, p. 59ff.). For a review of historical theories of imperialism, see Wolfe (1997).

[3] On the end-of-history debate, see the Melzer, Weinberger, and Zinman collection *History and the Idea of Progress,* which includes a chapter by Fukuyama that refers to how "Communism collapsed of its internal contradictions by the end of the 1980s . . . [with the result that] there were no competitive ideologies that could threaten liberalism on its own home turf" (1995, p. 15).

fore inevitable, and Hegel defines the measure of that progress as an increasing and self-conscious realization of Human Freedom: "The History of the
world is none other than the progress of the consciousness of Freedom; a
progress whose development according to the necessity of its nature, it is our
business to investigate" (p. 19). For Hegel, however, participation in History
on the road to Freedom is not open to everyone.

The deciding factor, according to Hegel, is a people's knowledge of the
Spirit of Freedom. For example, "The Orientals have not attained the knowledge of that Spirit—Man *as such*—is free; and because they do not know this,
they are not free" (1956, p. 18; Hegel's emphasis). I take his use of the present
tense with the Orient to suggest a lack of a past or a future, which comes of
its failure to know the World-Spirit and its Freedom. China and India are assessed as "*entirely* wanting in the essential consciousness of the Idea of Freedom" (p. 71, Hegel's emphasis). They are mired in a state of perpetual despotism, which is played against the West's historical achievement of liberty, and
thus deserve to be excluded from the progress of World History: "China and
India lie, as it were, still outside the World's History" (p. 116).[4] The Greeks
and Romans are portrayed as passing the torch of an awakened Freedom on
to the Germanic world, which through the additional vision of Christianity
realized the Spirit of Freedom as progress and History (p. 19). "The History
of the World travels," Hegel declares, "from East to West, for Europe is absolutely the end of History" (p. 103).[5]

Building his own great wall against the barbarians, Hegel created semi-
permeable time zones that fell between those in the civilized and historical
West and those who are said to exist outside History. Given his keen anthro-

---

[4] Romila Thapar has attacked the common view of oriental despotism by pointing out
how it overlooks the crucial historical role played in Indian history by "the renouncer," as
he names the ascetic figure who returned to society in the spirit of a freedom that effectively tugged at the moral and political authority of the state, and thus played a strategic
role in society's governance. Thapar further attacks the ideas associated with India's timeless despotism by pointing to both the urbanity and history found in the territorial texts
known as *janapada* (1992, pp. 17–20). Immanuel Wallerstein argues that India is an invention of what he describes as the modern world system, specifically the British colonization through which India's premodern history "is an invention of modern India" (1991,
p. 132).
[5] Hegel: "The consciousness of Freedom first arose among the Greeks, and therefore they
were free; but they, and the Romans likewise, know only that *some* are free—not man as
such. Even Plato and Aristotle did not know this. The Greeks, therefore, had slaves; and
their whole life and the maintenance of their splendid liberty was implicated with the institution of slavery. . . . The German nations, under the influence of Christianity, were the
first to attain the consciousness that man, as such, is free: that it is the freedom of Spirit
which constitutes its essence" (1956, p. 18; Hegel's emphasis).

pological interests, he allows that India is "rich in intellectual products, and those of the profoundest order of thought," but it "has no History; and in this respect contrasts most strongly with China—an empire possessing one so remarkable, one going back to the most ancient times" (1956, p. 61). History goes backward for the Chinese—as "no people has a so strictly continuous series of Writers of History"—but fails to go forward: "Early do we see China advancing to the condition in which it is found today" (p. 116).[6] The point is subtle and profound. With Hegel's theory of relativity, a large part of the globe does not participate in the progress of time experienced by the West, creating a differentiating time-space continuum that further ensures the lasting division of the world in the Western imagination.[7]

As one might expect, unfortunately, Africa presents a simpler case for Hegel: "What we properly understand by Africa, is the Unhistorical, Undeveloped Spirit, still involved in the conditions of mere nature and which had to be represented here only as on the threshold of the World's History" (1956, p. 99). Africa is "shut up," "the land of childhood" (p. 91): "It is no historical part of the world; it has no movement or development to exhibit" (p. 99). This remarkably unsettling judgment was to become the all too familiar fate allocated to Africa by the West well into this century.[8] It should take no more than a few lines of Conrad's *Heart of Darkness* to bring this pervasive theme of Africa's timelessness back to mind:

---

[6] Hegel condemns the Chinese for failing to take advantage of gunpowder ("The Jesuits had to make their first cannons for them"); for being unable to represent "the beautiful, as beautiful" despite a "remarkable skill in imitation"; for refusing to apply their knowledge of the magnet and the art of printing; and for missing out on an astronomy that has any claim as a form of knowledge (1956, p. 137). He notes a certain sense of meritocracy in China that he quickly dismisses as a wanting of maturity, as part of the scheme of matching historical and human development: "And though there is not distinction conferred by birth, and everyone can attain the highest dignity, this very equality testifies to no triumphant assertion of the worth of the inner man, but a servile consciousness—one which has not yet matured itself so far as to recognize distinctions" (p. 138).

[7] Johann Fabian uses the phrase "the denial of coevalness" in describing the impact of this idea on the development of anthropology (1983, p. 31). For a critique of this continuing denial of coevalness in anthropology, see Thomas, who claims that the effect of Geertz's work is to make of other cultures, such as the Balinese, "a picturesque, transhistorical presence, radically different from Western society" (1994, pp. 90–95).

[8] In his examination of Africa and history, Steven Feierman has described how previously among academic historians the tendency was to "appropriate bits of African past and place them within a larger framework of historical knowledge which has European roots" (1993, p. 169). History books in Swahili that were sent to the colonial schools of Africa described how Africa practiced slavery until colonialism brought *uhuru*, or freedom (p. 195). Feierman still finds it necessary to remind his colleagues that "history can no longer be written as a single clear narrative of the spread of civilization's arts from the *ecumene*, the historical heartland, to Africa and other parts of the world" (p. 171).

We were wanderers on prehistoric earth, on an earth that wore the aspect of an unknown planet. We could have fancied ourselves the first men taking possession of an accursed inheritance, to be subdued at the cost of profound anguish and of excessive toil. . . . We were too far and could not remember, because we were traveling in the night of first ages, of those ages that are gone, leaving hardly a sign—and no memories. (1973, p. 51)

The radical historical consequence of this Hegelian progression of consciousness is a world divided among people who live inside and outside history. The West remains consumed with its own sense of accelerated progress. Here nothing stands still, as people are quick to assert that change is the only constant and the news is a staple. Meanwhile, other parts of the world are marketed to the West as an escape from the overwhelming bustle. They are said to exist in a timeless space where the tomorrow people wake up to is yesterday. Hegel constructed his philosophy of history on this principle of inequitable participation in History, which is not a given of human experience; it is a privileged mode of being in the world.

What makes that historical privilege possible, for Hegel, is the nation-state. The nation is the necessary vehicle for realizing the World-Spirit and for participating in Universal History, given its unique ability to work toward "a moral, political organization" (1956, p. 75).[9] The nation alone is capable, for Hegel, of mediating between individual and Spirit. Universal History is an expression of "the Spirit of a People" that finds its form in "the 'National Spirits' of History" and the "National genius" (p. 53). This makes the historian (no less than the teacher of history) first among nationalists. If history, modernity, and freedom are defined in nationalist terms, then to be born beyond the coterie of European nations is to live outside the pale, outside the Spirit of the World and its Universal History. Adding to the weight of this national identity, Hegel identifies the "moral Whole, the State, which is that form of reality in which the individual has and enjoys his freedom; but on the condition of recognizing, believing in, and willing that which is common to the Whole" (p. 38). This theme of Government completing Freedom was,

---

[9] This was Hegel's contribution to the relatively late articulation of German nationalism. In Germany's case, national consciousness was largely the work of what Liah Greenfeld describes as "a peculiar class of educated commoners, [and] professional intellectuals" (1992, p. 277). Germany's colonial holdings were also acquired considerably later than those of the other European powers, playing largely a symbolic rather than an economic role in the development of the German state (Hobsbawm, 1987, p. 67). Hegel's nationalist philosophy of history, as Hayden White points out, demonstrates the rare virtue of making explicit how essential the *legal* status of the state was to the formation of a historical narrative (1987, p. 30).

for Hegel, "the real theater of History" (p. 99). The individuals were to be be-
holden to the state: "It constitutes their existence, their being," Hegel writes.
"Each unit is the Son of his Nation" (p. 52). This form of extreme nationalism
was to figure in future debates about Hegel's influence on the fascist state.

An empire, in Hegel's estimation, could offer a gratifying sense of destiny to a nation's citizens, further evincing their historical place in the world:
"Every Englishmen will say," Hegel imagines at one point, "We are the men
who navigate the ocean, and have the commerce of the world; to whom the
East Indies belong and their riches" (1956, p. 74). More than that, the British
student of this history can turn to the success of the empire as proof of national worth and destiny: "A Nation is moral—virtuous—vigorous—while it
is engaged in realizing its grand objects" (p. 74). The nation-as-instrument-of-
history played its part in imperialism, serving as proof of an advanced civilization worthy of a global expansion that would bring such tools of modernization as nationhood to the rest of the world.[10] During the rise of
Victorian imperialism in Great Britain, Thomas Macaulay wrote his monumental history of England, the National Portrait Gallery was founded, and
the massive publishing projects behind the *New English Dictionary on Historical Principles* (which later became the *Oxford English Dictionary*) and the
Dictionary of National Biography were initiated. These mighty works retro-
actively assembled a historical foundation for a nation worthy of a global empire. The rise of the West was the story of its heroic nations, and this casting
of history as a national project was to become the centerpiece of teaching history in school.[11]

After Hegel, we must constantly ask, at what points have we begun to
move beyond what he made of history and the world? How far are we from

---

[10] When nationalism became a tool of colonial liberation during this century, it was then
viewed, in Partha Chatterjee's terms, "as a dark, elemental, unpredictable force of primordial nature threatening the orderly calm of civilized life" (1993, p. 4). Chatterjee goes on to
complain that "history, it would seem, has decreed that we in the postcolonial world shall
only be perpetual consumers of modernity. Europe and the Americas, the only true subjects of history, have thought out on our behalf not only the script of colonial enlightenment and exploitation, but also that of our anticolonial resistance and postcolonial misery"
(p. 5).
[11] Robert Young observes that "Hegel articulates a philosophical structure of the appropriation of the other as a form of knowledge which uncannily simulates the project of
nineteenth century imperialism" (1990, p. 3). Wolfgang Mommsen, in reviewing theories
of imperialism, places Hegel's specific contribution among those who treated imperialism
as a necessary element of economic expansion, while quoting from Hegel's *Philosophy of
Right:* "The inner dialectic of civil society thus drives it—or at any rate drives a specific
society—to push beyond its own limits and seek markets, and so its necessary means of
subsistence, in other lands which are either deficient in the goods it has over-produced, or
else generally backward in industry" (cited by Mommsen, 1980, p. 30).

the assumption that the West stands at the source of the history that matters? How far are we from Hegel's geographically determined historicism when we read about the dynamic Asian economies that have catapulted Singapore and Malaysia into the twentieth century, or about the eternal tribal warfare that besets the politics of Africa in Rwanda or Somalia? Paul Gilroy ascribes a "decidedly Hegelian belief" to Frederick Douglass and a number of other African Americans of the nineteenth century in their faith "that the combination of Christianity and a nation state represents the overcoming of all antinomies" (1993, p. 35). Through whose suffering has the West developed its self-conscious sense of freedom, if not through those who have been denied that freedom, whether through slavery or apartheid, in the name of that Historical right that Hegel identified with the West? Our history lessons have plotted the progress of freedom and nationhood as a Western rite of passage; modernity has been set against the primitive and despotic ways of the rest of the world. The West has defined a single path to modernity, civilization, and the idea of a fully developed nation. "Historically, modernization is the process of change," S. N. Eisenstadt has written, "toward those types of social, economic, and political systems that developed in Western Europe and North America from the seventeenth century to the nineteenth" (1966, p. 1).

The legacy is such that critiques of Hegel often find themselves swimming in their own Hegelianism.[12] For example, my own critical efforts with Hegel engage their own version of the "great man" ("World-Historical Individual") theory of intellectual history closely associated with the rise of the European nation-state (1956, p. 29). This pursuit of History's imperial framework, through Hegel, seeks its own form of the Spirit of World History. Like Hegel, I have stretched a large canvas to convey the global scope of imperialism; I have turned to the historicizing of ideas and peoples in search of the greater Rationality that would make sense of the world today. That imperial sense remains stretched between the poles of primitive and civilized in one direction, and of East and West in the other. Although philosophers Jean-François Lyotard (1988) and Richard Rorty (1995) ask us to forsake such "master narratives," we cannot readily walk away from this historical education in

---

[12] Robert Young: "You cannot get out of Hegel by simply contradicting him, any more than you can get out of those other Hegelian systems, Marxism and psychoanalysis, by simply opposing them: for in both your opposition is likewise always recoupable, as the workings of ideology or psychic resistance" (1990, p. 6). Jacques Derrida speaks of "the very self-evidence of Hegel one often thinks oneself unburdened of" (1978a, p. 251). However, Charles Taylor speaks of an end of Hegelianism through modernity's technological domination of nature, which precludes a Hegelian synthesis of nature and reason, one of the philosopher's claims for the West (C. Taylor, 1979, p. 139).

favor of the recommended local knowledge and small experiments intended
to replace this grand theorizing of the world. By all means, let us break with
modernist aspirations for telling the whole truth of history, rejecting, as Rorty
recommends, "the romance of world history" and the idea that we can "grasp
the shape and movement of History" (1995, pp. 213, 211). But it is, above all,
the commonplaces of our own historical understanding that remain, of which
I consider the Hegelian conception of the West's self-conscious progress toward Freedom a persistent example and a heady leftover from the lessons originally designed to justify the West's domination and division of the globe.[13]
The desperately modern culture of Europe, relying on Sovereign Reason
rather than faith, was constantly generating accounts of itself and its actions.
And so the intellectual labors that I have reviewed in the previous three chapters, from the classification of species to the building of colonial schools, were
taken to justify Western expansion and colonialism.

The Subject of Imperial History

Let me move forward, then, from Hegel's lectures in the Berlin of the 1820s to
Great Britain later in the century when historians were placing increasing emphasis on the purity and quality of a race destined to assert itself around the
globe.[14] In 1895, a contributor to the *Athenaeum* pinpointed the collusion between the political and scholarly forces underlying colonialism by claiming
that "our Imperialism of today is the combined work of Beaconsfield and of
Seeley, a curious couple of collaborators" (cited by Aldrich, 1988, p. 25). While
Benjamin Disraeli (earl of Beaconsfield) upheld Britain's honor abroad, Sir
John Seeley, as Regius Professor of Modern History at Cambridge from 1869
to 1895, strengthened it on the home front through his immensely popular
Expansion of England, which clearly set the nation's Spirit on an imperial tra-

---

[13] Among those following this Hegelian/post-Hegelian path of examining the imperial
complex as the master narrative is Gilroy, who recently advocated treating "the Atlantic as
one single complex unit of analysis . . . and us[ing] it to produce an explicitly transnational
and intercultural perspective" (1993, p. 15). He sees the Middle Passage, or black Atlantic,
as defining the Western sense of modernity, as black people "engaged in various struggles
toward emancipation, autonomy, and citizenship," giving real meaning to the Hegelian
sense of Freedom (p. 16).

[14] Hugh MacDougall does not hold back on naming the perpetuators of the racial myth in
English history: "Of all the professions none served the cause of progress and Anglo-Sax-
onism more faithfully than historians. Gifted commentators such as Lord Macaulay,
Thomas Carlyle, John Kemble, Goldwin Smith, John R. Green, William Stubbs, James
Anthony Froude, Charles Kingsley, Edward Freeman, Lord Acton, dilated upon the greatness of the English race and its proud heritage. All were confident that their accounts were
somehow more objective than any that had come before, for history, it was believed, had
finally come of age as a critical science" (1982, pp. 91–92).

jectory. The historian was indeed seen as the curious collaborator with the politician in bringing Britain to "the climax of an empire," as James Morris (1968) characterizes the period.

Seeley proudly spoke of a "Greater" Britain treating its expansion as both innocent and natural. "The drift of our destiny towards the occupation of the new World," he wrote "grew up almost in our own despite," and he spoke of the colonies as Britain's "natural outlet for superfluous populations" (1884, pp. 14, 70). This was a history in which the British were carried along to empire as if by fate: "Nothing great that has ever been done by Englishmen was done so unintentionally, so accidentally as the conquest of India" (p. 179). The accidental empire entailed, he insisted, none of the barbarity of one community being "treated as the property of another . . . [for] we should be ashamed to acknowledge that in governing it we in any way sacrificed its interest to our own" (p. 66). The historical significance of this destined, innocent, and natural empire was not to be questioned: "This English Exodus has been the greatest English event of the eighteenth and nineteenth centuries" (p. 14). This biblical sense of exodus, with its vision of the promised land abroad, suggested a holy covenant between Britain and that one greater Empire.

Those with an educational interest in empire, such as Seeley, came to promote "imperial studies" for the schools, which had something of an interdisciplinary or social studies feel to it. Although this approach originated in Great Britain, its influence on history teaching was to be felt throughout the empire. The Rhodes Chair of Imperial History, established at the University of London in 1919, was initially held by A. P. Newton, who with J. Ewring authored the popular *British Empire since 1783* for use in secondary school and college history, geography, commerce, and economics classes (J. M. MacKenzie, 1984, p. 170). A number of public societies also sought to stir up loyalties for the empire through the schools using the themes of eugenics and motherhood, which, according to John MacKenzie, eventually created a space in the schools for the teaching of home economics (pp. 158–59). MacKenzie pays particular attention to the promotion of empire through the teaching of history, which became a compulsory subject for British schools only in 1900. Rudyard Kipling lent his support to this enterprise by contributing poetry to the 1911 textbook *A School History of England,* by Oxford historian C. R. L. Fletcher, a text that is still in print, having sold in excess of one hundred thousand copies. The book advises students that West Indians are "lazy, vicious, and incapable of any serious improvement," or, in a phrase, "quite happy and quite useless," whereas in India "our rule has been infinitely to the good for all the three hundred millions of the different races who inhabit that richly populated land" (Fletcher and Kipling, 1983, pp. 294–95). Although such was the

spirit of history teaching during the heyday of empire, this scholastic enthusiasm did not always impress the students, a point MacKenzie establishes by
drawing on the reflections of a member of the industrial classes who attended
school before the First World War:

> And how indeed did the nation's poor profit from the possession of em-
> pire? Compulsory State education had been introduced with overt
> propagation of the imperialistic idea. . . . What the undermass got ma-
> terially from empire, old and new, is hard to see, unless it was the ba-
> nana. (1984, p. 184)

The working class may well have enjoyed the fruits of imperialism when
it had the money, but the schools were intent on teaching the working class
that empire was so much more. What better way of integrating the young
into the empire than presenting the world as part of the mother country's
achievement, within which students from Calcutta to Canberra were invited
to find themselves and their places. Seeley advised that the teaching of history is best done by showing how history "affects our interests"; and until empire's end, the expansion of European imperialism and the rise of the West
were portrayed without qualm as being in just about everyone's interest (1884,
p. 307). Even after the European empires fell to the sweep of the independence movements in the colonies, the writing of history in the West retained
its more general Hegelian sense of the unfolding of an indomitable Spirit.

The Rise of the West in Our Time

A key work in sustaining this Hegelian theme during our own postcolonial
age has been William McNeill's widely lauded *The Rise of the West: A History
of the Human Community* (1963). This formidable book was briefly a *New
York Times* best-seller, and a second edition was issued in 1991. It falls in with
an American tradition of teaching Western civilization, originating from a
"war issues" course taught at Columbia University to the Students Army
Training Corps in 1918, which was intended to prepare troops to defend
America's stake in Europe (Allardyce, 1982). Richard Roberts has pointed to
how Western civilization textbooks tend to narrow the very sense of civilization until "it has become essentially a narrative history of Western cultural
elites and their ideas, propelled through time by the vagaries of politics and
the decline of empires" (1994, p. 58). I have alluded, in the first chapter, to
the recent battles at Stanford University over Western civilization courses, and
although there are clearly changes afoot because of multicultural education
initiatives, the general concept that the achievement of the West forms the
core of the educated imagination prevails, as well as the idea that "a history of

the human community" is about the rise of the West, as McNeill captures it in his title.

In his book, McNeill leads his readers from the "great darkness" of pre-history to the "Western explosion" of political, industrial, and cultural achievement in the modern era: "Hence 'The Rise of the West' may serve," he writes on the concluding page, "as a shorthand description of the upshot of the history of human community to date" (1963, p. 807). History in this book is laid out amid the detail and sweep of civilizations, each neatly encapsulated within the full rhetorical drama of a world history that places the greatness of others securely in the distant past, whereas the West has it all to enjoy here and now:

> Life in Demosthenes' Athens, in Confucius' China, and in Mo-hammed's Arabia was violent, risky, and uncertain; hopes struggled with fears; greatness teetered perilously on the brim of disaster. We belong in this high company and should count ourselves fortunate to live in one of the great ages of the world. (p. 807)

A second Hegelian feature of this familiar history is the universal quality of the West's cultural achievement. To bring this point home, McNeill offers an illustration of a Henry Moore sculpture depicting a reclining figure, which McNeill identifies in the caption as "Primordial Woman" before explaining how it gives "visual form to primordially primitive, inchoate dimensions of human femininity" (1963, p. 763). The resonant subconscious qualities of this female figure represent, for McNeill, "the highest intellectual sophistication," demonstrating "our twentieth-century scientific emancipation from the cultural parochialisms of the past" (p. 763). The sculpture's self-conscious sophistication has been artfully fabricated, we are led to believe, out of women's essentially primitive qualities. The historical ascendancy of the West, he appears to be saying, grows out of the achievements of a certain class of men who are able to reflect upon and transform into art the primal qualities found in others for the benefit of all.

In 1991, McNeill added an extraordinary retrospective essay as a preface to *The Rise of the West*. The piece, striking in its humility, attempts to shut the door on the Hegelian vision of the West, of which McNeill's book stands as something of a culminating moment in our time. He begins this new preface by identifying the scope of the American imperialism within which he came to write the book: "It seems obvious that *The Rise of the West* should be seen as an expression of the postwar imperial mood in the United States" (p. xv). He goes on to argue, against the main body of the book, that the common historical sense of discrete civilizations rising and falling across the stormy seas of time fails to represent what he now recognizes as an emerging world system marked by "a trans-civilization process" that has been blurring such artificial boundaries since the "the very beginning of civilized history" (pp. xxiv, xxix). He also questions the built-in bias of writing of history through the political units of nation and empire.[15]

McNeill's confession to these ideological sins in the new preface has a show-trial quality to it, and he allows that earlier he was only writing out of his own times, unaware of "the hand-in-glove fit between my review of the whole of human history and the temporary world role played by the United States." This self-serving historiography operated, according to McNeill, "if it operated at all, entirely at the subconscious level for all concerned" (1991, p. xvi). But it could still be said to be operating, as the historian concludes the 1991 preface by pledging his allegiance to the best Western conceptions of the historian's profession. "Historical scholarship has explored the globe as never before," McNeill writes, once more invoking imperial themes, only now, combined with "the evolution of historical concepts," we are afforded a "level of sophistication that makes older efforts at world history, even one as recent as mine, seem fundamentally outmoded and obviously in need of re-placement" (p. xxx). The ultimate triumph of History, as both discipline and profession, contains its own protective lesson against what is called into question and what must be allowed to stand. McNeill does not cite scholarship that comes from outside the West in the emendations and additions that his essay recommends for the original book. The self-correcting, truth-ensuring quality of Western knowledge that the 1991 preface offers, against the decid-edly ancient wisdom of the rest of the world, seems to me no less a part of the imperial legacy. So effectively naming the influence of his own location within an imperial structure, only to then take refuge in the sanctity of the historian's profession seems to ring hollow. At some level, his tale of the West's glorious rise still stands, even if flush with the new preface's inclusion of women and China. We need, then, to appreciate not only how such global histories have cast the world, but also how the academic disciplines might have a stake in such constructions.[16]

---

[15] McNeill credits the considerable work of Immanuel Wallerstein (1974–1988) for open-ing his eyes to this world system. Although he bolsters the place of China in his "history of the human community," McNeill appears willing to continue the Hegelian dismissal of Africa from the historical stage: although "the scholarship of the past twenty-five years [on Africa] has revealed a far more complex interplay of peoples and cultures . . . the con-tinent remained peripheral to the rest of the world, down to, and including our own age" (1991, p. xx).

[16] Michael Geyer and Charles Bright, providing a survey article on the fate of world histories, write of the relation between emergent non-Western scholarship and world his-

World History Today

To capture what students in the West face today when they approach the history of the world, I have selected three world history textbooks currently being used in the secondary schools of America, Canada, and Britain respectively. The textbook is a widely vetted curriculum resource that, although representing only a small part of any given student's educational experience, reflects the historical thinking of teachers, publishers, and education officials. In the case of texts on world history, the Hegelian influence on that thinking can be fully in the reader's hands before leaving the book's table of contents.

To begin with the American instance, *The Pageant of World History* (1986) is a seven-hundred-page textbook published by Allyn and Bacon. Its author, Gerald Leinwand, tells the story of the West as the history of the world, which does not concern me as much as what it makes of non-Western societies and their histories in the process. The book begins with a unit called "Discovering the Cradles of Civilization," which divides the world between "us" and "them" in the possessive forms *our* and *their*, beginning with "Our Debt to Ancient Greece" and "Our Roman Heritage," followed by "Their Ancient Splendors" (India and Southeast Asia) and "The Ancient Past of China, Japan, and Korea." It is tempting to point out how the cradle metaphor succeeds in making infants of those nations whose civilizations are seen to be "ancient." The historical contribution of these nations was to be a precursor for *the* civilization to come, while the people who lived in these lands entered a twilight zone outside history. The book's glossary defines *civilization* as "a term applied to a people who have reached a certain level of culture" (p. 713). It suggests a thoroughly nineteenth-century sense of uncivilized or previously civilized peoples somehow living with inadequate levels of culture. It offers nothing of the history of the term's use in organizing the world. The chapters on Africa and India have sections called "Contributions to Civilization," suggesting that even while outside a mainstream, while not forming part of "our debt" and "our heritage" (as in the case of ancient Greece

---

tories such as McNeill's: "There is no context within the world historical tradition to position these new histories, because world history, especially in its truncated form, has remained intimately linked to totalizing Western world images and stereotypes. The very act of mapping and thinking the world implicated historians from around the world in a nexus of histories of imperial power from which their 'other' worlds and histories were either excluded entirely—subaltern to the point of nonexistence—or rendered subordinate" (1995, p. 1036). Richard Rorty is most blunt about the motives in looking back from the end of Leninism, as he puts it, in ways that apply to both McNeill and my own work here: "Was our thirst for world-historical romance, and for deep theories about deep causes for social change, caused by our concern for human suffering? Or was it at least in part a thirst for an important role for ourselves to play?" (1995, p. 214).

and Rome), they have added some value to the civilization that we enjoy today.

After the book's global look at origins, the historical pageant on world history moves into a singularly European focus with units called "A Journey from Medieval to Modern Times" and "Democracy Triumphs over Absolutism in Europe." The chapters in these units describe the increasing realization of freedom and reason in Europe, abetted by overseas expansion. This leads to the unit "The Dominance of Europe," with its emphasis on nationalism, industrialism, and democracy, followed by "The Beginning of a Global Society," a unit that brings us to the latter half of the nineteenth century and into the heart of imperialism, with chapters called "Europe in Search of Empire: Imperialism in Africa" and "The Decline of Empire: Prelude to Global Conflict." If imperialism is portrayed as initiating a global society, which bears a certain truth while conveying little of the hardship unequally distributed in the process, the demise of imperialism is presented as a threat to world peace.

With the completion of the pageant from various ancient civilizations to *the* civilization, the book concludes optimistically with the unit "Toward a Global Peace," in which Asia returns rather ominously under the chapter rubric "Asia in Today's World: Sleeping Giants Awaken." The title's reference to the awakening giants suggests a looming threat to global order, evoking shades of oriental despotism and teeming masses associated earlier in this century with xenophobic "yellow peril" campaigns in North America. Without speculating on the educational effectiveness of dramatizing chapter titles, or on whether the images that lie dormant in, for example, the "sleeping giant" metaphor are available to the majority of today's students, I obviously think it worthwhile to introduce students to such traces of an imperial legacy in their history lessons.[17]

If the unit and chapter titles present one opportunity to critically examine the Hegelian heritage, the book offers another as it closes with a two-page world map that color codes 165 countries as "free," "partly free," or "not free" (1986, pp. 730–31). The map serves to validate the special concentration of World-Spirit that underscores the rise of the West and its benefits for the rest of the world. History comes down to this geopolitical dispersion of Freedom and Civilization. I do not mean to begrudge a nation's choice or struggle to be

---

[17] On the international front of U.S.-China relationships, *New York Times* columnist Thomas Friedman (1995) writes a new and self-censored version of the sleeping-giant metaphor: "We see China as the 800-pound gorilla that needs to be house broken. China sees itself as the 800-pound gorilla that should be able to sit wherever it wants."

"free" in this sense, but I think it only fair to consider how our common, schooled understanding of history measures the progress of the World. It must surely be the end of History when the whole of the world map is colored "free" by Western standards.

Now, I do not object to students taking their history lessons from this substantial textbook, any less than from the other two that I will go on to review here. Amid the increasingly limited resources allocated to public education, it does not make sense to think about abandoning existing resources, and *The Pageant of World History* is filled with much of educational value and historical interest. It is not so much a false history of the world as one that reflects a particular sense of time, history, and modernity that can be profitably called into question in trying to understand imperialism's educational legacy. There could well be supplementary lessons on the book's reading of the historical pageant, on the prominent gaps and featured moments, and on how this sense of history is being written otherwise in other texts, music, and artwork, often under postcolonial influence, thereby moving students beyond the textbook to find that influence is an educationally sound idea. Yet there are textbooks with something more of this postcolonial presence, including the one that I consider next.

The table of contents of Garfield Newman and Christian De Greer's *Odyssey through the Ages* (1992), a Canadian textbook for senior high school published by McGraw-Hill Ryerson, possesses the familiar pattern of fascinating ancient empires paving the way for a remarkable Western civilization. Taking up one of Marshall McLuhan's contributions to the modern lexicon, the book looks to the "Emergence of the Global Village" in its optimistic epilogue. But I wish to focus on the main body of the text, which both adheres to and questions the Hegelian tradition. The opening chapter, "Understanding the Past," takes considerable exception, for example, to traditional methods of doing history. Insisting that "history is not solely about political power-struggles and military campaigns," Newman and De Greer favor social history that "must endeavor to reflect the lives of men and women from all classes, for the poor as well as the rich have a past" (p. 3). The text includes the sidebar "Medieval History from a Woman's Perspective," based on the fourteenth-century *A Vision of Light*, by Margaret Ashbury.[18] This egalitarian commitment makes the rise-of-the-West narrative, which still dominates the organization of history in the book, all the more striking. Newman and De Greer label the

---

[18] *A Vision of Light* is introduced to demonstrate "the value of studying the history of all classes," although a reading of the excerpt reveals that Ashbury appears to be "rich, very rich" (Newman and De Greer, 1992, pp. 18–19).

Chinese "xenophobic," although they insist that "there was no antagonism toward the rest of the world—only a growing sense of superiority" (p. 162). The "Chinese world view" is described ahistorically as it is said to derive from the emperor's friendly or hostile relationship with the peoples of the surrounding countryside (pp. 163–64). Yet perhaps the most graphic instance of that Hegelian historical vision comes with the time line entitled "Major Events in Chinese History." The last specified event takes place in 1535 as the "Portuguese gain right to reside and trade in Macao" (p. 135).

In coming to address "The Modern Age," the authors of *Odyssey through the Ages* again show an initial sensitivity to the issues that I am addressing in this book. The chapter's key concepts, helpfully listed on the opening page, include globalization, acculturation, world economy, modern era, Europeanization, Christopher Columbus, capitalism, and Amerindians. "The pitfall we hope to avoid is that of presenting the Modern age as an age of modernization led by Europeans," Newman and De Greer write in introducing the chapter. "Instead we need to address this period of history from a broader perspective, taking into account the impact of contact on all cultures involved" (1992, p. 549). The key question at this point is whether these other cultures are thought to have entered the modern age or just to have come into contact with it as it went bounding by in its own historical time. This is the pitfall that above all needs addressing after Hegel, and the text does point to how "the term 'modern era,' applied to this period of history, reflects very much a Eurocentric bias, as it implies that progress and the export of European civilization were connected" (p. 550). The book supports its charges of Eurocentrism by comparing the Mercator projection of the world, which markedly amplifies the size of Europe in relation to the Southern Hemisphere, to the Peters projection, which reverses the distortion (p. 551). Newman and De Greer also take the bold step of stating that the idea of the West as the pinnacle of civilization is just that, an idea, and not a given fact, the origins of which they locate in medieval Christianity (p. 551). This all takes place in the introduction to the chapter on the "modern era," before the start of the real history that begins with Christopher Columbus. The prefatory comments on Eurocentrism serve as a supplemental lesson, a cautionary preview, of the sort that I have been advocating in this book. To call into question the biases of historians and geographers while showing a contradictory fidelity to the rise-of-the-West theme in the organization of the text, captures the intellectual play in this imperial legacy. Following Newman and De Greer's lead, students are to learn the history while keeping in mind how the discipline has put together the past in its own image. In this way, they stand to be greater students of their own education.

My example from Great Britain, a 128-page booklet, *Expansion, Trade, and Industry* (1993), by James Mason, published by Longman, goes even further in making clear to students the uses of history. If not itself a world history text, the series to which it belongs, A Sense of History, has global aspirations, with a "core" volume on the Roman Empire and "supplementary" texts on imperial China, India, and Islam. Judging by Mason's text, the series reflects the influence of the Schools Council Project 13–16 which, in pursuing the method of historical inquiry in preference to the presentation of a narrative, called the nature of history into question (Shemilt, 1980; Seixas, 1993). Mason encourages a critical stance toward the rise of the West that allows students to see, in a chapter such as "Images of Empire," that the rise was accompanied by relentless self-promotion. In writing about the empire's glory days, he repeatedly speaks of what the British *believed* at the time, effectively distancing himself, as historian, from these earlier and clearly prejudicial attitudes: "The British . . . believed they had a duty to spread Christianity and to help people live by its teachings" (p. 68). After calling such beliefs into question, the text also has its uncritical moments—Sir Stamford Raffles, Mason says, "treated the Javanese with respect and took a lot of trouble to learn about their history" before returning home "with 200 boxes of material weighing nearly 30 tonnes" (p. 71). Yet it also uses striking citations from the time, such as G. A. Henty's late-nineteenth-century stories for boys, to illustrate the British sense of racial superiority that accompanied its imperial exploits. Although Mason skillfully shows the motivational force of these attitudes in promoting the empire, he leaves little doubt about their morality.

Given my hope that this sort of thoughtfulness about the past would be turned toward the present, I was caught a little off guard by Mason's efforts to treat the racism fostered by imperialism as a thing of the past, as if to redeem the present moment. At one point, he cites Basil Davidson's *Into the Dark Continent,* which claimed in 1972 that "Britain in its age of power—from the mid-19th century—became racist, though of course with the very best intentions, and would so remain for almost 100 years until the imperial power was spent" (cited by Mason, 1993, p. 69). Davidson's "until" is the crucial point for me, because the racism did not neatly end with the collapse of empire, but remains part of an imperial legacy that continues to haunt British life to this day.

That much said, the strongest post-Hegelian feature of Mason's text comes when he turns to the writing of history itself. He points out how far into this century historians carried these earlier imperialist attitudes, using as his primary exhibit Jasper Stembridge's *The World,* which British schoolchildren began to study in the 1950s (1993, p. 73). Mason makes clear to students that histories can become as outdated as old clothes and music, although he falls short of inviting a critical judgment of his use of Davidson, for example. Mason appears to stand with McNeill in suggesting that, although it pays to retain a healthy skepticism about earlier histories and historians, we can trust today's professionals to have righted previous problems. Still, he establishes, as do Newman and De Greer, that there is a place in the history classroom for a critical understanding of what historians make of history. The next logical step, then, is to include a wider company of historians, including those from Africa and India who have reflected on imperialism, such as P. G. Okoth, Partha Chatterjee, and Gyan Prakash from among those cited in this book. The state of permanent revision I am invoking, as I alluded to earlier, is drawn from among the redeeming features of Western knowledge. I ask in return only that my own minor contributions to the triumph of the West be treated no less skeptically than those of the historians.[19]

To summon history to account will not be an easy process. Students, no less than the rest of us, are rarely in a position to call any academic discipline into question. All the more reason, therefore, to use the resources of the school, as well as personal experience, to think about what historians make of the nation in schoolbooks and in the popular imagination. It can begin by comparing the stories told over different generations of history textbooks or the history represented in different periods of film and other popular forms. Underlying it all is an effort to see what we have made of history after all the years we have spent tracing the brave voyages of the great explorers, studying the scientific and artistic accomplishments of the Newtons and da Vincis, and making the pilgrimages to London and Paris, Cambridge and Oxford.

In our own education and in history classes today, we can consider how historians have distributed people among premodern, modern and postmodern periods; we can ask how history works in conjunction with geography to create space-time continuums that, although they add fascination to study and travel, do so principally through the production of difference and the building of boundaries that seem only to naturalize the distances between people. In turning to the work of philosophers and historians in this way, we

---

[19] For the common ground between "new historians" and progressive educators, see Seixas (1993). The result of such an alliance could mean a far more encompassing vision of the past for the history class, with which teachers and students of history are invited to engage by joining the "community of inquiry" that for Seixas defines the field (p. 241). The recently announced National Standards for United States History, produced under the auspices of the United States government, also reflect this sense of broadening historical inquiry to include overlooked segments of the population, such as women and immigrants; the transformative impact of technology; and critical thinking skills ("Overhaul," 1994).

find both the weight of the scholarly contribution to these differences and the first steps in moving scholarship beyond these particular constructions of difference. We have yet to disentangle the nature of the encounter between the French sailors who arrived with Cartier and the Iroquois who met them along the St. Lawrence River, between the Jesuits who followed with their mission schools and the Hurons who attended them. We are struggling to find a way of teaching about the category of race, which has been, in large part, according to historian James D. Anderson, "distorted or omitted in the writing and teaching of American history" no less than in histories of other places (1994, p. 87). Anderson attributes this failure to the inability to face the past squarely, laying some of the blame at the feet of historians who tend to engage the issues of "race among themselves while excluding the masses of learners and citizens from this discussion by omitting it from high school textbooks" (p. 87).

For my part, I am not sure that we have fully worked out how profoundly the Western division of the world continues to hold the imagination in thrall, even as its sense of racial and national boundaries make less and less sense within what are increasingly global communities. In a similar manner, we need to pause over the role played by nationalism as an affair of land, loyalty, identity, and education, especially as it continues to serve in schools as an implicit disavowal of those "from away," to use a Newfoundland expression.

More than four centuries before Hegel opened his first lecture on the philosophy of history in Berlin, Ibn Kuldûn prepared a similar set of talks on universal history that were published as *The Muqaddimah* (1967). Ibn Kuldûn spent a lifetime moving between Granada and Tunis, across an intercontinental cultural bridge, coming finally to write his major historical treatise in a land that for Hegel lay beyond the reach of history and civilization. This Islamic scholar begins his fifteenth-century treatise by discussing the fallacies of a thousand years of Arab historiography, and he precedes Hegel both in his valorization of the temperate zones as the seat of civilization and in making history the reflection of national character. For Ibn Kuldûn, the historian must explore the "conditions affecting the nature of civilization, as for instance, savagery and sociability, group feelings, and the different ways by which one group of human beings achieves superiority over another" (p. 35). Ibn Kuldûn is a cautious and subtle historian, no more so than when he boldly declares that "there are many sciences," and proceeds to ask where, then, are the sciences of the Persians, Chaldeans, Syrians, Babylonians, and Copts? "The sciences of only one nation, the Greeks, have come down to us, because they were translated through al-Ma'mûn's efforts" (p. 39). It becomes the historian's trade, as Ibn Kuldûn describes it, to acknowledge the selectiveness and intermingling of the traditions within which we live. There needs to be this vigilance about what has been lost and what has been brought forward as "history." In the rise of the West, the achievement of superiority has been accomplished not only by the sword and cross, but also by a philosophy of history that has used time and place as conceptual tools for dividing the world according to the interests of imperialism.

Mappa mundi, in Isidore of Seville's Etymologiae *(Augsburg, 1472).*
Courtesy University of British Columbia Library.

GEOGRAPHIES OF DIFFERENCE

D
rawing on the records of da Gama, Columbus, Cabot, Vespucci, and Magellan, cartographers were able to construct remarkable maps of the world that, in their detail and decoration, stood like great stained-glass windows illuminating the annunciation of empire, the return to Eden, and the crossing into promised lands. These beautiful world maps, found in the palaces of popes and princes, could not fail to stir the imagination and pride of imperialism's faithful. Yet, more than a source of inspiration, the map was a technology of empire, an indispensable graphic interface for navigating and managing the world. It provided a running record of imperialism's reach, rendering shorelines and contours, sea by isle, bay by river, latitude by longitude. Through this projection of discovery and conquest, the world was gradually outlined, filled in, and renamed in imperialism's image. The increasing precision and subtlety of the map elevated geography to the premier art and science of imperialism. Yet the increasingly sophisticated maps of new and distant worlds did remarkably little to disrupt what for the European mind was the oldest of global divisions. In a rather different tack in this chapter, I want to show how advances in an imperial geography were dedicated to preserving and elaborating a remarkably ancient manner of dividing the world that remains with us to this day.

Long before Gerardus Mercator etched his influential maps in the sixteenth century, medieval cosmography gave rise to what I would posit as the most powerful, if least graphically nuanced, of world maps. It went by the Latin name *mappa mundi* and was to dominate European mapmaking for a thousand years. This map typically portrays the earth as a circle bounded by an ocean, with the land divided into three parts by bodies of water that form a T. Asia occupies the upper half of the circle (atop the watery T), which is designated as east. It is separated from Europe by the Don River and from Africa by the Nile, and those two continents are divided from each other by the Mediterranean. Some versions of the map offer a stark geometry, whereas others have varied shorelines and are illustrated with cities, animals, legends, saints, castles, and monsters. The continental boundaries of these early maps take the shape of a partial cross (T) with Jerusalem at its center, giving the world the imprint of the mapmaker's faith (Turnbull, 1989, pp. 42–43).[1] In the fifteenth century, Italian merchant-poet Goro Dati was still offering schoolchildren a verse rendering of the map in his celebration of maritime adventure: "A *T* within an *O* shows vividly / How all the world is cut up into three" (cited by Grafton, 1992, p. 67). The map also took the form of a sphere, which can be seen in the portraits of Holy Roman Emperor Charles V and England's Queen Elizabeth, celebrated as "the worlds Empresse." As they hold the "rule of orb," it symbolizes a righteous taking of the world in hand. The orb had a jewel-encrusted band circling the sphere around the middle and over the top, a three-dimensional *mappa mundi,* with a cross mounted on the top marking Jerusalem (Yates, 1975, p. 60).

The *mappa mundi* was only gradually supplanted during the Renaissance by a revival of Ptolemy's map from A.D. 150, which had been preserved and improved upon by Islamic scholars such as ash-Sharīf al-Idrīsī during the twelfth century. Then began to appear the far more practical *portolan* charts that could actually guide ships between merchant ports. The cartographic Renaissance that followed, however, did not undo the continental divides of the *mappa mundi,* and so we continue to imagine a world in which the continents of Europe, Asia, and Africa are natural divisions that signify as much the radical distance between races, as the division of landforms. It now seems beyond recall to think that, as Henri Baudet reminds us, Europe was no more than "a promontory, an outpost on the continent of Asia," to which he adds that "no consciousness, no definition distinguished West from East until, three thousand years ago, the Greek spirit emerged" (1965, p. 3).[2] It has fallen to the arts and sciences, geography not least among them, to find that distinguishing boundary, to establish that consciousness that set West from East. Or, as Edward Said puts it in his own overly determined style, one of orien-

---

[1] Editions of the *mappa mundi* included biblical events and depicted the monstrous races of Africa (Whitfield, 1994, p. 18).

[2] Herodotus complains in the fifth century B.C. about the seemingly arbitrary divisions between Europe, Asia, and Africa (Libya): "For my part I cannot understand why three names, and women's names especially, should ever have been given to a tract which is in

talism's great features was "a proclivity to divide, subdivide, and redivide its subject matter without ever changing its mind about the Orient as being always the same, unchanging, uniform, and radically peculiar object" (1978, p. 98).

We have then, on the one hand, to think of how firmly Europe is set apart from Asia in our minds, and, on the other, to consider how hardpressed we might be, after all those school days spent coloring maps and working with atlases, to mark on a map the precise line that geographically divides Europe from Asia. What was so clearly separated by water, often designated as the Don River, on the *mappa mundi* is nothing more than an imaginary racial boundary neither typically marked on the map nor tied to a single geographical feature (but roughly following the Black Sea, Caucasus Mountains, Kazakh steppes, and Ural Mountains). The geographical confusion over the boundary between Europe and Asia troubled Voltaire, who noted, in commenting on his much-admired Russia, that "one doesn't know any more where Europe finishes and Asia commences" (cited by Wolff, 1994, pp. 16–17).[3] These geopolitical formations were confounded by Russia's eighteenth-century leap into the circle of European civilization and its later imperial push to the Pacific. If the continental divide is difficult to locate geographically, it is easy to imagine in almost every other sense. In Western eyes, China is at the far end of the earth. Children in England, Canada, and New Zealand, as it turns out, imagine that to dig right through the earth is to end up in China, an idea that the China Syndrome, relating to nuclear meltdowns, scientifically encoded.

The West's sense of distance and difference is no less formidable in relation to Africa. Here the continental divide was handed down from the an-

---

reality one, nor why the Egyptian Nile and the Colchian Phasis (or according to others the Maeotic Tanais and Cimmerian ferry) should have been fixed upon for the boundary lines; nor can I even say who gave the three tracts their names, or whence they took the epithets" (H. 45). What does seem clear is that the Greek names for these lands and peoples (Africa is also thought to derive from the Greek) were to become part of their destiny. Sir Walter Raleigh, in his *Historie of the World* of 1614, was still tracing the journeys of Noah's descendants through Asia, Europe, and Africa, linking Amerindians to this biblical history and thus preserving the pattern that appears on a number of *mappae mundi* (Grafton, 1992, p. 209). The discovery of the New World may be thought to have disrupted this continentalism, yet neither the Amerindians, across two continents, nor the Aborigines in Australia have had the sort of common and total continental identification that distinguishes Europeans, Asians, and Africans.

[3] Wolff goes on to say that "this declaration of continental confusion was, in fact, an accurate account of the state of 18th century geography, for the border between Europe and Asia—though all agreed that it had to cut across Russia somewhere—was a subject of controversy. Our own cartographical convention, that the Ural Mountains mark the border,

cient Greeks, only to be further exaggerated as late as the nineteenth century by, for example, the denial of African influences on Greek culture (Bernal, 1987). The geographic arts, which did much to abet the expansion of European interests, had a way of building their scientific structures and elaborate maps on existing and inherited beliefs. It may not be all that surprising that the arts and sciences worked so hard to establish what had long been assumed, yet the educational legacy of imperialism is often about how a world of learning came to be based on setting out who fits where in the order of things. So I would return to the classroom's unfurled maps and ask, what geography lessons on this georacial understanding of the world, so critical to the work of imperialism, do students still acquire? Although not the least of those lessons is how the *mappa mundi* vision of the world lives on, there is much to be learned from following the course of geography from ancient times to today's classrooms.

Geographical Formations

The study of geography in the West had its Hellenic precedents, with Strabo's *Geography* offering directions for the drawing of spherical world maps, and Ptolemy's world maps from the second century A.D. featuring the use of latitude and longitude. It was Ptolemy who insisted that "the first principle and chief ground in all geography . . . is the history of travel" (cited by Lach, 1977, pp. 473–74). With the age of reconnaissance, although without being named as a discrete discipline, geography proved to be at the heart of what it meant for science to be empirical, for, as J. R. Hales puts it, "The first scientific laboratory was the world itself," and geography was there to take the full measure

---

had only just been proposed in the 18th century as one solution among several, and the maps of the period offered a variety of alternative borders, some beginning at the Don River [*mappa mundi*] and some farther east, at the Volga" (1994, p. 17). Arnold Toynbee attempts an historical explanation of the division in his BBC radio talks *The World and the West* by pointing out that Russia has "never been Western Christian" and that "Eastern and Western Christianity have always been foreign to one another . . . as Russia and the West unhappily still are today" (1953, p. 4). However, for Jalal Al-e Ahmad, West and East have no political or geographical meaning, or, as he explains in his *Weststruckness:* "The West means the countries with the full stomachs, and the East means the ones that are hungry" (1988, p. 12). More recently, Samuel Huntington, who has argued that "fault lines between civilizations are replacing political and ideological boundaries of the Cold War," draws such a line for Europe at the eastern boundary of Western Christianity in the year 1500 (1994, pp. 29–30). Finally, giving evidence of the racial roots in the fixing of these geographical divisions, geneticist Michael Crawford explains that studies of DNA prove that "there is no dividing line where on one side you can say it is Asia and on the other side it's Europe" (cited by Wheeler, 1995, p. A15). This cutting of geography with history is an important feature of the imperial legacy.

of that world (cited by D. Livingstone, 1992, p. 34). Writing in 1577, Richard Wiles captures the enthusiasm of the day for geography in his *Historie of Traveyle:* "Through the discovery of the fare Indies, the Moluccaes and new founde landes, of late to be wondered at . . . I dare to be so bold to say, that generally all Christians, Jewes, Turkes, Moores, Infidels, and Barbares be this day in love with Geographie" (cited by Lach, 1977, p. 474).[4] Wiles was given to complaining that geography did not receive the support it should in the universities, all the while asking, "Of whom doe we learne howe to divyde the world into partes?" Geography had been treated as a subfield of mathematics when Wiles studied it at a Jesuit college. He rested his case, as well, on geography's place in gathering "intelligences of the situation and strength of any cities" (p. 482). Here, amid images of divide-and-conquer, geography found its academic footing. By the end of the sixteenth century, most western European courts had geographers in their employ, and scientific geography was being taught at Louvain and Paris (pp. 478, 480, 488).[5]

In the eighteenth century, geography was not named as part of the "Detailed System of Human Knowledge" described in Diderot's *Encyclopédie,* whereas Benjamin Martin's *Philosophical Grammar,* from the same period, lists it as a branch of geology. By the early years of the next century, however, under a second wave of imperialism, geography come into its own as a full and accomplished field of study. In France, the Société de Géographie de Paris formed in 1821, which was but the most notable of the many geographical societies that, Olivier Soubeyran has argued, "constituted significant pressure groups in favor of colonization," with their number increasing exponentially toward the end of the century and the emergence of "the new imperialism" (1994, p. 246). In Great Britain, the Royal Geographical Society, which took shape in the 1830s, grew out of the Association for the Exploration of the Interior Part of Africa that had been founded in 1788. The society's active promotion of geography's vital contribution to the British Empire is nowhere made so plain as in this excerpt from a letter sent to the society's president, Roderick Murchison, in 1852:

---

[4] David Livingstone points out that "Columbus himself admitted that cosmography, cartography, and astronomy were predominantly Jewish occupations" and that "this specifically Jewish style of science practiced in sixteenth-century Portugal provided the template for English science in the period and 'the catalyst inducing the emergence of modern science in Western Europe'" (1992, p. 61). This always ambiguous sense of the Jew, as at once one with the West and apart from it, continues to work as an excellent purgative in dissolving the assumptions of geographic division.

[5] Lach notes that the method of teaching geography at the time appears to have been through dictation of contemporary materials, among them those of the Jesuits on Japan and of Vasco da Gama's voyages to India (1977, p. 481).

Geography lays open to the Government and to the Capitalist the hidden resources of the remote parts of this great Empire and teaches the one how to govern it at the least cost, and the other how to apply profitably the surplus capital and labour of the Country to objects which thru' the RGS [Royal Geographical Society] may be made known sooner than thru' any other means. (Cited by Stafford, 1989, p. 215)

Geography was a discipline prepared to serve the political economy of colonialism. Geographers were a source of sound advice on founding plantations, locating gold deposits, and improving acclimatization, given that among the more pressing questions of the age was whether the white races could settle in the tropics (D. Livingstone, 1992, p. 11). Geography was an applied science intended, as Richard Symonds puts it, to "build a bridge between the natural sciences and the study of humanity" (1986, p. 142).

Thomas Holdich, superintendent of frontier survey and prominent member of the Royal Geographical Society, was among those who observed the geographical relation between clime and character: "The indolent sun-loving people of the Southern latitudes have everywhere proved more easy to dominate than those nurtured in a colder atmosphere" (1916, p. 13). Real fears were expressed about the deterioration of character that might be suffered by colonists in the tropics; thus, one finds John Scott Keltie advising in 1897 that European children "must be sent home to England, otherwise they will degenerate physically and morally" (cited by Hudson, 1977, p. 16). One of the big geographical questions of the time was "the expansion of the white race," as Holdich put it, and the search for suitable "dumping grounds" for the "excess" and the restless working class of Europe (1916, p. 245). Whatever problems this would pose, as Holdich envisioned in a deeply disturbing image, would "find a partial solution in the extermination of many of the dark-skinned races" (p. 245). While one may well want to dismiss such extremism as the exception rather than the rule, Brian Hudson notes that in the year following Holdich's talk of final solutions, he was elected president of the Royal Geographical Society (1977, p. 17).

In 1875, as the Second International Congress of Geographical Sciences was being held in Paris, geography became an "examined" subject in the elementary schools of Great Britain. At the time, heroic explorers of the period such as H. M. Stanley could be heard making rousing speeches to the public on the educational and entrepreneurial value of this subject:

And whereas you owe so much to geographical knowledge you must cherish that knowledge, and go on acquiring it, you must teach it to your youths, that when they arrive at manhood each may know that beyond these islands there lie vast regions where they also may carve out fortunes as their forefathers did in olden times. (Cited by Hudson, 1977, p. 15)

Geography was to move from the province of a learned society to a full-fledged university discipline through the combined and telling sponsorship of the Royal Geographical Society and the British military forces (Hudson, 1977, p. 14). Together, they funded Oxford's first readership in geography in 1887. The *Times* of the day did not hesitate to weigh in on the imperial importance of Oxford's new discipline: "The serious mistakes made and the risks of war incurred by geographical ignorance have often been referred to; with the establishment of this school there will be no excuse for such ignorance among those who have the conduct of the Empire's affairs" (cited by Hudson, p. 14). The initial appointment was Sir Halford Mackinder, a man credited by Symonds as the founder of modern imperial geography. On his appointment, Mackinder made a point to bring the "new geography," as he termed it, to schoolteachers by holding the first summer vacation courses for them at Oxford, just as he found opportunities to instruct senior army officers in the analysis of the lands and peoples of the empire. During his seventeen years at Oxford, Mackinder published a series of popular works on the order of *Britain and the British Seas,* reflecting his patriotic sense of the geographer's duty not only to bring the world home to his students and readers, but also to aid the nation in realizing its global destiny.

A Schooling in Imperial Geography

The real success story of imperial geography was found in the schools of Britain and the empire abroad. Oxford University Press and other publishers sold millions of geography textbooks on and to the empire, full of predictably disparaging comments about colonized peoples, while offering a more encouraging view of the empire's natural wealth (Symonds, 1986, p. 145).[6] In this way, geography was launched as a school subject with unmistakable fervor, catching the full swell of the British Empire during the decades around the turn of the century. Geography was at the heart of the imperial studies movement, spearheaded by the League of the Empire, the Victoria League, and the Royal Colonial Institute, the latter being active in the colonies, such

---

[6] From *The Oxford Survey of the British Empire* of 1914: "The average Ceylonese (except members of the highest castes) dislikes responsibility and does not readily rise to it as does a capable European," and "Immigrants from the United Kingdom are specially desired [in Canada] not only for their inherent qualities, but to balance the foreign element, and to help Canadians to preserve the traditions and characteristics of the British race, and to maintain that spirit of loyalty to the British empire which pervades the country in such a marked degree today" (cited by Symonds, 1986, p. 147).

as South Africa, as well as in the motherland. The aim of "empire education," as Lieutenant Colonel Elsdale of Natal outlined it in 1895, was reciprocal between England and colony: "Thus, while England is careful to train her children to a better knowledge of each distant colony and its needs, the colonies should apply themselves to learn more of the position and requirements of England" (cited by Wesso, 1994, p. 319). As an aside, I should point out that this was not the only version of geography available to teachers of the day. The anarchist Peter Kropotkin addressed a Teachers Guild conference in Oxford in 1893 with the admonition that geography "must teach us, from our earliest childhood, that we are all brethren, whatever our nationality" (cited by D. Livingstone, 1992, p. 254). But if this theme of a common humanity was not denied outright by empire studies, it was out of keeping with the discriminating tendencies of both science and education.

By the 1920s, British rationales for geography offered that "travel and correspondence have now become general; the British dominions are to be found in every clime and these facts alone are sufficient to ensure that the subject shall have an important place in the school timetable" (cited by Goodson, 1988, p. 168).[7] Students were taught to look out onto "our empire and its neighbors," as the title of a Canadian textbook referred to it, an empire in which "no other nation controls such a curious jumble of people" (McDougall and Paterson, 1937, p. 1). The creative assignments in this textbook took the form of an "open forum," following a discussion of life in India and Kipling's "East is East and West is West," for example, with two remarkably frank points presented to young adolescents for discussion: "1. Is European exploitation being welcomed by the 'backward' races of the East? 2. Should the people of India be more grateful to Britain for what she has done to raise their standard of living?" (p. 87).

Students might also be asked to view the empire through nationalist eyes. *We Are Canadian Citizens,* for example, explains that

> the British Empire now occupies about one-quarter of the surface of the whole world and its population is approximately one-quarter of all the people in the world, being about 490,000,000, of which number approximately 70,000,000 are white people. . . . Canadians form but a small part of the British Empire, yet for other reasons our country is one of the most important units of the Empire. (Goldring, 1937, p. 222)

---

[7] In his history of the subject, Goodson (1988) does not credit the inspiring role of imperialism as I do, preferring to explain geography's place in the university as resulting from its having found a place in the schools. We agree, however, that the schools were working, through geography and history classes, to bolster nationalism and related imperial attitudes far more thoroughly than were the universities.

As the book then turns to the Roman Empire, students are left to wonder whether this matter of Canada's "white people" was part of its importance as a unit of empire.

By the 1950s, as self-determination among the colonial states was finally being understood as a political right rather than an act of ingratitude, a new tack was taken in schools across the empire and the Commonwealth. Jasper Stembridge's *The World,* for example, tried to strike a certain balance between disavowal and embrace in the fulfillment of the imperial spirit in world history:

> The rights and wrongs of "the scramble for Africa" on the part of European powers lie outside the field of geography. But the significant fact remains that the Europeans have brought civilization to the peoples of tropical Africa, whose standard of living has, in most cases, been raised as a result of their contact with white peoples. (Cited by MacKenzie, 1984, p. 193)

Thus, during a period of great African self-determination, we find Stembridge seeking to set aside judgments on the European "scramble" for the continent while still claiming that colonization benefited Africans in most cases. Students of geography need their history.

I know that, in my own case, as a child of the empire learning about Canada's place within the Commonwealth in the 1950s, I felt a certain pride sitting before the once and former empire, done up in pink in the *Oxford Junior Atlas.* I was like Marlow in Joseph Conrad's *Heart of Darkness,* who, as "a little chap . . . would look for hours at South America, or Africa, or Australia" and lose himself "in the glories of exploration" (1973, p. 11). Year after year, we studied the great British and French explorers, tracing their journeys with different colored dotted lines across ocean and continent, in ship and on snowshoe, as they trod across what they took to be lands that were theirs for the civilizing. The indigenous peoples of Canada showed up as guides and backdrops in the book's sketches of explorers such as Jacques Cartier and Simon Fraser, that being the whole of what was offered by way of understanding their stake in, or feel for, the land. We spent long hours coloring the nations of Africa and South America, saving our pinks (the mapping color of a healthy and robust white dominion?) for the British Empire and Commonwealth, in what seemed to me until recently the most innocent of school busywork. The shading of mountain and coastline along boundary after borderline added a therapeutic moment to the school day. Maps were an art form that even the artistic underachievers could reasonably achieve, all the while bringing us along on this great historical ride that left the world a colorful mosaic, with consequences that we might spend the rest of our lives figuring out and living through.

We were to intended to acquire "simple geographic understandings" from textbooks such as *Old World Horizons* (1944), composed by British Columbia school inspector John Gough and meant to instill in us Old World horizons on this far edge of the New World. The book, reprinted well into the 1950s, provided lessons on such a "valuable British possession" as India:

> India is one third the size of Canada yet it contains thirty times as many people. Several hundred different tongues are spoken throughout the land and only one native out of every ten can read or write. Caste barriers prevent groups of classes from mixing and the son of a carpenter, potter, or blacksmith must learn the trade of his father. Unfortunately, this system is supported by the Hindu faith to which the majority belong. The natives in the northwest follow the teachings of Mohammed; those in the northeast worship Buddha. These are but a few of the problems that face those who seek to unify the people of India and give them self-government. (p. 121)

Might "those who seek to unify . . . and give . . . self-government" be benevolent but perhaps misdirected British overlords? The book, still in use a decade after Indian independence, presented a patronizing picture of a land overwhelmed by chaotic and primitive forces. That Hinduism was "unfortunate" and that those who sought to "give" the people self-government faced seemingly insurmountable problems in what was still claimed as a "valuable possession," was only part of the mystery of the world that we were left to fathom, supported by tinted photographs of bathers gathered on the ruined steps leading down to the Ganges.

Although some of us in those Commonwealth classrooms were part of the "curious jumble of people," that is, not Englishmen, we were still encouraged to survey this former empire and newfound Commonwealth as our own. We were to offer up thanks to the bravery of those indefatigable explorers Cabot, Drake, Cook, Vancouver, and Livingstone, no less than to the fruitfulness of the colonial plantations that brought to our doorstep rubber, cocoa, silk, tea, and coffee. Whatever else we knew ourselves to be, distinct from the geography book's assumptions about our desire to be of British descent, we gratefully suspended as we pored over our place in the world as part of the empire, observing everywhere our good fortune and in that sense coming to know ourselves better. Geography, as a discourse of difference, was about learning to attribute that difference to a people within their landscape.

"If there were not relationships between what people do and the place conditions where they live," Neville Scarfe writes in *Geography in School,* "there would be no point in studying the separate conditions as geography" (1965, p. 7). For Scarfe, whose name graces the faculty of education building in which I currently work, geography's mandate is the studied division of humanity by place. Geography fixes people to a given place in the world. We learn to read a people through their time and place within the modern and premodern matrix of the world. People outside their assigned landscape evoke a sense of dislocation, with the lingering connection with their "land of origin" signified by racial qualities. The West alone has been able to free itself from this geographical determination that leaves a people place-bound. To this day, this remains the focus of geography, as R. A. Harper would have it in a recent defense of the subject's contribution to general education: "The *raison d'être* of geography is that the earth's environment and the peoples that inhabit it vary from place to place" (1992, p. 124). Finally, in a recent and far-reaching review of geography as a school subject, Sister Madeleine Gregg and Gaea Leinhardt come to the conclusion that "the fundamental concept that results from the scope of geography" is that "physical and cultural realities influence the ways that people in particular places think about and attempt to solve the problems of society" (1994, p. 320).

People certainly do vary in customs and cuisine, and these differences can often be traced to the geography of their origins, to available resources and climatic conditions. Yet this manner of tying non-Western lives to a particular patch of the earth reduces people to a reflection of their environments, and, in the spirit of Hegel discussed in the previous chapter, it ignores how they have worked with their world over time. Along this line, David Livingstone identifies a tradition in geography, from the nineteenth century, of treating climate as part of a "moral economy for the purpose of regionalizing racial character" (1992, p. 231). So one finds the geographical features of travel literature, illustrated magazines, and classroom materials encouraging an identification of the other with a certain landscape, designated as that place which, in its distance, is other than here. In this scheme, the concept of culture is used to characterize a people's response to their environment, with this category taking its place alongside race and nation in the global mapping of identity. Culture amounts to a collection of practices and artifacts that, in defining difference, effectively distinguishes one group of people from another (C. Herbert, 1991, p. 150). If "race" was the gift of biology and the natural sciences to imperialism, and "nationhood" and "nationality" were that of politics, then geography could be said to have made as its contribution "culture" and its anthropological study. No less than race and nation, culture is, as Christopher Herbert identifies it in his history of the idea, "a product and instrument of the modern imagination" (p. 204).

The study of culture contributed to a geographical determinism that was thought to hold for the non-Western world in its own version of social Darwinism (Peet, 1985). After all, Westerners had proved their global transcendence and adaptability, as well as their ability to apply their cultural solutions to the "particular places" that geographers favor, from the South Pole to the source of the Nile. It was as if the very knowledge of geography, of the two-dimensional projection of the world against which other people could be located, was enough to free Westerners, enough to allow them to move across those determinations and into history. Geography transformed the world into a readily navigable space for the educated imagination of the West in a theme I will now pursue through the pervasive educational influence of *National Geographic* magazine and a brace of contemporary Canadian geography textbooks.

National Geographic

Of all the subjects studied in school, geography alone has been supported to this day by an educational artifact that has thrived since its origins in the age of empire. Whether in the home, school, or dentist's waiting room, it has no educational match as it goes about creating an engaging spectacle out of anthropological differences that were first articulated within imperialism's making over of the world. *National Geographic,* which in 1989 had a worldwide circulation of 10.6 million and subscription levels in the United States surpassed only by *TV Guide* and *Reader's Digest,* is published by the National Geographic Society, founded in 1888. The society formed during the brief era of American imperial annexation, amid the rise of anthropology as an academic pursuit and the age of the international expositions.

There is no better analysis of the magazine than Catherine Lutz and Jane Collins's study (1993) which describes how the National Geographic Society has since grown into the largest scientific-educational organization in the world.[8] The magazine's dramatic photo-realist take on the world was initially to assert, as they put it, "America's vision of its newly ascendant place in the world" (p. 19). For them, as for many of us, the magazine continues to bring the whole of the world within easy and engaging reach, inside school and outside: "Our parents and grade-school teachers led us to *National Geographic* magazine, and there we found immense pleasure in the views of fantastically decorated forest people, vivid tropical fishes, and the expansive sense of a

---

[8] The society's educational force is testified to by a North Carolina State Department of Public Instruction official who has described the society's well-funded campaign to have its materials adopted as part of the geography curriculum—although this is, of course, no more than a major publisher of educational materials could be expected to do these days (Kramer and Reid, 1994, pp. 11–12).

world large, diverse and somehow knowable" (p. xi). It was a packaging of the educational fantasy of colonialism, or, as Howard Abramson recalls of the *National Geographic* experience, it was "always perceived as a nice homespun organization that publishes that distinctive yellow-bordered magazine that features . . . those trademark harmless photographs of all those memorable brown breasts" (1987, p. 5). Harmless to whom? one wants to ask, as the struggle against colonialism was going on throughout the world served up in those memorable pages.

The magazine was intent on introducing students of geography to the childlike innocence and exoticism of natives, who were without resistance or knowing in the face of this inquiry into their lives. These lives were then made available to our wide-eyed sense of mastery, as we stood before the mystery of a difference that was sexual, racial, cultural. It was a white man's world, we could see that. However, in her review of the prewar life of the magazine, Tamar Rothenberg cites a 1943 *New Yorker* profile of the magazine's policies, which, given that it was "read by a great many ladies," included running "occasional photographs, or paintings, of handsome young men . . . in next to nothing" (1994, p. 172). The magazine's treatment of native populations, which Rothenberg cites from those years, is dismal, with descriptions on the order of "innocent nudity decked with barbaric ornaments"—this in spite of a commitment to print "only what is of a kindly nature" (p. 165).[9] The sexual regard for native women was rendered inoffensive by playing on the assumption that they were "a breed apart" from white women, as Rothenberg puts it (p. 172). Once you were emperors, the magazine suggested to its readers, and such was your domain. The world portrayed in *National Geographic* reflects a nostalgia for nature and empire.[10]

Determined not to cease from exploration, *National Geographic* continues to circle the globe in an inexhaustible educational project. It offers a serialized global library, as Lutz and Collins note, designed for a permanent place on the bookshelves. Still, the magazine has changed with the times. With the end of colonialism, for example, the number of Westerners photographed in non-Western settings fell off dramatically (1993, p. 40). Lutz and Collins also

---

[9] The principles governing *National Geographic,* first set out in 1915, could well be mistaken for those of the typical geography curriculum: "(1) Nothing must be printed which is not strictly according to fact. . . . (2) Abundance of beautiful, instructive and artistic illustrations, (3) Everything printed in the Magazine must have permanent value. . . . (5) Nothing of a partisan or controversial nature is printed, (6) Only what is of a kindly nature is printed about any country or people" (cited by Lutz and Collins, 1993, pp. 26–27).
[10] Rothenberg cites Susan Sontag's *On Photography:* "When we are afraid, we shoot. But when we are nostalgic, we take pictures" (Sontag, 1971, p. 15).

point to the disappearance of pictures portraying porters carrying Westerners and their equipment, whether across raging rivers or up mountainsides, which has the effect of obscuring "the photographic encounter" that continues to define the relationship between distinct worlds (p. 40).[11] This take on geography is about preserving the radical empiricism of the photograph as the omnipresent and invisible eye on the world. It suggests a line that can be imagined running from the Arawak native exhibited by Columbus at the Spanish court to the photograph of the Kurdish soldier on the *National Geographic* cover five hundred years later. Can students see how it is their privilege to witness the primitive nobility of the native, as it once had been for Queen Isabella, while understanding that this experience is intended to constitute an educational advantage against the loss of a primal association with a world already gone? Once, the world was called upon to give up its truths to the imperial gaze; now we have to consider how that has changed and how it has remained the same.

National Geographic's mix of aesthetic presentation and scientific objectification only obscures how photographs, no less than other forms of representation, focus, distance, caption, and compress the lives of others for, in this instance, educational ends. The magazine is about the convenient engagement and self-improvement of the viewer, and it plays on a fascination with human difference that has long become the educational masking of the non-Westerner as an object of fascination and desire. The Kurdish soldier does walk away from the camera, whereas the Arawak could not leave the Spanish court. Yet the photograph continues to represent the transformation of the anonymous man into a symbol, even as it seems so literally true-to-life, of what the reader is not and yet commands by virtue of this educational experience. The one portrayed, however, is neither expected nor invited to participate in the knowing afforded the viewer. In a description of photography that seems especially applicable to this magazine, Susan Sontag speaks of how "to photograph people is to violate them, by seeing them as they never see themselves, by having a knowledge of them they can never have; it turns people into objects that can be symbolically possessed" (1971, p. 14).

In light of their study of the magazine, Lutz and Collins recommend that

---

[11] In their study of *National Geographic,* Lutz and Collins point out the relevant politics of inclusion and representation: "In the heyday of colonial culture, the inclusion of Westerners in the photographs of the colonized served to establish a sort of authenticity—to demonstrate that the photographer was 'really there.' By the late 1960s, however, the colonial and postcolonial relationships that permitted *National Geographic* to photograph the world had become a site of struggle, and reference to them was studiously avoided" (1993, p. 182).

teachers "search for ways of teaching about the third world that [do] not objectify and [are] not paternalistic but [foster] both a sense of how lives around the globe are interconnected and a capacity for empathetic understanding" (1993, p. 3). The struggle to find a nonpaternalistic or objectified regard for the "third world," whether in textbooks, news media, development agencies, or tourist promotions, speaks to the legacy of imperialism, which once made it so easy to teach the whole of the world to students. It speaks to an exclusion of voices and representations from a place that is seen as the world beyond the West. The educational motif here becomes that what has been learned has to be learned again.

As with the history textbooks discussed in chapter 5, I am not about to propose the abandonment of a magazine to which so many happily subscribe. Rather, I think the educationally wise path is to focus on the truth of the magazine's claim that "no other publication evokes as much trust, integrity, or believability" (*National Geographic*, 1994, p. 29). We have to ask ourselves what the magazine appeals to within us, as daring adventurer-photographers (and their editors) perpetuate a masculine colonizing of the other in the name of "trust, integrity, or believability." We have to watch ourselves. We have to attend to our own responses, to the fascination, wonder, desire, and pathos that arise from the magazine's framing of the world. Such critical self-reflection marks the path being pursued by those intent on resetting anthropology in light of its own postcolonial crisis (Thomas, 1991; Carrier, 1992). Lutz and Collins's sampling of what the magazine's readers have made of its treatment of cultural difference could well inspire students of the subject to conduct their own inquiries into what Mary Louise Pratt (1992) has identified as the monarch-of-all-I-survey perspective that has long been the hallmark of European and American travel writing and corresponding geographic sensibility. They might begin, as I will now, with how this attitude washes through the schoolbooks that define geography for the young today.

Contemporary Lessons on Canadian Geography

The two textbooks that I will examine are currently used at the middle school level in Canadian schools to teach geography within the interdisciplinary subject area of social studies. One text has a national and the other a global focus, and both seek to provide a fair treatment of indigenous peoples and multicultural issues, to name two postcolonial topics of some importance to my work. To demonstrate the distance that still needs to be traveled in moving beyond what I have identified as geography's imperial legacy, I take up two elements common to such books, namely, a discussion of a cultural artifact and an illustration of a cultural event.

In the first of the books, *Exploring Our Country* (1983), Daniel Wood tells the story of a girl named Morgan McCloskey who climbs through her television to visit six Canadian communities, focusing on their particular contributions to the nation. Through a familiar geographical genre, the students reading this elementary school text are asked to assume the pose of an interested tourist faced, in this case, with such chapter-title questions as "How Does Weyburn Help Feed Canadians?" and "What Do Cape Dorset's Artists Teach Canadians?" To stay with the Cape Dorset chapter, Wood places the prints of Inuit artists on a level with the wheat and oil of other communities. The economics of producing and selling the artwork are realistically presented, from the artists' co-op to the city gallery. Art is admirably presented as part of the economic profile of the nation, a vital cultural resource. Wood also demonstrates respect for the Inuktitut language spoken in Cape Dorset by making it clear that the discussions with the artist Kenojuak have been translated into English. These are small pedagogical points that acknowledge what has otherwise gone missing from the way this land has been taught to the young.

However, the legacy of imperialism remains a part of the story in the book's treatment of Kenojuak Ashevak's beautiful prints. Wood has Kenojuak tell the book's imaginary tourist that she is "drawing pictures of spirits" (1983, p. 100). Later she explains how the artists of Cape Dorset have "show[n] life in the Arctic" and are "about the old times showing how the Inuit hunted and fished." The book adds that "some of Kenojuak's drawings [are] about her daydreams" (p. 102). Here is the power of primitive art to mobilize spirits and daydreams, with its ability to capture, with "unspoiled" freshness, the profound "spiritual" quality that has long represented native art for the colonizer. However, as I found in Jean Blodgett's book on the artist, Kenojuak actually prefers to distance herself from assumptions that she must represent primitive spiritualism: "I stay away from trying to use the old-fashioned stories from the oral tradition," she says pointedly. "And rather what I do is try to make things which satisfy my eye, which satisfy my sense of form and color" (cited in Blodgett, 1983, pp. 34, 37). She speaks, first of all, as an artist concerned with individual expression, appealing to the eye rather than the spirit world. Although Woods names her an artist, he cannot resist, in the spirit of geography I have discussed, locating her art within the ascribed shape of the land and culture of the native. Thus, she is made to tell students that her art is "pictures of spirits," and the very young begin to absorb the fundamental structures of the imperial imagination.

Wood also glosses over the formation of this art. In Blodgett's book, Kenojuak describes being introduced to Western printmaking techniques by

James Houston in the late 1950s: "At the time, I was frightened, or nervous, about the idea of trying to express myself in that way but I ended up doing it because he requested, or in our culture, he formally requested, that I try this" (1983, p. 33). Kenojuak is describing a special reenactment of the colonial encounter, still lopsided in the direction of the cultural exchange, yet it was an undeniably productive exchange much appreciated by both Houston and Kenojuak. "I would have to say," Kenojuak adds, "that I consider myself to have been helped on the road, to have been placed on that road, by James Houston" (p. 33). This theme of placement, of being set on the road to successful participation in Western economies, with its echoes of reserves and schools, has worked out well in this case, but that is no reason not to draw lessons on imperialism from "what Cape Dorset's artists teach Canadians," to return to the chapter's title.

Exploring Our Country does nothing to interrupt what Loretta Todd identifies, in a collection of art and essays presenting native perspectives on the Columbus quincentenary, as the constant application of the "discovery" theme to First Nation peoples: "Everything about us—from our languages to our philosophies, from our stories to our dances—has become material in a quest for further discovery, for new treasures" (1992, p. 71). These colonial themes haunt the educational system, from school to museum: "We are caught in the grasp of neocolonialism, in the gaze of the connoisseur or consumer, forever trapped in a process that divides and conquers" (p. 75). This legacy of discovery continues, as well, to pervade the lives and textbooks of the young. It can be countered only by turning the gaze back onto itself, by considering with students how our educational materials are so ready to attribute, for example, primitivism to native art, when sometimes a picture of an owl is an exercise in design.

The neocolonial gaze identified by Todd is also encouraged in *Communities around Our World* (1984), by Donald Massey. This textbook shares both the possessive pronoun and the tourist motif of Wood's book, expanded to take in the world: "The best way to learn about any community is to make a visit to it" (p. 8).[12] The text presents a series of colorful snapshots of eight communities from around "our world," focusing on one family in each. The focus on family and community in itself represents for me a positive step away from placing the focus on national and cultural divisions, although

---

[12] Leslie Roman (1992) describes how this pattern of playing "intellectual tourist" and "voyeur" marks the social sciences in general and ethnography in particular, suggesting the continuity of this stance as not simply a problem of curriculum materials prepared for children.

these categories are certainly present. Students work with charts, stories, and pictures designed to introduce them to the combined traditions of travel writing, anthropology, geography, and economics in the study of the other. In their "travels," they come, through the vibrant photography, to appreciate the breadth of difference signified by race, religion, poverty, and primitivism. Although this educational technique appears to dissolve distance and to instill a sense of "being there," the result makes the differences more strongly felt, in what was once called living color.

This neocolonial gaze, which otherwise remains invisible, on occasion creeps into the book's picturing of the world, if one looks closely. The "visit" to what was once Zaire in *Communities around Our World* features a photograph of a circle of men sitting in an open-walled hut, the real focus of the picture being on a small collection of beans, corn, and vegetables at the center of the hut, with a caption stating that "these people are meeting to give thanks for a good harvest" (1984, p. 93). Sound familiar? In this case, one of the men is not attending to the harvest at the center of the hut and the picture, but is looking intently at the camera. His face reflects a sense of the photographer's intrusiveness and clearly falls short of expressing anything like, "Thanks for stopping by with the camera." By returning the gaze, this anonymous farmer serves as a reminder of how such pictures are carefully staged ("Please don't look at the camera"), perhaps, like the study of geography as a whole, to obscure the relationship between knower and known.

If students were to pause over this aspect of the photograph and look into those questioning eyes before turning the page, they might see how their geographical gaze into the lives of others is neither weightless nor invisible. To catch sight of how the camera is reproducing not just an image but the imperial imagination in action as it captures the "colorfulness" of the other, might further break down the colonial hold on education. The sense of difference that infuses these textbooks has its roots in how certain communities were studied with an eye to colonial administration and an understanding of noble and deteriorated savagery, leaving a legacy with which people are still struggling all over the globe. As much as this and many similar social studies textbooks eschew stereotypes and seek a balance in their representation of gender and race, they do not begin to present students with an understanding of how these differences came to be prejudicially structured in the making of "our world."[13]

---

[13] To give a brief instance of the difference in tone and focus that is sometimes achieved by geography texts for older grades, *Towards Tomorrow: Canada in a Changing World*, which is used in grade 11, treats the use of "appropriate technologies" in developing countries by

It is certainly fair to ask whether children in middle school can be expected to find these disruptive moments in the photographs and exercises with which they work. Do I imagine them operating as little Roland Bartheses, cleverly uncovering the common mythologies that underwrite their textbooks as Barthes has done with modern society, noting how, for example, "nature [rather than the photographer] seems spontaneously to produce the scene represented" (1971, p. 45)? If that seems unlikely, consider how perfectly reasonable it is to assume that the young in our schools will understand that the non-Western peoples depicted in their geography textbooks are less than they are, less fortunate, less civilized, less educated, even as these people are said to form part of the students' world.

Thus, I would argue for giving some thought to how this sense of difference and otherness has come to be historically produced within imperial regimes, regulated as a body of knowledge, and taught to succeeding generations of students under the rubric of geography. There is little in the students' geography lessons that looks forward to a community among knower and known, little that looks back to how aspects of this difference, such as discrepancies in resources, are not geographical in nature, as implied, but the product of a global system of economic inequality initially established by imperialism. In trying to make sense of the material and cultural differences they are confronted with in this and other textbooks, students might well slip into a form of social Darwinism that blames or pities those represented in their apparent failure to evolve. Thus, there needs to be a way to interrupt in class the neocolonial gaze that otherwise defines the picturing of the other. There also needs to be a way of recognizing that students in the class who possess roots in one of these seemingly unconnected communities around our world are living both within and outside the world depicted for, and the world assumed of, the student.

For these reasons, a critical space needs to be created in the classroom that allows students to stand apart from this representation of the world, to take issue with its inevitable and its readily avoidable limitations in peering into and rendering sensible the lives of others. As educators and educated, we need to think about how we can arrive at an account for these lessons that make sense of race, gender, nation, culture, yet leave us unable to comprehend recent events such as the massive refugee camps in the former Zaire.

---

pointing to the international agency the Intermediate Technology Development Group and its work with women in Sri Lanka in assembling hand pumps, concluding that, "overall, technology in less developed countries, with their large populations, should put improving production ahead of savings on labor costs" (Dunlop, 1987, p. 183).

Calling into question the textbooks and our own educations may seem a slight beginning in thinking about how we are here and the Zairean camps are there. It will not account for the camps, nor our responsibilities toward the people in them, but it can add to our education in how geography has mapped and divided the world.

This brief sampling of Canadian geography textbooks should make apparent that the privilege of studying lives-so-removed-from-our-own can turn students, from the earliest age, into educational tourists. My hope is to augment the strengths of this education in geography with lessons on how we tend, through such books, to picture the larger world as an exotic wonder within easy reach of unobjectionable—if not unobservable—study, travel, and economic advantage.

Although I favor an intellectual recycling of schools' existing texts, there are also alternative perspectives available for geography or social studies classes. To take one promising example, the Victoria International Development Education Association has produced *Colonialism in Asia: A Critical Look* (1993), the most recent in a series that includes comparable booklets on Africa and the Americas. Our guides to this booklet by Susan Gage are two cartoon characters: a blond teenage boy, who begins by declaring Columbus "awesome," and a teenage girl who asks him, "Let's look at the world though my eyes. Asian eyes. OK?" (p. 1). She meets his resistance ("Does that mean," he asks, "that you have to do a smear job on Europeans?") with an illustrated and lively journey through colonialism, from definitions through early contacts to case studies of India, Vietnam, and the Philippines:

> HIM: It sounds like the invasion of the killer tomatoes! Europeanism creeping over the earth?
> HER: Well, it was a bit. European powers were always trying to protect the border of their colonies, and that was an excuse to keep spreading outwards. By the 20th century, almost all of the world was either colonizer or colonized [supported by chart showing 84.5 percent of world land surface in 1914 covered by Europe and its possessions].
> HIM: But why are we talking about this when it's over? What difference does it make now?
> HER: Well to understand how yesterday's colonialism is related to the world today, we're going to have to have a good look at the building blocks of colonialism [later identified as "grabbing the cash," "raw deal," "holding up hierarchies," and "West is best"]. (p. 7)

The study of the Philippines, for example, uses cartoons, quotations, brief descriptions, statistics, and provocative questions ("Why do you think priests would become involved in armed revolution?") to examine the struggle for independence, first against the Spanish in the nineteenth century and then against the Americans, before finally arriving at the economic legacy of colonialism found in the free trade zones, which provide havens of cheap, largely female, labor typically union-free for Western manufacturers (1993, pp. 21–30). These teaching materials, with their unapologetic and unequivocal critique of colonialism and capitalism, also call for their own critical reading. Nevertheless, this integration of geography and history, with its pointed lessons on the imperial legacy, offers a healthy contrast with traditional textbook treatments for understanding how schools have tended to shape knowledge in relation to other advocacy groups.

In considering what can be done, Edward Said has opined in his study of orientalism that "systems of representation . . . carry with them the kind of authority which, to my mind, has been repressive because it doesn't permit room for interventions on the part of those represented" (1990, p. 95). Given that obviously there is no escaping representation, Said wonders whether such acts can at least be more "participatory and collaborative, noncoercive" (p. 95).[14] What would moving beyond the tyranny of representation look like in the geography class? It could mean, say, that a student undertaking a typical geography class project in Vancouver on "Chinatown" would consult with members of the community on their interpretation of its special features. Yet the project would still be in danger of constituting the educational act as a voyeuristic gaze on the exotic-in-Canada, with the Chinese in Canada being "transformed into a 'witness' of otherness," in Stephen Greenblatt's terms (1991, p. 112).[15]

What more will it take, we might then ask, to break the colonizing hold on the study of the other, especially when that other is, in some sense, oneself?

---

[14] This is also Said's thesis in *Orientalism:* "Political imperialism governs an entire field of study, imagination, and scholarly institutions—in such a way as to make its avoidance an intellectual and historical impossibility" (1978, p. 14). He develops this idea into a critique of representation: "The *act* of representing (and hence reducing) others, almost always represents violence of some sort to the *subject* of the representation, as well as a contrast between the violence of the act of representing something and the calm exterior of the representation itself, the *image*—verbal, visual, or otherwise—of the subject. . . . The action or process of representing implies control, it implies accumulation, it implies confinement, it implies a certain kind of estrangement or disorientation on the part of the one representing" (1990, p. 94). See Lutz and Collins for a fascinating topography of the gaze in *National Geographic* (1993, pp. 187–216).

[15] Kay Anderson writes in her study of Vancouver's Chinatown that "Chinatown points up once again the more general principle that a negotiated social process lies behind the apparently neutral-looking taxonomies of census districts and world regions. More importantly, perhaps, the manipulation of racial ideology by institutions is additional testimony to the fact that a set of power relations may underpin and keep alive spatial categories" (1991, p. 250).

Just to pose the question could turn a class's attention from documenting differences to comparing how a community has sought to represent itself and how it has been represented by others. Students could collaborate and cowrite with a member of the community materials for use in the life of the community, all of which could advance the degree of cultural exchange and understanding between community and school. Students could work with members of the community on compiling, organizing, preserving, and presenting different senses of the community's experiences. Such a project could lead to an understanding of how communities have been mapped, as well as to a remapping of the communities and their positions in the world. To return to this chapter's opening motif, the map of the world that we carry within ourselves would do well to include the boundaries of its own cartography. It has to allow for the myriad overlays placed across the surface of the globe during the last few centuries. If there is a geographic determinism of the world, it lies in how we have learned to imagine distance and difference. There is no true geography of this world underlying the historical overlays. We have to understand how such global maps are nothing less and nothing more than "our world."

Folio from Hartmann Schedel, Liber Chronicarum *(Nuremberg, 1493),*
which provided a narrative of human history for medieval readers.
Courtesy Rare Books Division, New York Public Library,
Astor, Lenox, and Tilden Foundations.

SEVEN

SCIENCE AND THE ORIGIN OF RACE

"I have not found the human monsters which many people expected,"
Columbus wrote of arriving on what he thought were the far shores of
Asia. "On the contrary, the whole population is very well made"
(1969, p. 121). Columbus would have expected to find human monsters because monstrous races were said in current and reliable reference books of the
day to occupy the outlying regions of the world. Even as Columbus was making his way across the Atlantic, Hartmann Schedel was completing his great
encyclopedic work, *The Nuremberg Chronicle,* which included an illustrated
guide to just such monstrous races. He lifted his material from Pliny's *Naturalis historia,* which in turn had borrowed much from the Greeks (Grafton,
1992, p. 36). The Romans and Greeks had identified monstrous races in
Ethiopia and other parts of Africa, setting them apart from the true Africans,
who were depicted in classical art and literature as praiseworthy for their
beauty, wisdom, and fierceness, and for their religious beliefs.[1] Throughout
the medieval period, Ethiopia was portrayed in legend as paradise and the
home of *le bon éthiopien,* most notably the priest-king Prester John (Baudet,
1965, pp. 14–20). The monstrous races were something else altogether.

In Schedel's *Chronicle,* the monsters include a man with a dog's head, another with a single eye, another with no head, and yet another with his feet
pointing backward, and on it goes through fourteen variations. The accompanying woodcuts, from dog head to elephant ears, all appear to be variations

---

[1] Snowden concludes that for the classical world, "in science, philosophy, and religion,
color was not the basis of widely accepted differences concerning the inferiority of blacks"
(1983, p. 108).

on the same (Caucasian) man. Race, in this sense, was a fantasy of deformity, allowing one to peer across the boundary of the human. Meanwhile, the "very well made" Arawak were being depicted by such accomplished engravers as Theodore de Bry in the manner of well-made classical Greek statuary. Natives were distinguished from Europeans in these illustrations not by physical characteristics but by their nakedness (which only further exposed the similarities), adorned with perhaps a feather headdress and, more likely, holding a human limb, indicating cannibalism. The physical differences between native and colonizer that were initially ill defined were not to be left at that. Enter the science of race.

Race became natural history's great contribution to naming human difference. In the eighteenth century, Linnaeus had used race to divide up humanity in his grand taxonomy. He began, in the manner of Pliny, with two: *Homo sapiens* and *Homo monstrous.* But by the tenth edition of his *Systema Naturae,* published in 1758, the number of races had grown to six, still including the monstrous (such as dwarfs and giants) in a mix of humans and primates.[2] Not all Europeans were prepared at the time to accept this radical division of humankind. In 1791, Johann Gottfried von Herder wrote that he hoped "the distinctions between the human species that have been made from a laudable zeal for discriminating science, [were] not carried beyond due bounds," for "There are neither four or five races," as *"All mankind are only one"* (1968, pp. 5, 7; Herder's emphasis). But Herder's caution was the exception, and his work on national identity and genius ("Every nation is one people") was to become its own version of the racialized nation (p. 7). The difference that race made was subject to an increasingly elaborate mixture of scientific and moral distinctions.

Although the science of race persists to this day, it had been largely discredited by the latter half of this century. Still, I don't think this misguided episode should be swept away as an embarrassing interlude in science's historic pageant. In earlier chapters, I surveyed the wide range of science's enthusiastic and productive engagement with imperialism, and at this point I want to focus on how the scientific construction of race offered the most monstrous of imperialism's lessons, down to the era of my own education, with some carryover into contemporary schools. What I found in looking at

---

[2] Linnaeus divided *Homo sapiens* into six subspecies that included not only *americanus* (red choleric, erect), *europaeus* (white, ruddy, muscular), *asiaticus* (yellow, melancholic, inflexible), and *afer* (black, phlegmatic, indulgent), but also *ferus* (four footed, mute, hairy) and *monstrous* (further subdivided to include deviant forms from several regions), and *troglodytes* (including "Orang Utan"). These summaries are taken directly from Banton (1987, p. 4).

today's high school biology classes is that the presence of the scientific construction of race is both obscured and present. It is *obscured* by a curriculum that fails to acknowledge science's part in making race a fixed point of human difference, even as the weight of those distinctions to which science once lent such credence are still *present* in the lives of students.

A Science of Race

The first thing to note about this science was how replete with hope it was as scientists during the nineteenth century thought that in it lay the secret of human nature. "In fact what makes the history of race science so interesting," Nancy Stepan writes in her history of the topic, "is that so many of the outstanding scientists of the past believed that biological races were the key to the most pressing problems of the day—the future of the Americas, the fate of the Europeans in the tropics, the extinction of peoples, the role of Britain in Europe" (1982, p. xvi). Stepan makes equally clear that it was with the ending of slavery in the British Empire, through the Emancipation Act of 1833, that the scientific study of race began in earnest, shedding what had earlier appeared to be a humanistic and egalitarian disposition, in favor of dissecting human racial difference. It might well seem that, with abolitionists finally winning the day on the fundamental human rights issue of slavery, it now fell to the natural sciences to reestablish the boundaries that demarcated the unequivocal superiority of the European races. One might then wonder if the science of race managed to reduce, in effect, the moral cost of imperial expansion and exploitation in the same way that Daniel Headrick (1981) has argued that nineteenth-century technologies—from quinine to breechloader rifle—made global domination irresistibly affordable for imperial powers.

It would be misleading, however, to suggest that nineteenth-century scientists took the leading hand in making race one of imperialism's organizing principles. Race was thoroughly an interdisciplinary enterprise. Among its major statements stands Gobineau's notorious *The Inequality of the Human Races,* published from 1853 to 1855, which is said to have inspired Hitler's thinking on racial purity. Gobineau drew on a wide range of philosophers, historians, and anthropologists to fill out scientific "findings," such as those of American craniologist S. G. Morton correlating brain size and cultural development, or those of the French anatomist Georges Cuvier measuring differences among white, yellow, and black races (Young, 1995, pp. 101, 103). In the book's dedication, Gobineau positioned race at the forefront of history: "I was gradually penetrated by the conviction that the racial question overshadows all other problems of history, that it holds the key to them all, and that the inequality of races from whose fusion a people is formed is enough to explain the whole course of its destiny" (1967, p. xiv). It was to prove a self-fulfilling prophecy of the highest order, although there is little original in Gobineau's claims of the superiority of European civilization—("everything great, noble, and fruitful in works of man on this earth, in science, art, and civilization" [p. xv]) and in his corresponding denigration of the savage and oriental races, what distinguishes Gobineau's argument, if we are to appreciate the force behind race science, is the alarm it raises about the threat of race pollution: "Civilization . . . will certainly die on the day when the primordial race-unit is . . . broken up and swamped by the influx of foreign elements" (p. 25). Here, then, was the need for the boundaries of race to be clearly demarcated, the differences firmly established, and the risks of border-crossing made perfectly clear, especially for those embarking on this global venture.[3]

Colonialism, as Robert Young describes it in his book on imperialism and hybridity, "produced its own darkest fantasy—the unlimited and ungovernable fertility of 'unnatural' unions" (1995, p. 98).[4] A vigilance was called for in managing Europe's racial superiority against what was otherwise an empire of desire. This intersection of race, sexuality, and science became a meeting place of home and empire. As Ann Laura Stoler puts it in her recent book on race and the education of desire, "It is imperial-wide discourses [of the nineteenth century] that linked children's health programs to racial survival, tied increased campaigns of domestic hygiene to colonial expansion, made child-rearing an imperial and class duty, and cast white women as the bearers of a more racist imperial order and the custodians of their desire-driven, immoral men" (1995, p. 35).

Although Gobineau held that an initial fusion of the races was necessary to civilization (with an Aryan infusion central to all past great civilizations), he warned against the obvious threat of the white drive for civilization being overrun and decimated by a racial "adulteration" of the blood. In the face of such a threat, race science sought to quantify and qualify the distinctions that would warrant imperial exploitation while strengthening the boundaries of

---

[3] Paul Gilroy also cautions that "science did not monopolize either the image of the black or the emergent concept of biologically based racial difference" (1993, p. 8). He points out that science was part of a far broader racial determination of the true, the good, and the beautiful across the full range of Western intellectual interests, which in itself points out science's willing collaboration with the other disciplines in setting what is, for Gilroy, the cornerstone of modernity.

[4] Young cites Thomas Hope's *An Essay on the Origin and Prospects of Man* from 1831, which, after much disparaging treatment of Africans, turns to the "Nubian nations," concluding, "Their complexion indeed still is dark, but it is the glossy black of marble or of jet, conveying to the touch sensations more voluptuous even than those of the most resplendent white" (cited by Young, 1995, p. 97).

differences: "It is only with modern times," the early anthropologist Edward B. Tylor claimed in 1891, "that the distinctions among races have been worked out by scientific methods" (1930, p. 1:2). The scientists who responded to the call proved full of theories to set the races further apart, not least among them the proposition that the races constituted distinct species, with the requisite evidence found in the supposed infertility of the offspring of interracial marriages. The idea gained such ground that Charles Darwin felt compelled to critique it in *The Descent of Man,* published in 1871. Although Darwin allowed that fertility between the races was no guarantee of a common species, especially among domesticated types, he pointed to three factors that suggested a single species among humankind: the easy association of the human races in places such as Brazil; the inconstancy of so-called race characteristics within a given race; and, ultimately, the way in which the races "graduate into each other, independently in many cases, as far as we can judge, of their having intercrossed" (n.d., pp. 533–36). This intersection had been the source of much disagreement among the learned about the number of races, which ranged in Darwin's day from Kant's quartet to Burke's sixty-three races. What is fascinating about Darwin's case that humankind constituted, from its origins, a single species, is just how far it goes in undermining the reliability of race as a stable scientific category.

Still, Darwin was prepared to build upon the idea of "savage races" for whom "humanity is an unknown virtue," even as he set Europeans apart, in a racial sense, from the Jews living in their midst (n.d., pp. 487, 551).[5] It is but a small step from this sense of racial distinctiveness, Stepan notes, to a casting of the races along an evolutionary scale (1982, p. 55), covering what Darwin's archdefender Thomas Huxley identified as "the gulf between civilized man and the brutes" (cited by Shipman, 1994, p. 65). Although reluctant, in his retiring way, to become involved in the social disputes surrounding his theory, Darwin did eventually come to the support of his cousin Francis Galton, who was advocating eugenics as evolution's applied science of human improvement. Thus, it might seem that, if anything, biologist Ruth Hubbard understates the situation with her warning that "when we use science to investigate subjects like race and sex, which are suffused with cultural meanings and embedded in power relationships, we need to be wary of scientific descriptions and interpretations that support, or even enhance, the prevailing political realities" (1995, p. 185).

---

[5] The subtitle of *Origin of Species* speaks of "favored races"—*By Means of Natural Selection or the Preservation of Favored Races in the Struggle for Life*—yet in *The Descent of Man,* an earlier work, race is made equivalent to "hereditary varieties" among plants and animals (Darwin, n.d., p. 20).

To claim that the biological and anthropological study of race was infused with the popular prejudices of the day hardly seems extraordinary. This is only to concede the humanity of the scientists involved. Yet race science is commonly treated today as an aberration or mutant science. In her history of race science, Pat Shipman, for example, holds that eugenics, especially as implemented in Nazi Germany, represents "the dreadful maiming of evolutionary theory" (1994, p. 140). Whether it was a maiming of theory or the tendency of science to find "truths" that serve the hopes and sins of the age is, for me, just the sort of question that students of science need to ponder in turning back to this history.[6] Do theories have their proper applications, their inherently moral consequences, beyond which scientists are absolved from responsibility for the misuse and maiming of their work? The question has certainly plagued the atomic scientists of this century. In the case of evolution, one needs to appreciate how well this most robust of scientific ideas, for all the consternation it caused among the church's faithful, suited the intellectual habits and needs of Victorian England during the age of empire. Evolution made natural history the perfect complement of imperialism. If Darwin hadn't "discovered" it, other Englishmen were ready to make it up. Thomas Malthus had spoken of naturally occurring population checks (which had inspired Darwin), and Herbert Spencer used the phrase "survival of the fittest," whereas Protestantism more generally regarded worldly success as reflecting heavenly selection (Shipman, 1994).

This is only to say that social Darwinism need not be seen as science slipping off course and being dragged willy-nilly into the political realm. The scientific invention of race is thoroughly one with a European zeitgeist consumed with mastery of nature on a global scale.[7] At one level, this is simply to historicize science, which is important enough for each generation learning the ways of this respected enterprise. But in reviewing both well-known and lesser-realized instances in the scientific construction of race, I am arguing that something more important is at stake. I want to show how science education has tended to step around its contribution to the construct of race, leaving the young to find themselves at the mercy of this powerful concept with little idea of how it has taken on such importance. They are left to imag-

[6] It is also worth considering Shipman's warning that "antiracist" scientists are torn between their moral and scientific beliefs: "In the face of the patent evil of Nazi Darwinism, some scientists raced to the other extreme" (1994, p. 174). On the response of Jewish race scientists, who, without calling the category into question, fought race science with race science in the decades leading up to the Nazi regime, see Efron (1995).
[7] As Donna Haraway has put it, in her critique of the discovery and invention themes in science, "We both learn about and create nature and ourselves" (1991, p. 42).

ine that race is, at some level, a natural division among humankind that has given rise, at times, to horrifying historical effects.

One aspect of this biological and social correspondence was to use gender in writing the racial equation. As Stepan spells it out, "In short, lower races represented the 'female' type and females the 'lower race' of gender" (1990, p. 40). Gender was often treated by scientists as directly analogous to the developmental scale of race, equally aimed at interpreting new social relations. Stepan describes not only the ascriptions of character (primitive, childlike) but also the elaborate anatomical measurements (brain weight, jaw protrusion) that were devoted to "linking lower races and women" in the anthropological, biological, and medical literature of the 1860s and 1870s (pp. 39–42). This, too, forms part of a scientific legacy obscured yet present in students' lives. Science served imperialism well through its scholarly and learned counsel on how to divide humankind in a fashion that corresponded well with European interests in global domination. Science proved itself a public utility, and it profited by the patronage it received in service to official policies and popular sentiments.

During the twentieth century, race science led to the deeply disturbing relationship that sprang up between American and German eugenics movements in the 1930s. Stefan Kühl (1994) argues that the Nazis took their "scientific" inspiration from American eugenicists, including those who were later to speak out against the rise of Nazi racial policies and practices. America offered the example of scientifically recommended sterilization programs, which had been legislated in sixteen states, the earliest in Indiana, dating back to 1907. However, American and British scientists were not long in recognizing that the boldness with which Nazi Germany pursued eugenic practices clearly threatened the good name of this science. This, combined with Germany's Aryanization policies, made it apparent to the international scientific community that something was amiss in the association of the fascist state and the scientific profession. In response, the British formed the Race and Culture Committee in 1934, which set out to pronounce on "the racial factor in cultural development," as the Royal Anthropological Institute described its mandate (Barkan, 1992, p. 286). As it turned out, the committee excluded Jewish anthropologists and biologists, questioning their ability to be objective in such matters, and, after a futile two years, failed to agree upon a scientific definition of race (p. 287).

In America during the same period, Franz Boas, throwing to the wind his Jewish lack of objectivity in such matters, became an outspoken critic of scientific racism. This respected social scientist undermined the standard anthropometric studies of race with figures that showed substantial intergenerational differences within so-called races. He proposed "culture" and "population" as scientific alternatives to the concept of "race," while fighting against statutes that prohibited interracial marriages on the grounds that assimilation ("dilution") would eliminate racism (Degler, 1991, pp. 61–84). But, of course, the American struggle against racism began at home, and Boas found his work dismissed as "propaganda" by the Harvard anthropologist Ernest Hooton, who accused him, in his correspondence with colleagues, of taking "a very extreme point of view on the subject of race, since he is a radical environmentalist and a Jew" (cited in Barkan, 1992, p. 317). A number of leading scientists during this period were prepared to dissociate themselves from the racial policies of Nazi Germany without embracing what was commonly understood as the other extreme—full racial equality.[8] It might well seem that it took the liberation of the concentration camps to make the ethical dimensions of this science fully and terribly transparent.

As indebted as I am to Elazar Barkan's history of race science during this unsettling era, I have to disagree with his conclusion that a complete break with "the scientific credo on race" took place after World War II with UNESCO's Statement on Race produced by a small group of concerned scientists, including Claude Lévi-Strauss and Ashley Montagu (1992, p. 341). In turning to this UNESCO document, one is tempted to think, if only matters were that simple. The initial statement in 1950 affirms that "scientists have reached general agreement in recognizing that mankind is one: that all men belong to the same species, *Homo sapiens*" (Montagu, 1972, p. 7). If that seems too obvious, it is worth pointing out that as late as the 1930s, the single-species position was still being challenged by the respected British anthropologist Reginald Gates (Barkan, 1992, p. 291). The scientific consensus aside, the fifth of fifteen paragraphs in the UNESCO statement tries to distinguish between the science of race and what most people mean by the term (Montagu, 1972, p. 8). From this protected scientific perspective, "most anthropologists agree" that humankind is divided among "Mongoloid," "Negroid," and "Caucasoid" (p. 9). Therefore, a nation is not to be mistaken for a race, nor do Catholics, Protestants, or Muslims form a race, and "people who are culturally Turkish or Chinese or the like [are not] thereby describable as races" (p. 8).

However well-intentioned the UNESCO statement is, I would propose that claiming that people are culturally Chinese but racially Mongoloid is not

---

[8] For evidence of a postwar effort to exonerate American science, with claims, for example, that "American scientists undertook to refute the Nazi nonsense and to insure that the public had some reasonable understanding of the concept of race," see Light (1968, p. vii).

helpful in coming to understand either the scientific basis or the importance of such distinctions. Even the statement's most valiant efforts to separate "the biological fact of race and the myth of 'race'" seems to me to betray the scientists' desire to clear their name by setting themselves apart from what was otherwise being made of race, as if scientists had not contributed to the making of the myth (Montagu, 1972, p. 10). It will not work to restrict the term to the use of qualified experts. This shows little understanding of science's influence and flies in the face of the record, which reveals that such experts were the instigators of many abuses of the race concept. Although these scientists wanted to curtail the damage done in the name of race, their failure to acknowledge that biological categories are the product of human interests let the felt reality of race stand as a way of understanding the world.[9]

Since the time of the UNESCO reports, no one has done more to make apparent the repeated fallacies in the scientific study of race than Stephen Jay Gould. In his searing *The Mismeasure of Man,* one of America's best-known biologists easily catches out a number of respectable scientists who sought, in Condorcet's words from the nineteenth century, to "make nature herself an accomplice in the crime of political inequality" (cited by Gould, 1981, p. 21). Gould exposes the bankrupt notions that underwrote such ill-fated scientific pursuits as craniometry during the nineteenth and into the twentieth century.[10] He also holds up to the light the faulty assumptions underlying the IQ testing movement of more recent times, bringing his attack on Charles Spearman's measure of general intelligence up to contemporary times with an epilogue on Arthur Jensen, whose substantial effort to refute charges of bias in mental testing came out in 1979 and who has continued to publish, amid

---

[9] UNESCO's "Athens Appeal," coming some decade later, concedes that "modern racism is rooted in certain nineteenth-century scientific theories, particularly those relating to the evolution of the species and the classification of human population groups," yet it also holds to science's innocence by warning that it "can in this way find itself being used" (UNESCO, 1983, p. 153). The appeal reiterates the positivist faith that "objectivity . . . will ensure that [scientists'] work and conclusions cannot be used as the basis for falsifications and interpretations detrimental to mankind" (p. 155).

[10] Although measurements of brain size in relation to race may seem a matter of the nineteenth century's failed science, it is sobering to find allusions to craniometry in a colonial textbook such as *The Malayan Story* (1956), by Philip Nazareth, which was used in Malaysian schools: "The Malays belong to the Mongolian race, which has straight, black hair and narrow eyes. . . . The modern Malay is a very different kind of man from the simple Jakun, though they once had the same ancestors and were of the same race. Men have measured the skulls of the Malays, and they say the Malay has a bigger skull than the other races of the peninsula. Thus he has a bigger brain and is more intelligent. This is because the Malay, as a dweller and wanderer in the Archipelago, has mixed with other people" (cited by Watson, 1993, p. 168).

much criticism, his research on IQ-score differences among African American and white students (Jensen, 1985). In Gould's estimation, Jensen is guilty of "two of the oldest cultural prejudices of Western thought: the ladder of progress as a model for organizing life, and the reification of some abstract quality [such as IQ] as a criterion for ranking" (1981, p. 318). Finally, Gould turns to the fallibility of race as a biological category. He points out that the "overall genetic differences among human races are astonishingly small," citing studies by the geneticist Richard Lewontin, which show that of "variations in seventeen gene codings for differences in blood . . . only 6.3 percent of the variation [can be] attributed to racial membership" (p. 323).[11] By the book's end, Gould has undermined the principal claims made about racial difference and drained the race category of its scientific utility. The rigor and clarity of his head-clearing deconstruction of the scientific work on race has the effect of redeeming science as a whole. Gould's critique, however, was not to signal the end of a mismeasured race science, as we shall see later in this chapter.

The Origin of Races, circa 1962

Whatever level of general agreement among anthropologists to fight racism was represented in the UNESCO statement after the Second World War, it appears, at this distance at least, to be an instance of wishful thinking, or so I discovered on coming across the work of Carleton S. Coon. In 1962, after serving as president of the American Association of Physical Anthropologists, this distinguished professor from the University of Pennsylvania published his magnum opus, its title, *The Origin of Races,* resonating with Darwin's epoch-making work of a century before. I want to dwell on Coon's controversial study because it is such a late and exemplary model of how science continued to "do" race in what must seem now to be a reckless manner. His work was part of the intellectual climate in which many of us were educated, even as it offers itself today as the perfect exercise for students of science who wish to understand how categories of race have been given their polished edges up to the most recent of times. Coon's work was certainly contested by the leading figures of the time as the last gasp of a passing science, yet it had its supporters and stood as an influential statement on the nature of race.[12]

---

[11] A good indication that such statistics remain a questionable source of reliable distinctions, on both sides of the debate, is Peterson and Goodall's point that chimps and humans have 99 percent of their genetic material in common (1993, p. 25).

[12] Shipman's dramatic reading of Coon's career and the controversy surrounding it is well worth attending to, although her theme that he "was a man betrayed by history" is worthy of debate in the sort of science class I envisage resulting from this study (1994, p. 173).

In the preface to *The Origin of Races,* Coon carefully establishes the currency of his own work, holding up his worldwide investigations funded by the National Science Foundation and the U.S. Air Force and supplemented by "every scrap of existing information about every single fossil-man bone and tooth in the world" (1962, p. viii). He then opens the book by placing his persistent theme of separate-but-not-equal-races into the requisite historical context: "At the dawn of history, which is another way of saying 'beginning with Herodotus,' literate people of the ancient world were well aware that mankind was divided into a number of clearly differentiated races" (p. 3). His manner is every bit the friendly armchair commentator as he speaks of some people "tucked away in odd corners of the earth" (p. 91) and others who are, in evolutionary terms, "the simplest to follow and the most archaic today" (p. 371). The text is accompanied by photographs of pygmies, aborigines, and old-world monkeys, many of which were taken during his own travels, scattered among the cranial diagrams and pages of anthropometric statistics. In the book, Coon lays out the progenitors of five human races that, according to his extraordinary thesis, are older than the species itself, having "evolved in parallel fashion" on different timescales through history (pp. viii–ix). A scientist could hardly do more to envision a sense of unbridgeable distance and difference between races, short of using the discredited "speciation" argument. Having divided humankind into thirty races in his earlier work, Coon was returning to a simpler, five-race scheme similar to the one Johann Blumenbach had proposed in 1775, which was based on skull measurements, a classification method that Blumenbach introduced into the incipient science of race (1865). Among the fundamental problems of this science is just how one counts the races and, thus, just how many races count.[13]

Although Coon acknowledges that the category of *race* lacks the clear bi-

---

[13] Coon's typology of thirty races is found in Coon, Garn, and Birdsell (1950). Theodosius Dobzhansky's *Mankind Evolving* cites this earlier count and adds four more races, arguing that "while race differences are objectively ascertainable facts, the number of races that we choose to recognize is a matter of convenience" (1962, p. 279). Dobzhansky's defense of racial classification includes "to make diversity intelligible and manageable" and "to facilitate communication among students of man"; finally, "Race is also the subject of scientific study and analysis simply because it is a fact of nature." He recognizes, however, that "the ideal classification of the races of man is yet to be proposed" (p. 280). Gould reports that J. B. Birdsell eventually dropped the racial categories that he studied with Coon, in favor of "multivariate analysis of gene frequencies for blood types," expressing the belief that "the pleasure of classifying man [may] fall away, perhaps, forever" (cited in Gould, 1977, p. 236). Finally, among the discouraging finds in this inquiry is the citation of Coon's *Races of Europe* in the second edition of the *Oxford English Dictionary* entry on *ethnic:* "The Jews are an ethnic unit, although one which has little regard for spatial considerations. Like other ethnic units, the Jews have their own standard racial character."

ological function of *species* and "that all men belong to the same species," he adds that he knows this to be true "not only because all races are interfertile, but also because some individuals among them interbreed, although others oppose mixture" (1962, p. 13). Such is Coon's manner of keeping his values from influencing the presentation. For Coon, racial designations are determined by a scientific process that can tap a creature's essence: "Zoologists now base their decisions on all the characteristics that can be identified and measured, characteristics which together give an animal its essential character, its (to borrow a psychological term) *gestalt*" (p. 13). These devices are set alongside a sometimes confusing mixture of scientific and common parlance. Although he regards "Negroid" as a "condition" rather than a geographical subspecies or a race, and uses "Congoid" to designate the race from central Africa, he goes on to use "Negro" as if it were one of the races under discussion. However, the amazing feature of this story of humankind's origins is that each race was transformed at a different period from *Homo erectus* into *Homo sapiens* (pp. 29–30). With some equivocation over the evidence for whether the Mongoloid or the Caucasian race was the earliest in making the transition, Coon favors the Caucasian as first, whereas the Negroid and Australian races are depicted as latecomers to humanity.[14]

Coon opens his chapter on Africa, which is subtitled "The Darkest Continent," with an anecdote in which he is asked by "a Negress born shortly after emancipation . . . 'Professor, who were *my* ancestors?'" Coon frankly admits to her that he does not know, leading him to his point that "the origin of the African Negroes and of the Pygmies, is the greatest unsolved mystery in the field of racial study" (1962, p. 588). One can only wonder to what sort of speculation (mutations, aliens?) such unsolved mysteries were intended to give rise. Still, the professor feels confident enough in his reading of recent archaeological findings to conclude the chapter with the supposition that "if Africa was the cradle of mankind, it was only an indifferent kindergarten. Europe and Asia were our principal schools" (p. 656). At the very least, Coon's work offers readily accessible lesson material for introducing students to science's involvement in the racism that grew out of imperialism and formed part of the popular educational materials only a generation or two removed from their own schooling.

In the book's closing pages, Coon rewards the patient reader by coming clean on what he sees as the scientific case for racial segregation. He affirms that "racial intermixture can upset the genetic as well as the social equilibrium," making racial prejudice a natural force exemplified, in his mind, by

---

[14] I am indebted to Shipman's critical reading of these sections (1994, pp. 204–5).

the attitudes of Jews, Negroes, and Europeans (1962, p. 661). "To me, at least," he concludes, "it is encouraging to know that biochemistry divides us into the same subspecies that we have long recognized on the basis of other criteria" (p. 662). This ability to "distinguish races almost at a glance" (p. 662), with its trusting of the eye's unequivocal testimony—*as anyone can see*—remains the bedrock of empiricism's transcending truth. Or, as Donna Haraway affirms, "Biology has been pre-eminently a science of visible forms, the dissection of visible shape, and the acceptance and construction of visible order" (1991, p. 21). Science constructed a biological order out of the seemingly natural perception of race, one that ran far deeper than the surface of the skin.[15] If Coon proudly sets the science of race on the side of common sense, it is worth recalling that other scientists, from Galileo to Einstein, have worked to disrupt familiar perceptions of the world (Wolpert, 1993). Coon's daring was to base the great divide on the distinct racial origins that divided humankind. If his theory did not survive the times, it still serves as a stark reminder of the scientific sponsorship by which racism benefited within recent memory.

This major statement on the profound and permanent barriers between the races from a respected author (Coon) and publisher (Alfred Knopf) suggests that the credo of scientific racism did not end in 1950, as Barkan suggests. Certainly the horrors of the Nazi regime brought home to many people the consequences of this misanthropic science of race, which is to say that the reviews of Coon's book were mixed. The claims of its staunch defenders that it was "a major contribution to our knowledge of evolutionary theory" were buffeted by open accusations of racism (Hulse, 1963). The book's critics bluntly identified it as "the darling of segregationist 'Committees'" (Opier, 1962). The geneticist Theodosius Dobzhansky—who turned from friend to critic of Coon on the basis of *The Origin of Races*—put a fine and generous

---

[15] Anthropologist William Howells, drawing on Coon's work, notes in *Mankind So Far* that "many writers justly point out that there is no such thing as a Jewish race, but they are apt thereby to lose the confidence of every reader who knows perfectly well that he can pick out a fair percentage of people of Jewish descent by their looks and who may have been told a few pages before by the same writer that this is the general process by which one does discern a race" (1947, p. 241). Howells's explanation is essentially that "the Jews developed, with their religion, both a strong nationalism and an exclusive social system which, biologically, expressed themselves in inbreeding and a refusal to mix with others" (p. 241). John Baker, in *Race*, also devotes a section to the Jews, holding that they are not a distinct subspecies or race, although he makes clear, by identifying physical features in less than flattering tones, that neither are they "Europoids": "The lower lip [of the Jew] is everted so as to appear thick, but it is not swollen like that of a Negro; on the contrary, it tends to be flattened." The accompanying illustration is of what seems to be a fifty-year-old "Armenid [Jewish] type" and a twenty-year-old "non-Armenid type" (1974, pp. 238, 240).

turn on the controversy in his *Scientific American* review of "this important book" (1963) when he allowed that "Professor Coon states some of his conclusions in a way that makes his work susceptible to misuse by racists, white supremacists and other special pleaders." I still find that this sense of a "misused" science reflects a professional defensiveness that fails to deal with the relationship and responsibility that hold between science and society. Montagu's telling complaint against Coon was that he failed in his career to offer "the slightest disavowal and repudiation . . . of the uses to which his views have been put" (1964, p. 232).[16]

What now of Coon's *Origin of Races?* The publisher, Knopf, has a current physical anthropology textbook by Clifford Jolly and Fred Plog that carefully dissociates itself from Coon's theory: "We do not subscribe to the view that human subspecies corresponding to the five traditional races of human classification ever existed" (1987, p. 281). However, Jolly and Plog suggest that the idea has yet to be scientifically repudiated and is still open for subscription.[17] Although they advise students to look at race only as it has "enhanced our understanding of human variation," they do not delve into just how "useful" the scientific study of race has been to constructing the moral order that underwrote Western expansion and exploitation during the nineteenth and twentieth centuries (p. 488). They do not consider that since the 1970s, there has been a marked decline in references to race in physical anthropology textbooks, which might be interpreted as a way of avoiding a little critical self-reflection on the nature of the discipline (Littlefield, Lieberman, and Reynolds, 1982). Jolly and Plog do, however, include a sidebar on the Jewish and Chinese immigrants who, in the early years of this century, were subjected to English-language intelligence tests by officials on arriving in America, with predictable results. Aside from this moment of historical reflection on the bu-

---

[16] Shipman cites Coon on his sense of scientists' responsibility to attack not the misusers of their work but the misquoters, among whom Coon names Dobzhansky (Shipman, 1994, p. 209).

[17] A far franker assessment of Coon can be found in Ashley Montagu: "Professor Coon's views give great comfort to racists, but they find no support among scientists" (1972, p. 39). However, I find that Montagu's subordinate clause undoes his primary claim through its inaccuracy, as once again a scientist tries to clear the good name of the profession. Coon is cited supportively by, among others, Dobzhansky (1962) and Baker (1974). Coon's final work, *Racial Adaptation,* on racial adaptation to climate and culture, which included not only cranial capacities in relation to the division of labor, but also comparisons between endocrine gland weights across races, was published posthumously in 1981. Finally, among the recent texts used in university teaching, Robert Juriman and Harry Nelson's *Introduction to Physical Anthropology* presents Coon's views along with the idea that "today three racial groups are recognized by anthropologists," to which they add, "However, there is hardly consensus on this point" (1994, p. 119).

reaucratic misuse of science, the authors fall into the pattern of leaving up in the air the current scientific function and status of race.

Today, the remnants of race science are found mainly within the study of sociobiology and the work of a very small, but hardly insignificant, segment of the profession.[18] The most sensational instance of a scientific engagement with race in recent years has come with *The Bell Curve: Intelligence and Class in American Life* (1994), by the late Harvard psychologist Richard J. Herrnstein, working with social scientist Charles Murray. The book made the best-seller list and the cover of a number of newsmagazines by drawing dour political implications from the well-known correlations between IQ and race (working with a mix of categories that ranged from Asian to Ashkenazi Jew). The authors deploy, without explicitly embracing, a eugenic argument that holds that the nation represents a gene pool threatened in its intelligence quotient by differing rates of reproduction at the low and high ends of the intelligence measure. The growing divide between the rich and poor and the associated rise in crime are shown to be statistically associated with race and IQ distributions.[19] Herrnstein and Murray do not hesitate, based on a faith in the fixed and determined quality of IQ and equipped with highly controversial figures and findings from the biological and social sciences, to write off such equity programs as Head Start and to denounce other forms of social support as inherently dangerous and simply poor investments.

Nonetheless, the book did manage to move the liberal press to once again ask about the scientific status of race, and science's contribution to the state in its work as a futures broker (S. A. Holmes, 1994). A cover story in *Newsweek* ran with the subtitle "Surprising New Lessons from the Controversial Science of Race," only to report that the 1972 findings of Richard Lewontin on the very small differences between races have merely been added to by the findings of the Human Genome Diversity Project (Begley, 1995, p. 67). Although many scientists are now outspoken in attacking the scientific status of race, as the *Newsweek* story points out, they are still working against the enormous intellectual force that science brought to the fixing of those racial divisions during this and the preceding centuries. The questioning of race in the media and the vociferous debate surrounding *The Bell Curve* speak to the continuing scientific controversy surrounding the issue. Students of science have the

---

[18] For a review of the "new racism" represented by sociobiology, see Barker (1990). Ziegler, Weizmann, Weiner, and Wiesenthal (1989) include a listing of scientific journals, such as *Annals of Theoretical Psychology* and *Mankind Quarterly*, that regularly publish this work.
[19] Among the many critical reviews, Beardsley's coverage in *Scientific American* (1995) provides a good summary.

opportunity, if not the responsibility, to learn how this research on race continues a legacy that once prevailed and, however discredited, still survives.

If science in the modern age became the new church, then we need to consider how race was part of its original dogma, part of what justified belief in the natural superiority of this (white) science. To look at this another way, Nancy Stepan captures the pervasiveness and commitment that marked the science of racial differences, as she charts the never complete "disappearance" of the race paradigm in science after the Second World War:

> For more than a hundred years the division of human species into biological races had seemed of cardinal significance to scientists. Race explained individual character and temperament, the structure of social communities and the fate of human societies. In fact commitment to typological races often appeared to have been deeper, because psychologically more necessary or satisfying, than the commitment to revolutionary change in science itself. (1982, p. 170)

We need to realize the authority that this scientific legacy continues to infuse into such primary categories of experience as race. How could such a legacy evaporate from a culture through a generation or two? Nor is it enough to wish that science finally and completely rid itself of race. This centuries-old scientific enterprise has contributed to the making of a racial world and must, in turn, become part of a responsible education in science if we are to have any hope of moving beyond that legacy.

An Education in Race

What do students learn about the scientific status of race in school today? What do science teachers and textbooks have to say about race? As it turns out, the message over the last few years is decidedly mixed. At the college level, extensive surveys have been conducted in the United States of both textbooks and professors in the fields of biology and physical anthropology by the team of Lieberman, Hampton, Littlefield, and Hallead (1992; see table 1). The striking differences between the two disciplines they surveyed provide an interesting perspective on how scientists, thought to hold common standards of objectivity, can come to differ on what might seem a fundamental and long-standing matter of basic classification. Categories are always more useful than real. Or is it that those engaged in biology and physical anthropology have varying levels of sensitivity to the social issues that touch on their work?

In pointing out the considerable movement away from the viability of race in physical anthropology textbooks, the authors of this study cite Franz Boas's identification of the discipline as originating in the efforts of "zoologists in the 18th century to measure and classify human races" (1992, p. 305). It is worth adding that the American Committee for Democracy and Intellectual Freedom, which Franz Boas helped found in 1939, conducted a survey of pre-war science textbooks only to find that a majority of them carried prejudicial concepts of race and a fifth of them embraced forms of white superiority (p. 306). The results from another survey a decade ago indicate that race lives on, in biology at least, in a thin majority of textbooks, and professors are relatively unshaken in their belief in the scientific validity of the concept. In physical anthropology, only a fifth of textbooks accept race as a fair division of humankind, although fully half of the faculty members surveyed in this field hold the category viable.

Table 1

Acceptance and Nonacceptance of the "Race Concept" in Textbooks and among Professors in Biology and Physical Anthropology, 1975–1984

"Race Concept"	*Biology: Animal Behavior*		*Physical Anthropology*	
	(1) *Textbooks* *1975–1982*	*(2)* *Professors* *1983–1984*	*(3)* *Textbooks* *1975–1982*	*(4)* *Professors* *1983–1984*
	% (N)	% (N)	% (N)	% (N)
Accepted	53 (11)	73 (108)	21 (7)	50 (73)
Indeterminate	38 (8)	15 (22)	39 (13)	8 (11)
Not Accepted	10 (2)	12 (17)	39 (13)	42 (63)
Total	101 (21)	100 (147)	99 (33)	100 (147)

Source: Data from L. Lieberman, R. E. Hampton, A. Littlefield, and G. Hallead, "Race in Biology and Anthropology: A Study of College Texts and Professors," *Journal of Research in Science Teaching* 29 (3): 312; reprinted by permission of John Wiley & Sons, Inc. Percentages may not total 100 because of rounding. $p < .02$ for columns 1 + 2 + 3 + 4; or columns 1 + 3.

One fascinating aspect of this division of scientific opinion is whether we should expect a democratic arrival at a definition of race's scientific status. Does the meaning of race require a majority decision? Does race work well for one discipline and not another? At the very least, such questions add to the sense that such categories, per se, are not only constructs of the mind but

also projections of disciplinary convenience. To gain some sense of the ob-
fuscation at stake, consider how Joseph Birdsell blithely claims in the first edition of *Human Evolution: An Introduction to the New Physical Anthropology*
that "today new races are in the process of being formed" (1972, p. 598), only
to announce in the next edition that the "use of the term of race has been dis-
continued because it is scientifically undefinable and carries social implications that are harmful and disruptive" (1975, p. 505). Simply expunging references to race in biology textbooks, as Lieberman's team found had happened
with the eight college texts they examined from 1987 through 1989, obscures
how the concept lives on in so many scientific and nonscientific forms. The
Lieberman team views this "as preferable to presenting race as if it were an
accepted concept but not as informative as presenting both the new information and the issues that have been debated" (1992, p. 310). Not only do I
side with this more informative approach, I want to see it introduced at the
high school level rather than reserving it, as Lieberman et al. do, for the limited number of students at college who take biology.

What, then, of the high school biology teacher and the teaching of race?
To gain some idea of what teachers today make of the topic, I turn to five experienced teachers and five student-teachers from the Vancouver area, evenly
divided by gender, each having studied biology at university, some very recently. They spoke about their own training, their ideas about race, and
where, if at all, they envisioned race fitting into the biology curriculum. Although hardly a representative sample, they articulated a range of positions
on race. The teachers were divided on the scientific status of race, as the
Leiberman team found at the university level, as well as on whether the concept had a place in high school biology. One encouraging source of doubt
about the viability of race as a scientific category came from these teachers'
own schooling, as one of the student-teachers conveys:

> As far as race goes, I think one of the most important things that I can
> recall about my education at the University of Manitoba is a professor
> who . . . asked us the question "Is there such a thing as race?" And that
> was a really important question and we debated it for a long time and
> resolved that really we are all part of the human race.

In a similar vein, an experienced teacher recalled having a professor who had
explained how craniometry, especially in its connection to race, was "an example of bad science, because of the methodology used."

On the other hand, a student-teacher, after complaining that "multiculturalism was just jammed down my throat" ("I was just like, 'What's the
point?'"), described how her education kept distinctions alive:

My professor was telling us that there is a scientific basis for differentiation of race based on genetic stuff, that actually the different races are different subspecies of the human species, but that you can't say that because it's not politically correct or proper. . . . He mentioned that interracial couples, like black and white, interracial couples when they have children, they have major orthodontic problems because the jaw is structured differently or the size is different or something so they have these problems.

She added that a course in evolution taught her that "yes, there is a scientific foundation and we are different, we can't dispute that, there are differences." Another student-teacher was confused about the relation between race and species: "I don't know if you can even, like I don't know if I would equate race and species together; I don't know if they're the same thing or different."

On teaching about race in biology class, the student-teachers expressed a level of discomfort that divided them from their experienced counterparts. One of those saying no ("I just think that [those discussing the science of race are] too emotionally charged, too full of opinions to really do anyone any good") did so after relating his own untroubled experiences growing up as an African Canadian: "There was a *big* difference between the First Nations population and the town population, and I always felt that was rather strange on how I fit in and someone of First Nations [ancestry] didn't in that town."

Only one of the experienced teachers, in his second year of biology teaching, shared the students' aversion to teaching about race. He felt it to be "social studies or something," for "it is more like personal development, it's not my job to get into that kind of thing here." His professional identification was with science: "I mean, I'm a scientist and I try to see things objectively, in a scientific way, and I just think that you can get into all kinds of things here that don't belong in science."

Among the experienced teachers, one explained how he teaches about both the physical and the genetic bases of race:

We talk about different features, such as shape of nose, thick lips, hair texture, and that basically there are four races, some people put it at five. I also talk about the idea of classification as a sort of a human thing, we look for basic characteristics, and basically there may only be, say, five or six genetic differences between races. We're basically the same species but there are significant differences in races and these probably originated as adaptations to different environments.

Part of what is fascinating within this teacher's often-taught account of race is how he both limits the reach of race—by allowing "classification as a sort of a human thing" and that there "may only be, say, five or six genetic differences"—and then extends the race boundary by referring to species and significant differences. Remember that these are the scientific perspectives to which students are exposed, even as they are bombarded by what can only be characterized as a wide range of attitudes toward racial difference in the society at large. Science teachers need to consider whether what they say about race can be taken as leaning either way, toward a strengthening or a weakening of the hold of biologically based racial divisions on our thinking.

Some of the experienced teachers also reflected on their high school students' interest in the topic of race. One teacher, with five years' experience, made clear that in his science class, students felt free to ask about the concept as a matter of managing difference and identity:

> Kids want to know what is the advantage of living in a more uniform environment. They want to know why Asian eyes are different, and what are the advantages and disadvantages to vision of these differences. About advantages and disadvantages of interracial marriages where there are children, are we moving towards a more universal person with all of these? I throw it back to them, ask what they think. They note that children who have one Chinese parent often look more Chinese than anything else.

To speak of looking "more Chinese than anything else" brings us back to the identity themes of the opening chapter, in which race operates within notions of nation and culture. Although this teacher seeks to turn the discussion back to his students, when asked about whether his own ideas about race had changed over the years, he responded that they were "definitely more fuzzy."

A teacher in his fifth year of teaching who felt it important to discuss race in science class was adamant that race "has nothing to do with biology." He made references to the Eve hypothesis, on humanity's descent from a common mother in Africa ("Some of the [scientists'] stuff was a little screwy and there were problems with it, but the concept itself was OK"), and was one of two teachers who cited the recent media attention paid to the psychologist Philippe Rushton's questionable work on race and brain size: "I got all kinds of questions about him: a lot of our kids are Asian, and there were a lot of questions [such as], 'Are kids from Asia smarter?' 'Do they have bigger brains?' "[20] His final words in the interview located the issue within his own life and his need for understanding:

[20] J. Philippe Rushton, a University of Western Ontario psychology professor, has become well known for a remarkable thirty-one–item table on "the relative ranking of races on diverse variables," comparing Mongoloids, Caucasoids, and Negroids on such questionable measures as cranial capacity, millions of excess neurons, IQ test scores, age of walking and

For me it's a big issue. I've seen a lot of racism in my time, and it really bothers me. . . . I remember when I was young my grandmother [a First Nations woman] coming to the house, and the neighbors burning a tire in front of our yard and telling the squaw that she should go back to the reserve. And when you're six years old this makes a big impression on you. I couldn't understand. This was my grandmother; why were these people mad at her?

Although it would be discouraging to think that it might take this level of personal experience for a teacher to feel that race warrants inclusion as part of a science class, this teacher does remind us of the magnitude of the issue and the corresponding need to develop an approach in science classes that helps students deal with the weight placed on race. Will the teacher be able to offer students some insight into the unstable and contested meaning of race; will they understand the part that science plays in that contest? This small sample of teachers offers a limited perspective on science education's take on race. The biology textbook provides a clearer idea of what the typical high school student is able to discover about the scientific status of race.

Race, Biology, and the State of the Text

When I went to high school in the 1960s, the topic of race was typically presented in biology class through a portrait gallery approach. We students were presented with a page of photographs, with each race represented by one figure shown in a head-and-shoulder shot. In William Gregory and Edward Goldman's *Biological Science for High School* from the period, the racial lineup features a well-groomed man in a suit as the final, Caucasoid figure in the set (1968, p. 483).[21] To see where race now stands in American and Canadian high schools, I reviewed fifteen biology textbooks from the 1980s. I found that race hardly appears at all. In only three of the twelve American and in neither of the two Canadian high school biology textbooks did I find refer-

---

first intercourse, size of genitalia, and state of mental health (1995, p. 2). Although allowing for "numerous sources of error" in his data, he holds that their overall consistency guarantees his conclusions about the civilized superiority of Mongoloids compared to Caucasoids, who, in turn, are more advanced than the Negroid races. Rushton portrays himself as a victim of political correctness, blaming decolonization and the civil rights movements for forcing upon science ideologies of egalitarianism (pp. 256–57). For scientific critiques, see Weizmann et al. (1991) and J. Anderson (1991); and for popular press coverage, Dolpin (1989). For a 1997 Web site devoted to critical coverage of "the return of racial science," see Marek Kohn's work at http://www.hrc.wmin.ac.uk/race gallery/.

[21] The Gregory and Goldman text proposes a basic division of humankind into three races or "basic stocks": Caucasoid, Mongoloid, and Negroid. In what appears to be a statement emphasizing equality among the races but is really a confusing mix of scientific terms, the authors stress that "dividing men into racial stock is just a convenient way of describing

ence made to race.[22] Avoidance has long been the schools' response to controversy, and the result is that young minds are often forced to deal with heavily contested ideas exclusively on an extracurricular basis. In this case, avoidance entails both a lost opportunity for intellectual engagement in the social implications of science and a failure to address the experiences of the young, who are living with race. As it turns out, the two American biology textbooks approved for use in British Columbia address race. The question for me, then, is to see whether some further sense can be drawn from these books that might make visiting the concept of race in a science class a less confusing and potentially misleading experience.

In grade 11, students in British Columbia typically use *Macmillan Biology,* which, in its chapter "Life in the Past," points out "that the concept of race has become increasingly blurred in the last few thousands of years" (Creager, Jantzen, and Mariner, 1986, p. 282). Here's a good point for jumping in to explore with students the fine distinctions that need to be made in the conceptualization of difference. Although the distinctions among once isolated peoples have by all means diminished, the *concept* of race has only gained in precision through scientific usage, beginning a little more than two centuries ago (Shipman, 1994). The contradictions continue with Creager, Jantzen, and Mariner's attempts to undermine racial classification ("We see that such systems fail to hold any real meaning") offset by their set of four photographs each depicting a modern family, in what is clearly meant to represent the mating of distinct racial types. The caption reads, "Selection, drift, and isolation were important factors that produced differences between early human populations" (p. 282). The visual reinforcement of distinctly modern racial differences in the photographs and the earlier claim about racial blurring can only leave a student wondering how to approach the textbook's question at the end of the section that asks why "biological definition of 'race' is based on allele frequency, not on appearance" (p. 283). The text supports the idea that science continues to have something to say about race and difference,

some outstanding physical differences" and that "there are no fundamental differences in the physiology of people no matter what the color of their skin, eyes, or hair" (1968, p. 484). The Lieberman et al. study makes passing reference to reports on the decline of race in biology textbooks used in high schools (1992, pp. 302–3). What is striking in their report on high schools is the books that, although focusing on "social issues," fail to consider race as a category to assess (p. 303).

[22] The three textbooks that make statements on race are Creager et al. (1986), Mader (1988), and Biological Sciences Curriculum Study (1987). The other textbooks in the sample are Barr and Leyden (1986); Galbraith (1989); Gottfried et al. (1983); Heimler (1981); Kaskel et al. (1981); Levine and Miller (1991); McLaren and Rotundo (1985); McLaren et al. (1981); Oram (1983); Ramsey et al. (1986); Slesnick et al. (1985); and Webster et al. (1980).

even if it would be difficult to say precisely what that something is. I do not doubt that as a student I would have read through this section without a second thought. Although my reading of the contradictions may be challenged, just such a discussion is needed in searching for the meaning of race in science.

When it comes to grade 12, biology students in British Columbia turn to *Inquiry into Life,* by Sylvia Mader (1988). Mader has no desire to blur the concept of race. She begins by pointing out that "all human races of today are classified as *Homo sapiens* . . . because it is possible for *all types of humans* to interbreed and bear fertile offspring" (p. 638; emphasis added). Mader's set of race-type photographs juxtapositions what appears to be a professional fashion shot of a young "Caucasian" woman with the more typical anthropological portraits labeled "Australoid," "Negroid," "American Indian," and "Mongoloid" (referred to as "Oriental" in the text). The caption for the photographs reiterates that "all human beings belong to one species, but there are several races," without specifying whether the five depicted are exhaustive or merely suggestive (p. 639). The chapter ends in an another excellent instance of trying to clear up a concern in a manner that raises as many questions as it answers: "While it has always seemed to some that physical differences might warrant assigning human races to different species, this contention is not borne out by the biochemical data mentioned previously" (p. 639).[23] Is one to think that wanting to assign those who differ to another species is a natural inclination despite the biochemical data? What is the point of the contrasting photographs, if not to suggest that an excellent student of science is an attentive reader of difference and distance? In both of these weighty biology textbooks, the matter of race takes up a very small section indeed. The majority of texts do not deal with the topic at all. My concern is that as part of what students learn about science, and in the face of the lessons on race that they bring to those classes, they need a better understanding of science's role in the making of this conceptual divide among peoples.

Fortunately, some science educators refuse to avoid and obfuscate the

---

[23] The seventh edition of Mader's text (1994) eliminates much of this discussion of race. It refers to skin color, from very light to very dark, illustrated by a "white husband and his intermediate wife" and their offspring (p. 437). In shades of Carlton Coon, Mader reports that theories of a single African origin for modern humans is discredited: "Others believe that the human races originated in several geographical regions, but they became one species because of gene flow" (p. 616). A sidebar called "U.S. Population Projections" includes reproductive levels for non-Hispanic whites, Hispanics, African Americans, Native Americans, and Asian Americans, pointing out that "the share of the population that is non-Hispanic white should decline steadily. . . . By 2050, a bare majority of Americans (53%) will be non-Hispanic whites" (p. 670).

issue of race. During the 1980s, a group of London teachers tapped into a segment of the scientific community that was actively working for social change, and developed an antiracist science curriculum. They went on to address questions of nutrition and management of world hunger, biology and the construction of race, and ecology and African game parks, as well as taking on issues of ability labeling and other evaluation practices that can have a racial impact on science teaching (Gill and Levidow, 1987). These educators assumed responsibility not just for teaching science, but for teaching about science's place within the prevailing economic and ideological system as well:

> Science teaching masks the real political and economic priorities of science; hides its appropriation of non-Western scientific traditions; [and] often attributes people's subordination or suffering to nature—be it biological or geographic factors—rather than to the way science and nature itself have been subordinated to political priorities. (p. 3)

With an interesting twist on the scientific theme of discovery, these authors turn students' attention, if sometimes with a heavy hand, to the political causes and consequences of scientific concepts such as race. This approach becomes another way of learning about the interests of the most objective of disciplines.[24]

This critical approach to race and science has also managed in more recent years to find its way into more traditional textbooks. An excellent instance of at least an introduction to the topic is the Wiley general science textbook *Science Probe 10,* which is used in many of British Columbia's schools (Bullard et al., 1992). This Canadian text includes in its chapter on recent advances in genetics an extended warning note under the title, "The Potential for Misuse of Genetic Ideas" (pp. 428–29). In two pages, the book presents a brief history of the eugenics movement, including its origins in Francis Galton's work, the sterilization and antimiscegenation laws passed during the 1920s and 1930s in North America and Europe, and the emergence of eugenics in Nazi Germany amid ideas of a master race. The book's explicit stand is that there are no pure races, yet it also casts doubt on the scientific determination of any reliable racial boundaries. It also identifies the continuing support that eugenics receives from "a certain number of scientists and others" (p. 429). The book stands apart in asking students to remain vigilant against abuses of new developments in genetics. Otherwise, it claims, it will be easy "once again for a few people to mislead others with their biased and narrow-

---

[24] A second valuable work in this vein, a manual for teachers and educators, is *Race, Equality, and Science Teaching* (Thorp, 1991).

minded ideas" (p. 429). The image of informed citizenship and historical awareness that the book encourages is admirable, although holding "a few people" responsible for the eugenics movement is a debatable point, given the broad basis of the Americas' "fitter families" contests, "race betterment" conferences, and international congresses on eugenics that were held earlier in this century (Rydell, 1993, pp. 38–58). Yet to have a textbook raise the issue of responsibility among students, to allow such points of discussion to be raised, seems a worthwhile extension of the meaning of science class.

Having found some encouraging initiatives in the realm of science and race, I want to make at least passing reference to a related dimension of imperialism's educational legacy that is also excluded from the science curriculum. Maurice Bazin has developed science programs that introduce to students the "science in every civilization which the colonists destroyed" (1993, pp. 36, 45). Thus we find, for example, that the pre-Columbian preparation of rubber by the Amerindians of South and Central America is a form of knowledge that was handily exploited and incorporated into Western pharmaceutical and industrial chemistry. In working with multicultural classrooms in Brazil and California, Bazin has introduced education's missing scientific traditions, including "observing the moon the way the Mayans did or the height of the sun the way the Egyptians did," and "sand drawings with curves to exemplify what we call topological properties" done by Tchokwe children from northeast Angola (p. 44). I should reiterate here that my aim is not to vilify the scientific endeavors of the West nor to condemn a basic human curiosity about the natural world, but to foster in students an understanding of how a global initiative such as imperialism can leave a significant impress on a human endeavor such as science.[25]

A second extension of this study of science's contribution to the organizing principles of racial difference is to realize that these practices are closely connected to those who participate in this powerful social enterprise; as Sandra Harding asks, "What can be done to enhance the democratic tendencies within the sciences and inhibit their elitist, authoritarian, and distinctly androcentric, bourgeois, Eurocentric agendas?" (1991, p. 217). Donna Haraway

---

[25] For additional work on multiculturalism in science education, see Barba's review of the issues (1993), Hodson's rationale for multicultural science education (1993, with critique in H. Williams, 1994), and Alcoze et al. (1993) for reading and activities in multiculturalism in math, science, and technology. With the current force of economic imperialism, Sandra Harding points out how the ignorance of scientists about the military and industrial utility of a "pure" science such as physics may well be "carefully planned and cultivated" (1993, p. 17). On this note of global competitiveness, she also notes how the "keep U.S. science strong" movement has meant "recruiting more women and racial minorities into science careers as fewer and fewer white males enter the sciences" (pp. 2–3).

offers one answer in her feminist physical anthropology and primatology, which has "stressed principles of organization for bodies and societies that do not depend on dominance hierarchies," bringing to light instead "matrifocal groups, long-term social co-operation rather than short-term spectacular aggression, flexible process rather than strict structure" (1991, p. 19). The dominance by gender applies no less to race, in the transformation of a political principle into the legitimating realm of scientific theory (p. 19). As should be clear by this point, my hope for reversing some of the damage done by this dominance is to make science's confounding role in maintaining these divisions part of a science education.

In the 1950s, UNESCO called for a moratorium on the use of the term *race* (Montagu, 1972). This happened, in effect, among the majority of high school biology texts of the 1980s. I remain convinced, however, that this is as much a disservice to students who are learning about science today as was the earlier, often confused and prejudicial treatment of race provided to a previous generation of science students. Students need to treat race as a way of working through the nature of the discipline and its social implications. All that is named and classified represents a tireless effort to render difference sensible, to work with an unsettled and shapeless world that can be brought to order through language, the civilizing force. Where precisely the sense of subspecies can be said to reside—in the eyes of the beholder or in the creatures themselves—could bring students to the brink of epistemology. To question the nature of knowledge and the knowledge of nature will spill over into a questioning of other ways in which the world and experience are divided. It appears that, apart from this compulsion to classify, the "racialization" of the West has meant, in Michael Banton's compact formulation, that "race, like class and nation was a concept first developed to help interpret new social relations" (1977, p. 13). But it was not "first developed," just like that, for these concepts were mobilized through enormous intellectual and educational labors that made race, like gender, class, and nation, work within the close association of knowledge and power.

Science's assistance in the racial and gendered ordering of social relations needs to be promoted for the science curriculum and the preparation of science teachers. It needs to form an aspect of current concerns about scientific literacy and the new educational programs that link science, technology, and society. I am asking that students face the ongoing questioning of race's viability as a biological category as well as the unsavory history of race science (Barzun, 1937; F. B. Livingstone, 1964; Gould, 1977). Students find themselves living within racial designations, and we have the potential to provide them with some of the intellectual background for why that is so. It is true that, during their education in science, many students are introduced to the fallacy of the science of craniometry, the devastating impact of the eugenics movement, and the controversy surrounding IQ testing. My hope is that these lessons are seen within the historical framework best described as imperialism. I think it is helpful to understand that scientific racism was not simply a freak event, a mutant science carried out only by so-called scientists. It had and continues to have too many of the markings of real science, from research grants to statistical tables. Thus, there remains a need to introduce students to the fragile nature of truth, to the moral dimensions of this inquiry, and to the responsibilities we have as practitioners and students of science. This is to propose an education concerned with the historical dimensions of universal truths.

As with other subject areas, science teachers can often begin to share this history with students simply by visiting the school's book room, where old biology textbooks can reveal science's changing regard for race. In addition, one group of students can pursue the continuing controversies surrounding race and science that crop up in the popular media, most recently about the issue of IQ (Begley, 1995), while others could gather and compare selections from the scientific debates about race that have occupied this and the previous century (Harding, 1993). They may well find, as I have found, that the scientific constitution of race in the West brought greater force and precision to the significance of difference, to the naming of the other. It further ordered European interests in dividing the world to its advantage and in placing those divisions on a scientific basis. Yet to realize the scientific inadequacy of this concept is not to deny race's continuing meaning as a point of identity. I do not assume that an understanding of what science has made of race can or should put an end to anyone's racial self-identification. My aim is to give students an account of how science has worked in consort with other social forces in bringing us to this point in the complex and polysemous meaning of race. I believe that a science curriculum that obscures the discipline's contributions to the meaning of race is incomplete and irresponsible. The obscured yet present legacy of race science, if it were made part of the curriculum, would have the potential of serving both those students who understand race as a part of who they are and must be, and those who have learned to think of race as someone else's problem.

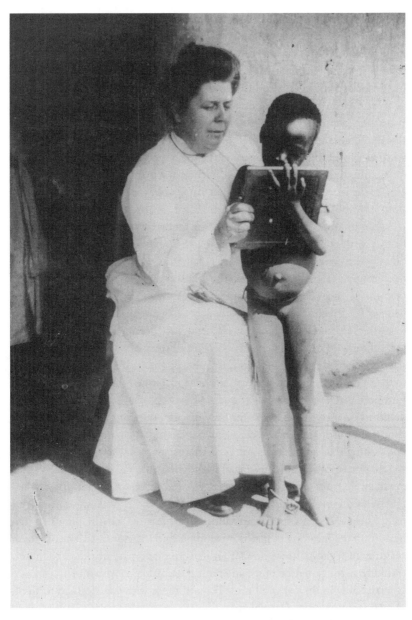

Photograph of a British missionary teaching in Africa in the 1890s.
Courtesy Church Mission Society.

EIGHT

LANGUAGE, NATION, WORLD

Gordon Peters, vice-chief of the Assembly of First Nations and a member of the Delaware Indian Band, stood before an audience of linguists and educators at a Toronto conference entitled "Multilingualism in an Interdependent World" and described his determined efforts to learn his native language after a lifetime of speaking English. The Delaware language had fallen out of use in his family, and now only his mother spoke it with a few of her friends and the band elders. After two years of working at learning his mother tongue, he explained, he was still finding it hard going. His goal, he said, was to be able to think in Delaware, which he felt would allow him to recover a spiritual understanding of the Delaware people that was otherwise lost to him.

When the talk came to a close, Peters was asked by a member of the audience what it felt like to speak English. It was one of those awkward questions for which it is hard even to imagine an answer. Peters responded by describing his admiration for the elders' ability to speak Delaware with such feeling and how, when he had asked his mother why she had not taught him the language, she told him how hard it had been for his father to find work as an Indian, even in the factories. As he spoke, one could feel her earnest efforts to render his nativeness invisible so that he would not have to suffer this identity. Peters then told listeners that he wanted to learn Delaware so that he could know the true names of things, including his own true name. This was, he frankly explained, his way of coming to terms with the great rage he had come to feel during his school years, when he must have learned that becoming invisible was neither the deal he wanted nor what the school could deliver.

This was how he described what it felt like to speak English. Like water to a fish, English did not feel like anything, except that these linguistic waters were not somehow his own, as if English was both his knowing and his unknown.

As I and others listened to Gordon Peters that evening, I'm sure a number of us must have given some thought to the lost languages of our own families. I know I began to consider the Yiddish and Polish that at least some of my great-grandparents had brought to this continent in the nineteenth century. Except for an exasperated Yiddish *oyvey-schmeer* or a deeply condemning *drechk,* I could recall only the sound of English floating among the four generations of my family around me when I was growing up. Although tempted by such nostalgia to mourn the loss of these tongues, I also thought about reluctantly trudging off to Hebrew school classes after long days of regular school. The Hebrew classes had been largely wasted on those of us who could not imagine why we would want to speak the language of Jews from long ago in biblical times or far away in Israel. This was now and we were here. Hebrew-schme-brew, we figured, without realizing our debt to Yiddish. Languages are not lost by accident or unwillingly forsaken. They give way to other desires, desires to join and be heard in other conversations, which left us happy enough to leave behind the accent and inflection of our former history and geography.

At the very least, the lessons that Peters set before us that evening supported the importance of schools' recognizing the value of students' mother tongues. In reviewing the education of minority language students in Canada, Yvonne Hébert has found that whereas once children might be punished for using their mother tongue at school if it was not English, "today violence in minority education occurs less crudely, with educational programs promoting the majority language and devaluing the minority language and culture" (1992, p. 62). She understands this form of symbolic violence against the child to be a human rights issue. One's mother tongue is a vital aspect of one's person. In Canada, what are known as "heritage" language classes have been established in schools, often on an after-hours basis and only after considerable struggle by parents (Cummins, 1989). Although the educational benefits of providing initial schooling in a child's mother tongue have been established by research on bilingualism, the practice in the United States, typically involving Spanish, is under assault by the "official English movement." The status of the language we speak and of the language in which the young are educated form no less a part of the legacy of imperialism. The degree to which English, as well as French and Spanish, is spoken around the world is not simply an incidental aspect of empire.

Language has long ridden aside the forces of expansion and conquest, whether in Greek, Latin, or Chinese. The "barbarian" is the one who does not speak Greek, the one "living outside the pale of the Roman empire and its civilization," as the second edition of the *Oxford English Dictionary* "historically" defines this term. In 1492, Spain not only saw Columbus off to a new world and expelled its Jews and Islamic populations, but also witnessed the launching of a new sort of linguistic dominion. In what needs to be celebrated as the birth of a national standard for language, Antonio de Nebrija proposed to the Spanish court that Castilian be made the official language of the land and a "consort of empire," as he presciently put it in dedicating his *Grammatica de la lengua castellana* to Queen Isabella (Illich, 1979, p. 35). His book was a set of rules for Castilian that would ensure that it served Spain as Latin had the Roman Empire. In Ivan Illich's analysis, Nebrija was offering the Spanish Crown an educated tongue that would effectively communicate its authority to the farthest reaches of nation and empire while minimizing the likelihood for any back talk. In those early days of the European empires, the Portuguese also sought to spread their language, with the help of the Franciscan monks and other missionaries who carried religious books to India and Abyssinia¹ that the indigenous peoples might receive the word of God in the language in which they were to be governed. João de Barros observed in the sixteenth century that a language that teaches salvation must surely be easy to learn, a project he assisted by producing woodcut-illustrated alphabet and word books for use among the barbarians abroad (Lach, 1977, p. 505). Within a generation or two of Columbus, it seems, language instruction materials had become part of imperialism's educational apparatus. To realize one's place in this centuries-old instructional landscape, whether as a student or a teacher of what were once empire's official languages, seems an eminently educational act.

This chapter's sampling of linguistic history is a way of thinking back through the lost languages that many of our families once spoke. It is a reminder of the humility with which we might approach the teaching of the English language. It is simply too easy to teach English as if it were the soul of civilized knowing, the heart of great literature, and the very tongue of democracy. English is some part of this and more. But the story of its dominion reminds us that it is also less than that. With the expansion of the British Empire, English was made an instrument of domination and silencing; it was used to regulate and police access to authority and knowledge among colonized peoples. If we need to temper our celebration of English's cultural achievements, it is only to make good, in accord with the theme of this book, on our promise to give an account of what education and empire have made of language over the centuries. We need to face the historical role of schools in expediting the loss of languages in one generation after another in a colonial project that needs serious reconsideration after the age of empire. More than righteous indignation over the schools' violation of the right to a voice is called for. At issue is the immediate task of mastering language skills that make a difference, that are heard and attended to, while appreciating the winding road that has led to this linguistic juncture, to lives being lived out through these first- and second-language lessons. In this chapter, I have organized the scope and substance of our responsibilities in teaching about language through three aspects of English: as a second language, as a national language, and as a world language.

English as a Second Language

Without a doubt, one of the most challenging educational issues today in what is known as the English-speaking world is how best to work with students for whom English is a second language. Vancouver, where I live, may seem an extreme example, with more than half of the students in the schools today speaking a language other than English as their mother tongue, but most urban centers are experiencing a tremendous growth in what are known as ESL students. The search for the best method of teaching ESL students has often limited the educational discussion to one of efficiencies in assimilation. Students certainly have the right to effective teaching, and I do not want to underestimate the importance of teaching students the language in which they will be schooled and very likely employed. I only want to add that students also have a right, as part of their education in the language, to see that what they are experiencing with the English language forms part of a history that they are both reliving and changing.[1]

When students move from Hong Kong to Vancouver, from what was the last major British colony to a Commonwealth dominion, as many have done in recent years, they are part of a postscript to the British Empire. They are often made to feel, as I outlined in the first chapter, that this move is out of the ordinary, a reversal of the historical colonial patterns that made this land

---

[1] I take my lead here from Alastair Pennycook's critique of the field's obsession with facilitating linguistic proficiency through the pursuit of ever newer methods (1989, pp. 597–98). The literature on teaching methods, he points out, reveals a centuries-old recycling of techniques, conducted amid confused conceptions of teaching methods. The pursuit of method has effectively distracted the educator's attention from the "interests served by particular forms of knowledge," as Pennycook puts it, citing the inclusion of language teaching in development packages and the American defense department funding of structural linguistics and audiolinguistics as part of a concerted effort, as one supporter put it, in the "war for men's minds" (pp. 609–10). In response, Pennycook calls for an education engaged in "validating and investigating students' knowledge and cultural resources and developing language skills within a transformative critique" (1990, p. 311).

English-speaking. The Chinese language that they bring with them is made to seem particularly out of place in this otherwise bilingual land. Their English lessons do not include historical and current perspectives on language distribution and status; they do not allow students to gain a critical and historical distance from colonialism's patronizing stance toward teaching English as the key to civilization.

As it now stands, English as a second language classes are taught as if language learning operated outside history, with a focus on being able to function in social and academic settings. Just how this is sympathetically conceived by ESL educators is conveyed by Mary Ashworth, a leader in this field, when she asks us to imagine "the psychological effect of a new immigrant being able to produce a few words in halting English and to understand the reply," or "the contribution to a developing nation of a native-born technician trained overseas after first learning the new language of instruction in his own country" (1985, p. 3). This psychological sense of belonging, of having a command of the language, is certainly what it is all about, and well should student and teacher feel the pride of accomplishment in the acquisition of English. However, these lessons in English for "new immigrants" and "developing nations" grow out of a historical context that, if introduced into this education, could only add to the sense made of this experience. Ashworth herself is not oblivious to the educational value of this history. She calls "for educators to keep the past and the present in their minds as they plan for the future," and she points to the "disempowering" lessons that came of poor second-language teaching, the denigration of home languages, and the more general effects of racism felt by First Nations, African Canadian, and Chinese Canadian children: "The public's fear of minority groups far exceeded its love of humankind and its concern for justice" (1992, pp. 124, 131).[2] Although she asks educators to take these lessons to heart, she does not ask that this history be included in the language education of those who, if they will not have to suffer as they once might have, still deserve a full account of this process. To acquire the English language is to have a stake in its claim as a world language; it is to be party to a history that runs from the colonial past that first planted English across the globe to the postnational futures of English on the global electronic network known as the Internet.[3]

---

[2] See Eliot Judd (1983) for another approach to the political situation of ESL teaching; he asks teachers to consider how their work relates to the loss of other languages and cultures and how it contributes to the training of power elites in certain countries while providing low-level language skills in others.

[3] The status of English as a colonizing force on the Internet has been seen, up to this point, largely as a threat to the hegemonic claims of French, although Bill Gates has defended

In raising the specter of a language curriculum that actively seeks to name its own place in the devolution of colonialism, it also needs to be made clear why this work is not only for minority-language students. There is as much, if not more, reason to be concerned about the education of students born into the English language who will go on to inhabit increasingly multi-lingual communities. The frame of mind in which teachers and students listen to those who speak other languages than they do, and the frame of mind in which they understand their own position in the world as English speakers may still bear traces of the history of imperial conquest and dominance. The distinguished linguist Joshua Fishman observed in 1977 that "unfortunately, we know far more about how to help the world learn English (little though that may be), than we do about how to help native speakers of English learn about the world" (p. 335). To become aware how language has figured in this ongoing state of global interdependence requires a review of a history that, I am arguing, still has a hold on our imaginations. My educational premise remains that we need to understand how the world was divided by the intellectual project of imperialism and how those divisions continue to weigh on our thinking about, in this case, native speakers and the learning of English.

The Native Speaker

One important aspect of this second-language question is the standard set by the "native speaker." The concept has been perhaps most vigorously addressed by Thomas Paikeday, editor of *The New York Times Everyday Dictionary* and *The Penguin Canadian Dictionary.* His book *The Native Speaker Is Dead!* (1985) is an innovative instance of bookmaking that consists of a Socratic dialogue made up of the responses of forty linguists who responded to Paikeday's inquiries about who and what is a "native speaker."[4] The book's principal antagonist is Noam Chomsky, who considers the scope of sentences possible within the English language to be defined by what is "acceptable to a native speaker." In one of the epigraphs of the book, Paikeday quotes the editorial director of the Merriam-Webster dictionaries, who insists that the two requirements of a dictionary editor are that "he should be a native speaker of English and he should have at least a bachelor's degree from a reputable col-

---

the multilingual potential of the Internet and work is being done on expanding its current character-set capacity (Stackhouse, 1995; Pollack, 1995).

[4] Thomas Paikeday's use of computer databases to prepare and assess dictionaries was responsible for setting me off on the fascinating study of lexicography.

lege or university" (p. xiv). Paikeday, having been born in Calcutta, realizes that he will never be allowed to regard himself as a native English speaker, which gives this theme a personal and poignant turn, especially as he feels compelled to include in his book readers' testimonials on the quality of his nonnative editing of *The New York Times Everyday Dictionary.* Although he does not explicitly address the relation between foreignness and race, he makes apparent the considerable operating expenses accrued by those made to suffer such distinctions. Paikeday offers examples of "native" and "nonnative" specimens, anecdotes, and informal experiments, all of which point to the bankruptcy of the concept as a reliable guide to so-called proper usage. His position is simply that there is no such thing as a "native speaker" in the sense of a person being able to claim an inherent hold on the full extent of the language. The editor of a successful dictionary should know.

In *The Native Speaker Is Dead!* Paikeday's learned correspondents slip and slide over the definition and usefulness of the native speaker concept. For example, Randolph Quirk makes clear that the survey of English usage was restricted to the "mature educated native speaker," as he puts it without a touch of irony, because it was thought to reduce the risk of gathering "imperfect" samples for the survey (Paikeday, 1985, p. 6). Chomsky holds that "everyone is a native speaker of the particular [language] that person has 'grown' in his/her mind/brain," showing little interest in Paikeday's concerns about language as a marker of social origins (p. 58). The point among these linguistic scholars appears to be that for their scientific investigations, those whom they can identify as "native speakers" are the only reliable informants of the language. That we are native to one language as we are to one mother and, for that matter, one land, carries with it a trace once more of that overdetermination of character that I have reviewed in the previous chapters. Paikeday's book establishes the degree to which the concept of the native speaker lives on as "a myth propagated by linguists," even as it operates as the unattainable ideal for students of English (p. xiv). The native speaker of English, it appears to be assumed, has been born into a white family or at least a white country. Or so I am tempted to imagine when I read in the local newspaper about a group of young students, having been raised in Urdu and English bilingual homes in India, coming to Canada and finding themselves mistakenly placed in English as a second language classes (Kurl, 1993). Paikeday proposes that "Indian English may be only as much of a dialectical entity as Boston English" (1985, p. 26). On the other hand, Braj Kachru, who is listed as professor of English as a world language at the University of Illinois, has no trouble referring to the English spoken in India as a nonnative variety, as if to insist once again on the national basis of the English language as native to England and America (1992b, p. 57).[5]

Native speakers alone are presumed to have a right to contribute to the growth of the language, to open metaphorical spaces, create new diction, and unearth new meanings through their work on the page. Native speakers use an English that holds hope for universal and global communication through their redoubtable standard. At the same time, they are capable of preserving the language and the culture that stands behind it. Native speakers are, after all, particularly sensitive to solecisms, maintaining standards of diction, pronunciation, and grammar. This discriminating sense comes, of course, not through some natural or native-born sensitivity, but through a thoroughly institutionalized process of family discipline and formal education in the language. This lack of linguistic tolerance, bred into the bone by education, appears to have little to do with levels of communication among native and nonnative speakers, as nonnative speakers have proved in at least one comparative study to be the most effective users of English on a global scale.[6] This sense of a special need to maintain the language's proper grammar is by no means restricted to English, of course, and Aimo Seppänen (1981) has argued that compared to other European languages, the norms of English allow a higher level of grammatical flexibility than is typically recognized by defenders of the standard. Still, it is safe to conclude that the English language's "doctrine of correctness," which arose during the eighteenth century, continues to have an impact on how speakers of the language are identified across a number of qualities (Leonard, 1962). Native speakers may assume it their duty to maintain standards for a language of which they are the sole protectors, but they will be standards that continue to coincide with the maintenance of privileges by nation, race, gender, and class.[7]

---

[5] Another instance of this second-class treatment in the professional literature occurs with the concept of nonnative "varieties" of English, further reifying the distinctions between speakers of the English language along the lines established by the imperial regimes. Rodney Moag (1992) describes a "life cycle" of nonnative varieties that includes transportation, indigenization, expansion, institutionalization, and restriction.

[6] In an attempt to assess this claim, if only with a "pilot study," Larry Smith (1992) has investigated the level of intelligibility, comprehensibility, and interpretability obtained among three groups: native, nonnative, and mixed speakers. His preliminary results suggest that native speakers are among the most limited in their global participation in this world language: "Native speakers (from Britain and the United States) were not found to be the most easily understood, nor were they, as subjects, found to be the best able to understand the different varieties of English. Being a native does not seem to be as important as being fluent in English and familiar with several different national varieties" (p. 88).

[7] On gender, the Cameron collection (1990) is a fine guide, and class is dealt with in Crowley (1989).

My concern is that the linguistic chauvinism embodied in this notion of the native speaker sustains a colonizing division of the world that ultimately makes countries where English is the mother tongue less welcoming for those from other lands and languages who seek a new life there. We also need to think back to how native speakers first brought English lessons to the colonies, investing the language with a sense of cultural mission. The schools have always made clear to students just where they stand and speak within the center and on the periphery of these languages, where civilization begins and ends. The intricacies of the European languages represented the unattainable ideals of this civilization for all but those who could claim an untroubled identity of European ancestry and mother tongue. Among those who have attempted to specify the moral dimensions of this continuing political history of the language, Homi Bhabha offers a theoretically and parenthetically rich reading of language that is well worth decoding:

> Culture-as-sign articulates the in-between moment when the rule of language as semiotic system—linguistic difference, the arbitrariness of the sign—turns into a struggle for the historical and ethical *right to signify.* The rule of language as a signifying system—the possibility of speaking at all—becomes the misrule of discourse: the right for only some to speak diachronically and differentially and for "others"—women, migrants, Third World peoples, Jews, Palestinians, for instance—to speak only symptomatically or marginally. (1992, p. 49, Bhabha's emphasis)

To speak "only symptomatically" is to speak always as an "other"; it is to speak only as a "woman" or a "migrant," and that, in itself, places in the margins what one is actually saying. The history of the right to speak as oneself does appear in the schools within the great story of democracy's unfolding. There is no reason why this liberating tale cannot be expanded to include the linguistic place of English as a national and world language, as if to learn a language is to learn about its hold on the world.

English as a National Language

The English language is itself the product of invading Teutonic peoples, as the amalgam of its imported Anglo-Saxon absorbed the further weight of Latin and Norse and French invasions, all the while chasing the native Celtic languages into the hinterlands of what would later become, at least in name, the United Kingdom. By the end of the first millennium, there were the rudiments of an identifiable language, and a people, known as "English." The nation, however, has not been England for centuries now, and the overwhelming majority of English speakers live far from the once-English nation. To study English is to pursue Shakespeare, yes, but it is also to read Dickinson, Atwood, Morrison, Okri, and Rushdie. English is a transnational national language, not strictly native to any place in particular.

Not long ago, when Randolph Quirk sought to identify the civilizing link between language and nation, he turned to the necessary unity between them: "We have come to take it as axiomatic," he assures us, "that the norm of national unity is linguistic unity: One nation, one language, with its standard determined by and emanating from the nation's capital—the seat of political authority, as well as authority in other respects (taste in architecture, literature, couture)" (1982, p. 57). Although this makes perfect sense, it can also be said that the capital seats of authority for English now extend to New York and Los Angeles as well as London and Washington. These cities operate transnationally; the unity and authority that they emanate are about the nation's global hegemony through English and American language and culture. To this initial identification of nation and language, Quirk adds that although nations can and do exist without a singular national language (all mother tongues, to his mind, deserving respect), ultimately those nations are indeed "fortunate in which the major language of daily currency is already one which (like English, French, Spanish, Arabic) is widely used beyond the frontiers of individual nations" (p. 71). Here, as you might imagine, I would add that these more widely used national languages did not spill over their frontiers through good fortune or linguistic advantage, but were part of deliberate campaigns of expansion of no small consequence for the languages and lives of those who felt the weight of those faraway capitals. Frantz Fanon has noted the geopolitical aspect of mastering extranational languages: "In France one says, 'He talks like a book.' In Martinique, 'He talks like a white man'" (1967, p. 21).

In reviewing how "national" languages were thought to sound the very soul of a people in the last century, Joshua Fishman (1972) holds up the example of the German philosophers Herder and Schleiermacher, who celebrated the organic authenticity realized in one's mother tongue. For both, language embodied the distinct culture of the state. Schleiermacher states that "language, thus, just like the Church or state, is an expression of a peculiar life" (cited by Fishman, p. 127), whereas Herder asks, in observing how the Chinese were held in "childish captivity" by their language, "Is not the language of each country the clay out of which the ideas of a people are formed, preserved, and transmitted?" (cited by Olender, 1992, p. 46). This linguistic romanticism simply added another dimension to the European fascination with the determination and division of peoples. It formed part of what Benedict Anderson (1983) has characterized as the bourgeois dream of the nation as an imagined community. Although both Herder and Schleiermacher put their faith in the spoken word of the people, the historian Anderson emphasizes how print culture can make a single vernacular the center of the nation-state: "The general growth in literacy, commerce, industry, communication and state machineries that marked the nineteenth century created powerful impulses for vernacular linguistic unification within each dynastic realm" (1983, pp. 77–78). Anderson offers a record of linguistic nationalism that swept Europe beginning with the Renaissance and led by a "golden age of vernacularizing lexicographers, grammarians, philologists and litterateurs" (p. 71). These language professionals and amateurs, followed by the reading classes, were able to bring about the institution of national languages in Hungary, the Balkans, Norway, and Finland (pp. 74–75). From the United Kingdom to South Africa, the nation-state had rarely evolved into the natural home of a singularly spoken people. The national tongue was far more often the result of the symbolic and literal violence required to forge and govern a standard language out of the vernaculars and dialects that marked the modern state.

The literati contributed as well, with writers singing the praises of their respective languages across Europe: "The 'national languages' in which they discovered the essential character of their nations," Eric Hobsbawm writes in *The Age of Empire, 1875–1914,* "were more often than not, artifacts, since they had to be compiled, standardized, homogenized, and modernized for contemporary and literary use, out of a jigsaw puzzle of local or regional dialects which constituted the non-literary languages as actually spoken" (1987, p. 147).[8] This growth of linguistic nationalism in Europe was also spurred on by the discoveries made abroad. What had begun as the random assembling of foreign word lists by Spanish, Portuguese, and Dutch seamen, missionaries, merchants, and soldiers had grown by this period into the scholarly pursuit of comparative grammars and the classification of language families (p. 70). These, in turn, led to speculations about evolutionary models of language development. Such was the classification and ordering of the world that defined a large part of imperialism's scholarly project.[9]

The English language's principal display case for that well-evolved linguistic perfection is the *Oxford English Dictionary (OED)*, a massive publish-

---

[8] On the making of standard English without the assistance of a state language academy, see Crowley (1989).
[9] See Olender for, among other aspects of this history, the relative demotion of Hebrew in the late eighteenth century as the language of origin and of paradise, giving way to Aryan,

ing project, led by James Murray, that was undertaken in the 1850s and finally completed in the early 1930s (J. Willinsky, 1994a). Whereas the French and Italians had scholarly academies to govern their languages, the liberty-loving English had come to rely on their dictionary editors to rule the word. Samuel Johnson's *Dictionary* had its day through the eighteenth and nineteenth centuries, but it was the *OED,* as the great Victorian engine of research, that carefully assembled a historical tapestry of the language by including citations from the language's great and small works dating back to the ninth century. James Murray and his associates used those citations to demonstrate just how distinguished a literary tradition underwrote this language at the center of a global empire.[10] The making of the *OED* provides its own lessons in how English was imagined as a civilizing beacon, a light to guide lesser peoples out of their own dark ages. This dictionary provided a gothic tower of suitable proportions to hold that light aloft, all the while asserting its linguistic dominion over nation and empire.

The Oxford dictionary that began as a nation-defining project in Great Britain continues to be directed at a worldwide market of speakers and students of the language. One might imagine that the Oxford dictionaries on sale in Kuala Lumpur, Calcutta, and Vancouver stand as artifacts of that otherwise diminished British authority. The plotless dictionary has a story to tell about an English that was carried into the world through the empire. The dictionary, once intended to define the national soul of the people, grew into a product for market export in a postcolonial world. Where once the *OED* brought a literary majesty to the language's history, with Shakespeare by far the leading source of citations in the dictionary, later editions of and supplements to this dictionary pursued the language of business, technology, and journalism, with an increasing proportion of its sampling of the English language coming from the United States.[11] The success of this linguistic marketing continues on a global scale, with the Oxford family of dictionaries cap-

---

Sanskrit, and Indo-Europrean research, with French philologist and historian Ernest Renan denying Hebrew the capability of evolving (1992, pp. 8–9, 53). Olender notes that in the 1800s, Renan, as well as Max Müller, spent decades working with race and language in regard to the concept of Aryanism, before cautioning against the racist implications that could be derived from comparative philology (p. 82).

[10] The concept of "invented tradition" as a European project of the last century is from Hobsbawm and Ranger (1983).

[11] In the period 1989–1991, the *OED* editors' sampling of English from outside the United Kingdom and the United States still fell short of 5 percent, whereas America's share had risen to 63 percent (J. Willinsky, 1994a, p. 236 n. 3). Given the habits of leading American dictionary publishers, it might be safe to say that the *New York Times* is the single most influential organ of the English language in setting a dictionary-led standard (J. Willinsky, 1988).

turing its share of the global market for English without yet creating a dictionary that adequately represents English as a world language. It remains a dictionary of two nations, housing a language that emanates from the linguistic capitals of the English language. The tattered paperback English dictionary that sits in students' desks around the world, although not necessarily an *Oxford,* symbolizes both the accessibility and the remoteness of this particular transnational tongue. The language is there to look up, even as it always comes from somewhere else. Where does this English stand? What sort of "peculiar life," to go back to Schleiermacher, does English engage in, if not one tangled up in the history of its dispersal? Since the collapse of the British Empire, the English language lives on as its legacy. It stands as a national and schooled language in a good number of countries.

Yet when it comes to linguistic nationalism, Anglo-American dictionaries pale before the recent movement to make English the official language of the United States (Peña, 1991; Baron, 1990). The Official English movement continues to gain national prominence, receiving legislative support in more than twenty states and standing behind a federal bill that in 1996 had passed the House of Representatives. English needs to be protected, the argument runs, to ensure the future of the nation and its democratic character. More pointedly and politically, the movement is intended to restrict support for the use of languages other than English in schools and other public institutions. Immigrants are seen as a threat to the English language, because too many of them are presumed to lack an interest in learning the nation's language. The fact is that they have shown a great deal of interest in learning English and often find themselves on enormous waiting lists for English classes—17,000 in New York City in 1993—leaving them frustrated about the skills and desires that cannot be realized for want of this language (D. Sontag, 1993). The Official English movement, which has been around in different incarnations since the First World War in America, is based, in Eileen Tamura's estimation, on "a doctrine of Anglo-Saxon superiority" (1993, p. 37). Examining how the issue was promoted earlier, in the education of children of Japanese descent, Tamura finds that the argument was clearly one of protecting not only "the future of American democracy" but "the survival of the English language and the dominance of the Anglo-Saxon 'race'" (p. 37). This reemergence of linguistic nationalism should give us pause, whether it comes on a T-shirt that reads, "Welcome to America—Now speak English," or with David Letterman joking on late-night television that solar flares are causing New York City taxi drivers to speak perfect English.

There is a troubling forgetfulness to it all, as if America had not already been built more than once by those who arrived without a word of English, and as if English itself were not a language that grew up with the benefit of exchanges with many tongues, translation playing an especially enriching role in the expansion of the vocabulary (J. Willinsky, 1994a, pp. 104–10). One interesting chapter in the linguistic history of America has been its own postcolonial struggle with distancing itself from England and, thus, the English language. The proposals in the early years of the nation were to make German and even Hebrew the official languages of the United States (Baron, 1982, p. 11). As it was, Noah Webster successfully instituted a number of spelling reforms (*colour/color*) through his dictionaries, as one means of establishing the greater reasonableness and independence of the American people. Now, it appears that the very coherence of the nation is threatened by a Babel of tongues. Yet Julia Kristeva, writing in France, sees another sort of fear lurking behind these apprehensions over newcomers: "Lacking the reins of the maternal tongue, the foreigner who learns a new language is capable of the most unforeseen audacities when using it—intellectual daring and obscenities as well" (1991, p. 31). For all that the schools and other mass media have done to bring a standard language to bear, the voices that fill a country have always spoken across many tongues and accents.

What is unsettling, however, is that those who promote the importance of ESL services make the same case as those who seek to restrict this opportunity, both tying English language skills to the fate of the nation. Consider this comment on the results of a literacy survey in the *New York Times* that indicated that immigrants scored poorly in English: "The test which included questions with a civics theme like jury-duty instruction or points of view on public policy issues, raised questions about whether these individuals lack even the most rudimentary of skills to be full participants in American society" (Celis, 1993). This could be read as a call for increased funding for ESL programs or a condemnation of immigration. Yes, these people may well have trouble with jury duty, but are they really wanting in "the most rudimentary of skills"—tempting us to imagine them as illiterate—necessary to participate in and make responsible judgments about American society? This is to ignore the degree to which America has long been a multilingual nation served by a multilingual press. It is to miss the educational opportunity of understanding how language is used to build, divide, and govern a community. Calling into question the role of education in affirming nationalist and linguistic associations that restrict opportunity and teach a narrowing of the nation, could well form part of a curriculum that pauses at some point to reflect with students on its own educational practices.

The Postcolonial National Language

The basic facts of colonialism's impact on nation and language are easy enough to assemble. In a world of some sixty-five hundred living languages, more than one hundred of the world's nations have selected English, French, or Spanish to serve as at least one of their official languages, with half of those nations choosing English (Mackey, 1991, p. 58 n. 10). This facilitates a greater degree of international communication while ensuring lingering dependencies on the part of the former colonies. As Robert Phillipson (1991) forcefully argues, the European nations have not missed out on this economic and cultural opportunity to retain an otherwise lost influence. In examining the map of European language-use, one is faced with how the postcolonial states, as R. B. Le Page explains, "owe their frontiers to the old colonial regimes which, for motives of their own—administrative convenience, or the geography of white exploration and settlement—gave a sometimes spurious unity to regions which had little otherwise to recommend them as national entities" (1964, p. 1). The language of the colonial administration was sometimes the only tongue in common across the cobbled-together regions of the colonies.

The nation that became Nigeria encompasses roughly four hundred indigenous languages. Two of those languages, Hausa and Yoruba, were able to support small weekly newspapers in 1991, whereas English, the nation's sole official language, affords a dozen large-circulation dailies (Schmied, 1991, p. 43 n. 1). The nation's business is conducted largely in a language that is not native to the majority of citizens but that has popular support when it comes to education, for example (pp. 30, 42). In what sense, then, is English a national language? This has not prevented the Nigerian author Wole Soyinka from winning the 1986 Nobel Prize for a body of literature that he wrote in English, even as he advocates Swahili as an African lingua franca. At the height of the colonial independence movements, the Second Congress of Negro Writers and Artists, which met in Rome in 1959, passed a series of resolutions on language and the African states: "(a) that independent African countries should not adopt European languages as national languages; (b) that a pan-African language be chosen and fostered; (c) that a team of linguists be selected to modernize that language" (Schmied, p. 121).

To set this struggle on a more personal level, we might consider the deliberations of African writers confronted with the question whether to write in English. Chinua Achebe commented on the challenges he faced in the 1960s as a Nigerian novelist whose mother tongue was Ibo, even as he was educated in English: "Is it right that a man should abandon his mother tongue for someone else's? It looks like a dreadful betrayal; and produces a guilty feeling. But for me there was no other choice. I have been given the language and I intend to use it" (1975, p. 62). Two decades later, the Kenyan writer Ngugi wa Thiong'o put the issue in decidedly more forceful terms, referring to imperialism's "cultural bomb," which can "annihilate a people's belief in their names, in their languages, in their environment" and make them "want to identify with that which is farthest removed from themselves, for instance, with other people's languages rather than their own" (1986, p. 3). This vision is met, in turn, by Nigerian scholar Gaurav Desai, who holds, in poststructuralist fashion, that "any essentialist arguments which attempt to reject English because it is not 'African' are, I believe, romanticized treatises on some abstract (that is, ahistorical) notion of a monolithic 'Africa'" (1993, p. 10). But Desai's claim that "English is as much an African language as it is a British or American one" betrays its own level of ahistorical idealism that stands in the face of a regard for English in Africa as a dialect form (p. 10). For his part, Ngugi rejects this stance by pointing to the domination of English by a certain Anglo-American geography of cultural and national reference, especially in educational arenas. This debate about the writer's responsibilities to word and nation should remind us of the complex legacy out of which writers are struggling to bring forth a new sort of future.

The benefits of inheriting a national language of international currency are not as unequivocal as Quirk suggests in the earlier quotations. For example, there is no refusing this inheritance. Postcolonial India spent untold energy in trying to establish Hindi as the country's official language and thereby to break the administrative and educational dependency on English. The government sought to standardize Hindi through examination centers for schools and colleges, a board of scientific terminology, and a Hindi encyclopedia (Hobsbawm, 1990, p. 112). Yet, after setting aside fifteen years for the transition from English to Hindi, the country found itself forced to retain English as an official language, not least of all because of language riots protesting the imposition of Hindi as *the* national language in the linguistically diverse India (Fasold, 1984, pp. 20–30). Since then, Aijaz Ahmad observes, "English has proliferated, instead of declined," which he takes as indicating "the greater elaboration and deeper penetration of the state into all aspects of civil society" (1992, p. 74). The country's cities are occupied, he notes, by "an English-based intelligentsia for whom only the literary document produced in English is a *national* document . . . so that English emerges in this imagination not as *one* of the Indian languages, which it undoubtedly is, but as *the* language of national integration and bourgeois civility" (p. 75;

Ahmad's emphasis). Ahmad would as soon abandon English as give up the railway. He stresses, in a way consistent with this book, that with this embrace of English there needs to be an understanding of "the mode of its assimilation into our social fabric" and how "it is used in the process of class formation and social privilege, here and now" (p. 77).

It should at least be clear that there is no safe stance or right answer to take on language and nation. Even the politically correct pose, typically so easy to spot, does not make itself readily apparent in deciding how to relate to the linguistic past, to this division of local and international perspectives, while speaking to the future. Let us go informed and tentative, receptive and disruptive, into the play of language and languages that speak the world. Let us support people's choices of language. Let us advocate that lessons on languages of greater global currency include the historical forces that have created the unequal exchange value of this global linguistic economy. Otherwise, one might ask, how are students to withstand the sense that English has assumed its global status out of a natural superiority and the superiority of its native speakers? How are they to interpret English's status as a national language in so many states? How are they to resist judging people, and themselves, by how well they speak this one language, by how native a speaker of English they can be? English today is no less a source of linguistic identification and dislocation than its history has made it in the process of becoming a global phenomenon, and the point of an education in language is primarily to help in understanding that complex process.

English as a World Language

In the early years of this century, the anthropologist Franz Boas (1974) felt it necessary to insist that all languages should be regarded as equivalent in their development and sophistication. He did this in the face of what had become a common evolutionary ranking of primitive and civilized languages, and, with a number of his colleagues, he was gradually successful in establishing at least an anthropological equality of recognition for both the languages and the cultures that make up this world (Stocking, 1982). Today, this idea faces another sort of threat, with the general acknowledgment that English has assumed the mantle of "world language." My concern with this title is not how many people are said to be using English, especially as the figures cited in a typical piece on the topic range from 800 million to 2 billion (Kachru, 1992c, p. 357). What is important is the manner in which English is accorded this special honor, and how it reflects or moves beyond the fulfillment of an earlier imperial mandate that had something of the same presumption. English may well dominate in scientific literature, air traffic control, and the business correspondence of many multinational corporations. However, we have to watch whether the promotion of English as a world language carries within it the cultural, racial, and national legacy that I am associating with imperialism, and we have to insist that this legacy be explicitly addressed as part of a valuable and missing lesson for an education in language that is intent on not reproducing the colonial frame of mind.

It is easy enough to find distinguished scholars unabashedly promoting English in what Phillipson refers to as a "linguicism," which seeks "to legitimate, effectuate, and reproduce an unequal division of power and resources . . . between groups which are defined on the basis of language" (1991, p. 47). There is Randolph Quirk, who, in refusing to shy away from invoking the greatness that was the British Empire, refers to English as "*the* language on which the sun does not set" (1985, p. 1; Quirk's emphasis). Equally, Robert Burchfield, editor of the *Supplement of the Oxford English Dictionary*, appears prepared to call forth educational missionaries who will make it their business to relieve linguistic deprivation, with perhaps something of an imperial profit motive in mind for the dictionary:

> English has also become a lingua franca to the point that any literate educated person on the face of the globe is in a very real sense deprived if he does not know English. Poverty, famine, and disease are instantly recognized as the cruelest and least excusable forms of deprivation. Linguistic deprivation is a less easily noticed condition, but one nevertheless of great significance. (1985, pp. 160–61)

The other familiar figure in this set of English promoters is Braj Kachru, who, in making his case for the language's global status, is given to quoting John Adams, who, as the second president of the United States is said to have foreseen "the destiny of English" in 1780 when he stated that "English will be the most respectable language in the world and the most universally read and spoken in the next century, if not before the close of this one" (1992a, p. 2). In all three cases, there is a triumphant tone, as if the forces of evolution, to overstate it only somewhat, had awarded this tongue its natural place in the progress of humankind.

Kachru, for one, celebrates English's "universal" element while carefully distinguishing between native and nonnative speakers, or those for whom English is the "other tongue," whose ability he allows can vary "from broken English to almost native or ambilingual competence" (1992a, p. 3). English's cultural value as a universal language is unequally distributed between those who inherit this wealth through possession of it as a mother tongue in an

English-speaking country, and those who can only aspire to it, forever assigned to the purgatory of the nonnative speaker. Kachru holds that the spread of English is the result both of inherent qualities and of external factors, that is, "because of its literary heritage, because of the status it may confer on the reader or speaker, because of the door it opens on technology, science, trade and diplomacy" (p. 4). He goes on to support the claim of English with such evidence as the testimony of an Indian raj from the nineteenth century who asked that the British provide an education to his people in English rather than in Sanskrit, as had originally been planned, and the remarkable Japanese proposal of Mori Arinori in 1873 that English become the language of state and business in Japan (p. 5).

The English language may well have been welcomed, but it was also enforced across the empire, not least of all by the "colonial spiritual policemen," as Ngugi has termed those who brought an English education to the outreaches of the empire (1981, p. 34). Summing up the place of English in colonial Africa, Ngugi calculates that "the weapon of language [should be] added to that of the Bible and the sword in pursuit of what David Livingstone, in the case of nineteenth-century imperialism, called 'Christianity plus 5 percent' " (1990, p. 284).[12] Care needs to be taken in assessing English's ascendancy around the globe, its opening of doors to the future while holding the keys to the past, so that one does not lose sight of that history even as one seeks to move beyond the attitudes associated with that history.

It is not that I imagine the vast company of English-language educators currently serving around the world as a lost legion of colonial militia, armed with the jingoistic poetry of Kipling and Newbolt. But I do think that these educators need to go into this global language trade with their eyes open to English as a national-imperial language with a history that is not yet fully past but stands to be transformed. This understanding of what it means to teach English, of how teachers regard the multilingual resources that their students bring to class, and of how they encourage their monolingual and multilingual students to think of their own place within the nation, are all part of what follows from these representations of language and nation. Without discounting the advantages of international languages in developing a far more

---

[12] A nineteenth-century missionary such as Hope Waddell could feel assured that in Africa with "the aid of missionaries and schools [English] may be made the common medium of communication, yea, the literary and learned language of all Negro tribes as the Roman language was to the modern nations of Europe while yet the modern European languages were in an infantine and unwritten state" (cited by Batsleer et al., 1985, p. 23).

cooperative, if not interdependent, globalism, I think that we cannot shy away from critically examining the merits and consequences of the Anglo-centric dreams of a universal language that, like our prized credit cards, will be negotiable anywhere. Without my challenging anyone's aspirations to learn English or to participate in the world of this language, there remains a responsibility among educators to bring to these lessons an understanding of the English imperative and all that it entails. Such an approach could mean that students suffer a good deal less of the linguicism behind the language.

The education of language teachers, then, to extend this notion of a responsible curriculum, needs to include a critique of *method* as forming the core of their own professionalism. For example, Phillipson is critical of how many ESL classes allow only English to be spoken, questioning whether the use of other languages interferes with the process and whether native speakers are unquestionably the ideal teachers (1991, pp. 185–215). In a word, English is not taught as a *second* language but as the only medium of intelligible communication. The ESL educator's claim to professionalism, rooted in the academic discipline of linguistics, forms part of a larger Western project of intellectual mastery of the world that, in its applied science of language, can exclude a great number of the language lessons discussed in this chapter. Educators also need to be vigilant with the traces of a latent imperialism among far-reaching agencies such as the British Council and the Center for Applied Linguistics in Washington, which promote the teaching of English on a global scale. English has become an extremely successful cultural commodity, with such agencies operating like language marketing boards to ensure that its value continues to grow. The mandate of the British Council, as announced by the Prince of Wales in 1935 on its inauguration by royal charter, makes apparent its imperial roots:

> Our object is to assist the largest number possible to appreciate the glories of our literature, our contribution to the arts and sciences and our pre-eminent contribution to political science. This can be best achieved by promoting the study of our language abroad. (Cited by Phillipson, p. 138)[13]

---

[13] Half a century later, the council's 1987–88 annual report states that "the British Council promotes Britain abroad through educational, cultural, and technical cooperation" (cited by Phillipson, 1991, p. 140), and Phillipson reports that it has offices in eighty-six countries and fifty-five English teaching centers in thirty-two countries (p. 142). More recently, Caroline Moore of the council stated, "We are very concerned that English could be perceived as damaging to other languages," although she also expressed optimisim at its global status: "But we're mindful of what happened to French and Latin" (cited by Drohan and Freeman, 1997, p. D1).

Teachers also need to come into contact with the opposition that has arisen in the face of the unbridled enthusiasm for English's claim as a world language, exuded by the likes of Quirk, Burchfield, Kachru, and others. They might, for example, turn to Prayag Tripathi's biting piece "English: 'The Chosen Tongue'" (1992), which appeared in *English Today,* a journal given to covering the global phenomenon of English. Tripathi argues that "the notion of English as the most important language in the world is, I think, an ideological production, the creation of the native and non-native elite with a material and professional interest in the language, its retention and dissemination worldwide" (p. 3). Rather than picking up on the biblical overtones suggested by "the chosen tongue," he goes after another irony inherent in the sense of "choice": "Nothing could be farther from the truth, for the choice is hardly independent of the will of history and providence, aided by colonial headmasters who disallowed and punished the use of local languages in the school" (p. 3). Tripathi contrasts English-language boosterism with the declining reliance on the English language in India's schools.[14] His position finds support in the work of sociolinguists Andrew Conrad and Joshua Fishman, who conclude that, although the demand for English remains closely associated with "the political and economic hegemony of English-speaking powers," the rise in indigenous national languages will cause "a decline in English medium schooling at the primary and secondary levels" (1977, pp. 55–56). Still, they comment that English remains "the major link-language in the world today and that it alone shows signs of continuing as such, at least in the short run, while the use of local languages for official literacy/education related purposes is also likely to increase" (p. 56). What has happened is that English's status as the second language of choice for literacy- and education-related purposes has continued to grow at the expense not so much of local languages as of other former colonial languages, principally French. More recently, Richard Bailey, another who is, in his own words, "skeptical of English triumphalism," challenges the more optimistic figures on the number of En-

---

[14] One of the more gratuitously inflated statistical examples is Braj Kachru's "three concentric circles of English" that comprise lists of nations and their populations divided among an "inner circle" of English-speaking countries, an "outer circle" that ranges from Bangladesh to Zambia, and an "expanding circle" that includes, among others, China, Indonesia, Japan, and the USSR (1992c, p. 356). McArthur, in his review of models for English, notes only that Kachru's possesses "a unique demographic dimension," but his own model (without the numbers) is equally misleading in its use of concentric circles that place "World Standard English" in the center, with the next circle equally divided among British, American, African, Caribbean, South Asian, and Australian Englishes, followed by further divisions by region and nation, suggesting a great democracy with each constituent part contributing equally to the definition of a common standard (1992, p. 19).

glish speakers in the world, calculating that the proportion globally is perhaps "15 percent, *and declining*" (1991, p. vii; Bailey's emphasis).[15] Although Bailey's point about the decline of English is, in part, a factor of differing birthrates around the globe, it also represents the deliberate efforts of some nations to resist what might be seen as English's continuing quest for global cultural domination. The promotion of English as a lingua franca would make it the first tongue among equals, securing the cultural capital of its speakers in ways that spill over into other cultural and commercial areas.

To return to the reflections of Ngugi on the place of the English language in Kenya, he notes how he and others quickly learned that "the English language was the bearer of all knowledge in the arts and sciences," leading some students to the obvious conclusion that "English . . . was the language spoken by God" (1990, p. 286). He goes on to point out that his objection is not that English was taught using Oxford readers but that it was taught "as if Africa had no tongues except those brought there by imperialism" (p. 287). Although things have changed with the independence of Kenya and other African nations, Ngugi's essential point remains that "English and the African languages never met as equals, under conditions of equality, independence, and democracy, and this is the root of all subsequent distortions" (p. 287). Ngugi asks that we recognize that although English proudly stands as the language of democracy in England and America, it was a culturally destructive vehicle for imperialism abroad. If we are to consider a common language for the world—and the idea is tempting when thinking of a new global awareness and one-world sensibility—Ngugi insists that care be taken not to continue the damage that the European languages have already wrought on other cultures and languages (p. 291). This professor of comparative literature at New York University and well-established author calls for a new appreciation of translation, even as he himself has attempted to turn away from writing in English to writing in his native Gikuyu, which has no press to support it, speaking of "the struggle to move the center of our literary engagements from European languages to a multiplicity of locations in our languages" amid "the present conditions of a continent's disbelief in itself" (1993, p. xiv). But Ngugi also dares to nominate Kiswahili, a major language spoken in eastern, central, and southern Africa, as a candidate for a world language, offering by way of understatement that "this would symbolize the dawn of a new era in human relations" (1990, p. 293).

---

[15] David Crystal's *Cambridge Encyclopedia of Language* puts the number of first-language speakers of English at 350 million, or roughly 7 percent of the world's population (1987, p. 287).

Before throwing up one's hands at the slim prospects of changing people's attitudes toward such fundamental conceptions as language and nation, one needs to consider the reforms that feminists have effected in diction (and dictionaries) through a far-reaching analysis of the place of gender in language.[16] To have students see opportunities to challenge language norms and history has the potential to affect both who speaks and what is spoken, a point that seems all the more promising in an era marked by global change. At issue is a cultivated sensitivity to the ways in which the word inscribes authority and culture, identity and difference. These sensitivities to the political economy of language, on both personal and public levels, can inform the general approach of educators, students, and learning materials to language instruction. I am advising that, as an intellectual right and responsibility of the curriculum, we assist students in learning more about how language forms an integral part of a history that is still unfolding in a post- and neocolonial world. We can think back through lost languages to the imperial patterns of settlement and consider how education needs to be responsive to the words that others live by and responsive to its own role in reshaping lives through its schooling of language.

What would follow from introducing into the classroom this history of language, nation, and world cannot be predicted. To think of how language marks the flow of power through history could prove a source of humility that I think would only add to our teaching of the English language. To ignore these lessons, however, only adds to the price that many students have to pay in coming to a new land and language, even as it ill prepares the rest of the student body for living fruitfully on a multilingual globe. Granted, the global impact of imperialism on language forms only one chapter in the history of language, but given the weight felt by those trying hard to move beyond imperialism's definition of the world, it seems that a chapter on language and nation, native speaker and dictionary, is worth teaching. I recognize that these lessons must play a minor role in learning a language and that my coverage does not exhaust the issues raised by considerations of language education in an interdependent world. Yet I think that, in looking to the century ahead and at current tensions that we are having such difficulty moving beyond, we should work knowingly with a history that is, after all, unfolding through all of our lives and words.

---

[16] Zohreh Sullivan directly argues colonialism's race and gender connections, pointing to how "constructions of heroic masculinity were conflated with myths of cultural origins and common inheritance in order to create a unified idea of the Imperial mission" among the British (1989, p. 23). Julia Emberley calls for a "feminism of decolonization" that she finds present in the writings of Canadian native women (1993, p. 4).

CRUSOE DELIVERS FRIDAY.

Engraving by J. D. Watson in Daniel Defoe, The Life and
Adventures of Robinson Crusoe *(London: Routledge, 1869).
Courtesy University of British Columbia Library.*

NINE

LITERATURE AND THE EDUCATED IMAGINATION

"When asked to write a short essay on the good of the study of literature, I was stumped. What good is it?" Sally Hansen, a high school senior, was responding to a reading of Northrop Frye's *The Educated Imagination* (1963). She had come to realize that, after twelve years of literature classes, from Mother Goose to William Shakespeare, and now the distinguished literary critic Frye, she was hard-pressed to name what literature was worth. Her pointed question—"What good is it?"—might well cause an English teacher's life to pass before her eyes, which may be why more than a few teachers have assigned Frye's highly approachable defense of literature to their classes. The book offers a rare instance of high school students dealing directly with the reasons for studying what they study. Many of them may not have cause again to think about why literature matters. Given this prospect, I consider in this chapter the colonial legacy of literature that teachers and students would do well to consider when they think about literature's value. I do so by examining the case Frye made in 1963 for literature and students' responses to it three decades later, to see how English literature stands in an ostensibly postcolonial era.

I have used Frye's title—"the educated imagination"—more than once in this book to suggest what the study of the arts and sciences is held to achieve. There are, of course, many ways of educating an imagination, but for Frye the phrase reflects a particular form of engagement with literature and the arts that radiates from a Western canon to encompass traditions from around the world. In making this case, Frye still falls back, as I will make plain, on a colonial imaginary of island paradises, plantation economies, and evolutionary hierarchies. This imperial legacy lives on today as a trace element in our educational lives, not necessarily toxic in itself but worrisome as it goes unspoken and unexamined. Along with the English language, literature formed the core of the British Empire's for-export culture, and in many ways literature still holds a special place. Although English literature has its largest market within the classroom, Jane Austen has recently proved the darling of television screens and movie theaters, giving serious competition to a run of Shakespeare film productions. The pleasure we might take from these magnificent productions is also part of a history of literature's exploits in the former colonies. Literature survives the empire that first carried it abroad, but how, we might ask, has our thinking about the story told by literature been changed in the process?

In many university English departments, devoted as they are to finding new things to say about literature, a deliberately postcolonial regard has been introduced, concerned with how literature works across the geopolitical surface of the world.[1] The postcolonial critics—and there are not many—work with and against the prevailing variations of close reading that often entail the subtle removal of literature from the world, which Frye exemplifies without fully achieving, as we shall see. This belief in art's transcending and uplifting powers persists, despite the exaggerated postmodern rumors of its death. Still, a struggle over the nature of art has emerged, making for strange bedfellows. Witness America's recent and heated "culture wars" brought on by the attack of archconservative aesthetic sensibilities aligning with staunchly anti-intellectual forces in their rage over perceived politicosexual transgressions in the arts (Bolton, 1992). Then there is the Association of Literary Scholars and Critics, which formed in 1994 to save literature from the likes of postcolonial critics through its commitment to "literature as literature and not something else" (Fruman, 1995).

The high schools, where most people receive the whole of their literary training, are largely protected from the tempests of theory. The teachers working there often rely, as I have found, on their own original literary training. Thus, I think it worthwhile to consider the literary order that Frye represents, as it captures the training of more than one generation of teachers, a literary order that I, no less than many other students and teachers, learned to love and loved to learn, an order that has had a lasting influence on our edu-

---

[1] On postcolonial literary theory, a good starting point is the two Ashcroft, Griffiths, and Tiffin books on the topic (1989, 1995).

cated imaginations.[2] To that end, this chapter briefly introduces the colonial history of literature and literature teaching, before turning to what Frye made of the educated imagination in the 1960s. It was a formative period for a good number of today's teachers, amid the civil rights movement and the collapse of colonialism. Yet Frye's ideas about literature have hardly passed, and in the final section of this chapter, I draw on a contemporary engagement with Frye by a group of students who read *The Educated Imagination* during their final year at a high school in Ontario.

A Colonial Primer

The question how the writer's craft, as opposed to the arts of the shipwright and gunsmith, could further an empire has recently attracted the critical attention of literary scholars. In naming the creative energies that drove England's Renaissance, these critics have now set the exploration of America alongside the Reformation, the resurgence of classicism, and the rise of nationalism. Jeffrey Knapp (1992), for one, makes apparent how the possibilities of a New World empire, which emerged during the early and otherwise discouraging days of America's initial colonization, were imaginatively and encouragingly rendered by Spenser, Shakespeare, and More. It was the English writer, safely ensconced at home, who made plausible and attractive the idea of being at home in a larger world of England's own making. Preview the wonders through literature, these works offered; see and feel the adventure played out in *The Tempest* or *Utopia*. The colonial empire became one of the creative playing fields of English literature, and vice versa.

The fantastical literary voyages gradually gave way, as the world became increasingly "known," to the greater realism exemplified by Defoe's *Moll Flanders,* no less than his *Robinson Crusoe.* This literary realism was aligning itself with scientific empiricism in rendering the coherence of the expanded world (Fausett, 1993). Although it is tempting to credit postcolonial theory alone for finally naming the often overlooked colonial influence on the arts, that would not be accurate. In his life of the poet Richard Savage, Samuel

---

[2] See John Willinsky (1991) for the influence of Frye and other literary theorists on the teaching of English in the high schools of North America. See Walter Kendrick for a typical paradise-lost defense of close reading: "Academic criticism told us what poems meant. . . . The technique called close reading, required no theoretical buttresses. You paid the closest attention to what a poem said, to everything it said, and then you wrote your article" (1995, p. 12). The problem with this approach is that everything from the choice of the poems to the closenesses that were most prized, in their ambiguities and ambivalences, for example, was not without theory but an expression of theoretical underwriting and buttressing.

Johnson spoke of the settlement of the colonies "bewildering the imagination in delightful prospect," which "naturally fixed the attention, and excited the applause of the poet" (1975, p. 285). The poet, whom Johnson ranks here as something of a travel agent and emigration officer, "guides the unhappy fugitive from want and persecution to plenty, quiet, and security, and seats him in scenes of peaceful solitude, and undisturbed repose" (pp. 285–86). No less than the many treatises, ballads, sermons, and broadsides that extolled the benefits of empire, English literature rallied people to the imperial cause, portrayed the adventure, engaged in the abolition debate, and generally participated in the public discourses of the time, in measured prose or rhyme.

Literature had the advantage of keeping the play of gender at the forefront of the sense made of imperialism. In considering the fiction of empire, Jenny Sharpe sets out how "the figure of women [was] instrumental in shifting a colonial system of meaning from self-interest and moral superiority to self-sacrifice and racial superiority" (1993, p. 7). Certainly, a particular sexual tension pervaded the literary setting of European women among the "savages," from Prospero's charge against Caliban in *The Tempest* ("Thou didst seek to violate / The honor of my child") to the cave scene with Adela Quested in Forster's *Passage to India*. Literature evoked, in Sharpe's analysis, the striking of a racial boundary that, once crossed, in this imaginative public realm, carries the weight of a crime against nature, with all of its ensuing horror and fascination. Literature toyed with the imaginative frontiers, situating the dangers and tensions of this "living in sin," in a phrase from Paul Scott's more recent *Raj Quartet* to which Sharpe pays close attention (p. 157).

Literature was also able to offer up the particular sins and blundering ineptitude of expatriates abroad; it was a way for readers to avoid the prospect that colonialism was at root a hideous rather than a beneficent act. In her reading of eighteenth-century writers Aphra Behn, Jonathan Swift, and others, Laura Brown finds that "the threatening ambiguity of the native and the woman place them in a similar relation to the dominant, imperialist ideology" (1993, p. 17).[3] The key, for Brown, is literature's staging of identity for both natives and women, which, in the eighteenth century, often took place around commodification and conquest. The regard of colonized peoples as effeminate only confounded the colonists' sexual orientation toward the subaltern that underlay the literature and history of imperialism. So much of

---

[3] Brown summarizes her position as a "feminist reading of colonist ideology, which places women at the center of the structures of rationalization that justify mercantile expansion, to ground an account of the formal and ideological contradictions surrounding the representation of race and slavery" (1993, p. 62).

what held this system together was surrounded by a purposeful and "dead silence," which is also what followed Fanny Price's question to her uncle, Sir Thomas Bertram, about the slavery by which the family had profited, in Jane Austen's *Mansfield Park* (Said, 1993, p. 96). Even in its silences, literature seems capable of articulating the complex moral edifice by which some women were protected and others used, some were met with silence and others were silenced, within the global structure of beloved home and necessary colonies. English literature rendered sensitive and sensible the immediate world of civilized men and women, while imperial and industrial expansion remained the silent underwriter of domestic exploits. Literature and its attendant criticism identified and intensified a certain class of heart and hearth as the proper location of civilized attention.

Before letting go the postcolonial critical pose, it is important to see that it also applies to American writers. In a major work on race in the making of American literature, Eric Sundquist carefully sets out

> the degree to which writing about the problem of slavery—in particular, writing about slavery by African Americans—can be seen to have animated that rebirth [of American literature] not because it was central to every major literary text of the period but because it defined the overarching ideology of liberty which left the nation in a state of unresolved crisis while at the same time authorizing its cultural independence, territorial expansion, and the rise to world power. (1993, p. 30)

The case Sundquist builds, which is as subtle and complex as the quotation suggests, comes out of the intersection of Nat Turner, Frederick Douglass, W. E. B. Du Bois, Herman Melville, and Mark Twain. Another critic interested in Melville, John Carlos Rowe, gives even greater prominence to this literary figure's engagement with imperialism, as he argues that "Melville's *Typee* is one of the first U.S. literary texts to establish a connection between the institutions of slavery in the United States and the Euroamerican colonialism in Polynesia" (1994, p. 255). Rowe's interest is in literary renderings that encourage students "to find alternatives to the social, political and economic failures of the democratic promise" that was, after all, America's postcolonial starting point (p. 257). This theme of America's literary response to colonialism is sustained by Walter Benn Michaels (1993), who examines a later series of anti-imperialist novels, such as Thomas Dixon's *The Leopard's Spots,* from 1902. Michaels finds that these now forgotten but once popular works still managed, despite their assault on extensions of the American empire, to succumb to nativist efforts at fixing the boundaries of race *within* the nation.

At the outset of *Playing in the Dark,* Toni Morrison declares that "the

readers of virtually all of American fiction have been positioned as white"
(1992, p. xii). This positioning acts as a form of deracination that encourages
white readers to see their situation as "universal," just as educators tend to
hold that the school curriculum is color-blind.[4] Against this complacency,
Morrison describes a need "to discover through a close look at literary 'blackness,' the nature—even the cause—of literary 'whiteness'" (p. 9). Notice how
this is not a call to ban the classics, but to consider again their influence and
uses. Against what she identifies as the "studied indifference of literary criticism" to these issues, Morrison hopes that we can now raise the questions
"What parts do the invention and development of whiteness play in the construction of what is loosely described as 'American'?" and, more generally,
"What makes intellectual domination possible?" (p. 9). In this way, she dares
to name the colonial project in American literature as "the architecture of a
new white man" (p. 15; Morrison's emphasis). She vividly recalls the degree to
which freedom in American literature is achieved by the African presence:
"Africanism is the vehicle by which the American self knows itself as not enslaved, but free . . . not a blind accident of evolution but a progressive fulfillment of destiny" (p. 52). I would add to Morrison's account, especially as she
herself has taught literature in school and university, only the fact that literature does a good deal of its work in literature classes. The issue, then, is not so
much holding Hemingway responsible, as Morrison does, for being an architect of the American character. It is, rather to come to grips with the work
that his books continue to do in classrooms today. Not only is the story Hemingway tells important, but also the way in which his works continue to be
taught defines the nature of the American experience by gender and race.

Finally, in the meeting of literature and imperialism, there is that body of
"postcolonial literature" which came on the heels of colonialism's demise after
the Second World War. The category encompasses a geopolitical amalgam of
writers from among the many decolonized states. "It has become the project
of postcolonial literatures," writes one student of this literature, Helen Tiffin, "to investigate the European textual capture and containment of colonial
and postcolonial space and to intervene in that originary and continuing containment" (1995, p. 97). These are the sort of points that postcolonial critics
make, although the critical categories at stake have certainly left at least one

---

[4] Christine Sleeter, a leading figure in multicultural education, writes that "white teachers
construct race . . . mainly on the basis of their life experiences and vested interests" (1993,
p. 157). Although she is not optimistic about change, I think there is a need to introduce
teachers to how these race constructs are, in fact, grounded in academic disciplines rather
than in their own experiences, and that they take their basis from the very founding of social studies, English literary study, and modern biology.

such critic cold. "Not only was it [colonial literature] a ghetto," Salman Rushdie writes in his essay "'Commonwealth Literature' Does Not Exist," "it was an exclusive one" (1991, p. 63).[5] Still, if postcolonial literature and criticism, with their political interests in national status, go beyond what literature is supposed to do, threatening to spoil the purely private and personal pleasures of the text, they are also educational in their desire to expand the historical contexts that give rise to readerly desires, all of which brings us to the other side of the story, that is, to the largely colonial invention of English literature as a subject fit for the schools.

Colonial Literary Study

One can roughly date the launch of English literature classes in the British Empire with the passing of the 1835 English Education Act in India. The English Education Act made English the language of instruction in the Indian schools under British control. English was to serve the natives much as Latin served British students, in a ladder of learned ascendancy. As the reader will recall from chapter 4, the key figure is Thomas Macaulay, whose famous 1835 minute to the British government on education was based on his estimation that the whole of Indian literature was unworthy of a shelf of English writing. Nearly two decades later, in 1853, the orientalist Horace Wilson was able to advise the British Parliament that as "we initiate [the Indians] into our literature, particularly at an early age, and get them to adopt feelings and sentiments from our standard writers, we make an impression upon them, and affect any considerable alteration in their feelings and notions" (cited by Viswanathan, 1989, p. 48). Literature teaching was thought instrumental in shaping character. As it reflected the genius of a people, it not only would serve as a model of civilized being to others, but also would work upon students in the colonial schools as a "mask of conquest," in Gauri Viswanathan's phrase.[6]

What was proved in colonial schools was then thought fit for Great Britain. With the Foster Act of 1872, which furthered the compulsory education of British children, English literature found its place as part of a cur-

---

[5] This critical alignment with postcolonial literatures has been rightly questioned by critic W. J. T. Mitchell, who observes that although such criticism "tends to subvert the imperial authority," the authors at issue (he names J. M. Coetzee, Ian Wedde, and Toni Morrison) look on it "with wary fascination . . . unsure whether it is a friendly collaborator in the process of decolonization or a threatening competitor for limited resources" (1995, pp. 476–77).

[6] Viswanathan cites the following from the *Madras Christian Instructor and Missionary Record* from 1844: "The genius of literature . . . clearly sees . . . that she has found the men who are to extend her empire to the ends of the earth, and give her throne a stability that will be lasting as the sun" (1989, p. 166).

riculum devoted, in its own way, to forging a unified state and empire that included the most wayward elements of those far-off colonies and the industrial classes at home. Among English literature's great educational advocates at the time was Matthew Arnold, who brought together his capacities as literary critic and school inspector: "Good poetry," he advocated in his 1880 inspector's report to the Privy Council, "does undoubtedly tend to form the soul and character" (1908, p. 60).[7] English literature, as a discrete academic discipline, had a more difficult time finding a proper home in the great universities of Oxford and Cambridge, where it presumably was needed far less to shape character than in the common schools (Palmer, 1965).

During this period, Canada was the site of much educational activity on behalf of English literature, and was no less so after entering postcolonial nationhood in 1867. Judging from the evidence amassed by Robert Morgan (1990), English literature had a large role to play in the country's smooth transition from colony to dominion, whether one looks at the composition topics assigned at University College in Toronto ("The connection between literary excellence and natural greatness, as exhibited in English history") or listens to the declarations of educator Henry Scalding that Shakespeare was "virtually a type of colonist . . . appreciated among the junior members of the family of nations—among the human downrootings from the great mothertree of England" (cited by Morgan, pp. 209, 213). In advance of Matthew Arnold's recommendations, George Paxton Young, architect of English studies in Ontario, advised in his department of education report for 1867–68 that *The Merchant of Venice* "was a lesson in practical Christian Ethics . . . [that] can scarcely be read intelligently without entering into the soul and becoming part of its convictions for ever" (cited by Morgan, p. 203).[8] This sense of literature's educational mission was built on the language of spiritual salvation.

The successes of English literature in India and Canada notwithstanding, not all colonizers supported a literary education as ideal for the empire. The clearest instance comes from the British secretary of state for the colonies, L. S. Amery, who advised the Imperial Conference of 1926 to set literature aside in an effort to tailor schooling, in a more progressive manner, to the developmental state of the students:

---

[7] America had its educational champions of English literature in, for example, the *Atlantic Monthly,* although Matthew Arnold, through the sponsorship of Andrew Carnegie, did his part by coming to America to deliver a series of successful lectures on literature's behalf in the 1880s (Honan, 1980).

[8] So it is, perhaps, that this play, as I noted in chapter 1, was my high school introduction to Shakespeare in grade 9, as it has proved to be for my youngest son.

Our whole endeavor now is to substitute for a purely literary education, not suited to the needs of the natives, a type of education more adapted to their mental aptitude—a type of education which, while conserving as far as possible all the sane and healthy element in the fabric of their own social life, will also assist their growth and evolution on natural lines and enable them to absorb more progressive ideas. (Cited in Whitehead, 1988, p. 212)

This interest in making the native "useful in his own environment" was largely resisted with what Clive Whitehead characterizes as "the insatiable drive by many Africans for Western schooling after the 1930s" (1988, p. 221). Although such local interest might appear to exonerate Shakespeare from charges of an imposed cultural imperialism, the drive for Western schooling also reflects an African rejection of Britain's patronizing provision for "growth and evolution on natural lines." Certainly, Whitehead tries to dodge the charge of a "deliberate British policy to colonize the indigenous intellect" by pointing to the ineptitude and incoherence of policies at the time (p. 215). The result, however, was that the literature of Great Britain remained a mainstay of a colonial education in Africa and around the globe, the ambiguous reception of which is captured in the novelist R. K. Narayan's recollections of his own education in colonial India:

We had professors from English universities to teach literature, which I always feel was a blessing. But the professor's contact was strictly limited to the classroom. When he left the class, he rushed back to his citadel of professors' quarters and the English club where no Indian was admitted except to serve drinks. (1988, p. 231)[9]

Although official policies on literature's place in the modern curriculum at home and abroad were only rarely questioned, a few of those destined to join the literary canon, namely, Conrad and Forster, had already begun to question the cost of imperialism to those who practiced it. So it was that such troubling works as *Heart of Darkness* and *A Passage to India* were read, after a time, as part of a literary education in the English language. Although I have already called on both of these books to illustrate imperialism's legacy, it is tempting to hold up Conrad's novel again as proof of literature's unsettling powers in regard to imperial themes. For me, lessons on Conrad's 1902 novel might begin with T. S. Eliot's use of the line "Mistah Kurtz—he dead" as the epigraph for "The Hollow Men" (1971a). It is spoken in the novel by "the

---

[9] On a similar ambiguity at colonialism's literary influence, this time in the writing and forms of modern Bengali literature, see Nirad Chauduri (1987, pp. 149–59).

manager's boy," who "put his insolent black head in the doorway" and announced that this paragon of the colonial impulse gone mad had ceased to exist (1973, p. 108).[10] Conrad and Eliot appear to be offering a requiem for the emptiness of an age that seemed to die with Mistah Kurtz yet lived knowingly on: "We are the hollow men / We are the stuffed men." It is that stuffing—"headpiece filled with straw. Alas!" (1.4)—that I am asking after here, as did Eliot and Conrad, by turning, in this case, to the substance of a literary education. Certainly Eliot and Conrad formed part of the post-Kurtzian stuffing of a modern education in literature, writing as they did within and against the worst prejudices of their times.[11] They, and those who have taught their work to generations of students around the world, saw literature as calling civilization back from the expansive wasteland that occupied the souls of both the modern city dwellers and the colonizers, without slipping into the darkness thought to haunt African rivers. An education in literature was about rising above both the savagery and the hollowness within.

In the secondary schools of the English-speaking world, by far the more frequently taught "children's" version of Conrad's tale is William Golding's *Lord of the Flies* (1967).[12] In this novel, a planeload of schoolboys who are stranded on a proverbial desert island enact a similar sense of a repulsive yet fascinating reversion to a primitive state, presumably occupied by other savages at other times, without dealing with the responsibilities of colonialism. As much as Conrad and Eliot originally troubled the West in naming the horror and waste of the modern age, they were to become central to an education based on artfully and manfully exploring the soul of the West, lighting beacons along the way so that the rest of the world might find its way.

A literary education intent on imagining a world that has moved well beyond the age of empire would include what falls under the literary rubric of third-world and Commonwealth, immigrant and multicultural, with the ironies of association and dissociation integral to these counterformations. But this call for a postcolonial education is not about proscribing or policing any given piece of literature or form of literary criticism. What is needed is a return to our ideas about the value of literature, ideas that, after the centuries

---

[10] Eliot deleted Kurtz's famous final words in the *Heart of Darkness*—"the horror, the horror"—from the original epigraph of *The Waste Land*.

[11] On Eliot's anti-Semitism and prejudices, see Ricks (1988) and Julius (1996), and on Conrad's racism, see Achebe (1988).

[12] Arthur Applebee's research on the "most popular titles of book length works, grades 9–12" ranks *Lord of the Flies* in tenth place in America for public, Catholic, and independent schools (where, respectively, 54, 52, and 34 percent of schools use it). It rises to third place at the grade-12 level (1993, pp. 65, 68).

of literature's engagement with imperialism, are bound to bear something of a legacy devoted to civilizing the savage, to bringing sophistication of feeling and thought to the primitive. A student's literary education needs to include this historical role of literature as an educational tool that supported, and at times stood against, the expansion of empire. We need, then, to return to literary education's formative texts to gain some appreciation of how literature works with empire.

Frye's Educated Imagination

During the latter half of the twentieth century, Northrup Frye took a direct hand in the shaping of a modern literary education, gradually assuming the Arnoldian mantle of exemplary literary critic and educational overseer. While forging a reputation as a subtle and profound critic of Blake, Milton, and Shakespeare, as well as a major theorist of literary criticism itself, he also found time to serve as honorary president of the Ontario Council of Teachers of English and to edit a popular series of literature textbooks for Canadian and American high schools.[13] He was as much a teacher of English teachers as he was a critic's critic.

The Educated Imagination (1963), although hardly the whole of Frye's thinking on the subject, is one of the rare books on literary theory that is taught in the schools and, as such, continues to reach a far wider audience than discussions of the value of literature normally achieve. The book is based on the 1962 Massey lectures, which Frye gave on the Canadian Broadcasting Corporation (CBC) radio network. What has since become the nation's premiere lecture series had been initiated only the year before to honor the Rt. Hon. Vincent Massey, who as governor-general served as the first Canadian-born representative of the British Crown in Canada. Frye's radio talks located the nation in the imaginary space cultivated by English literature, where "English" remains an ambiguous designation of language, culture, and nation.[14] Although Frye achieved international stature as a literary critic, he was

---

[13] Frye's textbook series, Literature: Uses of the Imagination (1972), is published by Harcourt Brace Jovanovich.

[14] This chapter can be thought to extend, though perhaps only by a postcolonial footnote, Deanne Bogdan's considerable delineation of Frye's project in Re-educating the Imagination, which addresses the limits to Frye's vision of "identity as similarity," as she puts it, in which differences in power and location are "subsumed under the developmental assumption that wider and wider reading and more and more informed responses will inexorably propel the respondent into the third order of experience, where every other voice resonates as part of our own" (1992, p. 131). Whereas Bogdan argues for an extension of Frye's determination of literary study, I return to Frye himself, already far more expansionary in a colonial sense than was originally thought.

to hold a special place in the educated imagination of this country as a venerated intellectual who, until his death in 1989, gave cultural definition to a country that continued to wrestle with the English heritage of its colonial period.

Through his critical work and public stances, Frye did a great deal to foster the development of Canadian literature as itself an anti-imperial cultural formation against the press of British and American literature. He didn't shy away from invoking this country's colonial past, identifying what he termed the "garrison mentality" of "a closely knit and beleaguered society" that marked it (1971a, p. 225). Frye was part of what gave "here" its literary identity, part of what allowed Canadian works to take their place on school and college syllabi, although he never mistook them for the masterpieces that formed the great critical focus of his career. This form of literary nationalism, with an eye to the mother country, poses one sort of postcolonial response. As such, it has drawn its own critics, including "the most published Native author in the country," as Lee Maracle identifies herself in taking up Frye's notion of a garrison mentality: "Canadian writers still hover about the gates of the old forts, peek[ing] through the cracks of their protective ideological walls" (1992, p. 14). Maracle advises that "to resolve this colonial condition in literature we need to have Canada recognize that first it is our condition and second, Canada needs to view this condition as unacceptable" (p. 15).

Frye speaks to us about the value of literature from here, Canada, yet not from here. He is speaking, surely he would hold, from the place occupied by the imagination, which is not of this nation-bound earth. But Frye is also speaking from what was once known as a white colony and then a white dominion. How he speaks to the nation from this location is part of what can be known about the education of the imagination. Frye has noted elsewhere that the CBC's broadcasting mission "to promote Canadian unity and identity" was bound to be frustrated by the fact that "identity is local and regional, rooted in the imagination and works of culture; unity is national in reference, international in perspective, and rooted in political feeling" (1971b, p. ii). For his part, Frye roots the national imagination in transcendent forms of culture and politics rather than regional ones, and he does so in ways that I will explore according to the four themes of the uninhabited island, outside and other, the place of Canada, and the work of literature.

Imagining the Uninhabited Island

Frye's opening lecture in *The Educated Imagination,* "A Motive for Metaphor," begins with a small imaginary disaster: "Suppose you're shipwrecked on an uninhabited island in the South Seas" (1963, p. 2). Thus Frye subtly transports us to the colonial era, with the "South Seas" evoking Balboa's naming of this newfound ocean El Mar del Sur in the sixteenth century, Cook's opening of the South Seas to the British Empire in the eighteenth century, and working tours of the region by Robert Louis Stevenson and Paul Gaugin in the nineteenth century. For its part, the South Seas uninhabited island is a palimpsest that is always already written over with its own buried treasure of colonial imagery. The pastoral myth that opens this lecture is cut with the colonial theme of starting anew in a newfound land, of going back in time to an untainted version of the homeland.

There is something striking, then, in Frye's locating his island in the South Seas, far from Canada's own abundant supply of no less "uninhabited" territories, including many islands. Has our postcolonial nationhood brought this vast dominion within the "civilized" and thus "inhabited" world? The colonial vision is about gaining a distance that transforms a culture, offering what is, in effect, a blank page through the expansiveness of an overwritten civilization. The island is "uninhabited," of course, in relation to a European presence, with the (nomadic) occupation of indigenous populations erased or denied. Think of how the islands on which Columbus first set eyes in the Caribbean were unpossessed, and in that sense unoccupied, even as the native Arawak stood on the beach to watch this odd group of men come ashore and resolutely lay claim to their land in the name of their God and their queen.

In wrecking us upon a South Seas island, Frye uses colonialism's imaginative resources, with a nod to *The Tempest* and *Robinson Crusoe,* to remind us of Europe's civilizing mission. Prospero gives the gift of a civilizing language to an uncivil Caliban, whereas the ever resourceful Mr. Crusoe reprises, in short order, the industrious rise of the English to civilized existence, complete with an indentured, if not enslaved, savage named in imitation of God's own schedule for creation. Caliban and Friday remind us that the "uninhabited" islands were still the homeland of a people (with a single imaginary native standing for the many). When Rousseau finally allows Émile to begin reading at the age of twelve, what is his first book? "Is it Aristotle? Is it Pliny? Is it Buffon? No. It is *Robinson Crusoe*" (Rousseau, 1979, p. 184). Defoe's novel is the paradigmatic imperial adventure, offering its own schooling in a natural history of self-sufficiency and resourcefulness, a return to first things, as Crusoe, the recording angel of imperialism, moves from shipwreck and homestead to plantation and colony: "I descended a little on the side of that delicious vale, surveying it with a secret kind of pleasure (tho' mixt with my other afflicting thoughts) to think that this was all my own, that I was king and lord of all this country indefensibly, and had a right of possession" (1965, pp. 113–14).

The empire offers the European a second chance with the world, placing him once more in possession of paradise, an Adam before Eve. It is all that Rousseau would ask of his Émile: "I want it to make him dizzy. . . . I want him to think that he is Robinson himself" (1979, p. 185). Could there be any better teacher than Crusoe, this domesticator of wild islands and namer of men? "I made him know his name should be Friday," Crusoe records, "which was the day I saved his life" (Defoe, 1965, p. 209). The unquestioned right of possession comes in the face of the silent unwritten (unmapped) qualities of the island and the island people, protecting these proprietary privileges from questioning; civilization's representative retains the right of exclusion and intervention (on behalf of Friday). Derek Walcott, in "Crusoe's Journal," takes up the voice of the islander who ironically observes his subjection to the ostensible educator:

> Like Christofer he bears
> in a speech mnemonic as a missionary's
> the Word to savages,
> its shape an earthen, water-bearing vessel's
> whose sprinkling alters us
> into good Fridays who recite His praise,
> parroting our master's
> style and voice, we make his language ours,
> converted cannibals
> we learn with him to eat the flesh of Christ. (1986, p. 93)

In choosing the island metaphor, Frye suggests that to reach people where they live, one begins with their bookshelves, especially if one is speaking to them about literature. The South Seas island is more likely to suggest a colonial Eden in its seemingly unoccupied splendor ("the self-creating peace / of islands," in Walcott's poem [p. 94]), affording a time window on an earlier, simpler era of the sort celebrated by explorers, missionaries, anthropologists, and tourists. The deserted island has no less a home in popular culture, with the perennial cartoons of the shipwrecked sailor stranded with the voluptuous passenger, and highbrow variations such as the British Broadcasting Corporation's radio program "Desert Island Discs," which imagines escaping with the great monuments of culture—a return to Eden with a Walkman.

But for all of its sense of escape, the Western idea of the South Seas island also carries with it the hope of rescue and a return to one's proper home. The island offers writers and dreamers a fantasy of escape (from dreary winters and perhaps dreary families); it speaks to moments of uninhibited opportunities, of renewing the balance between innocence and experience. Above all, the island affords Frye, as it has served many before him, a clean slate on which to work the evolution of humankind. In this case, Frye inscribes his island with what he sees as the three stages through which language makes its civilizing progress: Language first affords a "consciousness or awareness" that leads to basic forms of self-expression. This is followed by the use of language in a "practical sense," which gives rise to technical terms. The process culminates in the imaginary realm as language is turned to poetry, plays, and novels (1963, pp. 3–5).[15]

Frye's island defense of literary study revolves around the evolutionary poles of the primitive and the civilized: "You find that every mother tongue, in any developed or civilized society, turns into something called literature" (p. 2). Frye's reference to "any developed or civilized society" is probably intended to include a yet-to-be-developed-but-surely-civilized China (questions about Frye's placing of China will be raised presently). He misses the chance here to allow that every language and culture has its literature, its imaginative retelling of the world and its ways, a point that Boas began to make, as I have pointed out earlier, at the close of the nineteenth century. Yet a few pages later, when Frye does make reference to the omnipresence of literature, he posits another evolutionary scale that carefully sets off primitive literature from the timeless classic: "Primitive literature hasn't yet become distinguished from other aspects of life: it's still embedded in religion, magic, social ceremonies" (p. 13).[16]

There are different conceptions of timelessness at work in Frye's imagination. Based on the principle "that every form in literature has a pedigree, and we can trace its descent back to earliest times," he charts the descent and disengagement of a true literature that may have begun in "war-songs, work-songs, funeral laments, lullabies" (p. 14). He continues the evolutionary motif by tying literature to the idea of cultural progress: "The more advanced a civilization, the more literature seems to concern itself with purely human problems and conflicts" (p. 22). Yet this developmental scale is also a matter of

---

[15] Ian Hunter, in analyzing literary education "as an arm of the emergent governmental educational apparatus," interprets Frye's island metaphor as part of an effort "to derive a 'total history' of culture and society from the split in the mentality of a castaway parachuted in from the aesthetic empyrean" (1988, p. 10).

[16] On the category of the "primitive," Bernard McGrane helpfully describes its anthropological invention as but a third phase in the European regard for an alien other that has continued to be formed since Columbus: "The alien Other is not fundamentally pagan, savage, and demonic from a Christian frame of reference, nor fundamentally ignorant and superstitious from an Enlightenment frame of reference; rather the Other is now *fundamentally primitive* from a progress and evolution frame of reference" (1989, p. 98; McGrane's emphasis). For the usefulness of "primitive" as a category in the realm of art, see S. Price (1989).

genre: "The most primitive nations have poetry, but only quite well developed nations can produce prose" (p. 51).[17] Frye then puts this scheme to pedagogical use, following the lead of Matthew Arnold, by asserting that it is only natural to start children on poetry before moving them into the more mature prose. In this way, the young of the West might recapitulate the ascent of civilization and overcome the stagnation of primitive and poetry-bound cultures.

The importance that Frye places on literature's "pedigree" is troubling only as it invokes the racial bearing of imperialism's long-standing division between primitive and civilized peoples. It troubles as well because this literary paternity suit gained prominence in Europe during the nineteenth century, when Matthew Arnold, Ernest Renan, and others were contrasting the Hellenic and Hebraic influences on the European disposition, the refined and cultivated Hellenic influences proudly being held in ascendancy. This was bound to have serious ramifications for the racialized identity of the Jewish people, who had been recently "emancipated" in England and elsewhere after a period of what can be aptly termed internal colonization.[18] Frye reaffirms Arnold's emphasis on the bicultural origins while playing the Hellenic favorite as Arnold did: "The basis of the cultural heritage of English speaking peoples is not in English; it's in Latin and Greek and Hebrew" (p. 49).

Little credit is given to the influential orientalism of Richard Burton, Edward FitzGerald, Ezra Pound, and William Carlos Williams, or to the Celtic imaginings of Walter Scott and James Joyce.[19] Frye also overlooks the millions of English-speaking people who bring to the language a literary heritage that is not Latin, Greek, or Hebrew. The educated imagination is still being constructed within a colonial imaginary that navigates among primitive and civilized islands, holding as its true course a direct descent from a golden age, however adrift it may seem to have been at various historical junctures. It is worthwhile comparing these island themes in popular and literary culture with the more recent experiences of "boat people," who, in a reverse migra-

---

[17] In this statement he echoes the Elizabethan Philip Sidney, who, in the first great defense of English literature, *An Apology for Poetry*, wrote of "the most barbarous and simple Indians where no writing is, yet have they their poets" (1970, p. 9).

[18] See Olender (1992). George Steiner gives a recent twist to the pedigree question in the final words of his review of the late poet Paul Celan, Jewish survivor of Nazi Germany: " 'We are all Greeks,' proclaimed Shelley. 'Every poet is a Yid,' replied Paul Celan with unplumbed bitterness and self-mockery. The old story: Athens and Jerusalem. Between them lies the uncertain advent of what remains of European language and literature" (1995, p. 4)

[19] On Pound's and Williams's modernist orientalism, including their dialogues with Chinese poets, see Zhaoming Qian (1995); and on Joyce's anti-imperialist Celtic interests, see Vincent Cheng (1995).

tion-exploration pattern, have sought to shipwreck themselves in North America. The opportunity of starting afresh on a new shore has not worked out as neatly in this direction. The Chinese hopefuls whose ship foundered off Queens in New York a few years ago ended up in jail awaiting deportation from their Manhattan island dream. The former colonizer cannot readily imagine being colonized.

In going over high school students' essays on *The Educated Imagination,* I found that a number of them took up the island metaphor, some, like Frye, pursuing it as a site for an evolutionary reckoning. They found Frye's advantage in using the island to create a world of their own making, both far away yet subtly attached to the known world. Kristy, for example, introduces "a small island" as part of her own thought experiment intended to demonstrate how nonfiction also extends the human imagination. In this way, she shows how effectively students can pick up both Frye's substance and method, as well as something of his dry wit, as she extols the power of the written word to expand our horizons:

> Through literature, Frye believes that our human experience will grow, and I feel this could not be more true. Not everyone in the world has the time or money to visit all different cultures, and lifestyles. By reading a book or an article on a specific place or time, we learn everything you could possibly need to know about that society. To stress this point, I would like to use a hypothetical situation. Let's pretend that you have been born on a small island and the only people on the island with you are your devoutly Catholic parents. Left on the island is a biology book from a shipwreck. Inside this book, you find many interesting scientific explanations for the phenomenon that your parents had originally explained in biblical terms. These few words that you read would definitely give your mind many things to think about and choices for you to make.

Equally present in this student's defense of literature and biology is the presumed responsibility of the educated to experience a world of different cultures, learning along the way "everything you could possibly need to know about that society." This sense of global mastery, of being in a position to know the other, and the related release from primitive superstitions, which permits one informed and superior choices, are part of what recommends the educated imagination as still bearing something of a colonial construct. Its coinciding with the thrust of imperialism's intellectual project is not grounds for condemnation but may, in Kristy's words, "give your mind many things to think about and choices for you to make." Without calling Kristy's intentions into question, it would still seem valuable to set such commonplace ideas as a sense of global masters within the context of the colonial imperative and its educational objectives. In this way, we can turn to the origins and implications of widely held views, setting them upon a larger historical stage as we explore the continuing play of the colonial imagination within the literary landscape.

A second student, Sam, understands that to engage the island metaphor is to raise the evolutionary opposition of primitive cultures versus evolved civilizations. The difference is that Sam is not entirely prepared to accept this as a development for the good. His pattern of initially resisting Frye's position, only to come around on the question of literature's contribution, was a pattern pursued by a number of students:

> Frye talks about a different person stranded on an island who has no intellect or let's say without literature, often he "feels lonely and frightened and unwanted in such a world." I must object to that. If you look and compare the primitive people, for instance aboriginal and civilized people, look at what people with intelligence have done to our world. They created a more dangerous place with pollution, over population and potential nuclear wars. It seems to me it's more peaceful to be less civilized.

Having realized the value of less civilized forms of life, Sam then moves on to the corollary of this challenge by pointing out literature's dangerous side in a manner that tends to confuse teacher and text, literature and hate literature. He raises the well-known Canadian instance of Jim Keegstra, an Alberta schoolteacher who for fourteen years taught his high school students in social studies about a Zionist global conspiracy until he was finally brought before the courts for spreading hate. Sam concludes that "studying literature can cause people to be dangerous. . . . Being intelligent from studying literature doesn't mean you're the most worthy." Sam is working critically from the fundamental imperial construct of the primitive and the civilized. But for all that, his essay finally arrives at an anthropological model of literary criticism that is similar to Frye's. For Sam, literature marks the advance of humankind and is ever a civilizing influence: "I realize now that literature brought us away from the primitive era when we used to live like the animals around us. And as we became more aware of literature we created civilizations."

Heather is another student who challenges the line that Frye draws between reality and the imagination. She resists that very posture of the colonial which imagines a nature that is hostile and in need of governance:

> Frye mentions being shipwrecked on an island and he sees the world on the island as objective and that it is "something set over against you and

not yourself or related to you in any way" (p. 2). I disagree with Frye because the world is not objective and when you are on the island one is more related to and a part of the world. . . . I feel people can make conversation in their own way with nature and its surroundings.

This conversation with nature, even with Heather and Frye both using the term "surroundings," still represents the empathetic reach across differences (rather than a conquest of them, or Frye's sense of "against"). She proposes a healing of the distances that set us apart from nature and native. Yet before I, in turn, thoroughly romanticize the views of this student of nature, I would also note how she goes on to agree ultimately with Frye's faith in the civilizing force of literature:

> Frye feels what comes naturally to humans is their civilization. I think Frye's arguments need to be revised into a form we are comfortable with and where civilization is the essence of what it is like to be a human being. Literature provides us with a vision for our lives. It lends a little more zest in our experiences.

It is not entirely clear from the rest of Heather's brief essay how she would comfortably revise Frye's arguments, except perhaps to mend this apparent breach with nature. Frye offers his own reconciliation between imagination and nature in a later lecture that I will presently discuss but that Heather was not assigned. In the final analysis, she does not take up the evolutionary narrative. To be human is to be civilized for Heather, and literature is an incidental aspect of that essential civilizing spirit. She is ready to question the sense of literary progress that might otherwise be thought to distinguish some humans from others, and thus she is moving beyond the habits of thought, if no longer the deep-seated beliefs, of a once-and-lingering colonial imagination.

Outside and Other

Frye's literary anthropology not only distributes humanity between primitive and civilized cultures, it also places the Orient on a distant horizon. At the moment of the initial shipwreck, he suggests that "if the ship you were wrecked in was a Western ship you'd probably feel that your intellect tells you more about what's really there in the outer world and that your emotions tell you more about what's going on inside you." Then he introduces the "other" possibility: "If your background were Oriental, you'd be more likely to reverse this and say that the beauty and terror was really there, and that your instinct to count and classify and measure and pull to pieces was what was inside your mind" (1963, p. 3). The superstitious quality he attributes to this oriental disposition becomes one of a series of points of contrast he establishes. A few pages later, Frye returns to this sense of the East's foreignness, drawing attention to what was clearly the wayward, unreliable, and nonliterary thinking of Ezra Pound in the (linked?) areas of "fascism and social credit and Confucianism and anti-Semitism" (p. 7).

Next, Frye shows his own literary range by linking the mythic theme of human flight in the Icarus story with *Sakuntala,* "an Indian play fifteen hundred years old," which he pulls in to illustrate how these imaginative ventures can lead to a "scientific civilization like ours" (p. 8). Frye's great learning, lightly seasoning his text, gives his claims a universal purchase even as he situates literature within an evolutionary scale that locates India and China in the past, or *as* past. When he addresses poetry's primitive qualities, he draws our attention to the poetic "singsong" of children's speech before contrasting the "Chinese language" (more properly Mandarin or Cantonese, the dominant spoken dialects), which has "kept differences of pitch in the spoken word," and the Canadians' "monotone honk" (p. 51). Although he does make a self-deprecating pun on the Canada goose, the association groups the primitive, the childlike, and the Chinese. Of course, Frye is writing not about Chinese civilization here but about the nature of poetry, using a convenient anthropological contrast. The slight matters little enough in light of Frye's enormous critical accomplishment, little enough against how he has helped us appreciate the achievement of literature. Yet, as a literary critic, he would have us attend to commonplaces, to the archetypal, and to the unique turns that distinguish a text.

Among the commonplaces to which Frye would have us attend are prejudicial uses of language: "Some years ago, in a town in the States, I heard somebody say, 'those yellow bastards,' meaning the Japanese. More recently, in another town, I heard somebody else use the same phrase, but meaning the Chinese" (p. 63). By locating racism in America, at least to begin with, Frye provides a reassuring answer for his oft smug Canadian audience to the question "Where is here?" We are not alone, of course, in this habit of locating unpleasantries on the other side of some border, diverting attention from, in this case, a Canada that in the past has succumbed to various waves of xenophobia over a "yellow peril" (Ward, 1990). Frye's ostensible point in recalling these incidents, however, is to eschew the mechanical and unthinking nature of this racist language: "There are many reasons not connected with literary criticism, why nobody should use a phrase like that about anybody. But the literary reason is that the phrase is pure reflex: it's no more a product of a conscious mind than the bark of a dog" (1963, p. 63). We need to grow conscious of the function served by distinctions between Occident and Ori-

ent that fall between discrimination and discriminating, because the prejudicial and the discerning are directed at establishing the other as a point of contrast and as something less. Although Frye allows that his literary objections
are not the whole of the matter, to equate this overheard virulence with a
dog's barking suggests that it is nothing more than the product of bad breed-
ing or poor training. Is Frye suggesting that racial prejudices are simply too
vulgar for the cultivated imagination? After all, he notes that the highly cultivated Ezra Pound's anti-Semitism is a prejudice whose place in literature
spans from Shakespeare's *The Merchant of Venice* to Eliot's "Burbank with a
Baedeker: Bleistein with a Cigar."[20]

Now, it can be fairly asked whether this sort of reading is too much to expect of high school students. One high school student, Sam, whose work is
cited earlier, comments on Frye's opposition of East and West: "Frye [was]
probably brought up learning some stereotypes as he mentions that Eastern-
ers and Westerners think differently because they are opposite to where they
live." The challenge is to work with students to arrive at a more nuanced reading of Frye that tests the basis of his distinctions while recognizing that Frye
was very much a global thinker and reader, dedicated to identifying the structural features common to all literature, just as the school anthologies he
edited included myths from many lands. Sam's recognition of Frye's contrasting the Orient with the West suggests that we might well ask students
and ourselves how, out of this colonial imaginary, some people and places
are made to serve the West's claim on civilization. The point is all the
more poignantly made when we realize that these other people, who stand as
the point of contrast, are no longer so distant, but are our neighbors, if not
ourselves.

Canada, Neither Here nor There

One of the most fascinating aspects of the postcolonial perspective is what it
makes of geography, and more particularly, what it makes of Frye's question
"Where is here?" The educated imagination is at once boundless and free-
ranging, while remaining attentive to the detail and nuance of place. It is also
located within a pedigree, a certain line of descent that runs, Frye reminds
us, from Jerusalem and Athens, through Rome to London, and then out into
the culturally "uninhabited" world settled by the British Empire. Where does
that leave a place such as Canada? It is not absent from Frye's lectures, but it
is not as firm or fertile a place for grounding a defense of literature as is the

---

[20] I have dealt elsewhere with anti-Semitism in English literature as an influence on the
Oxford English Dictionary (J. Willinsky, 1994a, pp. 140–56).

uninhabited island in the South Seas of the imagination. If Frye appears to recognize some debt to this nation—and he does speak to it in the Massey lectures—his uncertainty about what to do with this land provides the perfect entry point for thinking about lingering colonial sensibilities that will not be banished by the nationalism of a Canadian literature movement, itself a product, in many ways, of the age of imperialism.[21] But let us consider how the land lies for Frye.

In the opening of the lecture series, Frye includes Canada, this officially bilingual but in reality multilingual state, among the "English-speaking countries" (p. 2). This transnational language ensures a special cultural bond with things English, although this bond operates on a different basis across the racial differences between the former "white colonies" and the rest of the British Commonwealth. For Frye, "English means, in the first place, the mother tongue," although it is not clear whether this maternal reference is to the English mother country or to Canadian mothers, who all presumably speak English to their babies (p. 2). And so this complicated place begins to unfold like so many backdrops in a theater, each a transformation of the landscape in an evolving story. The educated imagination feels at home within a transported literature (forming its own cargo cult, one is tempted to say) that secures this country's place as a proper extension of English culture. The close identity with a British national culture that Canadians are at once part of and removed from is another reminder of how the study of literature is implicated in a cultural preoccupation that operates so effectively at a distance. We need to consider the blocking out of this cultural space among colonies and motherlands to see whom it includes and excludes and how it continues to operate on assumptions of the sort that Frye drew on in speaking to the requirements of an educated imagination.

In those moments when Frye deals directly with Canada, it is interesting to note his reconciling of nationhood with a perpetual displacement from the center: "When Canada was still a country for pioneers, it was assumed that a new country, a new society, new things to look at and new experiences would produce a new literature" (p. 15). It has not, however, and Frye ends up dismissing Canadian writers for originally imitating Byron and Scott and then moving on to "producing imitations of D. H. Lawrence and W. H. Auden" (p. 16). All is imitation and invisibility, determined by a center of

---

[21] The legacy of colonization on current understandings of immigration in Canadian culture is the subject of Roxana Ng's analysis of Canadian nationalism (1993). A postcolonial perspective on the Canadian landscape is well represented in Himani Bannerji's collection, in which Ng's essay appears.

meaning that is, in this case, an Anglo-American terrain in the imagination. But in this apology for Canadian literature, Frye again engages the invisible displacement of those who, at least ten thousand years before, began to inhabit this land.[22]

"The constructs of the imagination tell us things about human life that we don't get in any other way. That's why it's important for Canadians to pay particular attention to Canadian literature, even when the imported brands are better seasoned" (p. 53). This statement, which Frye follows with reflections on Lincoln's Gettysburg Address, needs to be weighed against his failure in the lectures to credit a single Canadian writer by name. Although it is easy enough to speak of the imagination as unbounded, Frye is actually retracing through these lectures the well-trod path from Homer to Wordsworth, which was also followed in ships' cabins, plantation mansions, and schoolhouses around the colonial empire. Where precisely is Frye to be found, then? Broadcasting from the radio towers of this former colony, but not necessarily here in mind. At the University of Toronto, Frye trained generations of Canadian students, many of whom went on to be English teachers. He trained them in an English literature that was imagined to form the natural order of our mother tongue. The imagined community, which Benedict Anderson (1983) wisely identifies with the formation of the nation, is marked in this postimperialist world by the cultural tensions of former colonies and motherlands. "Here" is not so much a place as an intersection of lives and imaginations, languages and narratives. Where Canada figures in this scheme, with its history as both colony and colonizer, is still being struggled over, through aboriginal land claims and multicultural policies. In responding to Frye's lectures, none of the high school students found reason to comment on where their Canada fits into the defense of literature.

The Real Work of Literature

It's true that Frye makes only passing references to South Seas islands, China, and Canada on his way to situating literature's contribution to the educated imagination, and I know that I must seem to be making too much out of too little. Yet these traces of an imperial legacy situate the center and the periphery, the civilized and the primitive, I have tried to show, in Frye's identity question "Where is here?" In trying to understand how literary study still works the rhetoric of empire, we arrive, finally, at the complex relationship of literature to life, which forms the core of Frye's concerns. Frye believes literature

---

[22] Julia Emberley writes about the nature of the postcolonial imagination, which native women writers such as Lee Maracle are exploring (1992, p. 47).

is both a form of writing removed from the world and an imaginative guide to living in it. He repeatedly distances literature from the real—"Literature belongs to the world that man constructs, not the world he sees" (1963, p. 8)—suggesting that it is simply naive to relate literature "directly to life or reality" (p. 39). In Frye's terms, to imagine literature's involvement in such a worldly matter as imperialism is to make a mistake of category: "In the world of the imagination anything goes that's imaginatively possible, but nothing happens. If it did happen, it would move out of the world of the imagination into the world of action" (pp. 5–6). Rejecting a sense of literary and critical agency, Frye secures a space for literary study that is safely bounded by literature's recurring mythopoetic structures and protected from earthly cares. Frye's professional calling is to hive off literature from "ordinary life" (p. 9). I recall my father doing much the same with his medical practice. Although he often enjoyed discussing "interesting cases" with the family, he always acted surprised when we interrupted his disembodied presentations to ask questions about the actual lives of the patients. He'd offer their approximate age and perhaps their gender, but we seemed to him to be missing the point.

The professional sensibility begins with detaching literature (or medicine) from life. At the same time, however, Frye celebrates Defoe's ability to write the nation's history through the life of a single, stranded sailor. Literature is a lens: "The whole cultural history of the nation that produced it comes into focus" (p. 52). After distancing the imagination from the reaches of this earth, we can see the cultural history of the nation by looking through that imagination. In this, Frye and I are not so far apart. We both want to talk about literature as *apart from* yet *a part of* the world.

To grasp this subtle relationship between imaginative and worldly realms, we need to return to the proverbial island that gave rise to Frye's three-story evolution of language. The linguistic escalator begins at the garden level, with the creation of a human realm separate from the rest of nature, making a home out of an environment (p. 4). We then ascend to the second level, where language works the world in very practical ways, extending human control over it. When we finally reach the third level, we construct our own world in a language that, in its completeness, returns or reconnects us to the world that we have come to know otherwise as outside ourselves: "We recapture, in full consciousness, that original sense of identity with our surroundings, where there is nothing outside the mind of man, or something identical with the mind of man" (p. 9). There is, in this final level, "an identity between the human mind and the world outside of it," which suggests the global expansiveness of the European educated standard that I read as part of imperialism's intellectual legacy (p. 12).

To assist us in understanding this rather elusive identity, Frye uses both religious and scientific analogies. First, he states that "there can never be any religion of poetry or any set of beliefs founded on literature" (p. 31). I would agree that literature, as a whole, tends toward a certain antidogmatic mutability and equivocation. Yet I also think that, if specific beliefs cannot be founded on particular works of literature, Frye nevertheless appeals to literature's spiritual value in warning his listeners that "if we shut the vision of [literature] completely out of our minds, or insist on its being limited in various ways, something goes dead inside of us, perhaps the one thing that is really important to keep alive" (p. 33). A little later in the lectures, he adds that "literature gives us an experience that stretches us vertically to the heights and depths of what the human mind can conceive, to what corresponds to the conceptions of heaven and hell in religion" (p. 42). Similarly, when he speaks of literary criticism as "the activity of uniting literature with society" (p. 55), the critic begins to sound like the church bringing the word of God to humanity. The study of literature carries its own spiritual rewards, just as it has lessons to teach about the good life. If beliefs cannot be founded on literature, perhaps a religion can still be made of it, a religion founded first in the colonial schools, where literature was held to redeem those who imbibed it.[23]

Turning to science, Frye points to literature's particular dedication to dream-testing ideas in "the laboratory where myths themselves are studied and experimented with" (p. 67). Experiments in laboratories do, on occasion, lead to actions of some consequence in the world. The literary treatment of colonialism was given to narrating old and new myths about human difference, about ways of dividing the world. These works of the imagination can also be expected to have had an impact on how people imagined the possibilities of imperialism, just as their authors were influenced in turn by the news from the empire. The "constructive power" of literature, from *The Tempest* to *A Passage to India,* was given to notions of race, culture, and nation that have outlived their time, and it will continue thus unless there is a concerted effort to retest, as I am attempting here, the moral fabric of those originating myths.

---

[23] There are strange parallels to be found between this call for a mind-stretching, heaven-and-hell literary experience and the "total universe" that Susan Sontag identifies with the pornographic imagination (1982, p. 112). If the pornographic imagination represents a "spectacularly cramped form of the human imagination," it still possesses " 'a wider scale of experience' than healthy-mindedness" (p. 116). "No wonder, then," she notes, "that the new or radically revamped forms of the total imagination which have arisen in the past century—notably those of the artist, the erotomane, the left revolutionary, the madman—have chronically borrowed the prestige of the religious vocabulary" (p. 114).

For their part, the high school students responding to Frye's essays did not hesitate in situating literature's proximity to life. Heather, for example, wrote that literature "teaches one about times, dress, work, and homes," and Jeremy divided literature between its educational and its transcendent qualities: "We study literature to improve our imagination, our vocabulary, to get away from reality and escape to another world or another time." Patricia extended Frye's stance, as she pushed his idea of literature as a laboratory for humankind toward an anthropological field test made possible by literature's vicarious and spiritual powers:

> For example, we may read a book and gain an understanding of the plight of a black slave. In this way and others literature helps us grow, spiritually and mentally. Our political attitude is improved because literature gives us a more worldly view. Without literature we would not be influenced by or introduced to new societies or attitudes.

If somewhat more than Frye would comfortably subscribe to, Patricia's caricature of growth-through-literature does capture literature's bridge to a better world, leading the way in finding what is not yet part of ourselves. I have no desire or reason to be smug about this faith. My work shares the same inclination, using, in my case, books such as Forster's and Frye's to "help us grow," in a worldly striving to move beyond that earlier global turn of imperialism and all that it has come to mean for literature and education.

Finally, there is the student who set Frye's educated imagination within the metaphorical powers of the expanded horizon: "Literature awakens one's imagination, it brings one's attention to things they hadn't ever thought of before. With this in mind one could say that literature helps to broaden our horizons. Frye and I both agree on this." This statement seems much closer to imperialism's educational project in its call to awakening the imagination to what hadn't been seen or thought before the broadening of our horizons. Literature borrows from the imperial metaphor, making similar claims for the educational benefits of an expanded world. The extended horizon developed into an empire on which the sun, it seemed, was never to set. For students, no less than myself, to use the tired metaphors of an earlier age is no great crime, I hope, when we consider how they speak to what the language carries forward and what it allows to slip from sight. Literature's lasting power, as Frye suggests, is both to transcend the routines of the day and to crystallize moments of history and culture. But for all of that power, it falls to education and the educated imagination to decide where the attention to literature should be placed.

Toward the end of the lectures, Frye explains how the Tower of Babel has been the organizing myth for his lectures, with its underlying theme of a lost universal language—"the language of human nature" (p. 68). What was lost finds its expression for Frye in the "authentic poets," Shakespeare and Pushkin, and in the "social vision" of Lincoln and Gandhi (p. 68).[24] Here the crux of cultural discrimination comes not only out of this global sense of a brotherhood of genius, but also in his insistence that the language of human nature "never speaks unless we take the time to listen in leisure, and it speaks only in a voice too quiet for panic to hear" (p. 68). This refined sense of listening to a radio talk, such as Frye's, in the evening after dinner, returns us to the book's opening image of civilization as "a little cultivated world with a human shape, fenced off from the jungle" (p. 9). It takes little enough to see that the props and imagery furnishing Frye's ideal world of literature are leftovers from the jungle-conquering age of empire. It is here that we find "the affinity," as Gayatri Spivak names it, "between the imperialist subject and the subject of humanism" (1987, p. 202). It is here as well that we find literary claim to the "universal," to use a term that Chinua Achebe has objected to (in the context of "colonialist criticism" of African literature) as nothing more than "a synonym for the narrow, self-serving parochialism of Europe" (1995, p. 60).[25]

If we are to get beyond this way of imagining literature, we need to begin with how our own imaginations were educated, and how this gives literature much of its place in the world. I hope there will always be books that are able to remove us in some way from the world; we need not forsake that experience by acknowledging how literary study and its object have long contributed to the writing of the colonial world as a dream recalled, a paradise lost and regained on the page. The complex relationship between literature and world that Frye inscribes, with our imaginations ascending and returning ("We are not getting any nearer heaven, and . . . it is time to return to the earth" [1963, p. 68]) could be turned to examining how deserted islands and

---

[24] Arun Mukherjee explores the universalist credo of Western literary criticism using Frye's references to a "a single international style" as an instance, and taking exception to, among other things, the way in which Western literary criticism tends to "deradicalize" the "fiercely political confrontations in the works from the Third World" (1988, p. 13).

[25] Mukherjee describes her undergraduate students' reading of "The Perfume Sea," by Margaret Laurence, which deals with a beauty salon in Ghana during the country's achievement of independence, as largely stepping over the historical moment in favor of "the anxiety and hope of humanity," as one student put it (1995, p. 449). The students were able "to efface the differences between British bureaucrats and British traders, between colonizing whites and colonized blacks, and between rich blacks and poor blacks" (p. 449). The pursuit of the universal found its echo in the textbook's editorial preface to Laurence's story, which warned that "feminine vanity is presented as the only changeless element in a world of change" (p. 450).

lost empires still figure in our reckoning of the world. What is it that we still understand through difference and distance? How is it that "here" still bears the legacy of concepts that took their form during the age of empire? We owe students a sense of literature's part of that legacy, a legacy that still seems to protect our place in the world, as though we were snails who seldom wonder how it is that they are housed. I realize, however, that these will always be difficult, trying points to consider with a class of students. In their readerly pleasures, no less than in their belabored readings, students of literature need to imagine how time spent with accomplished works of art positions them in the ways that Toni Morrison and Northrop Frye have suggested, that is, as (white) beneficiaries of an educated imagination that promises to set them apart from the jungle. The inquiry of this legacy that I am advocating can only renew connections between education and the arts as an intellectual enterprise of consequence in the world. My educational hope is that, once these literary assumptions about primitive islands and white readers are raised as at least a part of literature's story, the divisions remaining from those colonial days will not be able to work in quite the same way.

Frontispiece engraving from Peter Kolb, Present State of the
Cape of Good Hope *(London, 1731). Kolb's account of the customs
and natural surroundings of the "Hottentots" of South Africa
was a key early ethnographic text for European audiences.*

TEN

OUT OF THE PAST

In a Vancouver school not long ago, a teacher invited his grade 7 class to discuss the nature of racism and what could be done about it. The students were not at a loss for words or ideas, judging by the videotape one of them made of the discussion.[1] Whereas some students in this ethnically diverse class used the Rodney King beating and other well-publicized incidents of racism in the United States to make their point, others brought the argument home by insisting, for example, that "racism is in Canadian society because other people want Canada to be one country and one color." Another student pointed to Canada's part in the Underground Railroad, which helped American slaves on the road to freedom in this country, although a classmate countered with Canada's imposition of a Chinese immigration tax, before allowing that "it's getting much better right now, because there's not lots of news about racism anymore."

Some also spoke from their own experience, with one describing the job discrimination suffered by his two aunts who had emigrated from Hong Kong. Another rattled off the racist names he had been called, before identifying what he felt was the racism in his own family in the selection of suitable marriage partners. Among the many caring and thoughtful comments made by the students, I was ultimately struck by the final words recorded on the video, which pose a particular challenge to this book. What was said suggested that turning to history was not the way forward. "Let's just forget

---

[1] Excerpts from the videotape are drawn from Leslie Roman and Timothy Stanley (1994; 1997).

what's happened in the past," George Hepler stated. "Remember that we are all unique individuals and live the rest of our lives without racism." The student spoke into the camera with feeling, his words coming across as a hopeful conclusion to the film. Would it not be better to put yesterday's sins behind us, to step away from a troubled past and start afresh? The question certainly needs to be asked of this book.

My dwelling on scholarship's disturbing contributions to the age of European imperialism does seem an odd manner of building a greater level of inclusion in the classroom. Is this the best way to expand a curriculum long bound by ideas that grew out of Western expansion? What it might mean to move forward, I argue, cannot be assessed unless we understand what education has already made of difference and diversity through race, culture, and nation. What might be written off as the remote history of imperial adventures and misfortunes has to be considered as still working on the educated imagination. As if among the hunting trophies I was once surprised to find mounted on the walls of the Harvard Club in New York some years ago, we sit comfortably and pleased with the prizes long after distancing ourselves from the practices. The solution, however, is not simply to redecorate. Before selling off the glassy-eyed trophy kills of that colonial past, let us ask what else of that original adventure in learning decorates the clubhouse of our education.

We need to consider what we have learned about a world that was, in no small measure, divided and instructed under the sponsorship of imperialism. We have to ask what the young learn of the question "Where is here?" and the part that schooling has long played in defining who belongs where. This is my call to history, to not forgetting but reconsidering how the past remains present in the way we tend to see the world. It is my way of asking whether we can take greater charge of what we carry forward from this inevitably persistent past. Yet this call comes at a time when the very idea of history faces the intellectual ferment of a postmodern "crisis of representation." According to those waving the postmodern banner, we have reason to be decidedly shaken in our ability to discover—and represent—a transcending truth for such a globally complex phenomenon as imperialism. And while these postmodern enfants terrible treat history as so much narrative that suffers from aspirations to the truth, very late Hegelians are busy writing end-of-history obituaries.[2] Taken together, these critiques cannot help but seriously undermine what we have come to count on and use as "history." What is it, then,

---

[2] On posthistory, see Lutz Niethammer, who sees it as not "the end of the world but the end of meaning" (1992, p. 3); and on history as narrative, see Hayden White (1987).

that I can reasonably hope to do with the past, now that it no longer stands before us like a chronologically ordered shelf of books, waiting to be opened and read? Is there still a *nonfiction* section to be found? Such questions, in light of what I have argued for up to this point, call for further reflection on history and schooling, on the idea of a useful past that can serve the schools in a new way. To this end, I will draw on comments from a final sample of schoolchildren to suggest that the account that I think is called for is not so far removed from what the young already know.

History, Finally

It was once enough for Francis Bacon to claim that "historians make men wise" (1909, p. 151). And although this claim seems dated in this cynical age, the recently proposed national standards for history teaching in the United States begin by quoting Thomas Jefferson's advice that history prepares us for the future, and Étienne Gilson's idea that history is a laboratory for testing the consequences of thought.[3] Yet it is too easy to point out how this faith in history stands in the face of the century's principal horrors, from the First World War to the Persian Gulf War, all of which were launched by those who did not want for an education in history. If I fear that forgetting the past will leave me ill prepared for the future, I still cannot count on the ready-made value of recalling what came before. The idea of returning with a critical eye to the history that we have inherited is not only about what has gone missing in the story of the past, but also about a history that has remained all too present as a force in our lives; which is to say that more or better history teaching, including the history of imperialism, does not in itself point the way forward.

In one sense, my approach to history comes down to a further wrestling with Hegel. "What experience and history teach," Hegel writes in *The Philosophy of History*, "is this—that people and governments never have learned anything from history, or acted on principles deduced from it" (1956, p. 6). For my part, I have been arguing that most everything people know about the world at large has come down to them from the past, and in that sense they are nothing if not students of history. How does a child first come to know the world, if not out of the history of meaning posed by family and school? How does the child grow into the meaning of the world if not through the interpretations established by the prominent voices of previous

---

[3] Jefferson and Gilson are invoked under the heading "The Significance of History for the Educated Citizen" in *National Standards for World History* (National Center, 1994, p. 1).

generations that pervade the morning papers and evening TV? People become carriers of this history, transforming it, rewriting corners of it, acting on it, keeping alive their connections with it. It can also be said that what is made of this history is finally something broad and philosophic. Long after the school lessons on Columbus and Cook are forgotten, people retain their historic encounters with difference, read across such two-dimensional spectrums as civilized and savage, West and East, white and black. These history lessons, the details having been lost, are elevated to universal principles. History becomes poetic in Aristotle's sense, as poetry, compared to history, has a greater claim to truth. "Poetry is something more philosophic and of graver import than history," he writes in *Poetics*, "since its statements are of the nature rather of universals whereas those of history are singulars" (1947, p. 636).[4] In just this poetic way, the historical distinctions that the imperial powers used to establish colonies, divide races, and distinguish cultures are transformed into universals of nature. These universals then become what people and governments do indeed learn from history.

Of course, there is no return to a pre-Columbian world, no place to be found outside this history of history. "We have no language—no syntax and no lexicon—which is foreign to this history," writes Jacques Derrida, who has tried as hard as anyone to write beyond the borders of what came before. "We can pronounce not a single destructive proposition which has not already had to slip into the form, the logic, and the implicit postulations of precisely what it seeks to contest" (1978b, pp. 280–81). The search for a prelapsarian Eden, for a time or a state of mind before the fall, was itself part of the colonial project in all of its destructive contradictions, a point George Steiner forcefully renders in discussing the nostalgia for the Absolute: "Possessed, as it were, by some archetypal rage at [our] exclusion from the Garden of Paradise, by some torturing remembrance of that disgrace, we have scoured the earth for vestiges of Eden and laid them to waste wherever we have found them" (1974, p. 32).

The past is not forgotten, but it is used to invest the present with meaning. Its transformation into universal truths makes for better mental storage and access, we might say today in light of advances in cognitive psychology. Thus, we view a typical newspaper photograph of the white cow sitting in the streets of an Indian city as the timeless truth of that country's collapsed

---

[4] I am indebted here to M. I. Finley's discussion of ancient Greek historiography, in which he helpfully points out that *historia*, which refers simply to inquiry into the past, was "invented" by Herodotus "to preserve," in Finley's words, "the fame of the great and wonderful actions of the Greeks and barbarians" (1986, p. 30).

and ancient civilization. The challenge before us, in the face of this "actual" photograph, is to arrive, and to help students arrive, at an understanding of how history renders the world sensible, a history that seems above all to dictate the meaning of difference. What I see in photographs of India has been produced by the lifetimes of hard, deliberate work that went into engineering the intellectual infrastructure of European expansion. When Derrida insists that we cannot step beyond the historical encoding of the world, beyond what he names elsewhere (1982) a "white mythology" that holds many of us in its educated grasp, he is speaking to a history that inscribes what has become the nature of the body. The perception of race, you may recall Carlton Coon reassuring his readers in *The Origin of Races,* is only natural (1962, p. 662).

Well, the human perception of difference per se is natural enough. We cannot live but by making distinctions. But the significance invested in any given difference forms an order of work, history, and discourse, that then passes as "only natural." The specific differences that we learn to attend to with acuity—such as those grouped under the heading "race"—and the extremely consequential burden of meaning that we learn to assign to those differences are the result of a historical process that each of us is educated within. To change the significance of those differences will take an educational effort at least equal to the one required to put those meanings in place to begin with. My modest proposal is to supplement our education with a consideration of imperialism's influence on the teaching of history, geography, science, language, and literature in the hope that it will change the way this legacy works on us.

These additional lessons are intended to help all of us understand and question why it is perfectly natural for Kathy Chin, the student introduced in the first chapter, to understand that although she was born and grows up in Canada, she is—and not just of her own volition—"Chinese." We do not yet have an education prepared to deal with what has gone into the making of the boundaries between East and West, between races and cultures, that we still live within. My intention is not to free Kathy from the complex suppositions of identity nor to deny her the opportunity to choose how she would identify herself, whether within or against how others identify her. My argument is only that, as imperialism's legacy continues to contribute to what students learn of the world, its influence on learning deserves to figure far more explicitly as a topic for consideration in their formal education. Students have a right to see what the West, and its proud process of education, has made of them, even as this knowledge is bound to complicate and implicate their education; for one paradoxical implication of what I have assembled here is that I continue to count on the educational system to make us free, even as I question its entrenched complicity with imperialism. But after tracking just how entwined with imperialism modern education is, after five centuries of close association, I have to wonder whether education can ever stand completely apart from this imperial legacy. What are the prospects of turning education against a legacy that has contributed so much to our understanding of the educated imagination?[5]

There may be no better instance of the double bind that drives this project that turns on, even as it turns to, education, than the story told by Frederick Douglass of his own education as a slave. In his autobiography, which was published in 1845, he describes his surreptitious acquisition of literacy that came of tricking white children into sharing the letters of the alphabet with him. As he acquired the ability to read and write, it afforded him, as he puts it, "a new and special revelation, explaining dark and mysterious things, with which my youthful understanding had struggled, but struggled in vain." Of all that it did for him, he felt that the light it cast on slavery was foremost: "I now understand what has been to me a most perplexing difficulty—to wit, the white man's power to enslave the black man. It was a grand achievement and I prized it highly. From that moment, I understood the pathway from slavery to freedom" (1960, pp. 58–59). Douglass manages not only to affirm the fundamental faith in learning, which is no more than the missionaries of education had long sought to engender in their charges, but also to affirm whites' superiority by virtue of this lettered art. Such was basis for the European right, as some interpreted it, to enslave others. Although Douglass appears delighted with stealing the secret of fire from the gods, his statement also suggests the moral hollowness of those whose authority is based on inscribing letters on a page. To enslave a people by means of an alphabet, it needs to be asked, is precisely what sort of "grand achievement"? In Douglass's hands, at least, literacy lights a pathway to freedom (with its echo of Hegel's History-as-Spirit). Whatever education's complicity with power, whatever the paradoxical tension stretched taut between emancipation and entrapment, Douglass turns it against that power and into something to be prized as it liberates.

This is much the spirit of multicultural, antiracist, and feminist initia-

---

[5] In considering what can reasonably be asked in the face of this legacy, I would support Said's educational hope for an end of orientalism that would "ideally . . . go beyond coercive limitations on thought toward a non-dominative and non-essentialist type of learning," with an aim "not so much to dissipate difference itself—for who can deny the constitutive role of national as well as cultural differences in the relations between human beings—but to challenge the notion that difference implies hostility, a frozen reified set of opposed essences" (1995, pp. 4, 6).

tives that, in seeking to identify the obviously Eurocentric and patriarchal elements in the curriculum, are now part of what gets talked about in schools and universities. In support of that disruptive talk, I have focused on specific aspects of academic disciplines that gave modern form to such ideas as the rise of the West, aspects which need to be critically examined within Western education. Students need to see what science made of race and what orientalist scholars made of the East. These particular contributions to the formation of identity continue to affect their lives. An education in the arts and sciences needs to include what scholarship has made of the world. Despite the grade 7 student George's hopes and the philosopher Hegel's fears, a certain reading of the past is still very much with us; it courses through us with little review or reflection. "The past is never dead," William Faulkner has a character say in *Requiem for a Nun*. "It's not even past" (1951, p. 92).[6]

We still need to ask, What does it mean to be held in the throes of a past that we can no longer trust or be comforted by? How is a history of imperialism possible? Or rather, how can such a history be useful? Clearly, the study of history is not about achieving picture-perfect representations of an earlier reality. "Realism," which served as the principal intellectual goal of European thinking about history during the nineteenth century, is not the force it once was.[7] Not long ago, Roland Barthes took the decline of the historical narrative as "the sign [that] History is henceforth not so much *the real* as *the intelligible* (1988, p. 140; Barthes's emphasis). This is not to undermine the reality of what I have presented in this book. The Jesuits built schools in New France. Ojibwa students were beaten for speaking their native language in these schools. What is needed from this history is that which can make intelligible the struggle today over, say, native control of schooling. When the world history textbook terminates the time line of Chinese history in the six-

---

[6] Deborah Britzman writes that "in an odd turn of events, curricula that purport to be inclusive may actually work to produce new forms of exclusivity *if* the only subject positions offered are the tolerant normal and the tolerated subaltern" (1995, p. 160; Britzman's emphasis). In offering a similar warning for the discipline of comparative literature, Rey Chow asks that, despite "the euphoria of oppositional thinking," we not be misled into thinking that "by making the gesture of welcoming non-Western cultures and civilizations into our curricula, we are going to make real changes. . . . We need to remember that there has been a complicated history in the West of the study of non-Western, non-European languages; our Eurocentric multilingual comparatists have always had their counterparts in the great Orientalists, Sinologists, Indologists, and so forth" (1995, pp. 110–11).

[7] Hayden White: "Nineteenth-century European culture displayed everywhere a rage for a realistic apprehension of the world"; "each of the most important cultural movements and ideologies of the nineteenth century—Positivism, Idealism, Naturalism, (literary) Realism, Symbolism, Vitalism, Anarchism, Liberalism, and so on—claimed to provide a more 'realistic' comprehension of social reality than its competitors" (1973, pp. 45–46).

teenth century, as we saw earlier in this book, the problem is not simply that
it thereby misses the reality or truth of China. There is not going to be *a* historical truth of China (any more than a truth of imperialism) in any comprehensive or singular sense, no matter how exhaustive the historical coverage
of China (or imperialism). What is required of teachers is an explanation of
the textbook's suspension of Chinese history that would increase the intelligibility of the West's project with history and its teaching, a project that
reaches back, perhaps, to Hegel's notion that the non-Western world exists
outside History and the World-Spirit.

The educational approach to history that I am advocating here is best
described as "pragmatic." This book's focus is on the past's continuing presence. This approach may seem to use history crassly, as an instrument for
solving the problems of the present; "presentism" is what historians disparag-
ingly call it. It has been a common enough educational ploy for trying to convince students of history's timeless relevance (Seixas, 1993). Yet rather than
asking which history is most relevant to today's situation or asking that the
past be judged by the standards of the present, I am pursuing the history that
continues to trouble aspects of current educational practices. Imperialism is
but one trace element within this process. Such traces in, say, the field of geography can help us understand how human difference is structured and
given meaning by the educated imagination. Turning our attention to these
educational traces of imperialism might well speed up and direct the gradual
breakdown of this legacy that reflects centuries of intellectual labor. To pause
over a history textbook's obscuring of Chinese history can mean interrupting
the traditional division of the world (if not of the student) between East and
West. This historical exclusion of China contravenes the universalizing norms
of Western realism—how can a country exist outside time?—for no other apparent reason than to bolster the great divide. These lessons also seek to end
the exclusion that students who are identified as Chinese are made to suffer in
seeing China omitted from most of what is known as modern history. This
exclusion only confounds our best efforts to understand how these great divides continue to operate. Good teachers have long found supplementary
works on China to cover what's missing from the traditional program. But it
also needs to be made apparent to students that such exclusion is not simply
an oversight but a feature of how the disciplines of geography, history, science, language, and literature (as well as the arts and mathematics) have gone
about dividing the world since the age of empire.

That much said, it should be clear that more than the history of China is
at stake in Western schools. What is foremost, I would hold, is the historical
identity of the child. When Michel Foucault speaks of the "history of the dif-

ferent modes by which, in our culture, human beings are made subjects," it is not hard to imagine the imperial legacy doing its part to make subjects out of the young, who are and are not, for example, Chinese (1982, p. 208). Our subjectivity is written and named within the historically contingent texts of schools and popular culture. We are as we are named. The only hope of understanding and gaining some distance from this process appears to be to catch a glimpse of what has passed in the rearview mirror. In Foucault's terms, my historical inquiry into imperialism has been about how "human beings are made subjects" and how they are "divided inside [themselves] or divided from others." Such is the "government of individualization" (p. 212.). The Foucauldian imperative—"We have to know the historical conditions which motivate our conceptualizations"—calls for attending to the "dividing practices" by which knowledge and subjects, both school and individual, are constituted (p. 209). Learning to divide the world in this way is to be inscribed within, Foucault would say, a *régime du savoir* (p. 212). Although Foucault devotes little attention to imperialism, he comes close to posing my project's central question in his conclusion to *The Archeology of Knowledge*: "What is that fear that makes you seek, beyond all boundaries, ruptures, shifts, and divisions, the great historico-transcendental destiny of the Occident?" (1972, p. 210).

Teaching to this sense of destiny is precisely what E. D. Hirsch, Diane Ravitch, Arthur Schlesinger, and other contemporary defenders of a largely national cultural literacy in the United States are banking on to "unite" a fractured America. Their earnest directing of the school curriculum toward preserving "the great historico-transcendental destiny of the Occident" might make more students feel at home if it included a critical treatment of how that destiny was constructed on divisions that we are now working to overcome. As I described in the opening chapter, educators are responsible for developing an account with their students of what has brought us to seeing the world divided in this way. Imperialism's educational legacy, so prominent in my own schoolbooks decades ago, today exhibits far less prejudice toward the non-Western world. Current history textbooks, at their best, address how the legacy of imperialism has shaped the writing of history, although others, it is true, do not interrupt earlier traditions. Far fewer biology texts today carry the miscegenation torch, preferring to give the impression that the study of biology has had nothing to do with the concept of race.

For a teacher to give an account of imperialism's educational legacy means learning about how the world was divided as a result of the energetic study of the world. Given that this study of imperialism can hold no guarantee for decreasing racism, this inquiry finds its educational warrant in students' *right to know* where the material they study comes from and what it would make of them, rights that underlie the principle of educational accountability I have been advocating. In this way, this book is intended to demonstrate how much of what we mean by race, culture, and nation was shaped by imperialism, and how much of its legacy was the work of scholars and schools. It is hard to know what people will do with what they learn, but lack of assurance is hardly a reason to shy away from reflecting on what people educated in the spirit of European imperialism have made of the world in the past. Educators need to give an account of what their emerging profession (of learning) did during what was, for education as much as for any element in the West, the Great Expansion.

Lessons in Learning

Imperialism's great educational enterprise began in an effort to remake the world of learning. The Arawak people who greeted Columbus on the beaches undid what Europe had known of the world. These newfound people defied the strictures of Scripture (they were naked and not ashamed). They confounded the classical learning of science (they were neither hairy nor monstrous). They created a need for a supplement that would incorporate this New World into the old ways of understanding. Europe's great intellectual challenge, J. H. Elliott has argued (1970), was to assimilate the New World, as well as Asia and Africa, within a new European world order. The Europeans sought to place the people they met in the New World into a revised racial order, to convert them to Christianity, to teach them European languages, to rewrite their histories and laws, to rename them and their land, and to collect and preserve the artifacts of their culture. Europe sought to bring this other form of life into an ordering of the world that would amount to an elaborate supplement to the medieval *mappae mundi* that firmly set the divisions between Europe and Asia and Africa.

Earlier, I made it clear that I have faced my own imperialist dangers with this project, namely, in the sheer expansiveness of the suggested association of education and imperialism that I have engaged in explicating. The forces of imperialism might appear educational in their every purpose, and education during those years of empire must necessarily seem imperialist in its every intent. But given the shaping of educational practices (in English language and literature) and the initiation of disciplines (anthropology and modern geography) against the backdrop of imperialism, it is going to be extremely difficult to insist on clear, distinct boundaries between the metaphorical and the literal associations of imperialism and education. The Western thirst for learning in that earlier era was supported by, where it was not simply an extension of, the desire for colonial acquisition and political domination exercised by the European powers. Imperialism, in turn, fostered a global market for its own educational resources, as it sought to make the world into a storehouse of knowledge: "The sixteenth century collected facts as it collected exotic objects, assembling them for display in cosmographies like so many curios in a cabinet," Elliott writes (1970, p. 30). The West believed that it had a great deal to learn from the world but very little that it would credit others as having taught it, with few exceptions. Adventurous autodidacticism prevailed among the curious and the carefree who set off to teach themselves about these new realms, only to return home to interested audiences keen on learning what these self-made scholars made of the world. For all of the learning that went on abroad, Europeans showed little appreciation for their native teachers, who were as likely regarded as informants. There remains the ironic sense that the sophisticated learned from the naive, a role reversal that, it is assumed, was not fully appreciated by natives who served the colonists as temporary dressed-up "teachers."[8] After all, who was it who took those lessons on language, for example, and turned them into learned papers, dictionaries, grammars, and other works of scholarship? And how are we now to question the hold of the West on the role of global authority and educator?

Learning proved another way for the West to take the rest of the world in hand, whether by conducting geological surveys, preserving ancient texts, or setting up schools. None of this can be faulted, except that the globalization of Western understanding was always about a relative positioning of the West by a set of coordinates defined by race, culture, and nation. Although we cannot hope to ascertain the precise contribution of scientific efforts to advancing the colonial empires nor calculate the whole of imperialism's educational interests, we must still be prepared to challenge grade 7 student George Hepler's advice to "just say no" to history. We need to ask him whether this always partial inquiry does not at least hold out the hope of dislodging what too often passes as the human nature of difference. To trace the natural(izing) history of divisions that, for example, set one race apart from another is to call them into question. It reveals how these divisions were first cast by dedicated amateurs working hand in hand with champions of global expansion and racial domination. With time, an education system arose that encompassed the resulting systems of classification, the history of a triumphant West, the worldly powers of the English language, and the literature of island

---

[8] The race and class differences were kept present when, for example, Lt. Jerome Becker, stationed in the Belgian Congo during the 1880s, spoke of using "our black domestic servants . . . as language teachers" (cited by Fabian, 1986, p. 30).

paradises. A gilded dome of learning was constructed upon the columns of the colonized, who were held to be sheltered from their own savagery by this cover. And today, the educational legacy of imperialism extends across the cultural spectrum—whether in textbook treatments of Chinese history, Disney theme parks, or television reruns of *Wild Kingdom*. The imperial gaze is sustained in many tourist and educational enterprises, representing a certain domestication of imperialism while continuing its staking out of the world as a classroom of instruction and delight.[9] It is with caution, then, and an educator's ever-present hope, that I turn to the schools to consider the prospects of gaining a greater measure of critical distance from this educational legacy.

In School

As it turns out, George Hepler's recommendation to his classmates to forget the past is exactly what schools have often done and done very well, in the face of controversy. Standard practice for educators, always with brave exceptions, has been to shy away from subjects wherein life turns serious and fearsome. Educational programs on sexuality, substance abuse, and violence, for example, have been a long time coming. What, then, of imperialism's troubling legacy, especially as it implicates the arts and sciences? To say that race is no longer viable as a scientific category, which the majority of recent biology textbooks do by default, is one thing, but to ignore science's long service in the construction of race seems an act of miseducation, leaving students to wonder how race has taken on such weight as a nonbiological phenomenon. Although one science textbook has dealt with the eugenics movement (Bullard et al., 1992), science's larger contribution to the meaning of race has yet to find a place within what students can expect to learn about biology. Fortunately, this head-in-the-sand attitude has always struck some educators as irresponsible, and, far from the mainstream of educational publishing, they have created excellent support materials on the science of race and the economics of neocolonialism, to name two examples introduced earlier in this book (Gill and Levidow, 1987; Gage, 1993). It is this critical look at the arts and sciences that I see as an important addition to the considerable work that

---

[9] In writing of "the legacy of conquest" felt in the American West, Patricia Nelson Limerick describes the continuation of struggles over land and legitimation through cultural tourism, while portraying an ongoing educational treatment of this harsh heritage: "When Indian war dances became tourist spectacles, when the formerly scorned customs of the Chinese drew tourists to Chinatown, when former out-groups found that characteristics that had once earned them disapproval could now earn them a living, when fearful, life-threatening deserts became charming patterns of color and light, the war was over and the frontier could be considered closed and even museumized" (1987, p. 25).

is being done on numerous fronts in multicultural global education (Gold-berg, 1994; Sleeter and McLaren, 1995).[10]

This book has sought to ask readers to reflect on imperialism's educational legacy for their own education and that of the young. It does not pretend to provide adequate support for teachers who wish to introduce the themes of this book into their classrooms. My hope, however, is that it will provide a basis for teachers to sit down together to reflect on and compare educations. The starting point is to get a feel for how we think and see the world within the scope of this intellectual legacy. This reflection could lead, as I imagine the process, to the selection or development of specific supplements, for each of the subject areas, that encourage student and teacher to step back and examine how the subject has come to frame the world.[11] Although this approach is intended to change the way we envision the teaching of history, geography, and other subject areas, it does not mean that this legacy is all that one would want to teach or learn about. It becomes a way of situating the lessons, maps, textbooks, and films, that make up an education; it provides a sense of where these lessons came from and how, in trying to move beyond this legacy of colonialism, they need to change, to be viewed in a new way. Although this sense of change can be introduced through passing comments perhaps reflecting on one's own education, direct lessons on imperialism's educational legacy would form a postcolonial supplement to the curriculum. As a starting point in helping educators imagine, in a crudely schematic sense, what in the world might be taught to the young as a result of this book, I have drawn up a "postcolonial supplementary project grid" that gratuitously reduces this book to a snappy student activity sheet (fig. 1).

In considering what it would realistically take to make the educational legacy of imperialism part of the curriculum, classroom handouts aside, I can foresee three major objections that touch on what is both too remote and too

---

[10] See Peter McLaren, who, in the name of a "revolutionary multiculturalism," proposes that "we must actively help students to challenge sites of discursive hierarchy rather than delocalizing and dehistoricizing them," which will redeem us "from our finitude as passive supplicants of history" (1994, pp. 68–69).

[11] Derrida captures the educational value of the supplement in Rousseau's *Émile,* where "all education, [which is] the keystone of Rousseauist thought, will be described or presented as a system of substitution [*suppléance*] destined to reconstitute Nature's edifice in the most natural way possible" (1974, p. 145). He points out that the supplement "adds only to replace"; it "is *exterior* outside of the positivity to which it is superadded, alien to that which, in order to be replaced by it must be other than it" (p. 145; Derrida's emphasis). Just so, we need a history of imperialism to which is superadded imperialism's writing of history and other disciplines as an influence on the formation of the disciplines, as both alien to what has been meant by studying history and capable, in that way, of replacing some small part of it.

Figure 1. A Postcolonial Supplementary Project Grid

Identity Concepts
Gender   Race   Culture   Nation   Empire

Disciplines	*The Educational Legacy of Imperialism*	*Domains of Inquiry*
History	1) In the portrayal of the other	Students
Geography	2) In the treatment of distance from	Families
Science	the West	Teachers
Language	3) In the placement of the non-Western	Schoolbooks
Literature	outside history	Community
Others	4) In the suggestion of evolutionary differences along moral, cultural, and/or psychological lines	Popular Culture
		Informal
	5) In the construction of racial differences	Education
	6) In the equation of culture and/or nationality with race	Arts
		Literature
		Scholarship
		State

HOW THE PROJECT GRID WORKS: With any of the disciplines, the teacher can use instances from schoolbooks or popular culture to demonstrate how a discipline continues the educational legacy of imperialism, which has an impact on what are termed, for purposes of this grid, identity concepts and domains of inquiry. Examples beginning with the disciplines might include the following. The disciplines listed are only those that receive detailed treatment in this book.

(a) *History*: Students look at how the concept of *nationality* is presented in an *informal education* setting such as a museum exhibition on the American Revolution.

(b) *Geography*: Students interview members of the *community* about their understanding of the changing meaning of *culture*.

(c) *Science*: Students examine old biology *schoolbooks'* references to *racial identity* in humans.

(d) *Language*: Students examine the educational implications of the *state* language policies in the new South African constitution.

(e) *Literature*: Students review previous assignment questions, performances, and critical works on *Othello* for their treatment of race, gender, and miscegenation.

immediate about this topic. Some may say that imperialism's educational legacy, whether in geography's exotic representation of the other or in the use of literature to civilize, is simply removed from today's struggles against racism in the school yard and workplace. Imperialism seems a topic all the more wanting in relevance when thinking about American schools, until one makes vivid the colonial entanglement of conquest and slavery, and all that America did to construct an educated rationale for both. We need to help students appreciate how the ideas that took root in that context could still inform the way the world is divided, with the challenge before us being trying to relearn the world. By way of examples, I have tried to tie the persistence of this legacy to the most unassuming of ideas within our education. Perhaps the best instance is the geographically elusive boundary between Asia and Europe, which is otherwise so firm and fixed a great divide in our minds. Imperialism's intellectual accomplishments can be shown to be an immediate and present aspect of how the West continues to construct the world in an educational sense.

After imperialism's seeming remoteness, a second challenge facing educators is how to teach about this legacy when it is critical of the school subjects themselves. Placing the actual content and organization of the curriculum under scrutiny is a different order of dealing with controversial issues. Typically, as with sex and drugs, aim is taken at the teenage behavior that needs constraining. Asking the school to turn a self-critical eye toward its own practices and history, to how it has both participated in and managed to obscure the privileging of the West, is to ask the school for a level of educational courage that exceeds the level required to teach about safe sex or dangerous drugs. Yet what is so wrong with the West telling its best story to its young? Every society does; such ethnocentrism is only natural. Why not do it with pride rather than apology? Well, I would respond, this is where we are, and still I would ask that some allowance be made for the scale and proximity of this particular regime of ethnocentrism, that is, for the global educational consequences of imperialism's legacy within and beyond the West. In fostering this critical stance toward education, I have proposed that we begin with our own schooling, to see how matters of identity and difference have changed and have been retained since the collapse of colonialism. "We were born in an era when Europe still seemed to be—and perhaps was—Queen of the world," reflected Henri Baudet in 1959, "yet the West's great retreat from Asia and Africa, which spelled the visible end of our classic expansion and of Western mastery of the world has taken place within the space of less than one generation" (1965, p. 6). In taking this critical approach to the academic disciplines, those of us who fall today within that single generation's span are asking students to join with us in rethinking what we have inherited. As Baudet goes on say, "We have witnessed a tremendous event, requiring insight, interpretation, and explanation, even though we may, in the meantime, be unable to provide more than a mere provisional explanation of a very general nature" (pp. 6–7). My hope remains that the pursuit of such accounts will have an irreversible, if not exactly predictable, effect on imperialism's ways of dividing the world, to the educational benefit of all concerned.[12]

A third and final area of concern, also touching on the close and immediate spaces of teaching, comes from returning to what was most ugly about colonialism, the way people were divided at every turn as different, inferior. What impact will this have on racial awareness and tension in the classroom? What will this make of the color-blind classroom? Will it add to the backlash that has formed against the gains that have been made in gender equity, affirmative action, and other forms of redistributing power? I do not think we have any choice but to set aside the liberal hope for color blindness and to address the backlash with the undiminished sense of difference and distance to which the students are always already witnesses, working with them on the historical and interested construction of those categories of difference. It is bound to be disconcerting to delve into, for example, the Euro–American fixing of racial categories in the service of imperialism. Such work is bound to be filled with the awkward, discomforting moments that come of student and teacher bearing witness to truths that are difficult to find a way out from under. To give an intellectual and historical account of our education, which this book has sought to do, can fail to allow for how the personal experience of it is written on the bodies of those who are now asked to study it. This was brought home to me by Ceila Haig-Brown, who described how presenting her historical work on native residential schools to First Nations leaders convinced her just how inadequate academic account giving can be unless it also allows for a bearing of witness by those who suffered the outrages that were conducted in the name of cultural salvation and assimilation. My focus has been on *giving* an account, but what that presumes of its audience, of how

---

[12] More recently, James Fenton has written on what he terms the "unfinished nature of imperial business" through an examination of English poetry that comes to much broader conclusions: "Much as everyone might like it the empire does not collapse overnight. It collapses once. Then it continues to collapse. It breaks up once and then it breaks up again and again and again, and again. People's lives are ruined by it. Nations are ruined by it. People are still on the move, because there once was an empire and now the empire is no more" (1996, p. 62).

that history speaks to them, also has to form part of the pedagogy among students and teacher as a way of coming at these lessons.

What needs to be made clear is that, as the schools have contributed to racialized identities, so they need to be engaged in study of their own historical construction. This is no more than education's assuming responsibility for its own handiwork, no more than a faith in its ability and need to revise its faulty lessons, and to do so with the young because they may be the ones who suffer those earlier lessons. This embrace of history will also need to steer clear of the sort of "liberal transaction" that, as Glen Loury (1995) denounces it in the American context, portrays African Americans as no more than victims of historical injustices. Victimization forms yet another side of the imperial gaze. Rather, the aim here is to effect a series of course corrections in what we make of education. These would include, for example, examining how categories of identity are treated as facts of nature rather than products of history. This is too conceptual, perhaps, and I don't assume, as I've said, that it will end prejudice or inequality. Nor is it about denying what Loury terms "the saliency, the power, the inescapability of race" (p. 66). It is about helping students find what these categories have come to mean, and thus to find themselves, especially as many of them have crossed those historical divides of race, culture, and nation through their own lives.

If teachers can see their way past these obstacles, there remains the question how ready students are to attend to such histories. Where are students today in making sense of such history, culture, and difference? Well-publicized surveys regularly reveal the wealth of historical and geographical ignorance possessed by the young, which would seem to put the aspirations of this book into the category of the overly ambitious. Where do we start and how far can we possibly hope to go in disentangling what imperialism has wrought from what we know and what we would teach the young? There will be no definite answer to such questions, but I am not sure what it would mean to say that although we may owe the young an explanation for what we have made, they are not ready for it, and thus we are absolved of our responsibility.

As it is, I have been encouraged by what high school students from around the Pacific region have written about culture, language, history, and geography in a study that Lynn Thomas and I have been conducting.[13] They

---

[13] For a description of the study, see John Willinsky (1994b). More than a thousand students have participated thus far from twelve countries; for the first round of analysis on students' drawing and labeling maps of what they envision as the Pacific region, see Willinsky and Thomas (1994); and on ethnic tensions, see Thomas and Willinsky (in press). The work of paraticipating Japanese students reported here has been translated into English by Allan Bailey.

do not, as a rule, show a great historical understanding of this complex region, but out of the sheer range of their responses one finds expressed a certain awareness and vulnerability that could be coaxed into a more elaborate way of seeing what has been made of the world as a result of such phenomena as imperialism. By way of previewing our report on this ongoing study, I offer a sample of the students' comments on culture that convey just what they have already acquired about one of imperialism's more elastic concepts.

The reader can hear how students seek a place within the reality of categories, in this Hawaiian student's expression of bewilderment over how one is to be identified and where one feels one belongs, in a variation of that question "Where is here?":

> I feel that I belong to two cultures, but only one community. I am full Korean but I feel also a bit of Hawaiian since I live in Hawaii and [am] considered local, born and raised in Hawaii. I love the Hawaiian culture and their beliefs but most of that is gone due to the missionaries from the mainland, who gave them a new culture to go by. When I look at Korea, and how Koreans do things, I don't feel a part of it—like I am that culture, but not that culture. Does it make sense? My community is this local community here on Oahu.

This student chooses locality over race and the "fullness" of blood and genealogy, as if to recognize that against cultural loss and transformation, one is always and finally living locally, in the known world of one's own neighborhood. It is the other sense, of dislocation, that I want to help students better understand with this book's history work, in the hope that it may provide them with a sense of history to their feeling that "like I am that culture, but not that culture. Does it make sense?"

At a northern California high school where, judging by students' comments, there is a fair amount of racial tension, a student captured the struggle against an ascribed and dislocating identification:

> I'm from a group called Asian and most of the school students call us names and make fun of us. So, me and my friends stood up for ourselves and then some of the students told us to go back to where we belong, "Thailand." Most Asians don't like starting problems but we just [want] to get along, so if others can't we'll do the same back.

This student's regard for the label "Asian" suggests how coming to America can mean learning one is Asian. This is a called-name ("call us names and make fun of us"), an assigned identity, with the student setting off the presumed true home of Thailand in quotation marks, as if to point to the ignorance and absurdity at work here. The student seems to recognize that designation of identity is part of something larger, outside what can be challenged except to "do the same back." The rest of it, the local pushing around, name-calling, and pushing back, is also about disruptions and dislocations in the meaning of this place. It may seem little enough to say to these students that there is a history here that we can unpack, but this is what education does best.

Among the comments that we have collected up to this point, those of the students from the Solomon Islands, which achieved independence from Great Britain in 1978, present an especially poignant sense of how the legacy of imperialism might continue to haunt the education of those outside the West, just as it is often obscured in what are known as the former settler colonies; as one Australian student in the study put it, "I'd like to think that our culture included those of the Aboriginal people but we, as a community, basically ignore their way of life and concentrate on our own." The students in the Solomon Islands felt the tensions between colonial and postcolonial sensibilities, between an acceptance and a questioning of their assigned place in the world. More than one of the Solomon Islands students gave expression to Hegel's lesson on how the non-Western world exists outside history. "The Solomon Islands, a 'Paradise lost in time,'" is how one put it. The student's quotation may owe more to the tourism slogan than to postcolonial irony, but the critical stance does not seem out of reach. The students could imagine themselves, through European eyes, living in a "Paradise lost" that was meant to be the Eden that would redeem the imperial dream. They could find their place in the world through their relation to a distant center. Thus they wrote, "Unlike other European countries Solomon Islands only have two seasons a year, namely rainy and sunny seasons," and "Here we do not get serious illnesses like overseas." It might seem that these students have learned their lessons well, lessons that seem to be largely about distance and difference: "Far from the reach of Europeans, people here roam[ed] the forest for food, and other essential things for survival." The Solomon Islands students' sense of history and economy managed to touch on all the main themes of imperialism with a remarkably even hand:

> We depend mainly on our neighbor countries and we regard them as our bigger brothers. They are Australia, New Zealand, and Papua New Guinea.

> Geography has made us neighbors, history made us brothers and trade has made us partners. Primitive you might think we are, but civilized beings according to our culture, that's what we are. Though we are scat-

tered about, the bond that holds us together as Wantoks of the Pacific will last forever.

Before the 1500s, the Pacific was an isolated universe. Still a virgin, far from the hands of white men. Natives roamed over jungles. Eventually the age of discovery came. Men looking for new lands arrived. Explorers discovered our lands. It is a time of wonder and change for our ancestors. Captain Cook discovered the Cook Islands, Mendara the Solomons. The most spectacular event in the Pacific is when the white devils from the east came to our beautiful Pacific.

As the legacy of imperialism remains a viable and resisted presence in these students' lives, so it is still very much a part of the map of the Pacific: "In the past, the natives are known to be savages, but nowadays, they are very friendly and would flash their Pacific smile at anyone." With the West turning to the Pacific as its next New World of opportunity, educators have a special responsibility in teaching the young how the people of the Pacific came to be "known" as savage and primitive during that initial encounter, as a way of learning the region again in a new way.

One of the great educational claims of anthropology is that, in the study of the exotic native, we can be assured that "knowing them better does nonetheless help us to detach ourselves from our own society," which is how Claude Lévi-Strauss put it in reflecting on his study of Brazil's indigenous people (1961, p. 391). The anthem of detachment has long served the causes of anthropology, social studies, and cultural tourism. Yet it denies the dependence that Hegel describes as holding the master to the slave, as well as overlooking the resistance of those we would know. One might want to think about how "knowing them better" is really about affixing oneself to, not detaching oneself from, "our own society," as Lévi-Strauss puts it. This idea of ourselves as knowing others better than they know themselves has long been a source of Western identity and license. Lévi-Strauss is naming an ongoing history of identification for the learned, a history that has been wrapped up in imperialism's particular structuring of human difference and that this book has argued requires new lessons if we are finally to interrupt that structure.[14]

Yet postcolonial approaches to learning are emerging, including the "anti-anthropological" films of Trinh Minh-Ha, who calls for an educational

---

[14] Cornel West demonstrates how "'Whiteness' is a politically constructed category parasitic on 'Blackness,'" using the example of Irish and Sicilian immigrants arriving in America and having to "learn that they were 'White' principally by adopting American discourse of positively-valued Whiteness and negatively-charged Blackness" (1990, p. 29).

process that begins by naming the full and often forgotten extent of a colonialism that has long operated in the name of humanism:

> Maintaining the intuitive, emotional Other under the scientistic tutelage of the rational, all-knowing Western Subject is an everlasting aim of the dominant which keeps on renewing itself through a wide range of humanistic discourses. . . . Decolonization often means dewesternization as taught by the White man. (1991, p. 20)

I am not at all sure whether we can un-install the mammoth program of Westernization that the world has absorbed, nor would I want to decide that this is the best course of action on behalf of others. When it comes to the world we know, the best that we can hope for is to supplement what we know, to learn again, rather than to imagine walking away from being the educated subjects that we have become. Still, I hope I have made clear why it is fair and necessary to unsettle what we have for so long treasured as an educated and knowing perspective on the world, why it is only fair to reconsider, in light of this inquiry, the cultivated pleasures of the museum, the wildernesses turned into parks, the utopias envisioned and dramas written out of encounters with natives, the ruins visited in Malaysia and monuments climbed in Mexico. This idea of supplementary lessons on imperialism's legacy is about providing an account of how the West came to divide the world as it has, to draw on one of the more significant instances from this legacy.

To return to my own instance, where once, as Jews, we were a race apart from Europeans, many of us now find it easy enough to put this past behind us and to make ourselves one with this culture and its learning. This acceptance and forgetting, I have come to realize in writing this book, obliterates what this form of learning has made of the world and of the ways in which it has been divided. As one who has made his living through education, it is not enough to allow that this education has finally secured a place for me within its hold on the world. I have now to offer an account of what this education makes of others, those who continue to fall outside its measure of the world. This book has been written against the learned forgetfulness and complacency displayed in the face of history. How far we can go in seeing the world other than as we have inherited it, I do not yet know. The educational project always lies ahead.

This book began with questions of how we are known, questions that symbolized the way imperialism divided the world. The imperialism of colonial jurisdictions continues to fade away, hastened by Hong Kong's reversion to China and the close of the twentieth century. Yet imperialism of another sort lives on in how each of us is known and how each of us comes to know.

One resolution of the identity question in light of this legacy is to learn to "read [oneself] in quotation marks," to borrow Tzvetan Todorov's method of identification.[15] We are not anything so much as what we have learned to call ourselves. Learning to read ourselves within and against how we have been written, too, seems part of the educational project ahead. But learning to read oneself is also about learning to read the other, as we consider how to rewrite the learned and learn-*ed* perceptions of difference. How are we to overcome the foreignness that we have so often made of the other, if not by first finding it in ourselves, as we have made ourselves over through education and as we were all born foreign (ignorant, poorly spoken, barbaric)? Julia Kristeva (1991) answers the question by asking us to discover how we are strangers to (the idea of) ourselves. That may be enough to stir a certain compassion toward those officially defined as aliens, foreigners, immigrants. "The foreigner is within me," Kristeva insists, "hence we are all foreigners" (p. 192). We can better understand the shaping of that shared foreignness by studying the cultivation and manufacture, the cataloging and display of the categories that have done so much for nation and empire. In this way, we see how we are pierced by the persistent past. Lessons on this legacy will bring us back, it is true, to an educational project that was originally intended to profit and delight some at the expense of others, but it needn't continue that way.

---

[15] Todorov: "I can no longer subscribe to my 'prejudices' as I did before, even if I do not attempt to rid myself of all 'prejudice.' My identity is maintained, but it is as if it is neutralized; I read myself in quotation marks" (1995, p. 15). I am also cautioned in my approach to identity by Cornel West's advice that "education must not be about a cathartic quest for identity," which he writes in "Beyond Eurocentrism and Multiculturalism." Rather, "it must foster credible sensibilities for an active critical citizenry" (1993, p. 19).

WORKS CITED

Abella, I. (1996, November 21). A few last reflections on the Roux affair. *Toronto Globe and Mail,* A23.

Abramson, H. S. (1987). National Geographic: *Behind America's lens on the world.* New York: Crown.

Achebe, C. (1975). The African writer and the English language. In *Morning yet on creation day* (pp. 55–62). London: Heinemann.

———— (1988). An image of Africa: Racism in Conrad's *Heart of Darkness.* In C. Achebe, ed., *Hopes and impediments: Selected essays, 1965–1987* (pp. 1–13). Oxford: Heinemann.

———— (1995). Colonialist criticism (orig. 1974). In W. Ashcroft, G. Griffiths, and H. Tiffin, eds., *The post-colonial studies reader* (pp. 57–61). New York: Routledge.

Adas, M. (1989). *Machines as the measure of men: Science, technology, and ideologies of Western dominance.* Ithaca, N.Y.: Cornell University Press.

Advisory Committee on Native Education in the British Tropical African Dependencies (1979). Education policy in British tropical Africa. In B. Fetter, ed., *Colonial rule in Africa: Readings from primary sources* (pp. 130–32). Madison: University of Wisconsin Press.

Al Ahmad, J. (1988). *Gharbzandegi* (Weststruckness) (J. Green and A. Alizadeh, trans.). Lexington, Ky.: Mazdâ.

Ahmad, R. H. (1992). *Educational development and reform in Malaysia.* Paper given at International Conference on Educational Co-operation in the Asia-Pacific Region, Hiroshima, Japan.

Aijaz Ahmad (1992). *In theory: Classes, nations, literatures.* London: Verso.

Alcoze, T., Bradley, C. Hernandez, T. Kashima, I. M. Kane, and G. Madrazo (1993). *Multiculturalism in mathematics, science, and technology: Reading and activities.* Menlo, Calif.: Addison-Wesley.

Aldrich, R. (1988). Imperialism in the study and teaching of history. In J.A. Mangan, ed., *"Benefits bestowed"? Education and British imperialism* (pp. 23–38). Manchester, England: University of Manchester Press.

Allardyce, G. (1982). The rise and fall of the Western civilization course. *American Historical Review* 87: 724.

Altick, R. D. (1978). *The shows of London.* Cambridge: Harvard University Press.

Anderson, B. (1983). *Imagined communities: Reflections on the origins and spread of nationalism* (revised ed.). London: Verso.

Anderson, J. (1991). Rushton's racial comparisons: An ecological critique of theory and method. *Canadian Psychology* 32(1): 51–60.

Anderson, J. D. (1994). How we learn about race through history. In L. Kramer, D. Reid, and W. L. Barney, eds., *Learning history in America: Schools, cultures, and politics* (pp. 87–105). Minneapolis: University of Minnesota Press.

Anderson, K. J. (1991). *Vancouver's Chinatown: Racial discourse in Canada, 1875–1980.* Montreal and Kingston: McGill-Queen's University Press.

Appadurai, A. (1986). Is homo hierarchicus? *American Ethnologist* 13: 745–61.

———— (1993). Number in the colonial imagination. In C. A. Breckenridge and P. van der Veer, eds., *Orientalism and the postcolonial predicament: Perspectives on South Asia* (pp. 314–40). Philadelphia: University of Pennsylvania Press.

Applebee, A. (1993). *Literature in the secondary school: Studies of curriculum and instruction in the United States.* Urbana, Ill.: National Council of Teachers of English.

Aravamudan, S. (1993). Trop(icaliz)ing the Enlightenment. *Diacritics* 23(3): 48–68.

Archibald, J. (1993). Resistance to an unremitting process: Racism, curriculum, and education in western Canada. In J. A. Mangan, ed., *The imperial curriculum: Racial images and education in the British colonial experience* (pp. 93–107). London: Routledge.

Arendt, H. (1951). *Imperialism.* (Part 2 of *The origins of totalitarianism.*) San Diego: Harcourt Brace Jovanovich.

Aristotle. (1947). *Poetics.* In *Introduction to Aristotle* (I. Bywater, trans.; pp. 624–67). New York: Modern Library.

Armstrong, N. (1990). The occidental Alice. *Differences* 2(2): 3–40.

Arnold, M. (1895). *Poems: Lyric and elegiac poems.* London: Macmillan.

———— (1896). *Culture and anarchy: An essay in political and social criticism* (orig. 1869). New York: Macmillan.

———— (1908). *Reports on elementary schools, 1852–1882.* London: HMSO.

Ashcroft, B., G. Griffiths, and H. Tiffin (1989). *The empire writes back: Theory and practice in post-colonial literatures.* London: Routledge.

————, eds. (1995). *The post-colonial studies reader.* New York: Routledge.

Ashworth, M. (1985). *Beyond methodology: Second language teaching and the community.* Cambridge: Cambridge University Press.

———— (1992). Projecting the past into the future: A look at ESL for children in Canada. In K. A. Moodley, ed., *Beyond multicultural education: International perspectives* (pp. 115–33). Calgary: Detselig.

Bacon, F. (1855). *The novum organon or true guide to the interpretation of nature* (orig. 1620; G. W. Kitchin, trans.). Oxford: Oxford University Press.

———— (1909). Of studies (orig. 1625). In *The essayes and counsels civill and morall of Francis Bacon Lord Veruluam* (pp. 150–51). London: Dent.

Bagchi, J. (1994). Colonialism and socialization: The girl child in colonial Bengal. *Resources for Feminist Research (RFR/DRF)* 22(3–4): 23–30.

Bailey, R. W. (1991). *Images of English: A cultural history of the language.* Ann Arbor: University of Michigan Press.

Baker, J. R. (1974). *Race.* London: Oxford University Press.

Bakhtin, M. (1968). *Rabelais and his world* (H. Iswolsky, trans.). Cambridge: MIT Press.

Bal, M. (1991). The politics of citation. *Diacritics* 21(1): 25–45.

Banks, J. (1993). Australian coast and people (orig. 1770). In R. Hanbury-Tenison, ed., *The Oxford book of exploration* (pp. 406–10). Oxford: Oxford University Press.

Banton, M. (1977). *The idea of race.* Boulder, Colo.: Westview.

———— (1987). *Racial theories.* Cambridge: Cambridge University Press.

Barba, R. H. (1993). *A social reconstruction view of history of earth and space sciences.* Paper presented at the annual meeting of the American Education Research Association, New Orleans, Louisiana.

Barkan, E. (1992). *The retreat of scientific racism: Changing concepts of race in Britain and the United States between the world wars.* Cambridge: Cambridge University Press.

Barker, M. (1990). Biology and the new racism. In D. T. Goldberg, ed., *Anatomy of racism* (pp. 18–37). Minneapolis: University of Minnesota Press.

Baron, D. E. (1982). *Grammar and good taste: Reforming the American language.* New Haven, Conn.: Yale University Press.

———— (1990). *The English-only question: An official language for Americans?* New Haven, Conn.: Yale University Press.

Barr, B. B., and M. B. Leyden (1986). *Addison-Wesley life science.* Menlo, Calif: Addison-Wesley.

Barthes, R. (1971). *Image, music, text* (S. Heath, trans.). New York: Hill & Wang.

———— (1980). The plates of the *Encyclopedia.* In *New critical essays* (pp. 23–40). (R. Howard, trans.). New York: Hill & Wang.

———— (1988). The discourse of history. In *The rustle of language* (R. Howard, trans.; pp. 127–40). Berkeley: University of California Press.

Barzun, J. (1937). *Race: A study in a modern superstition.* New York: Harper & Row.

Batsleer, J., T. Davies, R. O'Rourke, and C. Weedon (1985). *Rewriting English: Cultural politics of gender and class.* London: Methuen.

Baudet, H. (1965). *Paradise on earth: Some thoughts on European images of non-European man* (E. Wentholt, trans.). New Haven, Conn.: Yale University Press.

Bazin, M. (1993). Our sciences, their sciences. *Race and Class* 34(4): 35–46.

Beardsley, T. (1995). For whom the bell curve really tolls. *Scientific American* 272(1): 14–17.

Bederman, G. (1995). *Manliness and civilization: A cultural history of gender and race in the United States, 1880–1917.* Chicago: University of Chicago Press.

Begley, S. (1995, February 13). Three is not enough: Surprising new lessons from the controversial science of race. *Newsweek,* 67–69.

Bello, W. (1992). *People and power in the Pacific: The struggle for the post–cold war order.* London: Pluto.

Benjamin, W. (1978). Paris, capital of the nineteenth century. In *Reflections* (P. Demetz, trans.; pp. 146–62). New York: Schocken.

Bennett, T. (1995). *The birth of the museum: History, theory, politics.* London: Routledge.

Bernal, M. (1987). *Black Athena: The Afroasiatic roots of classical civilization.* (Vol. 1, *The fabrication of ancient Greece.*) Baltimore, Md.: Johns Hopkins University Press.

Bhabha, H. K. (1992). Freedom's basis in the indeterminate. *October* 61: 46–57.

Biological Sciences Curriculum Study (1987). *Biological science: An ecological approach* (6th ed.). Dubuque, Iowa: Kendall Hunt.

Birdsell, J. B. (1972, 1975). *Human evolution: An introduction to the new physical anthropology* (1st and 2d eds.). Boston: Houghton Mifflin.

Bishop, A. (1990). Western mathematics: The secret weapon of cultural imperialism. *Race and Class* 32(2): 51–65.

Bitterli, U. (1989). *Cultures in conflict: Encounters between European and non-European cultures, 1492–1800* (R. Robertson, trans.). Stanford: Stanford University Press.

Blaut, J. M. (1993). *The colonizer's model of the world: Geographical diffusionism and Eurocentric history.* New York: Guilford.

Blodgett, J. (1983). *Kenojuak.* Toronto: Firefly Books.

Blumenbach, J. H. (1865). *The anthropological treatises of Johann Friedrich Blumenbach* (T. Bendyshe, trans.). London: Anthropological Society.

Boas, F. (1974). Anthropology. In G. Stocking, ed., *The shaping of American anthropology, 1883–1911: A Franz Boas reader* (pp. 267–82). New York: Basic Books.

Bogdan, D. (1992). *The re-educated imagination: Toward a poetics, politics, and pedagogy of literary engagement.* Portsmouth, N.H.: Heinemann.

Bolton, R. (1992). *Culture wars: Documents from the recent controversies in the arts.* New York: Free Press.

Boyd, D. (1994, October 3). Cost of providing ESL classes is eating up the education dollar. *Vancouver Sun,* B1.

Brandon, W. (1986). *New worlds for old: Reports from the New World and their effect on the development of social thought in Europe, 1500–1800.* Athens: Ohio University Press.

Breckenridge, C. A. (1989). The aesthetics and politics of colonial collecting: India at the world fairs. *Society for Comparative Study of Society and History* 31(2): 195–216.

British Columbia Ministry of Education (1990). *History 12 Resources Manual.* Victoria: British Columbia Ministry of Education.

Britzman, D. P. (1995). Is there a queer pedagogy? or Stop reading straight. *Educational Theory* 45(2): 151–66.

Brockway, L. H. (1979). *Science and colonial expansion: The role of the British Royal Botanic Gardens.* New York: Academic.

Brown, L. (1993). *Ends of empire: Women and ideology in early eighteenth-century English literature.* Ithaca, N.Y.: Cornell University Press.

Browne, J. (1994, August 12). Natural causes: "Old bones," the skeleton in the cupboard of evolutionary science. *Times Literary Supplement,* 3–4.

Bucher, B. (1981). *Icon and conquest: A structural analysis of the illustrations of de Bry's Great voyages* (B. M. Gulati, trans.). Chicago: University of Chicago Press.

Bullard, J., F. Cloutier, N. Flood, G. Gore, E. S. Grace, B. Gurney, A. J. Hirsch, D. Hugh, C. Madhosingh, G. Millett, and A. Wootton (1992). *Science probe 10* (2d ed.). Toronto: Wiley.

Burchfield, R. W. (1985). *The English language.* Oxford: Oxford University Press.

Burns, R. I. (1975). *Medieval colonialism: Postcrusade exploitation of Islamic Valencia.* Princeton, N.J.: Princeton University Press.

Cain, P. J., and A. G. Hopkins (1993). *British imperialism: Innovation and expansion.* (Vol. 1.) London: Longman.

Cameron, D., ed. (1990). *The feminist critique of language: A reader.* London: Routledge.

Cannadine, D. (1993). The empire strikes back. *Past and Present* 147: 180–94.

Carnoy, M. (1972). *Education as cultural imperialism.* New York: McKay.

Carrier, J. G. (1992). Occidentalism: The world turned upside down. *American Ethnologist* 19(2): 195–212.

Carter, P. (1987). *The road to Botany Bay: An exploration of landscape and history.* Chicago: University of Chicago Press.

Cassirer, E. (1989). *The question of Jean-Jacques Rousseau* (P. Gay, trans.). New Haven, Conn.: Yale University Press.

Castle, K. (1993). The imperial Indian: India in British history textbooks for schools, 1890–1914. In J. A. Mangan, ed., *The imperial curriculum: Racial images and education in the British colonial experience* (pp. 23–39). London: Routledge.

Celis, W., III (1993, September 12). Educators say new directions and resources are needed to raise literacy. *New York Times,* Y17.

Césaire, A. (1972). *Discourse on colonialism* (orig. 1955; J. Pinkham, trans.). New York: Monthly Review.

Chatterjee, P. (1993). *The nation and its fragments: Colonial and postcolonial histories.* Princeton, N.J.: Princeton University Press.

Chauduri, N. C. (1987). *Thy hand, great anarch! India, 1921–1952.* Reading, Mass.: Addison-Wesley.

Cheng, C.-C. (1992). Chinese varieties of English. In B. B. Kachu, ed., *The other tongue: English across cultures* (pp. 162–77). Urbana: University of Illinois Press.

Cheng, V. (1995). *Joyce, race, and empire.* Cambridge: Cambridge University Press.

Chomsky, N. (1993). *Year 501: The conquest continues.* Montreal: Black Rose.

Chow, R. (1995). In the name of comparative literature. In C. Bernheimer, ed., *Comparative literature in the age of multiculturalism* (pp. 107–16). Baltimore, Md.: Johns Hopkins University Press.

Civil rights: More anticlimax than crisis (1963, September 20). *Time,* 20.

Civil rights: The march's meaning (1963, September 6). *Time,* 15–17.

Clark, K. B. (1955). *Prejudice and your child* (2d ed.). Boston: Beacon.

Clifford, J. (1985). Objects and selves—an afterword. In G. W. Stocking Jr., ed., *Objects and others: Essays on museums and material culture* (pp. 236–46). Madison: University of Wisconsin Press.

Columbus, C. (1969). *The four voyages of Christopher Columbus: Being his own log-book, letters, and dispatches with connecting narrative drawn from the life of the admiral by his son Hernando Colon and other contemporary historians* (J. M. Cohen, ed. and trans.). London: Penguin.

Conrad, J. (1973). *Heart of Darkness* (orig. 1902). Harmondsworth, England: Penguin.

Constantine, S. (1986). *Buy and build: The advertising posters of the Empire Marketing Board.* London: HMSO.

Cook, J. (1993). Discovering and naming of Botany Bay (orig. 1770). In R. Hanbury-Tenison, ed., *The Oxford book of exploration* (pp. 410–13). Oxford: Oxford University Press.

Coolahan, J. (1993). The Irish and others in Irish nineteenth-century textbooks. In J. A. Mangan, ed., *The imperial curriculum: Racial images and education in the British colonial experience* (pp. 54–63). London: Routledge.

Coon, C. S. (1962). *The origin of races.* New York: Knopf.

——— (1981). *Racial adaptation.* Chicago: Nelson-Hall.

Coon, C. S., S. M. Garn, and J. B. Birdsell (1950). *Races: A study of the problem of race formation in man.* Springfield, Ill.: Thomas.

Creager, J. G., P. G. Jantzen, and J. L. Mariner (1986). *Macmillan biology.* New York: Macmillan.

Crowley, T. (1989). *Standard English and the politics of language.* Urbana: University of Illinois Press.

Crystal, D. (1987). *The Cambridge encyclopedia of language.* Cambridge: Cambridge University Press.

Cummins, J. (1989). Heritage language teaching and the student: Fact and friction. In J. H. Esling, ed., *Multicultural education and policy: ESL in the 1990s: A tribute to Mary Ashworth* (pp. 3–17). Toronto: OISE Press.

d'Alembert, J. (1995). *Preliminary discourse to the* Encyclopedia *of Diderot* (orig. 1751; R. N. Schwab, trans.). Chicago: University of Chicago Press.

D'Ambrosio, U. (1991). Ethnomathematics and its place in the history of pedagogy of mathematics. In M. Harris, ed., *Schools, mathematics, and work* (pp. 15–25). London: Falmer.

Darwin, C. (n.d.). *The origin of species by means of natural selection, or The preservation of favored races in the struggle for life and The descent of man and selection in relation to sex* (orig. 1859, 1871). New York: Modern Library.

——— (1962). *The voyage of the* Beagle (orig. 1845; L. Engel, ed.). Garden City, N.Y.: Anchor.

Dayal, S. (1996). Postcolonialism's possibilities: Subcontinental diasporic intervention. *Cultural Critique* 33: 113–49.

Debord, G. (1977). *The society of the spectacle.* Detroit: Black & Red.

de Certeau, M. (1988). *The writing of history* (T. Conley, trans.). New York: Columbia University Press.

Defoe, D. (1965). *The life and adventures of Robinson Crusoe* (orig. 1719). Harmondsworth, England: Penguin.

Dégerando, J.-M. (1969). *The observation of savage peoples* (orig. 1800, *Considerations on the various methods to follow in the observation of savage peoples;* F. C. T. Moore, trans.). Berkeley: University of California Press.

Degler, C. N. (1991). *In search of human nature: The decline and revival of Darwinism in American social thought.* New York: Oxford University Press.

de Kay, J. T. (1995). *Chronicles of the frigate* Macedonian, *1809–1922.* New York: Norton.

Derrida, J. (1974). *Of grammatology* (G. Spivak, trans.). Baltimore, Md.: Johns Hopkins University Press.

——— (1978a). From restricted to general economy: A Helgelianism without reserve. In *Writing and difference* (A. Bass, trans.; pp. 251–77). Chicago: University of Chicago Press.

——— (1978b). Structure, sign, and play in the discourse of the human sciences. In *Writing and difference* (A. Bass, trans.; pp. 278–94). Chicago: University of Chicago Press.

——— (1982). White mythology: Metaphor in the text of philosophy. In *Margins of philosophy* (A. Bass, trans.; pp. 207–72). Chicago: University of Chicago Press.

Desai, G. (1993). English as an African language. *English Today* 9(2): 4–11.

Descartes, R. (1960). Meditations (orig. 1641). In *Discourse on method and other writings* (A. Wollaston, trans.; pp. 101–72). Harmondsworth, England: Penguin.

Dickason, O. P. (1984). *The myth of the savage: And the beginnings of French colonialism in the Americas.* Edmonton: University of Alberta Press.

Diderot, D. (1991). Supplement to Bougainville's *Voyage* (orig. 1773). In *This is not a story and other stories* (P. N. Furbank, ed. and trans.; pp. 60–112). Oxford: Oxford University Press.

——— (1992). Extracts from the *Histoire des deux Indes*. In *Political writings* (J. H. Mason and R. Wokler, eds.; pp. 165–214). Cambridge: Cambridge University Press.

Dilke, C. W. (1869). *Greater Britain: A record of travel in English-speaking countries during 1866 and 1867.* New York: Harper.

——— (1890). *Problems of Greater Britain.* London: Macmillan.

Dobzhansky, T. (1962). *Mankind evolving: The evolution of the human species.* New York: Bantam.

——— (1963). Review of C. S. Coon's *The origin of races. Scientific American* 208: 169.

Dolpin, R. (1989, February 13). Race and behavior. *Maclean's,* 44.

Douglass, F. (1960). *Narrative of the life of Frederick Douglass, an American slave* (orig. 1845; B. Quarles, ed.). Cambridge: Harvard University Press.

Dreifus, C. (1996, January 7). The passion of Suu Kyi. *New York Times Magazine,* 32–37.

Drohan, M., and A. Freeman (1997, July 12). English rules. *Toronto Globe and Mail,* D1, D4.

D'Souza, D. (1991). *Illiberal education: The politics of race and sex on campus.* New York: Random House.

Dumont, L. (1966). *Homo Hierarchicus.* Chicago: University of Chicago Press.

Dunlop, S. (1987). *Towards tomorrow: Canada in a changing world: Geography.* Toronto: Harcourt Brace Jovanovich.

Eagleton, T. (1981). *Walter Benjamin: Towards a revolutionary criticism.* London: Verso.

Eberhardt, I. (1994). Figuig. In *Departures* (K. Hamdy and L. Rice, trans.; pp. 123–26). San Francisco: City Light.

Efron, J. M. (1995). *Defenders of the race: Jewish doctors and race science in fin-de-siècle Europe.* New Haven, Conn.: Yale University Press.

Eisenstadt, S. N. (1966). *Modernization, protest, and change.* Englewoods Cliffs, N.J.: Prentice-Hall.

Eliot, T. S. (1971a). *The complete poems and plays, 1909–1950.* New York: Harcourt, Brace & World.

———— (1971b). *Four quartets* (orig. 1943). New York: Harcourt Brace.

Elliott, J. H. (1970). *The Old World and the New, 1492–1650.* Cambridge: Cambridge University Press.

Emberley, J. V. (1993). *Thresholds of difference: Feminist critique, native women's writings, postcolonial theory.* Toronto: University of Toronto Press.

Fabian, J. (1983). *Time and the other: How anthropology makes its object.* New York: Columbia University Press.

———— (1986). *Language and colonial power.* Berkeley: University of California Press.

Fanon, F. (1963). *The wretched of the earth* (C. Farrington, trans.). Harmondsworth, England: Penguin.

———— (1965). *A dying colonialism* (H. Chevalier, trans.). New York: Grove.

———— (1967). *Black skin, white masks* (C. L. Markmann, trans.). New York: Grove Weidenfeld.

Fasold, R. (1984). *The sociolinguistics of society.* New York: Blackwell.

Faulkner, W. (1951). *Requiem for a nun.* New York: Random House.

Fausett, D. (1993). *Writing the new world: Imaginary voyages and utopias of the great southern land.* Syracuse, N.Y.: Syracuse University Press.

Feierman, S. (1993). African histories and the dissolution of world history. In R. H. Bates, V. Y. Mudimbe, and J. O'Barr, eds., *Africa and the disciplines: The contributions of research in Africa to the social sciences and humanities* (pp. 167–212). Chicago: University of Chicago Press.

Fenton, J. (1996). Goodbye to all that. *New York Review of Books* 43: 59–64.

Finley, M. I. (1986). Myth, memory, and history. In *The use and abuse of history* (pp. 11–33). London: Hogarth.

Fishman, J. (1972). *Language and nationalism: Two integrative essays.* Rowley, Mass.: Newbury House.

———— (1977). International societal bilingualism. In J. Fishman, R. L. Cooper, and A. W. Conrad, eds., *The spread of English: The sociology of English as an additional language* (pp. 329–36). Rowley, Mass.: Newbury House.

Flaubert, G. (1972). *Flaubert in Egypt: A sensibility on tour* (F. Steegmuller, trans. and ed.). Chicago: Academy Chicago.

Fletcher, C. R. L., and R. Kipling (1983). *Kipling's pocket history of England* (orig. 1911, *A school history of England*). New York: Greenwich House.

Forster, E. M. (1924). *A passage to India.* Harmondsworth, England: Penguin.

——— (1967). For the museum's sake. In *Arbinger harvest* (pp. 308–15). Harmondsworth, England: Penguin.

Foucault, M. (1970). *The order of things: An archeology of the human sciences.* New York: Vintage.

——— (1972). *The archeology of knowledge and The discourse on language* (A. M. Sheridan, trans.). New York: Harper.

——— (1979). *Discipline and punish: The birth of the prison* (A. M. Sheridan, trans.). New York: Vintage.

——— (1982). Afterword: The subject and power. In H. L. Dreyfus and P. Rabinow, eds., *Michel Foucault: Beyond structuralism and hermeneutics* (pp. 208–26). Chicago: University of Chicago Press.

Friedman, T. (1995, August 20). Fruit of the loom. *New York Times,* E13.

Fruman, N. (1995, June 23). A short history of the ALSC [Association of Literary Scholars and Critics]. *Times Literary Supplement,* 16.

Frye, N. (1963). *The educated imagination.* Massey lectures. Toronto: Canadian Broadcasting Corporation.

——— (1971a). Conclusion to *A literary history of Canada.* In *The bush garden: Essays on the Canadian imagination* (pp. 213–51). Toronto: Anansi.

——— (1971b). Preface to *The bush garden: Essays on the Canadian imagination* (pp. i–x). Toronto: Anansi.

———, supervisory ed. (1972). *Literature: Uses of the imagination.* (Multiple vols.). New York: Harcourt Brace Jovanovich.

Fukuyama, F. (1995). On the possibility of writing a universal history. In A. M. Melzer, J. Weinberger, and M. R. Zinman, eds., *History and the idea of progress* (pp. 13–29). Ithaca, N.Y.: Cornell University Press.

Furedi, F. (1994). *The new ideology of imperialism: Renewing the moral imperative.* London: Pluto.

Fusco, C. (1995). The other history of intercultural performance. In *English is broken here: Notes on cultural fusion in the Americas* (pp. 37–64). New York: Free Press.

Gage, S. (1993). *Colonialism in Asia: A critical look.* Victoria, B.C.: Victoria International Development Education Association.

Gaitskell, D. (1994). At home with hegemony? Coercion and consent in African girls' education for domesticity in South Africa before 1910. In D. Engels and S. Marks, eds., *Contesting colonial hegemony: State and society in Africa and India* (pp. 110–28). London: British Academic.

Galbraith, D. (1989). *Understanding biology.* Toronto: Wiley.

Gerbi, A. (1985). *Nature in the New World: From Christopher Columbus to Gonzalo Fernández de Oviedo* (J. Moyle, trans.). Pittsburgh: University of Pittsburgh Press.

Geyer, M., and C. Bright (1995). World history in a global age. *American Historical Review* 100(4): 1034–60.

Ghosh, S. C. (1993). "English in taste, in opinions, in words and intellect": Indoctrinating the Indian through textbook, curriculum, and education. In J. A. Mangan, ed., *The imperial curriculum: Racial images and education in the British colonial experience* (pp. 175–94). London: Routledge.

Gill, D., and L. Levidow (1987). *Anti-racist science teaching.* London: Free Association.

Gillispsie, C. (1959). *A Diderot pictorial encyclopedia of trades and industry.* (2 vols.) New York: Dover.

———— (1994). The scientific importance of Napoleon's Egyptian campaign. *Scientific American* 271(3): 78–85.

Gilman, S. L. (1985). Black bodies, white bodies: Toward an iconography of female sexuality in late nineteenth-century art, medicine, and literature. *Critical Inquiry* 12(1): 204–42.

———— (1986). *Jewish self-hatred: Anti-Semitism and the hidden language of the Jews.* Baltimore, Md.: Johns Hopkins University Press.

———— (1991). *The Jew's body.* New York: Routledge.

Gilroy, P. (1993). *The black Atlantic: Modernity and double consciousness.* Cambridge: Harvard University Press.

Gobineau, A. de (1967). *The inequality of the human races* (orig. 1853–55; A. Collins, trans.). New York: Fertig.

Goetzmann, W. H. (1986). *New lands, new men: America and the second great age of discovery.* New York: Penguin.

Goldberg, D. T., ed. (1994). *Multiculturalism: A critical reader.* Oxford: Blackwell.

Golding, W. (1967). *Lord of the flies.* Harmondsworth, England: Penguin.

Goldring, C. C. (1937). *We are Canadian citizens.* Toronto: Dent.

Goodson, I. F. (1988). Becoming a school subject. In *The making of curriculum: Collected essays* (pp. 160–83). London: Falmer.

Gossman, L. (1994). Philhellenism and antisemitism: Matthew Arnold and his German models. *Comparative Literature* 46(1): 1–39.

Gottfried, S., G. Madraso, M. Lamoine, P. Sinclair, G. Skog, C. D. Hampton, C. H. Hampton, and W. Leibel (1983). *Prentice-Hall biology.* Englewood Cliffs, N.J.: Prentice-Hall.

Gough, J. (1944). *Old World horizons: Great Britain, Australia, and New Zealand, Africa, Asia, and continental Europe.* Toronto: Dent.

Gould, S. J. (1977). Why we should not name human races—a biological view. In *Ever since Darwin: Reflections in natural history* (pp. 231–36). New York: Norton.

———— (1981). *The mismeasure of man.* New York: Norton.

Graff, G. (1992). Teach the conflicts. In D. J. Gless and B. Herrnstein Smith, eds., *The politics of liberal education* (pp. 57–74). Durham, N.C.: Duke University Press.

Grafton, A., with A. Shelford and N. Siraisi (1992). *New worlds, ancient texts: The power of tradition and the shock of discovery.* Cambridge: Harvard University Press.

Gramsci, A. (1971). *Selections from the prison notebooks of Antonio Gramsci* (Q. Hoare and G. N. Smith, trans.). New York: International.

Grange, M. (1995, September 25). Students ignorant of Canada's racist past, survey indicates. *Toronto Globe and Mail,* A3.

Greenblatt, S. I. (1991). *Marvelous possessions: The wonder of the New World.* Chicago: University of Chicago Press.

Greenfeld, L. (1992). *Nationalism: Five roads to modernity.* Cambridge: Harvard University Press.

Greenhalgh, P. (1988). *Ephemeral vistas: The* expositions universelles, *great exhibitions, and world's fairs, 1851–1939.* Manchester, England: Manchester University Press.

Greenlaw, J. (1993). The postcolonial conception of the high school multicultural literature curriculum. Ph.D. diss., University of British Columbia.

Gregg, M., and G. Leinhardt (1994). Mapping out geography: An example of epistemology and education. *Review of Educational Research* 64(2): 311–61.

Gregory, D. (1994). *Geographical imaginations.* Cambridge, Mass.: Blackwell.

Gregory, W. H., and E. H. Goldman (1968). *Biological science for high school.* Boston: Ginn.

Haig-Brown, C. (1988). *Resistance and renewal: Surviving the Indian residential school.* Vancouver: Tillacum Library.

Hakluyt, R. (1972). *Voyages and discoveries: The principal navigations, voyages, traffiques, and discoveries of the English nation* (orig. 1589–90, *Principal navigations, voyages, traffiques, and discoveries of the English nation;* J. Beeching, ed.). London: Penguin.

Hansen, K. T. (1992). White women in a changing world: Employment, voluntary work, and sex in post–World War II Northern Rhodesia. In N. Chaudhuri and M. Strobel, eds., *Western women and imperialism: Complicity and resistance* (pp. 247–68). Bloomington: Indiana University Press.

Haraway, D. (1989). *Primate visions: Gender, race, and nature in the world of modern science.* New York: Routledge.

——— (1991). *Simians, cyborgs, and women: The reinvention of nature.* New York: Routledge.

Harding, S. (1991). *Whose science? Whose knowledge? Thinking from women's lives.* Ithaca, N.Y.: Cornell University Press.

——— (1993). Introduction to S. Harding, ed., *The "racial" economy of science: Toward a democratic future* (pp. 1–22). Bloomington: Indiana University Press.

Harper, R. A. (1992). At issue: What is geography's contribution to general education? *Journal of Geography* 93(3): 124–25.

Hatem, M. (1992). Through each other's eyes: The impact of the colonial encounter of the images of Egyptian, Levantine-Egyptian, and European women, 1862–1920. In N. Chaudhuri and M. Strobel, eds., *Western women and imperialism: Complicity and resistance* (pp. 35–58). Bloomington: Indiana University Press.

Headrick, D. R. (1988). *The tentacles of progress: Technology transfer in the age of imperialism, 1850–1940.* New York: Oxford University Press.

Hébert, Y. (1992). Multicultural education and the minority language child. *Canadian Ethnic Studies* 24(3): 58–74.

Hegel, G. W. F. (1956). *The philosophy of history* (J. Sibree, trans.; orig. 1899). New York: Dover.

Heidegger, M. (1977). The age of the world picture. In *The question concerning technology and other essays* (W. Lovitt, trans.; pp. 115–54). New York: Harper & Row.

Heimler, C. H. (1981). *Focus on life science.* Columbus, Ohio: Merrill.

Herbert, B. (1995, July 14). Renewing black America. *New York Times*, A11.

Herbert, C. (1991). *Culture and anomie: Ethnographic imagination in the nineteenth century.* Chicago: University of Chicago Press.

Herder, J. G. von (1909). Ideen zur philosophie der geschichte der menschheit (orig. 1784–91). In *Sämmtliche werke*, vol. 14 (B. Supan, ed.; pp. 3–493). Berlin: Weidmannsche.

——— (1968). *Reflections on the philosophy of the history of mankind* (orig. 1784–91; T. O. Churchill, trans.). Chicago: University of Chicago Press.

Herodotus. (1910). *The history of Herodotus.* (2 vols.; G. Rawlinson, trans.). London: Dent.

Herrnstein, R. J., and C. Murray (1994). *The bell curve: Intelligence and class in American life.* New York: Free Press.

Hobsbawm, E. J. (1987). *The age of empire, 1875–1914.* London: Weidenfeld & Nicolson.

——— (1990). *Nations and nationalism since 1780: Programme, myth, reality.* Cambridge: Cambridge University Press.

Hobsbawm, E. J., and T. Ranger, eds. (1983). *The invention of tradition.* Cambridge: Cambridge University Press.

Hodson, D. (1993). In search of a rationale for multicultural science education. *Science Education* 77(6): 685–711.

Holdich, T. H. (1916). *Political frontiers and boundary making.* London: Macmillan.

Holmes, B. (1967). British imperial policy and the mission schools. In B. Holmes, ed., *Educational policy and the mission schools: Case studies from the British Empire* (pp. 5–46). London: Routledge & Kegan Paul.

Holmes, S. A. (1994, October 23). You're smart if you know what race you are. *New York Times*, E5.

Holmes, T. (1993). *Journey to Livingstone: Exploration of an imperial myth.* Edinburgh, Scotland: Canongate.

Honan, P. (1980). *Mathew Arnold: A life.* New York: McGraw-Hill.

Hooper-Greenhill, E. (1992). *Museums and the shaping of knowledge.* London: Routledge.

Howells, W. (1947). *Mankind so far.* London: Sigma.

Hubbard, R. (1995). Constructs of race difference. In *Profitable promises: Essays on women, science, and health* (pp. 179–86). Monroe, Maine: Common Courage.

Hudson, B. (1977). The new geography and the new imperialism, 1870–1918. *Antipode* 9(2): 12–19.

Hughes, R. (1993). *Culture complaint: The fraying of America.* New York: Oxford University Press.

Hulse, F. S. (1963). Review of C. S. Coon's *The origin of races. American Anthropologist* 65: 685.

Humbert, J.-M. (1994). The return from Egypt. In J.-M. Humbert, M. Panatazzi, and C. Ziegler, eds., *Egyptomania: L'Egypte dans l'art occidental* (pp. 251–56). Paris: Réunion des Musées Nationaux.

Hunter, I. (1988). *Culture and government: The emergence of literary education.* London: Macmillan.

Huntington, S. P. (1994). The clash of civilizations. *Foreign Affairs* 72(3): 22–49.

Hurd, D. (1997, July 11). When Britain left Hong Kong. *Toronto Globe and Mail,* A23.

Ibn Kuldûn (1967). *The muqaddimah: An introduction to history* (F. Rosenthal, trans.). Princeton, N.J.: Princeton University Press.

Illich, I. (1979). Vernacular values and education. *Teachers College Record* 81(1): 31–75.

Impey, O., and A. MacGregor, eds. (1983). *The origins of museums: The cabinets of curiosities in sixteenth and seventeenth century Europe.* Oxford: Clarendon.

Inden, R. (1988). *Imagining India.* Oxford, England: Blackwell.

Jacknis, I. (1985). Franz Boas and exhibits: On the limitations of the museum method of anthropology. In G. W. Stocking Jr., ed., *Objects and others: Essays on museums and material culture* (pp. 75–111). Madison: University of Wisconsin Press.

James, L. (1994). *The rise and fall of the British Empire.* New York: Little, Brown.

Jami, C. (1992). Western mathematics in China, seventeenth century and eighteenth century. In P. Petitjean, C. Jami, and A. M. Moulin, eds., *Science and empires: Historical studies about scientific development and European expansion* (pp. 79–88). Dordrecht, Netherlands: Kluwer.

Janofsky, M. (1995, July 23). For Aryan Congress, stridency and scrutiny. *New York Times,* Y8.

Jensen, A. (1985). The nature of black-white differences on various psychometric tests: Spearman's hypothesis. *Behavioral and Brain Sciences* 8: 193–263.

Johnson, S. (1975). *Lives of the English poets* (orig. 1779–81). London: Everyman.

Jolly, C., and F. Plog (1987). *Physical anthropology* (4th ed.). New York: Knopf.

Jones, E. L. (1981). *The European miracle: Environments, economies, and geopolitics in the history of Europe and Asia.* Cambridge: Cambridge University Press.

Joseph, G. G. (1990). *The crest of the peacock: Non-European roots of mathematics.* Harmondsworth, England: Penguin.

——— (1991). Foundations of Eurocentrism in mathematics. In E. Harris, ed., *School mathematics and work* (pp. 42–56). London: Falmer.

——— (1993). A rationale for a multicultural approach to mathematics. In D. Nelson, G. G. Joseph, and J. Williams, eds., *Multicultural mathematics: Teaching mathematics from a global perspective* (pp. 1–24). Oxford: Oxford University Press.

Judd, E. L. (1983). TESOL as a political act. In J. Handscombe, R. A. Orem, and B. P. Taylor, eds., *On TESOL '83: The question of control* (pp. 263–72). Washington, D.C.: Teachers of English to Speakers of Other Languages.

Julius, A. (1996). *T. S. Eliot, anti-Semitism, and literary form.* Cambridge: Cambridge University Press.

Juriman, R., and H. Nelson (1994). *Introduction to physical anthropology.* St. Paul, Minn.: West.

Kachru, B. B. (1992a). Introduction: The other side of English and the 1990s. In B. B. Kachru, ed., *The other tongue: English across cultures* (pp. 1–15). Urbana: University of Illinois Press.

———— (1992b) Models for non-native Englishes. In B. B. Kachru, ed., *The other tongue: English across cultures* (pp. 48–74). Urbana: University of Illinois Press.

———— (1992c). Teaching world Englishes. In B. B. Kachru, ed., *The other tongue: English across cultures* (pp. 355–65). Urbana: University of Illinois Press.

Karim, K. (1993, September 27). Feeding Aladdin's myths to a new generation. *Toronto Globe and Mail,* A21.

Kaskel, A., P. J. Hummer, and L. Daniel (1981). *Biology: An everyday experience.* Teachers annotated edition. Columbus, Ohio: Merrill.

Kendrick, W. (1995, December 24). Critics and their discontents. *New York Times Book Review,* 12–13.

Kennedy, P. (1987). *The rise and fall of the great powers: Economic change and military conflict from 1500 to 2000.* New York: Random House.

Kiernan, V. G. (1969). *The lords of humankind: European attitudes towards the outside world in the imperial age.* London: Weidenfeld & Nicolson.

Kimmelman, M. (1995, March 19). Art in aisle 3, by lingerie, and feel free to browse. *New York Times,* H43, H46.

Kingsley, M. H. (1965). *Travels in West Africa* (3d ed.). London: Cass.

Kipling, R. (1939). *Kim* (orig. 1901). Toronto: Macmillan.

Knapp, J. (1992). *An empire nowhere: England, America, and literature from* Utopia *to* The Tempest. Berkeley: University of California Press.

Kramer, L., and D. Reid (1994). Introduction: Historical knowledge, education, and public culture. In L. Kramer, D. Reid, and W. L. Barney, eds., *Learning history in America: Schools, cultures, and politics* (pp. 1–22). Minneapolis: University of Minnesota Press.

Kristeva, J. (1991). *Strangers to ourselves* (L. S. Roudiez, trans.). New York: Columbia University Press.

Krucik, K. (1995, June 14). Alas poor Kerrisdale, and those who loved it. *Toronto Globe and Mail,* A20.

Kühl, S. (1994). *The Nazi connection: Eugenics, American racism, and German National Socialism.* New York: Oxford University Press.

Kumar, D. (1990). The evolution of colonial science in India: Natural history and the East India Company. In J. MacKenzie, ed., *Imperialism and the natural world* (pp. 51–66). Manchester, England: Manchester University Press.

———— (1995). *Science and the raj, 1857–1905.* Delhi: Oxford University Press.

Kurl, S. (1993, July 10). Stranger in a strange land. *Vancouver Sun,* C10–C11.

Lach, D. F. (1977). *Asia in the making of Europe: A century of wonder.* (Vol. 2, bk. 3.) Chicago: University of Chicago Press.

Las Casas, B. de (1992). *The devastation of the Indies: A brief account* (orig. 1552; H. Briffault, trans.). Baltimore, Md.: Johns Hopkins University Press.

Latour, B. (1987). *Science in action: How to follow scientists and engineers through society.* Cambridge: Harvard University Press.

Leacock, S. (1941). *Our British Empire: Its stucture, its history, its strength.* London: Readers Union.

Lee, D. (1995, October 27). Certain monsters of Africa: Poetic voodoo in Keats' *Lamia. Times Literary Supplement,* 13–14.

Lee, F. R. (1993, October 10). An editor sees Asian-American identity as a work in progress. *New York Times,* E7.

Leinwand, G. (1986). *The pageant of world history.* Newton, Mass.: Allyn & Bacon.

Leonard, S. (1962). *The doctrine of correctness in English usage, 1700–1800* (orig. 1929). New York: Russell & Russell.

Leonowens, A. (1991). *The romance of the harem* (orig. 1873; S. Morgan, ed.). Charlottesville: University of Virginia Press.

Le Page, R. B. (1964). *The national language question: Linguistic problems of newly independent states.* London: Oxford University Press.

Levine, G. (1993). By knowledge possessed: Darwin, nature, and Victorian narrative. *New Literary History* 24: 363–91.

Levine, J. S., and K. R. Miller (1991). *Biology: Discovering life.* Lexington, Mass.: Heath.

Lévi-Strauss, C. (1961). *Tristes tropiques: An anthropological study of primitive societies in Brazil* (J. Russell, trans.). New York: Atheneum.

——— (1995). Saudades do Brasil. *New York Review of Books* 42(20): 19–26.

Li Y. and Du S. (1987). *Chinese mathematics: A concise history* (J. N. Crossley and A. W.-C. Lun, trans.). Oxford, England: Clarendon.

Lieberman, L., R. E. Hampton, A. Littlefield, and G. Hallead (1992). Race in biology and anthropology: A study of college texts and professors. *Journal of Research in Science Teaching* 29(3): 301–21.

Light, R. E. (1968). Foreword to M. Mead, T. Dobzhansky, E. Tobach, and R. E. Light, *Science and the concept of race* (pp. vii–viii). New York: Columbia University Press.

Limerick, P. N. (1987). *The legacy of conquest: The unbroken past of the American West.* New York: Norton.

Littlefield, A., L. Lieberman, and L. T. Reynolds (1982). Redefining race: The potential demise of a concept in physical anthropology. *Current Anthropology* 23(6): 641–55.

Livingstone, D. (1992). *The geographical tradition: Episodes in the history of a contested enterprise.* Oxford: Blackwell.

Livingstone, F. B. (1964). On the nonexistence of the human races. In A. Montagu, ed., *The concept of race* (p. xx). New York: Free Press.

Loury, G. C. (1995). *One by one from the inside out: Essays and reviews on race and responsibility in America.* New York: Free Press.

Lutz, C., and J. L. Collins (1993). *Reading* National Geographic. Chicago: University of Chicago Press.

Lyotard, J.-F. (1988). *The postmodern condition: A report on knowledge* (G. Bennington and B. Massumi, trans.). Minneapolis: University of Minnesota Press.

McArthur, T. (1992). Models of English. *English Today* 8(4): 12–21.

Macaulay, T. B. (1907). Warren Hastings (orig. 1841). In *Critical and historical essays,* vol. 1 (pp. 550–649). London: Dent.

——— (1909a). Education (orig. 1847). In *Speeches on politics and literature* (pp. 349–69). London: Dent.

——— (1909b). Government of India (orig. 1833). In *Speeches on politics and literature* (pp. 95–126). London: Dent.

——— (1971). Thomas Babington Macaulay on education for India (orig. 1835). In P. D. Curtin, ed., *Imperialism* (pp. 178–91). New York: Harper & Row.

McDonald, K. (1994, April 13). Charting biodiversity: Biologists propose effort to describe world's species before millions are extinct. *Chronicle of Higher Education,* A8–A9, A14.

MacDougall, H. A. (1982). *Racial myth in English history: Trojans, Teutons, and Anglo-Saxons.* Montreal: Harvest House.

McDougall, W. D., and G. Paterson (1937). *Our empire and its neighbors.* (Book 2, grade 8.) Toronto: Ryerson.

McGrane, B. (1989). *Beyond anthropology: Society and the other.* New York: Columbia University Press.

MacIntosh, P. (1990, winter). White privilege: Unpacking the invisible knapsack. *Independent School,* 31–36.

MacKenzie, C. G. (1993). Demythologizing the missionaries: A reassessment of the functions and relationships of Christian missionary education under colonialism. *Comparative Education* 29(1): 45–66.

MacKenzie, J. M. (1984). *Propaganda and empire: The manipulation of British public opinion, 1880–1960.* Manchester, England: Manchester University Press.

Mackey, W. F. (1991). Language diversity, language policy, and the sovereign state. *History of European Ideas* 13(1–2): 51–61.

McLaren, J. E., and L. Rotundo (1985). *Heath biology.* Lexington, Mass.: Heath.

McLaren, J. E., J. H. Stastik, and D. F. Levering (1981). *Spaceship earth: Life science.* Boston: Houghton Mifflin.

McLaren, P. (1994). White terror and oppositional agency: Towards a critical multiculturalism. In D. T. Golderg, ed., *Multiculturalism: A critical reader* (pp. 45–74). Oxford: Blackwell.

Macleod, R. (1987). On visiting the "moving metropolis": Reflections on the architecture of imperial science. In N. Reingold and M. Rothenberg, eds., *Scientific colonialism: A cross-cultural comparison* (pp. 217–49). Washington, D.C.: Smithsonian.

McMaster, G., and L.-A. Martin, eds. (1992). Introduction to *Indigena: Contemporary native perspectives* (pp. 11–23). Vancouver: Douglas & McIntyre.

McNeill, W. H. (1963, 1991). *The rise of the West: A history of the human community.* Chicago: University of Chicago Press.

Mader, S. S. (1988, 1994). *Inquiry into life* (6th and 7th eds.). Dubuque, Iowa: Brown.

Maracle, L. (1992). The "post-colonial" imagination. *Fuse* 16: 12–15.

Mason, J. (1993). *Expansion, trade, and industry*. London: Longman.

Massey, D. L. (1984). *Communities around our world*. Scarborough, Ont.: Ginn.

Melzer, A. M., J. Weinberger, and M. R. Zinman. (1995). *History and the idea of progress*. Ithaca, N.Y.: Cornell University Press.

Michaels, W. B. (1993). Anti-imperial Americanism. In A. Kaplan and D. E. Pease, eds., *Cultures of United States imperialism* (pp. 365–91). Durham, N.C.: Duke University Press.

Miller, D. P. (1996). Joseph Banks, empire, and "centers of calculation" in Hanoverian London. In D. P. Miller and P. H. Reil, eds., *Visions of empire: Voyages, botany, and representations of nature* (pp. 12–37). Cambridge: Cambridge University Press.

Milliken, R. (1993, December 23). Australians ratify deal with Aborigines. *Vancouver Sun*, A11.

Mills, S. (1991). *Discourse of difference: An analysis of women's travel writing and colonialism*. London: Routledge.

Minh-Ha, T. T. (1991). *When the moon waxes red: Representation, gender, and cultural politics*. New York: Routledge.

Mitchell, T. (1988). *Colonizing Eygpt*. Cambridge: Cambridge University Press.

Mitchell, W. J. T. (1995). Postcolonial culture, postimperial criticism. In W. Ashcroft, G. Griffiths, and H. Tiffin, eds., *The post-colonial studies reader* (pp. 475–80). New York: Routledge.

Moag, R. F. (1992). The life cycle of non-native Englishes: A case study. In B. B. Kachru, ed., *The other tongue: English across cultures* (pp. 233–52). Urbana: University of Illinois Press.

Mohanty, C. T. (1991). Under Western eyes: Feminist scholarship and colonial discourses. In C. T. Mohanty, A. Russo, and L. Torres, eds., *Third world women and the politics of feminism* (pp. 51–80). Bloomington: Indiana University Press.

Mommsen, W. J. (1980). *Theories of imperialism* (P. S. Falla, trans.). Chicago: University of Chicago Press.

Monet, D., and Skanu'U (Argthe Wilson) (1992). *Colonialism on trial: Indigenous land rights and the Gitksan and Wet'suwet'er sovereignty case*. Gabriola Island, B.C.: New Society Publications.

Montagu, A. (1964). On Coon's *The origin of races*. In A. Montagu, ed., *The concept of race* (pp. 228–41). New York: Free Press.

——— (1972). *Statement on race: An annotated elaboration and exposition of the four statements on race issued by the United Nations Educational, Scientific, and Cultural Organization* (3d ed.). New York: Oxford University Press.

Montagu, M. W. (1909). Inoculation for the smallpox (orig. 1763). In H. C. Lodge and F. Halsey, eds., *The best of the world's classics*, vol. 4 (pp. 63–65). New York: Funk & Wagnalls.

Montrose, L. (1993). The work of gender in the discourse of discovery. In S. Greenblatt, ed., *New World encounters* (pp. 177–217). Berkeley: University of California Press.

Morgan, R. (1990). The "Englishness" of English teaching. In I. Goodson and P. Medway, eds., *Bringing English to order* (pp. 197–241). London: Falmer.

Morris, J. (1968). *Pax Britannica: The climax of an empire.* Harmondsworth, England: Penguin.

Morrison, T. (1992). *Playing in the dark: Whiteness and the literary imagination.* Cambridge: Harvard University Press.

Mudimbe, V. Y., and K. A. Appiah (1993). The impact of African studies on philosophy. In R. H. Bates, V. Y. Mudimbe, and J. O'Barr, eds., *Africa and the disciplines: The contributions of research in Africa to the social sciences and humanities* (pp. 113–38). Chicago: University of Chicago Press.

Mukherjee, A. (1988). The vocabulary of the "universal": The cultural imperialism of the universalist criteria of Western literary criticism. In *Towards an aesthetic of opposition: Essays on literature criticism and cultural imperialism* (pp. 10–22). Toronto: Wallace.

——— (1995). Ideology in the classroom: A case study in the teaching of English literature in Canadian universities. In W. Ashcroft, G. Griffiths, and H. Tiffin, eds., *The post-colonial studies reader* (pp. 447–51). New York: Routledge.

Nandy, A. (1983). *The intimate enemy: Colonialism.* New Delhi: Oxford University Press.

National Center for History in the Schools (1994). *National standards for world history: Exploring paths to the present. Grades 5–12.* Los Angeles: National Center for History in the Schools.

National Geographic (1994, September 25). Connect. Convince. *New York Times Magazine,* 28–29.

Needham, J. (1954). *Science and civilization in China.* (7 vols.) Cambridge: Cambridge University Press.

——— (1964). Science and China's influence on the world. In R. Dawson, ed., *The legacy of China* (pp. 234–308). Oxford: Oxford University Press.

——— (1986). *The shorter science and civilization in China* (C. A. Ronan, ed.). (Vol. 3.) Cambridge: Cambridge University Press.

Neilsen, L., and J. Willinsky (1993). Literacy, knowledge, and power beyond the curriculum. Paper given at the American Educational Research Association Conference, Atlanta, Georgia.

Newman, G., and C. De Greer (1992). *Odyssey through the ages.* Toronto: McGraw-Hill Ryerson.

Ng, R. (1993). Sexism, racism, Canadian nationalism. In H. Bannerji, ed., *Returning the gaze: Essays on racism, feminism, and politics* (pp. 182–96). Toronto: Sister Vision.

Ngugi, T. (1981). Literature in schools. In *Writers in politics: Essays* (pp. 34–41). London: Heinemann.

——— (1986). *Decolonizing the mind: The politics of language in African literature.* London: Currey.

——— (1990). English: A language for the world. *Yale Journal of Criticism* 4(1): 283–93.

——— (1993). *Moving the centre: The struggle for cultural freedom.* London: Currey.

Niethammer, L. (1992). *Posthistoire: Has history come to an end?* (P. Camiller, trans.). London: Verso.

Nietzsche, F. (1969). *On the genealogy of morals and Ecce homo* (W. Kaufman, trans.). New York: Vintage.

Okoth, P. G. (1993). The creation of a dependent culture: The imperial school curriculum in Uganda. In J. A. Mangan, ed., *The imperial curriculum: Racial images and education in the British colonial experience* (pp. 135–46). London: Routledge.

Olender, M. (1992). *The language of paradise: Race, religion, and philology in the nineteenth century* (A. Goldhammer, trans.). Cambridge: Harvard University Press.

O'Neill, M. (1993, November 21). Why are we in Vietnam? *New York Times Magazine,* 71–79.

On Native Ground (1994, October 31). *New Yorker,* 18.

Opier, M. E. (1962, December 7). Review of C. S. Coon's *The origin of races. New York Herald Tribune Books,* 7.

Oram, R. F. (1983). *Biology: Living systems* (4th ed.). Toronto: Merrill.

Ornstein, M. (1963). *The role of scientific societies in the seventeenth century.* Hamden, England: Archon.

Osborne, M. (1994). *Nature, the exotic, and the science of French colonialism.* Bloomington: University of Indiana Press.

Overhaul of U.S. history urged. (1994, October 27). *Toronto Globe and Mail,* A2.

Paikeday, T. M. (1985). *The native speaker is dead!* Toronto: Paikeday Publishing.

Palmer, D. J. (1965). *The rise of English studies: An account of the study of English language and literature from its origins to the making of the Oxford English School.* London: Oxford University Press.

Panikkar, S. K. M. (1969). The view of an Asian scholar and diplomat. In R. W. Winks, ed., *The age of imperialism* (pp. 148–53). Englewood Cliffs, N.J.: Prentice-Hall.

Parekh, B. (1994, February 25). Superior people: The narrowness of liberalism from Mills to Rawls. *Times Literary Supplement,* 11–13.

Paxton, N. L. (1992). Complicity and resistance in the writings of Flora Annie Steel and Annie Besant. In N. Chaudhuri and M. Strobel, eds., *Western women and imperialism: Complicity and resistance* (pp. 158–76). Bloomington: Indiana University Press.

Peet, R. (1985). The social origins of environmental determinism. *Annals of the Association of American Geographers* 75(3): 309–33.

Peña, F. de la (1991). *Democracy or Babel? The case for official English.* (With a foreword by Alistair Cooke.) Washington, D.C.: U.S. English.

Pennycook, A. (1989). The concept of method, interested knowledges, and the politics of language teaching. *TESOL Quarterly* 23(4): 589–618.

——— (1990). Critical pedagogy and second language education. *System* 18(30): 303–14.

Peterson, D., and J. Goodall (1993). *Visions of Caliban: On chimpanzees and people.* Boston: Houghton Mifflin.

Phillips, A. (1993). The gates slam shut. *Maclean's* 106(24): 18–19, 22.

Phillipson, R. (1991). *Linguistic imperialism.* London: Oxford University Press.

Pollack, A. (1995, August 10). Cyberspace's war of words. *Toronto Globe and Mail,* A10.

Pollock, S. (1993). Deep orientalism: Notes on Sanskrit and power beyond the raj. In C. A. Breckenridge and P. van der Veer, eds., *Orientalism and the postcolonial predicament: Perspectives on South Asia* (pp. 76–133). Philadelphia: University of Pennsylvania Press.

Prakash, G. (1992). Science "gone native" in colonial India. *Representations* 40: 153–78.

Pratt, M. L. (1992). *Imperial eyes: Travel writing and transculturation.* New York: Routledge.

Price, S. (1989). *Primitive art in civilized places.* Chicago: University of Chicago Press.

Pyenson, L. (1989). Pure learning and political economy: Science and European expansion in the age of imperialism. In R. P. W. Visser, H. J. M. Bos, L. C. Plam, and H. A. M. Snelders, eds., *New trends in the history of science* (pp. 209–78). Amsterdam: Rodopi.

——— (1993). *French colonialism and the exact sciences.* Ithaca, N.Y.: Cornell University Press.

Qian, Z. (1995). *Orientalism and modernism: The legacy of China in Pound and Williams.* Durham, N. C.: Duke University Press.

Quirk, R. (1982). Language and nationhood. In *Style and communication in the English language* (pp. 54–72). London: Arnold.

——— (1985). The English language in a global context. In R. Quirk and H. G. Widdowson, eds., *English in the world: Teaching and learning the language and literatures* (pp. 1–6). Cambridge: Cambridge University Press.

Raby, J. (1983). Exotica from Islam. In O. Impey and A. MacGregor, eds., *The origins of museums: The cabinets of curiosities in sixteenth and seventeenth century Europe* (pp. 251–58). Oxford: Clarendon.

Race shapes health decisions, studies say (1993, August 26). *Toronto Globe and Mail,* A7.

Ragussis, M. (1994). The birth of nation in Victorian culture: The Spanish Inquisition, the converted daughter, and the "secret race." *Critical Inquiry* 20(3): 477–508.

Ramsey, W. L., L. A. Gabriel, J. F. McGurik, C. R. Phillips, and F. M. Watenpaugh (1986). *Holt life science.* Teachers edition. Toronto: Holt, Rinehart & Winston.

Ramusack, B. N. (1992). Cultural missionaries, maternal imperialists, feminist allies: British women activists in India, 1865–1915. In N. Chaudhuri and M. Strobel, eds., *Western women and imperialism: Complicity and resistance* (pp. 119–36). Bloomington: Indiana University Press.

Rayburn, A. (1994). *Naming Canada: Stories about place names from* Canadian Geographic. Toronto: University of Toronto Press.

Rayner, R. (1996, January 7). What immigration crisis? *New York Times Magazine,* 26–29, 46, 47, 52.

Rhodes, C. (1994). *Primitivism and modern art.* London: Thames & Hudson.

Richards, T. (1993). *The imperial archive: Knowledge and the fantasy of empire.* London: Verso.

Ricks, C. (1988). *T. S. Eliot and prejudice.* London: Faber & Faber.

Riding, A. (1995, October 29). "Primitive" no more, African art finds a proper respect. *New York Times,* 43, 46.

Riffenburgh, B. (1994). *The myth of the explorer: The press, sensationalism, and geographical discovery.* London: Belhaven.

Ritvo, H. (1990). The power of the word: Scientific nomenclature and the spread of the empire. *Victorian Newsletter* 7: 5–8.

Roberts, R. (1994). Teaching non-Western history at Stanford. In L. Kramer, D. Reid, and W. L. Barney, eds., *Learning history in America: Schools, cultures, and politics* (pp. 53–70). Minneapolis: University of Minnesota Press.

Robinson, J. (1990). *Wayward women: A guide to women travellers.* New York: Oxford University Press.

Rocher, R. (1993). British orientalism in the eighteenth century: The dialectics of knowledge and government. In C. A. Breckenridge and P. van der Veer, eds., *Orientalism and the postcolonial predicament: Perspectives on South Asia* (pp. 215–49). Philadelphia: University of Pennsylvania Press.

Rodney, W. (1981). *How Europe underdeveloped Africa.* Washington, D.C.: Howard University Press.

Roman, L. G. (1992). The political significance of other ways of narrating ethnography: A feminist materialist approach. In M. O. Lecompte, W. L. Hillroy, and J. Peissle, eds., *The handbook of qualitative research in education* (pp. 535–94). San Diego: Academic.

Roman, L. G., and T. J. Stanley (1994). Empires, emigrés, and aliens: Silenced antiracism and young people's negotiations of official and popular racisms in Canada. Paper presented at the annual meeting of the American Education Research Association, New Orleans, Louisiana.

——— (1997). Empires, emigrés, and aliens: Young people's negotiations of official and popular racism in Canada. In L. G. Roman and L. Eyre, eds., *Dangerous territories: Struggles for equality and difference in education* (pp. 205–31). New York: Routledge.

Rorty, R. (1995). The end of Leninism and history as a comic force. In A. M. Melzer, J. Weinberger, and M. R. Zinman, eds., *History and the idea of progress* (pp. 211–27). Ithaca, N.Y.: Cornell University Press.

Rose, G. (1993). *Feminism and geography: The limits of geographical knowledge.* Cambridge, England: Polity.

Rothenberg, T. Y. (1994). Voyeurs of imperialism: *National Geographic* magazine before World War II. In A. Godlewska and N. Smith, eds., *Geography and empire* (pp. 155–73). Oxford: Blackwell.

Rousseau, J.-J. (1979). *Émile, or On education* (orig. 1762; A. Bloom, trans.). New York: Basic Books.

Rowe, J. C. (1994). Melville's *Typee:* U.S. imperialism at home and abroad. In D. E. Pease, ed., *National identities and post-Americanist narratives* (pp. 255–78). Durham, N.C.: Duke University Press.

Rushdie, S. (1991). "Commonwealth literature" does not exist. In *Imaginary homelands: Essays and criticism, 1981–1991* (pp. 61–70). London: Granta Books.

Rushton, J. P. (1995). *Race, evolution, and behavior: A life history perspective.* New Brunswick, N.J.: Transactions.

Russell, A. G. (1945). *Colour, race, and empire.* London: Gollancz.

Rydell, R. W. (1993). *World of fairs: The century-of-progress expositions.* Chicago: University of Chicago Press.

Ryle, J. (1995, October 20). The anxiety of exoticism: How the Western idea of art impedes our understanding of Africa. *Times Literary Supplement,* 18–19.

Said, E. W. (1978). *Orientalism.* New York: Random House.

———— (1990). In the shadow of the West: Edward Said. In R. Ferguson, W. Olander, M. Tucker, and K. Fiss, eds., *Discourses: Conversations in postmodern art and culture* (pp. 93–104; P. Mariani and J. Crary, interviewers). Cambridge: MIT Press.

———— (1991). Identity, authority, and freedom: The potentate and the traveler. *Transitions* 54: 4–18.

———— (1993). *Culture and imperialism.* New York: Knopf.

———— (1995, February 3). East isn't East: The impending end of the age of orientalism. *Times Literary Supplement,* 3–6.

Sargant, E. B. (1914). Educational problems of the empire. In A. J. Herbertson and O. J. R. Howarth, eds., *The Oxford survey of the British Empire* (pp. 230–65). Oxford: Oxford University Press.

Sawchuk, K. (1992). Unleashing the demons of history: An interview with Coco Fusco and Guillermo Gómez-Peña. *Parachute* 67: 22–29.

al-Sayyid, A. L. (1979). Lord Cromer before history. In B. Fetter, ed., *Colonial rule in Africa: Readings from primary sources* (pp. 51–52). Madison: University of Wisconsin Press.

Scarfe. N. (1965). *Geography in school.* Normal, Ill.: National Council for Geography Education.

Schmied, J. (1991). *English in Africa: An introduction.* London: Longman.

Seeley, J. R. (1884). *The expansion of England: Two courses of lectures.* London: Macmillan.

Segregation's threat to the economy (1993, December 19). *New York Times,* E12.

Seixas, P. (1993). Parallel crises: History and the social studies curriculum in the USA. *Journal of Curriculum Studies* 25(3): 235–50.

Seppänen, A. (1981). On the notion of correct usage. *Moderna Språk* 75(3): 225–33.

Sharpe, J. (1993). *Allegories of empire: The figure of woman in the colonial text.* Minneapolis: University of Minnesota.

Shemilt, D. (1980). *History 13–16: Evaluation study.* Edinburgh: Holmes McDougall.

Sherlock, M. (1994). The year of the white bear. *Art Papers* 18(3): 31–37.

Shipman, P. (1994). *The evolution of racism: Human differences and the use and abuse of science.* New York: Simon & Schuster.

Shohat, E. (1992–93, winter). Staging the quincentenary: The Middle East and the Americas. *Third Text* 21: 95–105.

Shuttleworth, J. P. K. (1961). Privy Council considers Negro eduation. In P. D. Curtin, ed., *Imperialism* (pp. 192–208). New York: Harper & Row.

Sidney, P. (1970). *An apology for poetry* (orig. 1595). Indianapolis and New York: Bobbs-Merrill.

Simon, R. I. (1992). Forms of insurgency in the production of popular memories: The

Columbus quincentenary and the pedagogy of counter-commemoration. In H. A. Giroux and P. McLaren, eds., *Between borders: Pedagogy and the politics of cultural studies* (pp. 29–55). New York: Routledge.

Sioui, G. E. (1992). *For an Amerindian autohistory: An essay on the foundations of a social ethic* (S. Fischman, trans.). Montreal: McGill-Queen's University Press.

Sislian, J. H. (1967). Missionary work in Egypt during the nineteenth century. In B. Holmes, ed., *Educational policy and the mission schools: Case studies from the British Empire* (pp. 175–240). London: Routledge & Kegan Paul.

Sleeter, C. E. (1993). How white teachers construct race. In C. McCarthy and W. Chrichlow, eds., *Race, identity, and representation in education* (pp. 157–71). New York: Routledge.

Sleeter, C. E., and P. McLaren (1995). *Critical pedagogy and multiculturalism.* Albany: State University of New York Press.

Slesnick, I. L., L. Balzer, A. J. McCormack, D. E. Newton, and F. A. Rasmussen (1985). *Scott, Foresman biology.* Glenview, Ill.: Scott, Foresman.

Smith, B. (1960). *European vision and the South Pacific, 1768–1850: A study in the history of arts and ideas.* Oxford: Oxford University Press.

Smith, L. E. (1992). Spread of English and issues of intelligibility. In B. B. Kachru, ed., *The other tongue: English across cultures* (pp. 75–90). Urbana: University of Illinois Press.

Snowden, F. M., Jr. (1983). *Before color prejudice: The ancient views of blacks.* Cambridge: Harvard University Press.

Sontag. S. (1971). *On photography.* New York: Farrar, Straus & Giroux.

——— (1982). The pornographic imagination. In G. Bataille, *Story of the eye* (pp. 83–118). Harmondsworth, England: Penguin.

Soubeyran, O. (1994). Imperialism and colonialism versus disciplinarity in French geography. In A. Godlewska and N. Smith, eds., *Geography and empire* (pp. 244–64). Oxford: Blackwell.

South Viet Nam: Search for answers (1963, August 9). *Time*, 30.

Soyinka, W. (1981). *Aké: The years of childhood.* London: Arrow.

Spence, J. D. (1983). *The memory palace of Matteo Ricci.* New York: Penguin.

Spivak, G. C. (1987). Subaltern studies: Deconstructing historiography. In *Other worlds: Essays in cultural politics* (pp. 197–221). New York: Routledge.

——— (1991). Neocolonialism and the secret agent of knowledge: Interview with Robert Young. *Oxford Literary Review* 13(1–2): 220–51.

Sprat, T. (1959). *History of the Royal Society* (orig. 1667; J. I. Cope and H. W. Jones, eds.). Saint Louis, Mo.: Washington University Studies.

Spurr, D. (1994). *The rhetoric of empire: Colonial discourse in journalism, travel writing, and imperial administration.* Durham, N.C.: Duke University Press.

Stackhouse, J. (1995, December 4). Internet casts English shadow over world's use of French. *Toronto Globe and Mail*, A1, A9.

Stafford, R. A. (1989). *Scientist of empire: Sir Roderick Murchison, scientific exploration, and Victorian imperialism.* Cambridge: Cambridge University Press.

Stallybrass, P., and A. White (1986). *The politics and poetics of transgression*. Ithaca, N.Y.: Cornell University Press.

Steiner, G. (1974). *Nostalgia for the absolute: Massey lectures*. Toronto: Canadian Broadcasting Corporation.

———— (1995, June 2). A lacerated destiny: The dark and glittering genius of Paul Celan. *Times Literary Supplement*, 3–4.

Stepan, N. L. (1982). *The idea of race in science: Great Britain, 1800–1960*. London: Macmillan.

———— (1990). Race and gender: The role of analogy in science. In D. T. Goldberg, ed., *Anatomy of racism* (pp. 38–57). Minneapolis: University of Minnesota Press.

Sterling, S. (1992). *My name is Seepeetza*. Vancouver: Douglas & McIntyre.

Stocking, G. W., Jr. (1982). The scientific reaction against cultural anthropology, 1917–1920. In *Race, culture, and evolution: Essays in the history of anthropology* (2d ed.; pp. 270–307). Chicago: University of Chicago Press.

Stoler, A. L. (1995). *Race and the education of desire: Foucault's* History of sexuality *and the colonial order of things*. Durham, N.C.: Duke University Press.

Suleri, S. (1992). *The rhetoric of English India*. Chicago: University of Chicago Press.

Sullivan, Z. T. (1989). Race, gender, and imperial ideology: In the nineteenth century. *Nineteenth-Century Contexts* 134(1): 19–30.

Sundquist, E. J. (1993). *To wake the nations: Race in the making of American literature*. Cambridge: Harvard University Press.

Symonds, R. (1986). *Oxford and empire: The last lost cause*. London: Macmillan.

Tamura, E. H. (1993). The English-only effort, the anti-Japanese campaign, and language acquisition in the education of Japanese Americans in Hawaii, 1915–1940. *History of Education Quarterly* 33(1): 37–58.

Taylor, C. (1979). *Hegel and modern society*. Cambridge: Cambridge University Press.

Thapar, R. (1992). Ideology and the interpretation of early Indian history. In *Interpreting early India* (pp. 1–22). Delhi: Oxford University Press.

Thomas, L., and J. Willinsky (in press). Pacific Rim students' perception of racial and ethnic tension. *Canadian Journal of Education*.

Thomas, N. (1991). The curiosity of the gaze: Imperialism and anthropological postmodernism. *Social Analysis* 30: 20–31.

———— (1994). *Colonialism's culture: Anthropology, travel, and government*. Cambridge, England: Polity.

Thorp, S. (1991). *Race, equality, and science teaching*. London: Association for Science Education.

Tiffin, H. (1995). Post-colonial literatures and counter-discourse. In W. Ashcroft, G. Griffiths, and H. Tiffin, eds., *The post-colonial studies reader* (pp. 95–98). New York: Routledge.

Todd, L. (1992). What more do they want? In G. McMaster and L.-A. Martin, eds., *Indigena: Contemporary native perspectives* (pp. 71–79). Vancouver: Douglas & McIntyre.

Todorov, T. (1995). *The morals of history* (A. Waters, trans.). Minneapolis: University of Minnesota Press.

Torgovnick, M. (1990). *Gone primitive: Savage intellects, modern lives.* Chicago: University of Chicago Press.

Toynbee, A. J. (1953). *The world and the West.* Oxford: Oxford University Press.

Tripathi, P. D. (1992). English: "The chosen tongue." *English Today* 8(4): 3–11.

Trollope, J. (1983). *Britannia's daughters: Women of the British Empire.* London: Pimlico.

Turnbull, D. (1989). *Maps are territories: Science is an atlas.* Chicago: University of Chicago Press.

Tylor, E. B. (1930). *Anthropology: An introduction to the study of man and civilization.* (2 vols.; orig. 1891.) London: Watts.

UNESCO. (1983). *Racism, science, and peusdo-science: Proceedings of the symposium to examinine the pseudo-scientific theories invoked to justify racism and racial discrimination, Athens, 30 March to 3 April 1981.* Paris: UNESCO.

United Nations: Against the last white strongholds (1963, August 9). *Time,* 30.

United Nations: Words of dissent (1962, January 5). *Time,* 25.

Vasantha, A. (1992). The "oriental-occidental controversy" of 1839 and its impact on Indian science. In P. Petitjean, C. Jami, and A. M. Moulin, eds., *Science and empires: Historical studies about scientific development and European expansion* (pp. 49–56). Dordrecht, Netherlands: Kluwer.

Viswanathan, G. (1989). *Masks of conquest: Literary study and British rule in India.* New York: Columbia University Press.

Walcott, D. (1986). Crusoe's journal. In *Collected poems, 1948–1984* (pp. 92–94). New York: Farrar, Straus & Giroux.

Wallerstein, I. (1991). *Unthinking social science: The limits of nineteenth-century paradigms.* London: Polity.

Ward, W. P. (1990). *White Canada forever: Popular attitudes and public policy toward Orientals in British Columbia* (2d ed.). Montreal: McGill-Queen's University Press.

Ware, V. (1992). *Beyond the pale: White women, racism, and history.* London: Verso.

Watson, K. (1993). Rulers and ruled: Racial perceptions, curriculum, and schooling in colonial Malaya and Singapore. In J. A. Mangan, ed., *The imperial curriculum: Racial images and education in the British colonial experience* (pp. 147–74). London: Routledge.

Weatherford, J. M. (1988). *Indian givers: The continuing impact of the discovered Americas on the world.* New York: Crown.

Webster, V. R., G. S. Fichter, C. R. Coble, and D. R. Rice (1980). *Prentice-Hall life science.* Teachers' annotated edition. Englewood Cliffs, N.J.: Prentice-Hall.

Weizmann, F., N. Wiener, D. Wiesenthal, and M. Ziegler (1991). Eggs, eggplants, and eggheads: A rejoinder to Rushton. *Canadian Psychology* 32(1): 43–50.

Wesso, H. N. (1994). The colonization of geographic thought: The South African experience. In A. Godlewska and N. Smith, eds., *Geography and empire* (pp. 316–32). Oxford: Blackwell.

West, C. (1990). The new cultural politics of difference. In R. Ferguson, M. Gever, T. T. Minh-ha, and C. West, eds., *Out there: Marginalization and contemporary culture* (pp. 19–38). Cambridge: MIT Press.

———— (1993). Beyond Eurocentrism and multiculturalism. In *Prophetic thought in post-modern times: Beyond Eurocentrism and multiculturalism,* vol. 1 (pp. 3–30). Monroe, Maine: Common Courage.

Wheeler, D. L. (1995, February 17). A growing number of scientists reject the concept of race. *Chronicle of Higher Education,* A8–A9, A15.

White, H. (1973). *Metahistory: The historical imagination in nineteenth-century Europe.* Baltimore, Md.: Johns Hopkins University Press.

———— (1987). The question of narrative in contemporary historical theory. In *The content of form: Narrative discourse and historical representation* (pp. 26–57). Baltimore, Md.: Johns Hopkins University Press.

Whitehead, C. (1988). British colonial educational policy: A synonym for cultural imperialism? In J. A. Mangan, ed., *Benefits bestowed? Education and British imperialism* (pp. 211–30). Manchester, England: University of Manchester Press.

Whitfield, P. (1994). *The image of the world: Twenty centuries of world maps.* San Francisco: Pomegranate Books.

Whitney, C. R. (1996, January 7). Europeans redefine what makes a citizen. *New York Times,* 6E

Wigod, R. (1993, May 27). Immigrants form pool for disease, doctors say. *Vancouver Sun,* B1.

Williams, E. A. (1985). Art and artifact at the Trocadéro: Ars Americana and the primitivist revolution. In G. W. Stocking Jr., ed., *Objects and others: Essays on museums and material culture* (pp. 146–66). Madison: University of Wisconsin Press.

Williams, H. (1994). A critique of Hodson's "In search of a rationale for multicultural science education." *Science Education* 78(5): 515–19.

Willinsky, A. I. (1961). *A doctor's memoirs.* Toronto: Macmillan.

Willinsky, J. (1988). Cutting English on the bias: Five lexicographers in pursuit of the new. *American Speech* 63(1): 44–66.

———— (1991). *The triumph of literature/The fate of literacy: English in the secondary school.* New York: Teachers College Press.

———— (1994a). *Empire of words: The reign of the* OED. Princeton, N.J.: Princeton University Press.

———— (1994b). Pacific cultural literacy: An invitation. *Pacific-Asian Education* 5: 14–19.

———— (1996). Menchú's secret: Culture and education. In A. Carey-Webb and S. Benz, eds., *Teaching and testimony: Rigoberta Menchú in the North American classroom* (pp. 324–38). Albany: State University of New York Press.

Willinsky, J., and L. Thomas (1994). Imagining place and distance: When students draw the Pacific. *Pacific-Asian Education* 6(2): 31–40.

Winks, R. W., ed. (1969). *The age of imperialism.* Englewood Cliffs, N.J.: Prentice-Hall.

Wittgenstein, L. (1961). *Tractatus logico-philosophicus* (D. F. Pears and B. F. McGuinness, trans.). London: Routledge & Kegan Paul.

Wolfe, P. (1997). History and imperialism: A century of theory, from Marx to postcolonialism. *American Historical Review* 102(2): 388–420.

Wolff, L. (1994, November 13). "If I were younger I would make myself Russian": Voltaire's encounter with the czars. *New York Times Book Review,* 14–18.

Wollstonecraft, M. (1975). *A vindication of the rights of woman* (orig. 1792; M. Brody, ed.). Harmondsworth, England: Penguin.

Wolpert, L. (1993). *The unnatural nature of science.* Cambridge: Harvard University Press.

Wong, C. (1995, June 21). Paradise lost—or found? *Toronto Globe and Mail,* A18.

Wong, W. (1994). Covering the invisible "model minority." *Media Studies Journal* 8(3): 49–60.

Wood, D. (1983). *Exploring our country.* (Pt. 3 of *Explorations: A Canadian social studies program for elementary school* [kit]). Vancouver: Douglas & McIntyre.

Yates, F. (1975). *Astraea: The imperial theme in the sixteenth century.* London: Pimlico.

Young, R. (1990). *White mythologies: Writing history and the West.* London: Routledge.

——— (1995). *Colonial desire: Hybridity in theory, culture, and race.* New York and London: Routledge.

Ziegler, C. (1994). Planches de la *Description de l'Egypte.* In J.-M. Humbert, M. Panatazzi, and C. Ziegler, eds., *Egyptomania: L'Egypte dans l'art occidental, 1730–1930* (p. 257). Paris: Réunion des Musées Nationaux.

Ziegler, M., F. Weizmann, N. Wiener, and D. Wiesenthal (1989). Phillipe [sic] Rushton and the growing acceptance of "race-science." *Canadian Forum* 68(781): 19–22.

INDEX

JOHN WILLINSKY is professor of education at the University of British Columbia and the author of four previous books: *The Well-Tempered Tongue* (1988), *The New Literacy* (1990), *The Triumph of Literature/The Fate of Literacy* (1991), and *Empire of Words: The Reign of the OED* (1994).